# THE FRENCH LAUNDRY COOKBOOK

# THE FRENCH LAUNDRY COOKBOOK

THOMAS KELLER

with

Susie Heller and Michael Ruhlman

Photographs by Deborah Jones

Artisan

New York

Published by Artisan
A Division of Workman Publishing, Inc.
225 Varick Street
New York, NY 10014
www.artisanbooks.com

**Library of Congress Cataloging-in Publication Data**

Keller, Thomas.
The French Laundry Cookbook / by Thomas Keller with Susie Heller and Michael Ruhlman : photographs by Deborah Jones.
p.   cm.
ISBN-10: 1-57965-126-7
ISBN-13: 978-1-57965-126-8
1. Cookery, French. 2. French Laundry (Restaurant). I. Heller, Susie. II. Ruhlman, Michael, 1963–. III. Title.
TX719.K35 1999
641.5'09794'19—dc21                                                  99-32473
                                                                                      CIP

Printed in China

30  29  28  27  26  25  24  23  22

Design by LEVEL

To the memory of my mother, Elizabeth Marie

and

for my father, Edward James

**A c k n o w l e d g m e n t s** Few people move through their work as a solitary force, and no one in the service business does. As far as I'm concerned, my whole career has been a cumulative effort.

My mom, Betty, was and remains the biggest influence, if that's the word, in my life. Long before she put me to work, she taught me how to clean our home. Everything had to shine. That standard of perfect cleanliness was its own gift, given the work I'd choose. She was a focused, intense woman, the driving force of the family, and she taught through her own actions. I honestly don't know who I'd be if I'd been raised by, and had grown up watching, someone other than her.

My brother, Joseph, steered me in the beginning, even before I understood that my metier would be cooking, and for this I am grateful. He kept me on track when I could have gone in any number of less-productive directions.

Roland Henin was my chef. He hired me as staff-meal cook at the Dunes Club in Rhode Island, in the summer of 1976, when I was not yet twenty-one, and taught me what I needed to know to learn the rest.

During the years between Henin and the French Laundry, there was, among many others to whom I'm also grateful, Serge Raoul. He not only hired me in New York, he went on to give me a place to stay in France during my *stages,* and then, most important, provided the opportunity to establish the restaurant Rakel, which proved to be a transformative time for me.

I would like to thank all my partners; without them there would be no French Laundry.

When we were opening the restaurant, Laura Cunningham knocked on my door and handed me her résumé. She quickly took charge of the front of the house and has become more than a general manager and sommelier—she's as much a part of the heart and soul of the restaurant as I am. Her passions, standards, and character, as well as her capacity to express and teach hospitality, have been critical to the restaurant's success. For all this, and her ability to work so closely with me, I am more grateful than I can say.

In the kitchen, no one has been more dedicated and loyal, or more critical in shaping the French Laundry from its opening day, than French Laundry pastry chef Stephen Durfee. Sous chefs Eric Ziebold, Gregory Short, and Grant Achatz, who arrived with the opening of the new kitchen, have been important forces in developing the French Laundry into what it is today. They, along with Stephen, logged many hours quantifying and demonstrating recipes for this book. Pat McCarty has been more than the French Laundry's accountant—I see her more as the third leg of the front-of-the-house/kitchen/financial tripod that keeps a restaurant standing. I am grateful to her.

There are too many staff to thank individually. All of them make or have made the French Laundry the place that it is, and I thank every one, past staff and present.

For this book, Susie Heller is to be thanked above all. Few know that she and I have been talking about it for twelve years. (It began as a pop-up book!) And it was she who not only wrote and tested all the recipes with her able assistant, Angie Spensieri, but who marshaled the team that made this book: photographer Deborah Jones, with her assistant, Jeri Jones; writer Michael Ruhlman; and graphic designer Cliff Morgan, with his design partner David Hughes. Susie, Deborah, Michael, and Cliff became a part of the restaurant in order to transform its essence into a book. They're an extraordinary team; take any one of them away and this would have been a different book entirely.

Susan Lescher brought the book before the right people and found the best possible publisher and editor for this project, Ann Bramson. I'm also indebted to the team in New York—Deborah Weiss Geline, Judith Sutton, Dania Davey, Nancy Murray, and Tricia Boczkowski.

The French chef Fernand Point died the year I was born; in many ways his cookbook *Ma Gastronomie*—a book that conveyed his sense of humor and the totality of a life focused on dining—informed me early on about how a chef might live his passion.

I'd like to thank my entire family for their support and also for their understanding, because the life of a chef inevitably leads to areas of neglect in one's life. I am grateful to them.

Finally, I'd like to thank my colleagues. It's from you that I draw inspiration, and it's your cumulative talent that keeps me striving. Without the daily evidence of your skill and drive and passion, I would be a lesser chef.

# Pleasure and perfection

When you acknowledge, as you must, that there is no such thing as perfect food, only the idea of it, then the real purpose of striving toward perfection becomes clear: to make people happy. That's what cooking is all about.

But to give pleasure, you have to take pleasure yourself. For me, it's the satisfaction of cooking every day: tournéing a carrot, or cutting salmon, or portioning foie gras—the mechanical jobs I do daily, year after year. This is the great challenge: to maintain passion for the everyday routine and the endlessly repeated act, to derive deep gratification from the mundane.

Say, for instance, you intend to make a barigoule, a stew of artichoke hearts braised with carrots and onions, fresh herbs, oil, and wine. You may look at your artichokes and think "Look at all those artichokes I've got to cut and clean." But turning them—pulling off the leaves, trimming their stems, scooping out the chokes, pulling your knife around its edge—that is cooking. It is one of my favorite things to do.

Another source of pleasure in cooking is respect for the food. To undercook a lobster and serve it to a customer, and have him send it back, is not only a waste of the lobster and all those involved in its life, it's a waste of the potential of pleasing that customer. Respect for food is a respect for life, for who we are and what we do.

Carnaroli Risotto with Shaved White Truffles from Alba, page 88

The foie gras preparations in this book are among my favorites because foie gras engenders so many different feelings. It's luxurious. It's rare and expensive. It's visually and texturally rich, a very sensual thing. But the slow-cooking short ribs and oxtail and artichoke barigoule bring me some of the deepest pleasures of *cooking* I know. The process of braising, and the amazing aroma of floured meat in hot oil, is incomparable: taking the braising pan out of the oven to see the rich color of the liquid and the slow thick bubble of the deepening sauce, the beautiful clear layer of fat on top. When you've pulled your pot from the oven to regard your braise, to really see it, to smell it, you've connected yourself to generations and generations of people who have done the same thing for hundreds of years in exactly the same way. My mentor, Roland Henin, told me something long ago that changed the way I thought about cooking: "If you're a really good cook," he said, "you can go back in time."

Cooking is not about convenience and it's not about shortcuts. The recipes in this book are about wanting to take the time to do something that I think is priceless. Our hunger for the twenty-minute gourmet meal, for one-pot ease and prewashed, precut ingredients has severed our lifeline to the satisfactions of cooking. Take your time. Take a long time. Move slowly and deliberately and with great attention.

The idea of cooking and the idea of writing a cookbook are, for me, in conflict. There is an inherent contradiction between a cookbook, which is a collection of documents, and a chef, who is an evolving soul not easily transcribed in recipe form. A recipe has no soul. You, as the cook, must bring soul to the recipe. These recipes, a record of my evolution, have been painstakingly documented, but they should be used as tools rather than as exact blueprints.

I can tell you the mechanics—how to make a custard, for instance. But you won't have a perfect one if you merely follow my instructions. If you don't feel it, it's not a perfect custard, no matter how well you've executed the mechanics. On the other hand, if it's not literally a perfect custard, but you have maintained a great feeling for it, then you have created a recipe perfectly because there was that passion behind what you did.

These recipes, then, although exact documents of the way food is prepared at the French Laundry, are only guidelines. You're not going to be able to duplicate the dish that I made. You may create something that in composition resembles what I made, but more important—and this is my greatest hope—you're going to create something that you have deep respect and feelings and passions for. And you know what? It's going to be more satisfying than anything I could ever make for you.

In the spring of of 1992, I came to Yountville in the Napa Valley on the advice of a friend to look at the French Laundry. The grounds were enclosed by honeysuckle, and climbing roses covered an arched trellis leading into the courtyard. It seemed as if I'd been heading there my whole working life.

The French Laundry is a sixteen-hundred-square-foot structure, built in 1900 with the valley's river rock and timber. It's been many things to many people throughout its history—a residence, a French steam laundry, a saloon and brothel, and then a residence again before it became a restaurant: its best self, I think. The natural stone modesty comforts people who come here and helps us to focus on our work.

I have always maintained that the Napa Valley is a perfect place for a restaurant—it's the only place in the country where people come specifically to drink excellent wines and eat fine food. But there's more to its appeal: Thirty-five miles long and up to five miles wide, it is American bounty itself. Its first residents, the Wappo Indians, never learned to farm, because food just grew all year long. Their word *nappa* is sometimes translated as "plenty."

But the Napa Valley has not always been an emblem of rustic luxury, and the town of Yountville certainly hasn't. "An outlaw town," one valley resident called it. "Prostitution, gambling. Big, big party town. Things going on in unmarked buildings."

A North Carolina fur trapper founded Yountville in the 1830s, the first official town in the valley, and for most of its history it was anything but refined. The bulk of its population lived in the Veterans Home, which sheltered men returning from the Civil War and the Spanish-American War and continued this role right on through the Vietnam War, during which time Don Schmitt, a Fresno banker, and his wife, Sally, moved to town.

By then, 1967, Yountville's glamorous outlaw days had disintegrated into nothing more than a row of bars serving the veterans, trailers and ramshackle homes, and rooming houses. "It was a cesspool," said Don, who would become its mayor, orchestrate its regeneration, and, with Sally, open the French Laundry in 1978.

The late 1960s was an exciting time in the region, then a rugged territory of undeveloped farmland and abandoned prune and walnut orchards. Yountville sat like a quiet Mason-Dixon line between St. Helena lifting its eyebrows from the north at the townies of Napa in the south. And then a new wave of young winemakers arrived and tapped the power of The Grape. The grape to Napa is like the microchip to Silicon Valley, like oil to Texas. It would within thirty years transform the United States' wine business into a world-famous industry and turn the valley itself into the most sophisticated agricultural community on earth.

I gave the French Laundry a new life and it gave me a new life. I don't see us as being separate entities. Whatever the value of my skills, my knowledge, my sensibilities, they never would have come together in this book had it not been for the French Laundry.

A SAD HAPPY STORY Autumn 1990 was a sad time in my life. I was going to be leaving New York after ten years. I would be starting life over in Los Angeles, and my new employer there wanted me to prepare a dish for a food and wine benefit there that would really wow people.

Shortly before I moved, some friends took me to our favorite restaurant in Chinatown, and, as always, we went to Baskin-Robbins for ice cream afterward. I'd been nervous about this food and wine event; I guess it had been in the back of my mind for a while. I ordered an ice-cream cone. The guy put it in a little holder—you take it from a holder—and said, "Here's your cone."

The moment he said it, I thought "There it is! We're going to take our standard tuiles, we're going to make cones with them, and we're going to fill them with tuna tartare."

And that's what we did. Now I use salmon, but you can really use anything. Eggplant caviar and roasted red peppers or tomato confit make a wonderful vegetarian version. You can do it with meat—julienne of prosciutto with some melon. The cone is just a vehicle.

Because it was a canapé that people really began to associate us with, I decided that everyone who eats at the restaurant should begin the meal with this cornet. People always smile when they get it. It makes them happy. But I wouldn't have come up with it if I hadn't been sad. I had been handed an ice-cream cone a hundred times before and it had never resulted in the cornet. I had to be sad to see it.

## "CORNETS"
### Salmon Tartare with Sweet Red Onion Crème Fraîche

**CORNETS**

¼ cup plus 3 tablespoons all-purpose flour

1 tablespoon plus 1 teaspoon sugar

1 teaspoon kosher salt

8 tablespoons (4 ounces) unsalted butter, softened but still cool to the touch

2 large egg whites, cold

2 tablespoons black sesame seeds

**SALMON TARTARE** MAKES ABOUT ¾ CUP

4 ounces salmon fillet (belly preferred), skin and any pin bones removed and very finely minced

¾ teaspoon extra virgin olive oil

¾ teaspoon lemon oil (see Sources, page 315)

1½ teaspoons finely minced chives

1½ teaspoons finely minced shallots

½ teaspoon kosher salt, or to taste

Small pinch of freshly ground white pepper, or to taste

**SWEET RED ONION CRÈME FRAÎCHE**

1 tablespoon finely minced red onions

½ cup crème fraîche

¼ teaspoon kosher salt, or to taste

Freshly ground white pepper to taste

24 chive tips (about 1 inch long)

---

This is one of my favorite dishes to serve to large groups of people—it's fun to look at, it's distinctive, delicious, and doesn't require a plate or silverware. You can eat it standing up, with a glass of Champagne or wine in one hand. At the French Laundry, I use a specially made Lucite holder to serve these cones, but you might fill a bowl with rock salt, say, or peppercorns, and stand the cones up in this to serve them.

FOR THE CORNETS: In a medium bowl, mix together the flour, sugar, and salt. In a separate bowl, whisk the softened butter until it is completely smooth and mayonnaise-like in texture. Using a stiff spatula or spoon, beat the egg whites into the dry ingredients until completely incorporated and smooth. Whisk in the softened butter by thirds, scraping the sides of the bowl as necessary and whisking until the batter is creamy and without any lumps. Transfer the batter to a smaller container, as it will be easier to work with.

Preheat the oven to 400°F.

Make a 4-inch hollow circular stencil. Place a Silpat (see Sources, page 315) on the counter (it is easier to work on the Silpat before it is put on the sheet pan). Place the stencil in one corner of the sheet and, holding the stencil flat against the Silpat, scoop some of the batter onto the back of an offset spatula and spread it in an even layer over the stencil. Then run the spatula over the entire stencil to remove any excess batter. After baking the first batch of cornets, you will be able to judge the correct thickness; you may need a little more or less batter to adjust the thickness of the cornets. There should not be any holes in the batter. Lift the stencil and repeat the process to make as many rounds as you have molds or to fill the Silpat, leaving about 1½ inches between the cornets. Sprinkle each cornet with a pinch of black sesame seeds.

Place the Silpat on a heavy baking sheet and bake for 4 to 6 minutes, or until the batter is set and you see it rippling from the heat. The cornets may have browned in some areas, but they will not be evenly browned at this point.

Open the oven door and place the baking sheet on the door. This will help keep the cornets warm as you roll them and prevent them from becoming too stiff to roll. Flip a cornet over on the sheet pan, sesame seed side down, and place a 4½-inch cornet mold (size #35; see Sources, page 315) at the bottom of the round. If you are right-handed, you will want the pointed end on your left and the open end on your right. The tip of the mold should touch the lower left edge (at about 7 o'clock on a clock face) of the cornet. Fold the bottom of the cornet up and around the mold and carefully roll upward and toward the left to wrap the cornet tightly around the mold; it should remain on the sheet pan as you roll. Leave the cornet wrapped around the mold and continue to roll the cornets around molds; as you proceed, arrange the rolled cornets, seam side down, on the sheet pan so they lean against each other, to prevent them from rolling.

When all the cornets are rolled, return them to the oven shelf, close the door, and bake for an additional 3 to 4 minutes to set the seams and color the cornets a golden brown. If the color is uneven, stand the cornets on end for a minute or so more, until the color is even. Remove the cornets from the oven and allow to cool just slightly, 30 seconds or so.

To make the stencil:
Cut the rim from the top of
a plastic container. Trace
two concentric circles on the
lid, the inner 4 inches in
diameter, the outer about
4½ inches. Sketch a thumb
tab that will make it easy to
lift the stencil off the silicon-
coated Silpat. Trim around
the tab and outer circle.
Remove the inner circle so
that you have a hollow ring.
The batter gets spread to the
stencil's edges, then it's
lifted off, leaving perfectly
shaped rounds.

Gently remove the cornets from the molds and cool for several minutes on paper towels. Remove the Silpat from the baking sheet, wipe the excess butter from it, and allow it to cool down before spreading the next batch. Store the cornets for up to 2 days (for maximum flavor) in an airtight container.

FOR THE SALMON TARTARE: With a sharp knife, finely mince the salmon fillet (do not use a food processor, as it would damage the texture of the fish) and place it in a small bowl. Stir in the remaining ingredients and taste for seasoning. Cover the bowl and refrigerate the tartare for at least 30 minutes, or up to 12 hours.

FOR THE SWEET RED ONION CRÈME FRAÎCHE: Place the red onions in a small strainer and rinse them under cold water for several seconds.

Dry them on paper towels. In a small metal bowl, whisk the crème fraîche for about 30 seconds to 1 minute, or until it holds soft peaks when you lift the whisk. Fold in the chopped onions and season to taste with the salt and white pepper. Transfer the onion cream to a container, cover, and refrigerate until ready to serve or for up to 6 hours.

TO COMPLETE: Fill just the top ½ inch of each cornet with onion cream, leaving the bottom of the cone empty. (This is easily done using a pastry bag fitted with a ¼-inch plain tip or with the tip of a small knife.) Spoon about 1½ teaspoons of the tartare over the onion cream and mold it into a dome resembling a scoop of ice cream. Lay a chive tip against one side of the tartare to garnish.

PICTURED ON PAGE 5                    MAKES 24 CORNETS

## About the chef

by Michael Ruhlman

"The French Laundry is not new," Thomas Keller said the first time we spoke. "It's twenty years old. It's bigger than me. A lot of people make it what it is. I want this book to be about the French Laundry, not about me."

One of Thomas's main claims is that the French Laundry could not be what it is without his purveyors, and he wanted to include a few of their stories. I traveled from the mountains above Napa to the farmlands of Pennsylvania to the cliffs of Maine to talk to them. Almost all of them, I found, either led double lives or had fallen into purveying by accident. Ingrid Bengis, a seafood purveyor, was a writer of some notoriety in the 1970s; Keith Martin was a stockbroker before he was a lamber; and John Mood, hearts of palm grower, remains a commercial airline pilot. I found this extraordinary as the pattern emerged, but soon, it seemed almost inevitable. It was only this kind of person who might bring to the work a passion equal to that of the chef. And it was only this kind of chef who would satisfy this unusual kind of purveyor.

And so, Thomas told me, "Get the story. I want the story to be just as important as the food; otherwise, I'm not interested in doing a cookbook."

Thomas himself has an unusual story. How did a young man with no special food memories or even any real appreciation for food before the age of twenty become, two decades later, one of the country's best chefs? There are clues in the critical moments when Thomas learned important lessons that defined how he would work as a chef. Some of those revelations are in this book.

For me, Thomas's great gift is his example of how to be observant of the world and how food behaves and how we must react as cooks to that food. Largely self-taught, he is a good teacher, conveying not just information, but also how he got that information, as well as its broader meaning and possible uses. Thus, we have taken time to describe food technique, some basic (soups and braising), some refined (working with foie gras).

The recipes run the gamut from simple to difficult as well. Want a real challenge? Try the dish called "Head to Toe." Want simple? Make the Gazpacho, the Lemon Tart, or the Cream of Walnut Soup. Most of the recipes are time consuming; they require thought and, most important, involvement on the part of the cook. And therein lies the second gift from Thomas Keller. In this age of both intense interest in cooking and hurried, overly busy lives in which there is never enough time, he urges us to move slowly and deliberately, to fully engage ourselves in cooking, to regain the connection to food that we've lost in our craving for quick fixes, shortcuts, and processed ingredients. This is not fast food, nor is it four-star cooking simplified for home kitchens. It is four-star cooking, period. Cooking that teaches, that reminds us to return to classical French cuisine both for guidance in technique and for inspiration in creating innovative contemporary food. In the stories, in the techniques, in the recipes lies his call for cooks and chefs of every stripe to respect the food we have and to take more time and greater care in its cooking.

# When in Doubt, Strain: notes on how to use this book

by Susie Heller

The recipes in this book are the exact ones the restaurant uses daily, along with many tips to make them easier to reproduce at home. They have been tested by me, my assistant, Angie Spensieri, and home cooks in various home kitchens.

If the degree of difficulty of a dish exceeds your desire to make it, please remember that it's all right to do only part of a recipe. Most people, I'm guessing, will not try the pig's head preparation, but it would be a shame for anyone to miss the gribiche sauce that goes with it. It's so simple, and it's great with roast pork. The blini are simple—you need a tamis, but they'll be the best blini you've ever tasted.

So be flexible. If you don't want to make the tuile cone for the salmon tartare, serve the tartare on toast points. If you don't have the time for the stock-based sauces, turn to the glazes and the coulis—they're extraordinarily versatile. Yields are given for many subcomponents, the ones you may want to make on their own.

The recipes are built largely on basic techniques, so as you master them—making beurre monté, for instance, or understanding the glazing and deglazing process—the recipes will become much easier.

The portion sizes are small, based on the multicourse meals (at least five) the French Laundry serves. Most of the recipes can be doubled for larger portions.

Perhaps the most important piece of advice is to read the recipe through before you begin. Some require time and special equipment that you should be sure to have before you commit to the dish.

Sources for food and equipment are listed on page 315. Finding certain products may depend on where you live. We use gelatin sheets rather than powdered gelatin, for example, because they work better in the small quantities called for here. Many finer grocers carry the sheets; if they are not available, however, you can order them. Most hard-to-find items like gelatin, fleur de sel, and bottarga will last a long time.

I hope this book gives you a sense of what is possible in the home kitchen. I hope you get the same smile on your face that I've gotten making these recipes, that God-this-is-great smile when you can't believe how good it is, that real feeling of accomplishment.

## A FEW ADDITIONAL TIPS

STRAIN AND SKIM. When in doubt, strain. Not a single liquid or purée moves from one place to another at the restaurant except through some kind of strainer. And you must always be skimming—skim, skim, skim.

TAKE YOUR APPLIANCES INTO ACCOUNT. The recipes were developed and tested using a home gas stove. If you're using an electric stove, remember that the coil takes longer to go from high to medium-low than a gas flame. Oven temperatures vary considerably, so buy a reliable thermometer or have your oven calibrated.

USE GOOD EQUIPMENT. Get a few heavy-bottomed pots and pans—you don't need dozens. Buy two good baking sheets that don't buckle in the heat. And look for a great butcher and a good fishmonger with whom you can develop relationships.

TRUST YOUR INSTINCTS. Use common sense when following a recipe. If it calls for a pan on high heat, but the food is burning, it's probably too hot. If a piece of meat looks as if it's overcooking, it probably is, so take it out even if it hasn't been in as long as the recipe says.

SOME SPECIFICS. All eggs are large. All flour is all-purpose flour. Salt, unless specified, is kosher. All pepper is freshly ground. All butter is unsalted. All herbs are fresh. For oil, canola oil is an inexpensive, all-purpose cooking oil; vegetable oil is fine, grapeseed oil is preferable. Sugar is granulated unless otherwise specified. Staple vegetables (carrots, onions) and garlic are always peeled unless otherwise specified. All recipes include volume measurements, but learn to use a scale; weighing ingredients is the most accurate way to measure and will yield the most consistent results.

CANAPÉS

# The law of diminishing returns

Preceding page: "Bacon and Eggs," page 18. Above: White Truffle Oil–Infused Custard, page 16.

Most chefs try to satisfy a customer's hunger in a short time with one or two dishes. They begin with something great. The initial bite is fabulous. The second bite is great. But by the third bite—with many more to come—the flavors begin to deaden, and the diner loses interest. It's like getting into a hot bath or jumping into a cold pool. At first, the temperature is shocking, but after a few minutes, you get so used to it that you don't even notice it. Your mouth reacts the same way to flavors and sensations.

Many chefs try to counter the deadening effect by putting a lot of different flavors on the plate to keep interest alive. But then the diner can't focus on anything because it's confusing.

What I want is that initial shock, that jolt, that surprise to be the only thing you experience. So I serve five to ten small courses, each meant to satisfy your appetite and pique your curiosity. I want you to say, "God, I wish I had just one more bite of that." And then the next plate comes and the same thing happens, but it's a different experience, a whole new flavor and feel.

The way to keep the experience fresh is not by adding more flavors, but rather by focusing more on specific flavors, either by making them more intense than the foods from which they come, or by varying the preparation technique.

When I decide to make liver and onions, for instance, I might roast a whole foie gras and serve it with four different onion preparations—confit, roasted, glazed red, and glazed white. Or I might serve a calf's liver with just two of those preparations. The point is to isolate and enhance flavors, not confuse them. One lamb course might include five different lamb preparations, another might be simply a lamb chop with lamb sweetbreads.

When I combine flavors, I do so in traditional ways. Sometimes that lamb is served with eggplant and mint—a combination verging on cliché. But I roast the eggplant with butter until it is a virtual fondue, and I infuse the mint into a deep emerald oil.

My favorite dishes for inspiration are traditional ones like quiche lorraine, daube of beef, short ribs, sole Véronique. What is sole Véronique? Sole with grapes. At the restaurant, I serve a sole dish with a little more structure to it. I make a stuffing of sultana raisins (dried grapes) and brioche croutons, fold the sole around it to make a kind of package, and serve it with a classic *glaçage*. It still has the integrity of sole Véronique, but with a modern interpretation.

To achieve the effects I want, I serve courses that are small relative to portions you'll find at most restaurants. But small is not the point. The point is this: For every course, there is a perfect quantity. Some courses must be small because of what they are: A quail egg is small. One bite is enough; two eggs would be redundant. The scallops we get are about three ounces—nearly as big as a filet mignon. In a meal of five to ten courses, you don't need more than one scallop.

With foie gras, though, I serve just slightly too much of it, because I want people to know what foie gras is all about. I go overboard with truffles and caviar too, so that people who have perhaps only eaten truffles in stingy quantities can taste them and say, "Oh, now I understand."

# White Truffle Oil–Infused Custards with Black Truffle Ragout

**CHIVE CHIPS**

1 large russet potato

2 teaspoons Clarified Butter (page 125), melted

Kosher salt

About 20 chive tips (1½ inches long)

**CUSTARDS**

8 large eggs (with the paper egg carton)

⅔ cup milk

⅔ cup heavy cream

1½ tablespoons white truffle oil

Kosher salt

Freshly ground white pepper

**TRUFFLE RAGOUT**

⅓ cup Veal Stock (page 222)

1½ teaspoons finely minced black truffle
(from a whole truffle, pieces, or peelings)

Few drops of white wine vinegar

1 teaspoon unsalted butter

½ teaspoon white truffle oil

Kosher salt and freshly ground white pepper

Many ideas are created simply from the need to make use of something. When friends brought us an unexpected gift of farm-fresh eggs, we immediately thought to feature them in a custard. We had truffle scraps and truffle oil on hand. This dish is really that simple: two components, the most fundamental and the most rarefied, come together in an extraordinary way. We bake the custards in cleaned eggshells, then top them with truffle ragout and garnish each with a perfect chive potato chip.

FOR THE CHIVE CHIPS: Have all the ingredients ready when you begin and work quickly to prevent the potato slices from oxidizing (turning brown). One potato will make about 20 chips. You will need only 8 for this recipe; the extras make a great snack.

Preheat the oven to 275°F.

Peel the potato and use a paring knife to trim it into a Band-Aid shape (straight sides, rounded ends) approximately 4 inches long and 1 inch wide.

Brush two Silpats (see Sources, page 315) with the clarified butter and sprinkle each lightly with kosher salt. Place one Silpat on a baking sheet. Using a mandoline, cut the potato lengthwise into paper-thin slices. As you work, stack the potatoes in the order you cut them so that you will be able to match them up as closely as possible.

Lay the potato slices on the Silpat in pairs, keeping each one's match at its side. Place a chive in the center of one of the potato slices and cover each slice with its match. Use your fingers to press and smooth each chip, removing any air pockets between the two potato slices.

Place the second prepared Silpat over the potatoes, buttered side down, and top it with a baking sheet to weight the potatoes and keep them flat. Bake for 20 to 25 minutes, reversing the pan halfway through the cooking process. Remove the chips when they are golden brown. The chive chips can be baked up to 2 days ahead and kept in an airtight container.

TO PREPARE THE EGGSHELLS: Use an egg cutter (see Sources, page 315) to cut off the wider end of each egg. Or, if you don't have an egg cutter, rest an egg on its side on a towel. Holding the egg steady, use a serrated knife to saw halfway through the wider end. Lift the egg upright, remove and discard the lid, pour the egg into a bowl, and save the shell. Repeat with the remaining eggs, reserving 2 separately for the custard.

Rinse the inside of the eggshells under warm water and use your finger to loosen the inner membrane around the opening of the egg. Working all the way around the shell, carefully pull the membrane downward, remove it, and discard.

Break off any loose bits of shell from around the opening and make sure that the opening is large enough for a spoon to fit through it. Drain the eggshells upside down in the egg carton.

FOR THE CUSTARDS: Preheat the oven to 275°F.

Heat the milk and cream in a saucepan. As soon as it reaches a boil, remove the pan from the heat. Turn on a blender and pour in the milk and cream. Then add the truffle oil, the reserved 2 eggs, and salt and white pepper to taste. (Turning on your machine before adding a hot liquid will keep the liquid from splashing out of the machine; should the blender be turned off at any point, be sure to place the lid on the machine before turning it back on.)

Strain the mixture through a chinois (see page 73) into a small pitcher. Let the custard sit for a few minutes and then skim off any foam that has risen to the top. Turn the eggshells upright in the carton and fill each egg three quarters full with the custard.

TO COOK THE EGGS: Use a stainless steel or glass baking pan that is large enough to hold the egg carton and at least 4 inches deep. If you are using a stainless steel pan, fold a piece of newspaper to fit in the bottom; the newspaper will help to distribute the heat evenly. If you are using a glass pan, this is not necessary. Place the carton in the pan and fill the pan with enough hot water to reach two thirds of the way up the eggs, to form a bain-marie, or water bath. The water should be inside the egg carton as well as outside.

Cover the pan with a lid or baking sheet, place it in the middle of the oven, and bake for 40 to 45 minutes, or until the custard is set. (Allowing the custard to cook slowly prevents air pockets.) The finished eggs can be kept in the water in a warm place for up to 2 hours.

FOR THE TRUFFLE RAGOUT: Combine the veal stock, truffles, and a drop or so of vinegar in a small saucepan. You shouldn't taste the vinegar, but rather use it as you would use salt to enhance the other flavors. Simmer the ragout for 3 to 4 minutes, until it reduces to a sauce consistency and coats the back of a spoon. You will have 3 to 4 tablespoons of sauce.

TO COMPLETE: Swirl the butter and truffle oil into the truffle ragout and season to taste. Place each egg in an egg cup. Spoon about a teaspoon of ragout over the top of each custard. Gently stand a chive chip in each custard.

PICTURED ON PAGE 14                    MAKES 8 SERVINGS

## Soft Poached Quail Eggs with Applewood-Smoked Bacon

10 quail eggs (and their carton)

2 tablespoons white wine vinegar

1 to 2 slices thinly sliced bacon,
    frozen and cut crosswise into ⅛-inch strips

3 tablespoons Beurre Monté (page 135)

1 teaspoon water

2 teaspoons Brunoise (page 155)

Kosher salt and freshly ground black pepper

Serving a dish—whether a shrimp or a small spoonful of crème brûlée—already "plated" on the silverware creates an elegant impression even before you've tasted the food. I used to scramble a quail egg and serve it on a soup spoon; here I've replaced it with a poached egg. It's a great little bite. One night a customer told everyone this was so good he could eat ten of them. So we made ten of them and sent them out to him on a plate.

The best method for poaching eggs is in a deep pot of water. As the weight of the yolk pulls the egg through the water, the white encircles the yolk and sets. The deeper the water, the farther the egg travels before it stops, and the more the poached egg will resemble its original shape. You will want to cook a few extra eggs, as there might be some breakage.

In a deep pot, bring at least 6 inches of water to a simmer. Hold each egg on its side on a towel and use a serrated knife to cut halfway through the larger end of the egg. (It is important to cut the large end of the egg, as the yolk may not fit through the smaller end.) Lift the egg and remove the top. Stand the eggs in their carton until you are ready to poach them.

Once the water is simmering gently, add the vinegar. Pour the eggs from the shells into the water, adjusting the temperature as necessary to keep the water moving. Simmer for about 2 minutes, or until the whites are just set but the yolks are still runny. (If the whites are not fully set, they will break apart when touched.) Remove the eggs with a slotted spoon or skimmer to a bowl of ice water. After they have cooled, lift one egg at a time from the ice water and use a pair of scissors to trim their "tails" and excess whites. Return them to the ice water and refrigerate until ready to serve, or for up to 2 days.

Place the bacon in a nonstick skillet over medium heat and sauté for about 5 minutes, or until browned and crisp. Drain the bacon on paper towels.

TO COMPLETE: Remove the cold eggs from the water and place them in a saucepan with the beurre monté and water. Warm the eggs over low heat, then add the brunoise, along with salt and pepper to taste. The eggs can be held in a warm spot for several minutes, but be careful not to overcook them.

Place 1 egg on each of six spoons arranged on a platter. Top each egg with sauce and garnish the tops with the bacon. Pass the spoons to your guests while the eggs are hot.

PICTURED ON PAGE 13    MAKES 6 SERVINGS

NOTE: Applewood-smoked bacon or any fruitwood-smoked bacon is sweeter than bacon smoked with a hardwood such as hickory. Freeze the bacon to make it easy to slice. Poach the eggs ahead of time and then reheat them with beurre monté. The brunoise, a tiny dice of vegetables, adds bright color and additional flavor (see the photograph on page 202).

For "Oysters and Pearls," I float one or two plump oysters on top of tapioca custard, and garnish it with osetra caviar for what has become a signature dish. A lot of people think this is an unusual pairing, but for me it's logical: tapioca, pearls, pearls, oysters. Logical or not, it's a very sensual combination. (Choose oysters with the thickest shells; they have the most juice.)

Opposite: Preparing Cauliflower Panna Cotta, page 22. Above: Osetra caviar for "Oysters and Pearls," page 23.

# Cauliflower Panna Cotta with Beluga Caviar

3 oysters, scrubbed with a brush

8 ounces cauliflower, cut into large florets
    and stems trimmed

2 tablespoons (1 ounce) unsalted butter

About 1½ cups water

1 cup heavy cream

Kosher salt

1⅓ gelatin sheets (see Sources, page 315)

Freshly ground black pepper

1 to 2 ounces beluga caviar

I was hoping to make a cold lobster-cauliflower soup—cauliflower purée on the bottom with a clear "mirror" of lobster consommé on top, finished with caviar—but the cream in the cauliflower purée clouded the consommé. The dish's failure resulted in two terrific canapés: cauliflower panna cotta and gelled lobster consommé.

We prepare the cauliflower as a panna cotta (traditionally an Italian dessert of cooked cream), then coat it with gelled oyster juice, which adds a shine to the cream and creates a bright backdrop for the beluga caviar. The mellow creaminess of the cauliflower is enhanced by and contrasts the saltiness of the caviar.

TO SHUCK THE OYSTERS: Hold an oyster in a towel, to protect your hand, with the rounded side down. Lean the wider end of the oyster against the table for support. Push an oyster knife under the hinge at the narrow end of the shell. Don't jam the knife in, or you risk damaging the oyster. You will hear a "pop"; twist the knife to loosen the shell. Keeping the knife directly under the top shell, run the blade along the right side to cut through the muscle. This will release the top shell, which can then be removed. Slide the knife under the meat to detach the second muscle holding the oyster in place. Reserve the oyster and all its juices in a small bowl. Repeat with the remaining oysters.

Transfer the oysters to another small bowl. Strain the juices through a fine-mesh strainer into the bowl, pour ¼ cup of water over the oysters, and refrigerate them for several hours, or overnight.

TO PREPARE THE PANNA COTTA: Cut the florets of cauliflower vertically through the stems into ½-inch slices. Spread the cauliflower evenly in a medium saucepan and add the butter and 1½ cups of water, or enough to come just to the top of the cauliflower (it should not be completely submerged). Simmer for about 30 minutes, or until the

liquid is almost gone and the cauliflower is tender. Add the cream and simmer for another 10 minutes to reduce the cream and completely cook the cauliflower.

Transfer the cauliflower and cream to a food processor and blend until completely smooth. Strain through a chinois (see page 73). There should be about 1½ cups of purée. Taste for salt and add to taste.

Soak 1 gelatin sheet in cold water to cover for 2 to 3 minutes to soften. It should feel very soft, with no hard sections. Squeeze the excess liquid from the gelatin and stir it into the warm cauliflower mixture until dissolved.

Spoon about 2 tablespoons of the panna cotta into the bottom of each of twelve small serving bowls or small cups and refrigerate for at least an hour to set. This can be done several hours ahead.

Remove the oysters from the liquid (discard them) and strain the juice. You will need ¼ cup of oyster juice; refrigerate the juice.

Place the remaining ⅓ gelatin sheet and 2 teaspoons water in a small metal bowl set over a pan of hot water and stir constantly to dissolve the gelatin. Remove the bowl from the heat and add the oyster juice. Stir again to be sure that the gelatin and juice are completely combined. Add about 3 grinds of the peppermill.

Place the oyster jelly in the refrigerator and stir occasionally until it has thickened to the consistency of salad oil and the bits of pepper are suspended in the liquid. Coat the tops of the chilled panna cotta with 1 teaspoon of the jelly each, rotating the bowls to ensure an even coating. Return to the refrigerator until set or for up to 1 day.

To serve, garnish the top of each panna cotta with a quenelle (see page 274), or small oval scoop, of caviar.

PICTURED ON PAGE 20                    MAKES 12 SERVINGS

## Sabayon of Pearl Tapioca with Malpeque Oysters and Osetra Caviar

**TAPIOCA**

⅓ cup small pearl tapioca

1¾ cups milk

16 meaty oysters, such as Malpeque,
    scrubbed with a brush

1¼ cups heavy cream

Freshly ground black pepper

¼ cup crème fraîche

Kosher salt

**SABAYON**

4 large egg yolks

¼ cup reserved oyster juice (from above)

**SAUCE**

3 tablespoons dry vermouth

Remaining reserved oyster juice (from above)

1½ tablespoons minced shallots

1½ tablespoons white wine vinegar

8 tablespoons (4 ounces) unsalted butter,
    cut into 8 pieces

1 tablespoon minced chives

1 to 2 ounces osetra caviar

---

Timing is important in the completion of this dish. The cooking should be a continuous process, so have the cream whipped, the water for the sabayon hot, and the remaining ingredients ready.

FOR THE TAPIOCA: Soak the tapioca in 1 cup of the milk for 1 hour. (Setting it in a warm place will speed up the rehydration of the pearls.)
TO SHUCK THE OYSTERS: Follow the method for shucking described on page 22. Trim away the muscle and the outer ruffled edge of each oyster and place the trimmings in a saucepan. Reserve the whole trimmed oysters and strain the oyster juice into a separate bowl. You should have about ½ cup of juice.
TO COOK THE TAPIOCA: In a bowl, whip ½ cup of the cream just until it holds its shape; reserve in the refrigerator.

Drain the softened tapioca in a strainer and discard the milk. Rinse the tapioca under cold running water, then place it in a small heavy pot.

Pour the remaining ¾ cup milk and ¾ cup cream over the oyster trimmings. Bring to a simmer, then strain the infused liquid onto the tapioca. Discard the trimmings.

Cook the tapioca over medium heat, stirring constantly with a wooden spoon, until it has thickened and the spoon leaves a trail when it is pulled through, 7 to 8 minutes. Continue to cook for another 5 to 7 minutes, until the tapioca has no resistance in the center and is translucent. The mixture will be sticky and if you lift some on the spoon and let it fall, some should still cling to the spoon. Remove the pot from the heat and set aside in a warm place.
FOR THE SABAYON: Place the egg yolks and the ¼ cup oyster juice in a metal bowl set over a pan of hot water. Whisk vigorously over medium heat for 2 to 3 minutes to incorporate as much air as possible. The finished sabayon will have thickened and lightened, the foam will have subsided, and the sabayon will hold a ribbon when it falls from the whisk. If the mixture begins to break, remove it from the heat and whisk quickly off the heat for a moment to recombine, then return to the heat.

Stir the hot sabayon into the tapioca, along with a generous amount of black pepper. Mix in the crème fraîche and the whipped cream. The tapioca will be a creamy pale yellow with the tapioca pearls suspended in the mixture. Season lightly with salt, remembering that the oysters and the caviar garnish will both be salty. Immediately spoon ¼ cup tapioca into each of eight 4- by 5-inch gratin dishes (with a 3- to 4-ounce capacity). Tap the gratin dishes on the counter so that the tapioca forms an even layer. Cover and refrigerate until ready to use, or for up to a day.
TO COMPLETE: Preheat the oven to 350°F.
FOR THE SAUCE: Combine the vermouth, the remaining reserved oyster juice, the shallots, and vinegar in a small saucepan. Bring to a simmer and simmer until most of the liquid has evaporated but the shallots are glazed, not dry. Whisk in the butter piece by piece, adding a new piece only when the previous one is almost incorporated (as you would for Beurre Monté, page 135).

Meanwhile, place the dishes of tapioca on a baking sheet and heat in the oven for 4 to 5 minutes, or until they just begin to puff up.

Add the oysters and the chives to the sauce to warm through.

Spoon 2 oysters and some of the sauce over each gratin and garnish the top with a quenelle (see page 274), or small oval scoop, of caviar. Serve immediately.

MAKES **8** SERVINGS

PICKLING LIQUID

1 cup white wine vinegar

½ cup water

½ cup sugar

1 star anise

3 cloves

6 coriander seeds

3 stems dill

6 meaty oysters, such as Belon or Salutation Bay, scrubbed with a brush

"CAPELLINI"

1 English cucumber, peeled

½ teaspoon kosher salt

1 tablespoon rice wine vinegar

1 teaspoon chopped dill

About 3 cups seaweed or Rock Salt Mix (recipe follows)

1 ounce sevruga caviar (more or less according to taste and budget)

6 sprigs dill

Good concepts often re-create themselves in different forms. In this case a great canapé—"Linguine" with White Clam Sauce (page 25)—led to the creation of another. Pickled julienned cucumber replaces the capellini, dill replaces the thyme, and oysters replace the clams. Instead of being served hot in the clam shells on rock salt, this canapé is served cold in the oyster shells on a bed of seaweed.

FOR THE PICKLING LIQUID: Place all of the ingredients in a saucepan. Bring to a boil, remove from the heat, cover, and allow to steep for 30 minutes. This is enough liquid to pickle up to 2 dozen oysters.

TO SHUCK THE OYSTERS: Follow the method for shucking described on page 22.

Wash the deeper halves of the shells and reserve. Using scissors, cut away the muscle portion of the oysters and discard. Wash the trimmed oysters (the *noix*) under cold running water to remove the milky residue, which would coagulate with the vinegar in the pickling liquid and create an unwanted coating on the oysters. Add the oysters to the pickling liquid and refrigerate in a covered container for at least 12 and up to 36 hours.

FOR THE "CAPELLINI": Using a mandoline, cut ¹/₁₆-inch-lengthwise slices from one side of the cucumber until you reach the seeds. Turn the cucumber and continue to cut slices from all four sides of the cucumber. Stack the slices and cut them lengthwise into ¹/₁₆-inch julienne strips to resemble capellini. You will need 1 cup "capellini." Combine the cucumber strands with the kosher salt and rice wine vinegar in a bowl and allow them to marinate for about 30 minutes to extract excess liquid.

Drain the "capellini" and squeeze to remove excess liquid. Place in a bowl and toss with the chopped dill.

TO COMPLETE: Place a bed of the seaweed or rock salt mix on each of six serving plates. Twirl the cucumber with a fork, as you would pasta, and place a mound in each oyster shell. Remove the oysters from the pickling liquid and place an oyster on each mound of cucumber. Garnish each oyster with about 1 teaspoon of caviar and a sprig of dill.

PICTURED ON PAGE 26                    MAKES 6 SERVINGS

## ROCK SALT MIX

| | |
|---|---|
| Rock salt (see Sources, page 315) | Allspice berries |
| Star anise | Cloves |
| Bay leaf | Black peppercorns |

This is a decorative and practical base for clam and oyster dishes. The shells nestle comfortably in the salt, and if it's been heated, the mix will help keep the shellfish hot and give off a fragrant aroma. It can be kept indefinitely at room temperature.

There are no specific proportions or spices for this mix. Use the salt as a base and mix in as much of each spice as you wish.

Mix the ingredients, then store in a covered container at room temperature. The mix can be reused many times as long as if heated, it did not burn.

# "Linguine" with White Clam Sauce

**CLAMS**

18 littleneck clams, soaked in a few changes
    of cold water for several hours, drained,
    and scrubbed with a brush

2 large cloves garlic, unpeeled, slightly crushed

1 large shallot, roughly chopped

2 sprigs thyme

2 small bay leaves

$\frac{1}{2}$ cup crisp, dry white wine, such as
    Sauvigon Blanc or Muscadet

**SAUCE**

2 teaspoons Roasted Garlic Purée (recipe follows)

Reserved clam broth (from above)

12 tablespoons (6 ounces) unsalted butter,
    cut into $\frac{1}{2}$-inch pieces

Few drops of white wine vinegar

3 cups Rock Salt Mix (page 24)

2 ounces Pasta Dough (page 78),
    rolled out and cut into capellini

1 tablespoon chopped Italian parsley

$\frac{1}{2}$ teaspoon thyme leaves

Kosher salt and freshly ground black pepper

The Italian classic refined and reduced to a canapé size—clams steamed open in white wine infused with garlic and thyme, sauce made from the clam broth, butter, and more garlic. We use fresh capellini instead of linguini and whole littleneck clams, then serve the final dish in the clam shells. (Do not season the sauce until right before serving, as the clams add salt to the dish.)

TO COOK THE CLAMS: Place the clams, garlic, shallot, thyme sprigs, bay leaves, and wine in a stainless steel saucepan that holds the clams in one layer. Cover and bring to a boil over medium heat, moving the clams around from time to time to ensure even cooking. Remove each clam as it opens. This should take place within about 5 minutes; discard any unopened clams. Strain the broth through a chinois (see page 73) and set aside.

Remove the clams from the shells. Using a paring knife, loosen the muscle attached to the shell. Save the 18 largest half shells for the finished dish. Pull away and discard the muscle from each clam, leaving only the tender center section of the clam. Trim the clams as necessary for a smooth edge. The clams can be prepared to this point up to a day ahead. If you are not completing the dish, allow the broth to cool. Then place the clams in a container with the cooled broth and refrigerate.

Place the trimmed clams and the broth in separate small saucepans. Preheat the oven to 325°F.

FOR THE SAUCE: Whisk the garlic purée into the clam broth and bring to a boil. Simmer to reduce to 2 to 3 tablespoons. Whisk in the butter piece by piece, adding the next piece only when the last piece is almost incorporated. Season with white wine vinegar. Remove from the heat and strain into a bowl. Pour half of the strained sauce over the clams.

TO COMPLETE: Spread the rock salt on a baking sheet, place in the oven, and heat for about 5 minutes, or until hot and aromatic. Meanwhile, add the pasta to a large pot of lightly salted boiling water and cook for about 2 minutes, or until tender. Gently reheat the clams.

Drain the pasta, then toss it in the bowl with the remaining sauce, the parsley, and thyme leaves (chopsticks work well for this). Season to taste.

Place a bed of warm rock salt on each of six plates. Using a small fork, twirl a small portion of the pasta and place it in a reserved clamshell; repeat to fill all the shells. Top each portion of pasta with a warm clam and some of the sauce. Arrange 3 filled clamshells on each bed of rock salt.

MAKES 6 SERVINGS

## ROASTED GARLIC PURÉE

$1\frac{1}{2}$ tablespoons unsalted butter

3 large heads garlic
   (about 7 ounces)

1 teaspoon kosher salt

Preheat the oven to 300°F.

Place the butter on a double thickness of foil and smash it to make a base for the garlic. Top with the garlic and sprinkle with the salt. Fold over the sides to make a package and roast for $1\frac{1}{2}$ hours, or until the garlic is soft.

While it is still warm, scrape the softened garlic through a tamis (see page 73) or pass it through a food mill, leaving behind the skins. Roasted garlic purée should be used the same day it is prepared.

MAKES A SCANT CUP

You go out to an Italian restaurant, you order something like linguine with clam sauce, and think "Why don't I do this, reduce that, do this?" And you come up with a fun new dish—"linguine" with clam sauce served in the clam shells. People can relate to the concept and flavors because they already know how it will taste.

Opposite: Pickled Oysters, page 24. Above: "Linguine" with White Clam Sauce, page 25.

## THE MUSHROOM LADY: CONNIE GREEN

Bobcats and mountain lions have returned to the woods where mycologist Connie Green hunts, so she always keeps the blade of her picking knife open. She lives on the side of a mountain overlooking the Napa Valley, and in winter she prowls its hills hunting wild mushrooms for the restaurant. When she sees a fat chanterelle pushing out of damp leaves beside her driveway, she drops to the ground and caresses the great golden fungus—the "workhorse" of wild mushrooms. Connie often hunts at night, the best time to forage, especially for the black trumpet; its spore-bearing layer, she explains, gives off a phosphorescent glow in the beam of a flashlight.

Connie lives a kind of outlaw life, working only with wild, wild mushrooms—"act-of-God mushrooms," she calls them. And she has allied herself with an outlaw culture, a group of men and women called circuit pickers, who make their living on what's known as the Mushroom Trail, picking wild growths from Northern California up into the Yukon. They live largely outside society, in tents and cheap motels, and are known only by nicknames (Yankee Jim, Coke Bottle Danny). Connie meets them at a rickety motel they've dubbed the Mushroom Palace, where they stay up late drinking and telling stories of the trail, and in the morning Connie returns to Napa with their mushrooms—cèpes; morels; lobster mushrooms; matsutaki; the lacy, floral-scented cauliflower mushroom; and the remarkable, rare candy cap, a mushroom that smells and tastes like maple syrup.

"They use parts of your mouth you never knew you had," Connie says. —M.R.

# Soup

My favorite soups are the *amuse-gueule* soups, canapé soups, which we serve in demitasse or small soup cups: just two or three sips of intense lobster, of intense fennel, avocado, or watercress. It's the explosion of flavor that's so exciting—taking an ingredient and making it more than what it was to begin with.

Soup is simple. Identify your ingredient, cook it perfectly, and adjust the consistency. First, your main ingredient must be of prime quality: If you're making turnip soup, you want a really good turnip. When you have your ingredient, ask yourself, "How do I cook this best?" Carrots? They're a root vegetable, so you glaze them. If you glaze them perfectly, there's your soup—just adjust the consistency with stock or other liquid. Green vegetables? Start by "big-pot blanching," then purée, add liquid, and strain—there's your soup.

The liquid depends on your ingredient. If it's turnips, you can use chicken stock, because a turnip has a very sharp forward flavor that won't be lost beneath the chicken flavor. Favas, though, are so delicate and fresh you may not even want vegetable stock, maybe just enough water to bring the purée to the right consistency.

We try to make eight soups every day, and the single idea behind them is to intensify the flavor and color of the main ingredient. One spoonful of carrot soup should deliver the flavor of several carrots. A case of watercress makes only twelve ounces of purée. It then needs to be diluted, like an artist's paint that needs to be thinned with a neutral oil before it can be put on the canvas.

Certainly there are issues of finesse, such as adding cream. Cream tends to mute flavors, but it adds body and texture. Adding oils to soups finishes and enriches them; the pea soup with white truffle oil is a perfect example. We use lobster stock for two soups. For the consommé, we clarify it, gel it, and top it with crème fraîche. For the broth, we reduce the stock to a glace and cream it: the ultimate lobster taste.

**LOBSTER STOCK**

¼ cup canola oil

3¼ pounds lobster bodies (about 12 to 13 bodies, see page 124), quartered

1½ cups (6½ ounces) chopped fennel

1¾ cups (8 ounces) sliced carrots

3 cups (8 ounces) sliced button mushrooms

1½ cups (6 ounces) sliced shallots

1 cup dry vermouth

6 quarts water

4 cloves garlic

½ cup (1 ounce) tightly packed tarragon sprigs

4 pounds chopped tomatoes (7 cups)

**CLARIFICATION RAFT**

Generous ¼ cup (1½ ounces) chopped fennel

Generous ¾ cup (4 ounces) chopped carrots

⅓ cup (2 ounces) chopped onion

3 large egg whites

¼ cup lobster coral (roe; see page 33), at room temperature (optional, but recommended)

4 gelatin sheets (see Sources, page 315), soaked in cold water to soften

A small piece of lobster coral (optional)

½ cup crème fraîche, whipped

About 2 tablespoons Brunoise (page 155)

Be sure to have the correct amount of liquid before adding the gelatin; simmer the stock to reduce it to the exact quantity specified. Because this soup is extraordinarily rich—lobster essence, magnified—we serve it in very small bowls or demitasse cups, just two ounces per serving. This recipe will make four cups of consommé. I don't recommend reducing the recipe further, but any extra consommé can be frozen.

FOR THE STOCK: Heat the oil in a large rondeau, or deep straight-sided braising pan, over medium-high heat just until it smokes. Add the lobster bodies and sauté, turning often, until they turn red, 3 to 4 minutes. Be careful not to let them burn. (If your pot is not large enough to accomplish this easily, do it in two batches.)

Add the fennel, carrots, mushrooms, and shallots. Continue cooking, stirring occasionally, for about 10 minutes, to soften but not color the vegetables. Add the vermouth, water, garlic, tarragon, and tomatoes and bring to a boil, then reduce the heat and let the stock simmer for 2 hours.

Strain the stock through a China cap (see page 73), smashing the shells and vegetables with a wooden spoon to extract as much liquid as possible. Discard the shells and vegetables and pour the stock through a chinois (see page 73), tapping the top rim to help it run through. Do not stir or force any remaining solids through the strainer; they would cloud the stock. There should be approximately 4 quarts of stock. Let cool to room temperature. The stock can be refrigerated for up to 1 day.

Remove and discard any fat from the top of the stock, then place it in a heavy pot.

FOR THE CLARIFICATION RAFT: Finely grind the fennel, carrots, and onion in a meat grinder or food processor. Whisk the egg whites and the ¼ cup coral in a bowl until frothy, then stir in the ground vegetables.

Whisk the vegetable mixture into the cold stock. Place the pot over low heat and stir constantly with a wooden spoon until it reaches 128°F. Stop stirring and bring the stock to a simmer.

As the liquid begins to simmer, a raft will form over the stock. Cut a 1- to 2-inch "breather" hole in the side of the raft. You will be able to see the movement of the simmering stock through the hole. The raft acts as a filter to clarify the stock. The liquid may simmer up through the raft in a few spots, but it should never be at a full boil, which would break the clarification raft and cloud the consommé. Simmer for 1 hour. Be sure to keep the breather hole open.

Line a China cap with a damp towel or cheesecloth and set it over a deep container. Leaving behind as much of the raft as possible, ladle the stock slowly down the side of the cloth, starting at the top of the strainer. (Pouring it this way will keep the liquid from pushing through any fat or

Making consommé is an exacting process, but the results are amazing. The powerful lobster jelly melts in your mouth and the vegetables add a subtle bite. The coral is not only a color burst, it provides saltiness to the sweet lobster; and the acid in the crème fraîche makes all these colors and flavors and textures sparkle.

impurities that gather in the bottom of the China cap.) Tilt the pot as necessary to reach as much clear stock as possible. Leave behind any that doesn't look clear and discard it along with the raft. You should have about 2 quarts of consommé.

You will be able to see, floating on top, any fat remaining in the consommé. Gently lay a paper towel on top of the liquid and quickly glide it over the surface. Discard the towel and repeat several more times until there is no remaining fat (which could cloud the consommé).

Line a chinois with a clean towel or cheesecloth and strain the consommé one last time into a pot. Bring it to a simmer and reduce the consommé to 1 quart. Pour into a container.

Squeeze the gelatin sheets dry and stir them into the hot consommé until completely dissolved. Set in a larger container of ice and water and let cool to room temperature, stirring occasionally, then refrigerate, covered, for several hours, or overnight, to gel. The consommé will keep refrigerated for up to 3 days (after 3 days, it can be reboiled and kept for 1 to 2 more days). For longer storage, it can be frozen for up to 1 month;

when ready to use, defrost the consommé and bring to a boil, then cool as above and allow to re-gel in the refrigerator.

FOR THE LOBSTER CORAL (OPTIONAL): Wrap the coral in plastic wrap. Place it in a resealable plastic bag, pressing out any air from the bag, and seal the bag well. Submerge it in boiling water and cook the coral until it has turned bright red (you are making hard-boiled eggs!). Remove the coral from the bag and refrigerate it for an hour, or until it is cold.

Grate or grind the coral in a mini-blender or grinder. Store the ground coral in the refrigerator until ready to use, or for up to 1 day, or wrap well and freeze for up to several months. (The cooked coral can be frozen as a solid piece and then grated while still frozen when ready to use.)

TO COMPLETE: Break up the cold consommé with a spoon and place about ¼ cup in each serving cup or bowl. Top each serving of consommé with a quenelle (see page 274), or small oval scoop, of whipped crème fraîche and sprinkle with the brunoise and, if using, grated lobster coral.

MAKES 16 SERVINGS (4 CUPS)

## Creamy Maine Lobster Broth

¼ cup canola oil

3 lobster bodies (12 ounces total, see page 124), cut into quarters

1½ cups chopped tomatoes

½ cup chopped carrots

1 bunch tarragon (½ ounce)

2 cups heavy cream

Lobsters and cream is a luxurious combination, intensified here in the form of a canapé soup. I froth the broth before serving it.

When you are preparing lobsters, save the bodies to make this broth (freeze them if need be for future use). This is a very rich soup, best served in small portions.

Heat the oil in a large rondeau, or deep straight-sided braising pan. Add the lobster shells and sear over medium-high heat for 1 to 2 minutes per side, until they turn red. (If your pot is not big enough to accomplish this easily, do it in two batches.) Add the tomatoes, carrots, and tarragon, cover the shells and vegetables with water, and bring to a boil. Skim off any impurities that rise to the top. Reduce the heat and simmer over low heat for 1 hour. Strain the stock through a large strainer or a China cap (see page 73), smashing the lobster bodies with a wooden spoon to extract all the liquid, and then strain again through a chinois (see page 73) into a clean saucepan.

Return the strained stock to the stove and simmer until it is reduced to 1 cup. Add the heavy cream, return to a simmer, and cook, skimming occasionally, until the broth is reduced to 2 cups. Strain through a chinois into a container, discarding any solids remaining in the strainer. Cover and refrigerate the broth for several hours to chill, or for up to 3 days.

TO COMPLETE: Place the cold broth in a heavy saucepan and whisk vigorously over medium heat as you reheat it. The broth will froth as you whisk in air. Pour the hot broth into demitasse cups.

PICTURED ON PAGE 34          MAKES 6 TO 8 SERVINGS (2 CUPS)

## Gazpacho

1 cup chopped red onions

1 cup chopped green bell pepper

1 cup chopped English cucumber

1 cup peeled and chopped tomatoes

1½ teaspoons chopped garlic

1½ teaspoons kosher salt

¼ teaspoon cayenne

¼ cup tomato paste

1 tablespoon white wine vinegar

¼ cup plus 2 tablespoons extra virgin olive oil

1 tablespoon fresh lemon juice

3 cups tomato juice

Sprig of thyme

Balsamic Glaze (page 238), in a squeeze bottle

Don't always think of gazpacho as soup. Think of it as a sauce. Think of it hot as well as cold. It goes beautifully with grilled chicken or fish. Gazpacho is served in small portions as a canapé at the French Laundry, garnished with balsamic glaze, or as a sauce with the Salad of Globe Artichokes with Garden Herbs and Gazpacho (page 62). It can also be served in larger portions as a traditional cold soup. This soup couldn't be easier; it achieves its powerful flavor simply by overnight maceration, which is the only "cooking" involved.

Mix all the ingredients except the balsamic glaze together in a bowl or other container, cover, and let sit in the refrigerator overnight.

The next day, remove the thyme and blend all the ingredients in a blender until the gazpacho is smooth. You will have about 2 quarts. For a smoother texture, strain the soup to yield about 1 quart. Refrigerate the gazpacho until ready to serve.

TO COMPLETE: Ladle the cold soup into bowls and squeeze dots of balsamic glaze over the top.

MAKES 8 TO 16 SERVINGS

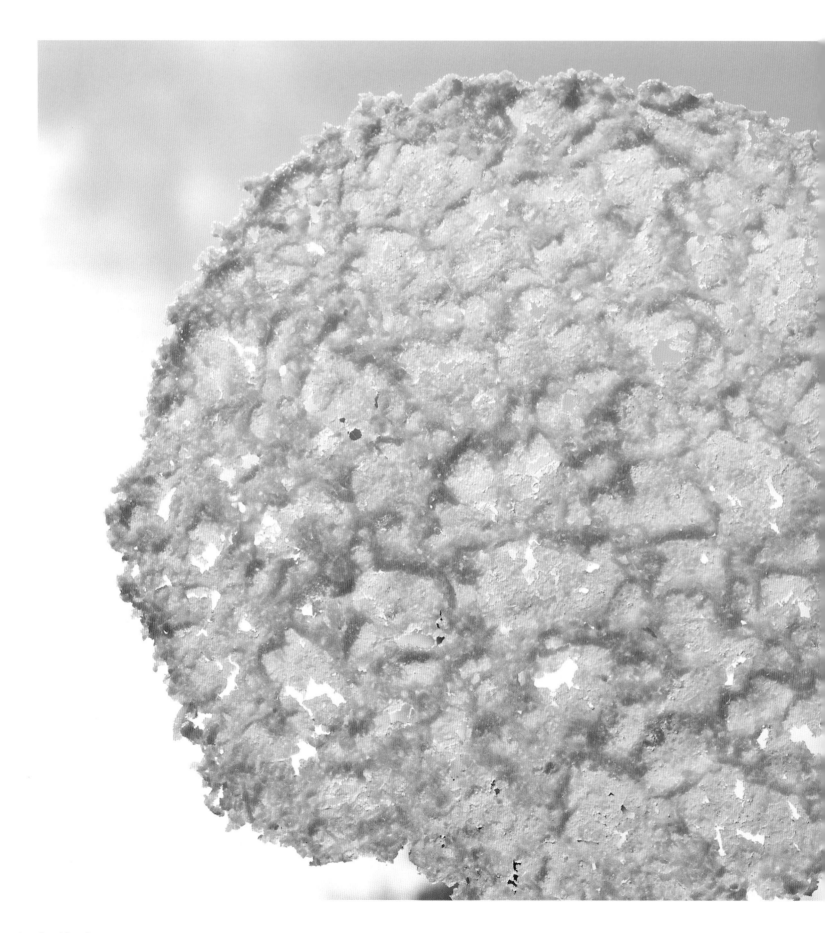

## Purée of English Pea Soup with White Truffle Oil and Parmesan Crisps

3 pounds English peas, shelled (about 3 cups)

7 quarts water

About 1 cup sugar

1½ cups kosher salt

¼ to ½ cup Vegetable Stock (page 227)

¼ cup water

Kosher salt and freshly ground white pepper

¼ cup white truffle oil

6 to 12 Parmesan Crisps (recipe follows)

(1 per serving)

This soup should be served the the same day it's made, as it will oxidize, or discolor, over time. The vivid green of the soup results in an extraordinary visual impact. The success of this recipe relies on the quality of the peas. Look for small sweet peas. Taste your peas for sweetness to determine the amount of sugar to add to the water (make this soup in early summer when English peas are at their peak). A Parmesan crisp is placed on each serving cup as a "lid"; be sure to make the crisps a size appropriate to your cups. This soup can be served hot or cold, but either way, I like to enrich it with white truffle oil, which enhances its luxurious flavor and texture.

Place the peas in a bowl, cover them with ice, and toss together to chill the peas (this step will help return their bright color).

Bring the water to a rolling boil in a large pot and add the sugar and salt. Lift up a small batch of peas with a strainer, letting the ice fall back into the bowl, and add them to the water. It is important that the water returns to a boil almost immediately to keep the peas a vivid green color; it may not if too many peas are added, so adjust the quantity added as necessary to maintain the boil. Cook the peas until they are tender and fully cooked, 7 to 10 minutes, depending on the quantity and quality of peas added.

While the peas cook, place a colander in a bowl of ice water. (This will make it easier to remove the chilled cooked peas from the ice.) When the peas are tender, remove them to the colander to chill as quickly as possible. Lift the colander from the ice bath and drain the peas well. Repeat this process until all the peas are cooked.

Purée the peas in a food processor, then scrape the purée through a tamis (see page 73). (If the vegetables are cooked correctly, some of the purée will stick to the bottom of the wire screen, and you will have to scrape it off.) You should have about 2 cups of purée.

Place ¼ cup vegetable stock and the water in a large blender (if your blender is small you may want to do this in two batches). Add the pea

purée and blend. (The color of the soup will lighten from the air blended into it, but it will return to dark green after it sits.) Check the consistency of the soup. If it is too thick and needs more liquid, add either more vegetable stock or more water, depending on how flavorful the soup is, and blend again. Add a pinch of salt, white pepper to taste, and blend again. Pour the soup through a chinois (see page 73). If you are serving the soup cold, stir in the truffle oil and refrigerate the soup in a covered container until serving. If you are serving the soup hot, reheat gently over low heat and stir in the truffle oil just before serving.

Serve the soup garnished with the Parmesan crisp "lids."

MAKES 6 TO 12 SERVINGS (ABOUT 3 CUPS)

### PARMESAN CRISPS

½ cup finely grated Parmigiano-Reggiano (from a moist piece of cheese)

These crisps can be made in any size, but it's important to use freshly grated Parmigiano-Reggiano. These are easy and have many uses—serve them with salads or soups, or use them to hold goat cheese mousse (page 49)—but be sure to make extra, because you'll want to eat a few while you're making them.

Preheat the oven to 325°F. Line a baking sheet with a Silpat (see Sources, page 315).

Sprinkle about 2 teaspoons of the cheese in one corner of the Silpat. Use your fingers to spread the cheese into a 2-inch circle. Repeat with the remaining cheese; you should have about 12 rounds.

Bake for 8 to 10 minutes, or until they are golden brown. Use a small spatula to transfer them to paper towels. They will still be soft when they are removed but will stiffen as they cool. Store the crisps in an airtight container for up to 2 days.

MAKES ABOUT TWELVE 2-INCH CRISPS

Opposite, right: Blini with Sweet Roasted Peppers and Eggplant Caviar, page 41

**Blini** are an elegant way to begin a meal. They're light, creamy, and refined, and they're a wonderful vehicle for garnishes, so we serve them six or seven different ways, treating them, in effect, like a luxurious potato. The blini almost dissolve on your tongue, leaving the flavors of the garnishes.

One way we serve them is with roasted peppers and eggplant caviar. Another is with bottarga, a bright tasty garnish, especially when paired with the rich, buttery tomato confit. But blini are great even with just a little fresh butter. Although we make them small, there's no reason you can't make them larger.

## Yukon Gold Potato Blini

1 pound Yukon Gold potatoes

2 tablespoons all-purpose flour

2 to 3 tablespoons crème fraîche, at room temperature

2 large eggs

1 large egg yolk

Kosher salt and freshly ground white pepper

I like to use Yukon Gold potatoes for these blini because they absorb more cream than other potatoes and thus result in the best possible texture. This recipe will make extra batter, but it's a difficult recipe to reduce. The batter is best when used immediately, but it can be made up to two hours ahead if stored in a warm place (the cream may clot if it gets too cold). Use a scale to weigh the proper amount of potatoes after puréeing them, and make the batter while the potatoes are still warm or the blini will not have the correct texture.

Place the potatoes in a saucepan with cold water to cover by at least 2 inches. Bring to a boil over high heat, reduce the heat, and simmer until the potatoes are thoroughly cooked and tender.

Peel the warm potatoes and press them through a tamis (see page 73). Immediately weigh out 9 ounces of puréed potatoes and place them in a medium metal bowl. Working quickly, whisk the flour into the warm potatoes, then whisk in 2 tablespoons crème fraîche. Add 1 egg, whisking until the batter is smooth, add the second egg, and then add the yolk.

Hold the whisk with some of the batter over the bowl. The batter should fall in a thick stream but hold its shape when it hits the batter in the bowl. If it is too thick, add a little more crème fraîche. Season to taste with salt and white pepper.

Heat an electric griddle to 350°F. Note, if you do not have a griddle, heat a large nonstick skillet over medium-low heat. Spoon between 1 and 1½ teaspoons of batter onto the griddle or skillet for each pancake. Cook until the bottoms are browned, 1 to 2 minutes. Then flip them to cook the second side, about 1 minute. The blini should be evenly browned with a small ring of white around the edges. Transfer the blini to a small baking sheet and keep warm while you make the remaining blini, wiping the skillet with a paper towel between batches. Serve the blini as soon as possible.

MAKES ABOUT 3 DOZEN SMALL BLINI

## Blini with Bottarga di Muggine and Confit of Tomato

¼ cup minced Tomato Confit (9 pieces) (page 64)

1½ tablespoons Vegetable Stock (page 227) or Chicken Stock (page 226)

2 teaspoons extra virgin olive oil

3 tablespoons Beurre Monté (page 135)

1½ teaspoons minced Italian parsley

Kosher salt

12 Yukon Gold Potato Blini (previous recipe)

Small piece of bottarga di muggine (see Sources, page 315)

Bottarga is the salted roe of cod or tuna. I use bottarga di muggine, from cod, because it has a milder flavor than the tuna, bottarga di tonno. It's sold by the piece and, kept tightly wrapped in the refrigerator, will last for months. It's salty and has a pleasant fishy taste, not unlike anchovies. In Italy, it's grated over pasta and is wonderful that way. It would also work perfectly as a garnish for risotto, or grated over salad.

Warm the tomato confit and stock in a small saucepan over medium heat. Stir in the olive oil and simmer for a few seconds. Reduce the heat and stir in the beurre monté, parsley, and salt to taste.

Place a spoonful of the sauce on each plate. Top each plate with 2 blini and grate bottarga over and around the pancakes.

MAKES 6 SERVINGS

# Blini with Roasted Sweet Peppers and Eggplant Caviar

2 tablespoons minced roasted yellow bell pepper
(see page 250)
2 tablespoons minced roasted red bell pepper
(see page 250)

1 1/2 tablespoons Vegetable Stock (page 227) or
Chicken Stock (page 226)
1 tablespoon Beurre Monté (page 135)
1 1/2 teaspoons minced chives

Kosher salt
1/4 cup Eggplant Caviar (recipe follows)
12 Yukon Gold Potato Blini (page 40)
About 1 1/2 teaspoons Pepper Confetti (page 97)

Combine the minced peppers and stock in a small saucepan and simmer over medium heat until most of the stock has evaporated. Reduce the heat and stir in the beurre monté, chives, and salt to taste. Remove from the heat.

Place a spoonful of eggplant caviar on each plate. Top with 2 overlapping potato blini and garnish each serving with a quenelle (see page 274), or small oval scoop, of roasted peppers. Sprinkle the plates with the pepper confetti.

PICTURED ON PAGE 39                                MAKES 6 SERVINGS

## EGGPLANT CAVIAR

1 large eggplant (about 1 1/4 pounds)
Kosher salt
1/4 cup extra virgin olive oil, plus extra for roasting
1/4 teaspoon very finely minced garlic (almost a paste)
1/2 teaspoon Dijon mustard

Cut the eggplant lengthwise in half. Score both halves on the flesh side, making a crisscross pattern about 1/4 inch deep. Sprinkle both halves with salt and place them scored side down on a baking sheet. Cover with another baking sheet and place a heavy object (such as a set of bowls) on top. Let the eggplant render its excess liquid at room temperature for 1 to 2 hours.

Preheat the oven to 350°F.

Rinse the eggplant, pat dry, and rub with some olive oil. Place the halves flesh side down on a lightly oiled baking sheet. Roast for about an hour, or until the eggplant is very soft and the skin is wrinkled; there should be no resistance when tested with a knife. Remove from the oven and let sit until cool enough to handle.

Scoop out the eggplant pulp and lightly chop it. Place the pulp in a double layer of cheesecloth and tie it securely into a bundle with butcher's twine. Leave the ends of the twine about 6 inches long so you can hang the bundle from a refrigerator shelf over a bowl, making sure it dangles freely. Or simply place the bundle in a colander set over a bowl and refrigerate. Let drain for at least 2 hours, or overnight.

Remove the eggplant from the refrigerator and hold the bundle over the sink. Twist and squeeze the cheesecloth to remove as much additional liquid as possible.

Place the pulp (you should have about 1/2 cup) in a small food processor or mini-chop. Pulse a few times to begin breaking up the eggplant. With the motor running, slowly pour 2 tablespoons of the olive oil through the feed tube. Continue blending for 30 seconds. The color and texture will begin to lighten. Stop the machine and add the garlic, mustard, and salt to taste. Blend again, then add the remaining 2 tablespoons olive oil. Continue processing for another minute, then taste and adjust the seasoning. Cover and store in the refrigerator until ready to serve, or for up to 1 week.

PICTURED ON PAGE 39                                MAKES 1/2 CUP

# The Importance of **Hollandaise**

My mother, a single parent by the time we moved to South Florida, managed restaurants. After I graduated from high school, I washed dishes at one of them, the Palm Beach Yacht Club in West Palm Beach.

When the chef there quit, Mom told me I was the chef. I called up one of my buddies and asked if he wanted a job. First thing we did in the morning was clean the bathrooms. Then we'd clean the dining room, then set up for lunch. Dinner too, on weekends. Together we ran the show—we did everything.

My older brother, Joseph, was a cook at an upscale French restaurant nearby, and when we were growing up, Joseph tried to keep good food on the table for Mom and my four brothers and, eventually, a stepdad and half-sister. But other than Joseph, no one was especially interested in food. As far as a trade, I tended toward carpentry, if toward any one way at all.

Now suddenly I was a chef. The year was 1975, and the yacht club's food was basic: hamburgers, French fries, sandwiches, eggs Benedict. When I didn't know how to broil lobster tail, I'd call Joseph and he'd tell me how. He told me how to cook a prime rib. I learned how to make omelets. I learned how to cook meat to the right temperature.

Then he walked me through making a hollandaise sauce. I'd just turned twenty. I was so excited by that first hollandaise that I ran out and told Captain John, the dock manager, about it. Hollandaise became the great daily challenge.

It started with the clarification of butter. I had no idea of the science of cooking, didn't know why butter clarified, so even this was something apparently ordained by the gods. "Will it clarify today?" I'd think. "Hope so."

And then the hollandaise itself. Again, I had no idea why the egg yolks and clarified butter came together. I never associated it with mayonnaise—I didn't know how mayonnaise was made. Hollandaise was just a mysterious thing that had a life of its own. You could screw it up in a second, and I was terrified every morning that, without reason, it would fall apart. Joseph taught me to whisk in a little boiling water if it broke—sometimes that worked, sometimes it didn't; I didn't know why.

To me, hollandaise sauce was magic. Nothing we did at the yacht club had that kind of mystery for me or was so critical as this centuries-old French emulsion sauce. I worked at the yacht club for two years and I made hollandaise every day. It was not only the high point of each morning, trying to get the hollandaise perfect; making hollandaise was the high point of those two years.

Today, I still get great pleasure from making a hollandaise sauce or any of its derivatives. I love a light béarnaise, hollandaise flavored with shallots and tarragon; I sometimes serve it at the French Laundry with rabbit. It has a real anchoring quality for me because of its importance during my first two years as a cook—every day of those two years, trying to perfect that hollandaise.

FRENCH LAUNDRY BÉARNAISE MOUSSELINE

A classical béarnaise should be as thick as mayonnaise. This recipe is in effect a standard béarnaise with whipped cream added at the end to make it light and pourable: Reduce red or white wine vinegar with chopped shallots, chopped fresh tarragon, and cracked black pepper until the pan is almost dry (the shallots and herbs should still have plenty of moisture). I do this over direct heat in a pan with sloping sides, but you may feel safer cooking it over a water bath. Add egg yolks and half an eggshell of water per yolk. Whip the yolks continuously over the heat; you'll see them tighten up and eventually form ribbons. When the eggs are thoroughly cooked—the ribbons should be thick, the mixture should taste cooked and be hot—remove the pan from the heat and whisk in clarified butter in a thin steady stream. When you've achieved the right consistency (about 8 ounces of butter for every 3 yolks), taste and season with salt and lemon juice, then strain through a chinois. Just before serving, add chopped fresh tarragon, finely minced shallots, and freshly ground black pepper, then stir in whipped cream—about a third as much by volume.

# Garden Canapés

Our garden canapés, which we serve to guests in the courtyard of the French Laundry, are meant to be simple and elegant bites you can eat standing, with a glass in one hand; they're especially delicious with Champagne before dinner.

Above: Shrimp with Avocado Salsa, page 66. Opposite, left: Truffle dip from "Chips and Dip," page 48; right: Gruyère Cheese Gougères, page 48.

Gougères are a classical preparation often served at wine tastings in France. The puffs are made from a savory pâte à choux, or cream puff dough—flavored here with Gruyère. They're best served hot out of the oven, offering that creamy-dough gratification. Don't add the cheese, and the puff is a base for a dessert.

"Chips and Dip" are, of course, the French Laundry equivalent of an American favorite, which we make a little more elegant by adding truffle to the chips and to the crème fraîche dip. The size and shape of the potatoes will determine how many chips each will yield. Once you begin cutting the potatoes, work quickly, as the potatoes will oxidize and discolor.

## Gruyère Cheese Gougères

1 cup water

7 tablespoons (3½ ounces) unsalted butter

1 tablespoon kosher salt, or more to taste

Pinch of sugar

1¼ cups (5 ounces) all-purpose flour

4 to 5 large eggs

1¼ cups grated Gruyère (5 ounces)

Freshly ground white pepper

Preheat the oven to 450°F. Line two baking sheets with Silpats (see Sources, page 315) or parchment paper.

In a medium saucepan, combine the water, butter, salt, and sugar and bring to a boil. Add all the flour at once, reduce the heat to medium, and stir with a wooden spoon for 2 minutes, or until the mixture forms a ball and the excess moisture has evaporated (if the ball forms more quickly, continue to cook and stir for a full 2 minutes).

Transfer the mixture to the bowl of a mixer fitted with the paddle and beat for about 30 seconds at medium speed to cool slightly. Add 4 eggs and continue to mix until completely combined and the batter has a smooth, silky texture. Stop the machine and lift up the beater to check the consistency of the batter. The batter in the mixing bowl should form a peak with a tip that falls over. If it is too stiff, beat in the white of the remaining egg. Check again and, if necessary, add the yolk. Finally, mix in ¾ cup of the Gruyère and adjust the seasoning with salt and white pepper.

Fill a pastry bag fitted with a ⅜-inch plain pastry tip with the gougère batter. Pipe the batter into 1-tablespoon mounds on the baking sheets, leaving about 2 inches between the gougères as the mixture will spread during baking. Sprinkle the top of each gougère with about ½ teaspoon of the remaining grated cheese and bake for 7 to 8 minutes, or until they puff and hold their shape. Reduce the heat to 350°F. and bake for an additional 20 to 25 minutes. When the gougères are done, they should be a light golden brown color. When you break one open, it should be hollow; the inside should be cooked but still slightly moist. Remove the pans from the oven and serve the gougères while hot.

PICTURED ON PAGE 47          MAKES ABOUT 4 DOZEN GOUGÈRES

## "CHIPS AND DIP"
## Potato Chips with Truffle Dip

TRUFFLE CHIPS

1 cup Clarified Butter (page 125), melted

Kosher salt

1 to 2 russet potatoes

24 to 48 thin slices fresh black truffle (1 to 1½ ounces)

TRUFFLE DIP  MAKES ⅔ CUP

⅓ cup crème fraîche

½ ounce fresh black truffle, finely minced

2 tablespoons white truffle oil

Kosher salt and freshly ground black pepper

Preheat the oven to 300°F.

FOR THE CHIPS: Place a Silpat (see Sources, page 315) on a baking sheet and generously brush it with clarified butter; sprinkle with kosher salt.

Peel the potatoes and trim them into long ovals approximately 2 inches long and 1½ inches wide. Using a mandoline, cut the potatoes into paper-thin ovals. As you work, stack the potatoes in the order you cut them so that you will be able to match them up as closely as possible.

Lay the potato slices on the Silpat in pairs, keeping each one's match at its side. Place one or two truffle slices each on half the potato slices and cover each with its match. Press and smooth each chip to remove any air pockets between the two potato slices.

Brush the potatoes generously with clarified butter and place a second Silpat over them. Top the potatoes with a baking sheet to weight them and keep them flat. Bake for 25 to 35 minutes, reversing the pan halfway through the cooking process. Remove the chips when they are golden brown and drain on paper towels.

FOR THE DIP: In a bowl set over a larger bowl of ice, whip the crème fraîche until stiff. Reserve 1 to 2 teaspoons of the minced truffle to garnish the dip and stir the remaining truffle into the crème fraîche. Add the truffle oil and season to taste with salt and pepper.

Spoon the dip into a serving bowl and sprinkle with the reserved truffles. Serve the chips on the side.

PICTURED ON PAGE 47          MAKES 24 TO 36 CHIPS

# Parmigiano-Reggiano Crisps with Goat Cheese Mousse

**PARMESAN CRISPS**

1 cup finely grated Parmigiano-Reggiano
(from a moist piece of cheese)

**GOAT CHEESE MOUSSE**

6 ounces fresh goat cheese
(or other soft goat cheese)

4 to 6 tablespoons heavy cream

1 tablespoon minced Italian parsley

Kosher salt and freshly ground black pepper

A clean egg carton

Here, these easy Parmesan crisps form small cups for a creamy goat cheese mousse. It's best to bake only half the crisps at a time, because they may harden while you're working with them.

Preheat the oven to 325°F.

FOR THE PARMESAN CRISPS: Line a baking sheet with a Silpat (see Sources, page 315), or use a nonstick baking sheet.

Place a 2½-inch ring mold (see Sources, page 315) in one corner of the Silpat and fill it with 1 tablespoon of the grated cheese. Using your finger, spread the cheese into an even layer. Repeat to make 8 rounds, leaving at least 1 inch between them.

Bake for 8 to 10 minutes, or until the crisps are a rich golden brown. Remove the pan from the oven and let cool for about 30 seconds to firm the crisps enough so you can remove them with a spatula. One by one, remove the crisps and gently press each one into a hollow in the egg carton to form a tulip shape. After a few minutes, remove the cooled crisps from the carton and make 8 more crisps.

FOR THE GOAT CHEESE MOUSSE: Place the goat cheese in a food processor and process (depending on the cheese used, it may look smooth or crumbly). Pour ¼ cup of the cream through the feed tube and continue to process until the mixture is smooth but will hold a shape when piped; if necessary, add a little more cream. Add the parsley and salt and pepper to taste and mix just to combine. Taste and adjust the seasoning. The mousse can be refrigerated for 2 to 3 days; let stand at room temperature for about 30 minutes to soften slightly before piping.

Place the mousse in a pastry bag fitted with a medium star tip. Pipe 2 to 3 teaspoons of mousse into each Parmesan crisp and serve.

MAKES 16 CRISPS

# Shrimp with Avocado Salsa

½ recipe Court Bouillon (recipe follows)

6 large shrimp (16 to 20 per pound) in their shells

**AVOCADO SALSA**

3 tablespoons very finely diced red onion

3 tablespoons very finely diced cucumber

¼ cup plus 2 tablespoons very finely diced avocado

1 teaspoon olive oil

Squeeze of lemon juice, or to taste

Kosher salt and freshly ground black pepper

12 tomato diamonds (see page 203)

Because both the shrimp and sauce are served on the fork, this is an excellent canapé to serve guests who are standing.

**FOR THE SHRIMP:** Bring the court bouillon to a simmer in a large saucepan, add the shrimp, and simmer for 1 minute. Remove from the heat, pour the shrimp and bouillon into a container, and let the shrimp cool in the liquid. Cover and refrigerate for up to a day before serving.

**FOR THE SALSA:** In a bowl, mix the red onion and cucumber together. Carefully fold in the avocado, taking care not to crush it. Season with the oil, lemon juice, and salt and pepper to taste.

**TO COMPLETE:** Peel the shrimp, removing the shells but keeping the tail tips intact. Dry the shrimp on paper towels. Cut each shrimp lengthwise in half down the back and use a paring knife to remove the vein that runs the length of the shrimp.

Spear each shrimp half on the tip of a fork. Place a spoonful of salsa on the fork behind each shrimp. Arrange the forks on a platter and garnish each mound of salsa with a tomato diamond.

PICTURED ON PAGE 46                                    MAKES 12 CANAPÉS

## COURT BOUILLON

2 quarts water

2 carrots, cut into ½-inch rounds

1½ cups coarsely chopped onions

2 leeks, split lengthwise, washed, and cut into ½-inch pieces (about 1 cup)

1 medium fennel bulb, coarsely chopped (about 2 cups; use only if cooking seafood)

1 Bouquet Garni (page 63)

6 black peppercorns

1 cup crisp, dry white wine, such as Sauvignon Blanc

½ cup dry white wine vinegar

1 lemon

Court bouillon means "short" bouillon, or quick stock—an acidic liquid flavored with vegetables and aromatics in which fish or shellfish are poached. The liquid is distinguished by fresh herbs and high acidity, so it's important to add that acid, whether in the form of wine, lemon juice, and/or vinegar, just before you cook the fish. This is enough to cook one Dungeness crab or 12 to 18 shrimp.

Place the water in a large pot. Add the vegetables, bouquet garni, and peppercorns. Bring to a boil, reduce to a simmer, and add white wine and wine vinegar. Halve the lemon, squeeze in the juice, and add the halves (acid stabilizes proteins in the seafood, giving it a better texture).

**TO COOK SHRIMP:** Bring the liquid to a simmer, add the shrimp, and simmer for 1 minute. Remove the shrimp to a bowl and pour the liquid over them. Let them cool to room temperature, then cover and refrigerate until chilled; or for up to a day.

**TO COOK DUNGENESS CRAB:** Bring the liquid to a simmer, drop in the crab, return the bouillon to a simmer, and cook for 4 minutes. Remove the pot from the heat and let the crab and liquid cool to room temperature. Transfer the crab and liquid to a container, cover, and refrigerate until ready to use.

MAKES ABOUT 2 QUARTS

FIRST

COURSE

Preceding spread, left: Dungeness Crab Salad, page 92. Above: Salad of Petite Summer Tomatoes, page 56; right: Vine-Ripe Tomato Sorbet with Tomato Tartare, page 57.

# Salad of Petite Summer Tomatoes with Vine-Ripe Tomato Sorbet

**TOMATO SORBET**

2¼ pounds tomatoes (6 to 7 medium tomatoes), peeled, seeded, and chopped into 1-inch pieces

1 tablespoon canola oil

⅓ cup finely chopped yellow onion

2 tablespoons red wine vinegar

Pinch of chopped tarragon

Pinch of cayenne

¾ cup plus 2 tablespoons Simple Syrup (page 271)

Julienned zest of ½ orange (removed with a zester; 1 teaspoon), brought to a boil in cold water, strained and repeated 2 additional times

Kosher salt and freshly ground black pepper to taste

**TOMATO COULIS** MAKES ABOUT 1 CUP

1 pound tomatoes (about 3 medium tomatoes), peeled, seeded, and chopped into 1-inch pieces

1 tablespoon balsamic vinegar

¼ cup extra virgin olive oil

Kosher salt and freshly ground black pepper to taste

**GARLIC TUILES** MAKES 2 TO 3 DOZEN

¼ cup all-purpose flour

2 tablespoons sugar

1½ teaspoons kosher salt

4 tablespoons (2 ounces) unsalted butter, softened but still cool to the touch

1 large egg white

2 teaspoons garlic paste (very finely minced garlic)

¼ cup finely grated Parmigiano-Reggiano

1½ teaspoons minced rosemary

1½ teaspoons minced Italian parsley

**CHERRY TOMATOES**

4 to 5 dozen (depending on size) assorted small cherry tomatoes, such as Sun Gold, Sweet 100s and Green Grape, at room temperature

Extra virgin olive oil

Kosher salt and freshly ground black pepper

Six ½-inch-thick 2-inch-round brioche Croutons (page 238)

Basil Oil (page 166), in a squeeze bottle

The most intriguing element of this dish is the tomato sorbet, a great example of reducing and concentrating the flavor of an ingredient so that it becomes more intense than the original. It's very refreshing, especially paired with a variety of cherry tomatoes (use as many different kinds as possible and the best available, preferably ones that are vine-ripened) set on a brioche crouton and garnished with a light, crisp garlic tuile. The garlic tuiles are best the day they are baked. They have an addictive flavor and can be eaten alone or as a garnish for salads. This recipe makes quite a lot, but it's difficult to mix less batter, and the excess can always be frozen for another time.

FOR THE TOMATO SORBET: Place the tomatoes in a saucepan and bring to a simmer over medium heat. Cook, stirring often, for about 45 minutes, or until the tomatoes have reduced by half; there may still be a small amount of liquid remaining.

Meanwhile, heat the oil in a skillet over low heat. Add the onions and cook gently for 7 to 8 minutes, or until tender.

Place the reduced tomatoes and the onions in a blender and purée them until very smooth. Press the mixture through a tamis (see page 73) (there will be about 1 cup of purée) and return it to the blender. Add the remaining sorbet ingredients and blend again. Strain through a chinois (see page 73). There should be about 1½ cups of sorbet base; cool the mixture in an ice-water bath or in the refrigerator until cold.

Freeze the sorbet in an ice-cream machine. Store the sorbet in a covered container in the freezer. Tomato sorbet is best eaten the day it is made, but it can be stored for up to 2 days; you will probably have some left over.

FOR THE TOMATO COULIS: Squeeze the chopped tomatoes in a kitchen towel to remove the excess liquid. Place the tomatoes in a blender with the remaining ingredients and blend well. Strain the coulis through a chinois. Store, covered, in the refrigerator. Bring to room temperature before serving.

FOR THE GARLIC TUILES: Mix together the flour, sugar, and salt in a medium bowl. Whisk the butter in another bowl until it is completely smooth and mayonnaise-like in texture.

Using a stiff spatula or spoon, beat the egg white into the dry ingredients until completely incorporated and smooth. Whisk in the softened butter by thirds, scraping the sides as necessary and whisking until the batter is creamy and without any lumps. Add the garlic and Parmesan, mixing until the batter is smooth and shiny. Transfer the batter to a smaller container, as it will be easier to work with, and set aside. The batter should be used within a day; any excess batter can be frozen.

Preheat the oven to 325°F.

Place a Silpat (see Sources, page 315) on the counter and spoon about ³⁄₄ teaspoon of the tuile batter into one corner of the Silpat. Use the back of a spoon to spread the mixture into a thin 2¹⁄₂-inch round. The batter doesn't have to be completely even—the Silpat can show through in sections; in fact, the baked tuiles look more interesting if there are gaps in the wafers. Continue to form additional tuiles, spacing them about 1 inch apart. Sprinkle each tuile with a small amount of rosemary and parsley.

Place the Silpat on a baking sheet and bake for 8 to 10 minutes, or until the tuiles are browned and crisp. Use a small narrow spatula to remove the tuiles from the pan and store them in an airtight container. Repeat to make more tuiles, or freeze the extra batter for another time.

FOR THE CHERRY TOMATOES: Blanch the tomatoes in a large pot of boiling lightly salted water for a few seconds, just until the skins have loosened. Peel the tomatoes with a paring knife. This can be done a few hours ahead and the tomatoes kept covered at room temperature.

TO COMPLETE: If the sorbet is very hard, remove it from the freezer for several minutes to soften slightly. Toss the cherry tomatoes and a splash of olive oil and season to taste with salt and pepper. Arrange a base layer of cherry tomatoes on each crouton and top with a second smaller layer of tomatoes. (The amount of tomatoes used will vary according to their size.) If the tomatoes are too large to balance, cut a thin slice from the bottom or one side of them as necessary to keep them from toppling.

Squeeze a ring of basil oil onto each plate. Fill in the center with a spoonful of tomato coulis. Carefully center a tomato-topped crouton on each pool of sauce. Set a quenelle (see page 274), or small scoop, of sorbet on top of the tomatoes, top each with a garlic tuile, and serve immediately.

## Vine-Ripe Tomato Sorbet
## with Tomato Tartare and Basil Oil

○

**TOMATO TARTARE**

1 vine-ripe tomato, peeled, seeded, and finely chopped

Fleur de sel

Kosher salt to taste

1 teaspoon extra virgin olive oil

¹⁄₄ teaspoon minced shallots

¹⁄₈ teaspoon red wine vinegar

¹⁄₂ teaspoon minced chives

Balsamic Glaze (page 238), in a squeeze bottle

Chive Oil (page 166)

Tomato Sorbet (page 56), made with Mandarin tomatoes
        or other vine-ripe tomatoes

Fleur de sel

6 Garlic Tuiles (page 56)

This tomato sorbet dish is simpler to assemble than the salad of petite or cherry summer tomatoes on page 56. The sorbet can be made in a variety of flavors and colors by changing the type of tomato you use; Early Girl, Green Zebra, and Mandarin are just a few that work beautifully. It has a very clean flavor, so it also works perfectly as a plated canapé or all by itself as an intermezzo, or palate refresher between courses.

FOR THE TOMATO TARTARE: Toss the tomato with a sprinkling of fleur de sel and allow it to drain in a strainer set over a bowl for 1 hour. Discard any liquid.

Combine the tomato with the remaining tartare ingredients and refrigerate for a few hours.

TO COMPLETE: Pipe dots of balsamic glaze along one side of each serving plate. Place a larger dot of chive oil in the center of each plate. Top each pool of chive oil with a spoonful of tomato tartare, place a quenelle (see page 274), or small scoop, of sorbet on the tartare, and sprinkle with a few grains of fleur de sel. Lean a garlic tuile on each quenelle of sorbet and serve immediately.

# Big-pot blanching

Blanching green vegetables in a big pot with a lot of water and a lot of salt until they are thoroughly cooked is critical to the finished product. It's entirely a color issue. I want green vegetables to be bright, bright green so their color can launch the flavor and impact of the entire dish. The old saying "We taste first with our eyes" is true. The faster a vegetable is cooked, the greener it becomes.

Raw green vegetables appear dull because a layer of gas develops between the skin and pigment. Heat releases this gas, and the pigment floods to the surface. But this happens fast, and pretty soon, as the vegetable cooks, the acids and enzymes in the vegetable are released, dulling the green color. At the same time, pigment begins to leach out into the water. So the challenge is to fully cook a vegetable before you lose that color, which means cooking it as fast as possible. There are three key factors to achieve this. First, blanch in a large quantity of water relative to the amount of vegetables you're cooking, so you won't significantly lower the boiling temperature when you add the cold vegetables. If you lose the boil, not only do the vegetables cook more slowly, but the water becomes a perfect environment for the pigment-dulling enzymes to go to work (these enzymes are destroyed only at the boiling point). Furthermore, using a lot of water means the pigment-dulling acids released by the vegetables will be more diluted.

Second, use a lot of salt—about a cup of salt per gallon of water. The water should taste like the ocean. Salt helps prevent color from leaching into the water. A side benefit is that the vegetables will be uniformly seasoned when they are done.

THE FINAL CRITICAL STEP: Stop the vegetables from cooking by plunging them into a large quantity of ice water. Leave them there till they are chilled through, then drain them. You can store them in a dry container for a day until ready to use.

The results are dramatic. You may need to be patient if your stove isn't strong and your pot is big, or you may have to do your vegetables in small batches. But it's not hard—you only have to decide to do it.

We don't give times for big-pot blanching in the recipes. There is only one certain way to tell if a fava or a bean or pea is done: Put it in your mouth and eat it.

Above: Bouquet Garni, page 63; right: Artichokes Barigoule, page 63

# Salad of Globe Artichokes with Garden Herbs and Gazpacho

12 red pearl onions, peeled and an X cut into
    the root ends
6 white pearl onions, peeled and an X cut into
    the root ends
2 cups water
1 teaspoon unsalted butter
1 teaspoon sugar
24 asparagus tips
1/4 cup plus 2 tablespoons diced haricots verts

12 yellow wax beans
24 carrot batons (1 inch by 1/4 inch, see page 203)
1/4 cup diced (1/4 inch) roasted red and yellow bell
    peppers (see page 250)
Extra virgin olive oil
Balsamic vinegar

1/4 cup plus 2 tablespoons Eggplant Caviar
    (page 41)

6 Artichokes Barigoule (page 63),
    cut crosswise into 1/4-inch slices
Gray salt
1/2 cup Herb Salad (page 97)
Extra virgin olive oil
Kosher salt
Balsamic Glaze (page 238), in a squeeze bottle
1/2 cup Gazpacho (page 35) (optional)

Cooking doesn't always mean creating something new. Sometimes cooking is combining separate preparations in new ways. This great vegetarian dish features artichokes barigoule and gazpacho. The rest is a garnish of vegetables to complete the salad; use any or all of those listed above. I think carrot and onion are important to feature because they are used to flavor the artichokes. As a garnish, they give the dish strength, logic, wholeness.

Trim the pearl onions as necessary so that they are uniform in size and will cook evenly. Place them in two separate small saucepans. Add 1 cup of water, 1/2 teaspoon of the butter, and 1/2 teaspoon of the sugar to each pan; the water should just cover the onions. Bring to a simmer and cook over medium heat for 20 to 25 minutes, or until the water has evaporated and the onions are tender and glazed but not browned. Remove from the heat and set aside.

One vegetable at a time, blanch the asparagus, haricots verts, and wax beans in boiling water until tender (see Big-Pot Blanching, page 58); chill in ice water; drain, and pat dry. Blanch the carrots in boiling water or strained barigoule liquid (reserved from the artichokes) until tender; chill, drain, and pat dry. Cut the wax beans on the diagonal into 1/4-inch pieces.

Lightly toss all the vegetables in a bowl with a few drops each of extra virgin oil and balsamic vinegar.

Place 1 tablespoon of the eggplant caviar in the center of each plate. Arrange about two thirds of the artichoke hearts around the spoonfuls of caviar. Artfully arrange the remaining vegetables, including the remaining artichokes, in a stack in the center and sprinkle with gray salt. Lightly dress the herb salad with olive oil and kosher salt and stack a small bunch on each salad. Squeeze dots of balsamic glaze around each plate.

If desired, spoon a generous tablespoon of gazpacho around each salad at the table.

MAKES 6 SERVINGS

# Artichokes Barigoule

2 cups water

2 cups dry white wine

4 cups Chicken Stock (page 226) or
    Vegetable Stock (page 227)

1½ cups olive oil

6 artichokes

2 lemons, halved

1 cup chopped sweet bunch carrots

1 cup sliced fennel

2 cups chopped onions

3 tablespoons minced shallots

1 tablespoon plus 1 teaspoon minced garlic

¾ teaspoon kosher salt

1 Bouquet Garni (recipe follows)

1 salt-packed anchovy fillet, bones removed,
    soaked in milk to cover for 1 hour, rinsed,
    and then soaked and rinsed two more times
    (optional)

A barigoule is a kind of stew of artichokes. A lot of restaurants serve it, but like tapenade, there's no standard proportion or classical recipe. We braise the artichoke hearts in olive oil, wine, chicken and/or vegetable stock, with carrots, onions, and garlic, thyme, and parsley. It's a wonderful marriage of flavors absorbed by the artichoke.

In a large container, mix together the water, wine, stock, and 1 cup of the olive oil.

TO PREPARE THE ARTICHOKES: Hold an artichoke with the stem end toward you. Pull off the very small bottom leaves. Break off the larger leaves by pushing with your thumb against the bottom of each leaf as you snap it off about ½ inch above its base, so you are well above the meaty portion (which will become part of the heart), pulling it down toward the stem. A small portion of the bottom of the artichoke leaf should be left anchored to the base. Continue removing the leaves until the only ones remaining are tender and yellow. Cut off the top two thirds of the artichoke, to where the meaty heart begins. Using a paring knife, cut away the tough dark green parts of the leaves to expose the tender heart. This is easily accomplished by first cutting around the artichoke bottom in a strip. Then, holding the knife with the tip at a 45-degree angle, trim the base of the artichoke next to the stem. Peel the stem and cut off the bottom.

Remove the fuzzy choke of the artichoke, using a spoon to scrape the heart clean. Squeeze some lemon juice over the artichoke and submerge it in the stock mixture. Repeat with the remaining artichokes.

Heat the remaining ½ cup olive oil in a pot large enough to hold the hearts in one layer. Add the carrots and cook over medium heat for 2 to 2½ minutes. Add the fennel and continue cooking for another 2 to 2½ minutes. Add the onions, shallots, and garlic and cook for 4 minutes, or until the vegetables have softened. Remove the artichokes from the liquid, reserving the liquid, and position the artichoke hearts stem side up over the vegetables. Sprinkle with the salt, cover the pot, and cook for 10 minutes. (Cooking the artichokes without liquid to start will help arrest the discoloration that normally occurs when the artichokes cook directly in liquid.)

Pour the reserved liquid over the vegetables and add the bouquet garni. Place a clean towel over the top of the artichokes to keep them submerged. Cook at a slow simmer for 15 minutes. If using the anchovy, dry it, chop it, and add it to the artichokes. Cook the artichokes for an additional 15 minutes, or until there is no resistance when a heart is poked with the tip of a sharp knife. Transfer the artichokes and their liquid to a container (the artichokes should be submerged in the liquid) and cool to room temperature, then cover and refrigerate. The artichokes can be stored for up to 1 week.

PICTURED ON PAGE 61                MAKES 6 ARTICHOKE HEARTS

## BOUQUET GARNI

3 outer green leek leaves, washed

5 sprigs Italian parsley

5 sprigs thyme

2 bay leaves

A bouquet garni is a classical combination of aromatic herbs and vegetables used to flavor liquids; because the herbs and vegetables are bundled with string, they can be removed easily from the liquid once they've given their flavor to it.

Lay out 1 leek green. Place the herbs on top and wrap in the remaining leaves to form a circular bundle. Tie the bouquet garni securely with string.

PICTURED ON PAGE 61

## Salad of Haricots Verts, Tomato Tartare, and Chive Oil

6 ounces haricots verts, ends trimmed and cut into
    1-inch lengths

**TOMATO TARTARE**

½ cup finely chopped Tomato Confit
    (about 24 pieces) (recipe follows)

1½ teaspoons finely minced shallot

1 teaspoon minced chives

½ teaspoon balsamic vinegar

**RED WINE VINEGAR CREAM**

⅓ cup heavy cream

1 teaspoon red wine vinegar

¼ teaspoon kosher salt, or to taste

Freshly ground black pepper

Chive Oil (page 166), in a squeeze bottle

1½ cups frisée (tender leaves only)

Extra virgin olive oil

Kosher salt

Tomato Powder (page 233)

Blanch the haricots verts in boiling salted water until they are just cooked through (see Big-Pot Blanching, page 58), 2 to 4 minutes, depending on the age and size of the beans. Chill the beans in ice water, drain, and dry on paper towels.

FOR THE TOMATO TARTARE: Combine the tomato confit, shallot, chives, and balsamic vinegar in a small bowl. Refrigerate until shortly before serving.

FOR THE RED WINE VINEGAR CREAM: Whisk the cream in a bowl set over a larger bowl of ice just until it thickens slightly and you can see the trail of the whisk in the bowl. Using the whisk, fold in the red wine vinegar and season with the salt and pepper to taste. Do not overbeat the cream, as it will continue to thicken when it is tossed with the beans.

TO COMPLETE: Place a 3-inch ring mold (see Sources, page 315) on a serving plate. Squeeze a ring of chive oil around the inside of the mold. Place about 4 teaspoons of the tomato tartare in the center and use the back of a small spoon to spread the mixture so it fills the bottom of the mold. Gently lift off the ring mold and repeat with the remaining five plates.

Toss the beans with just enough of the cream mixture to coat them. Stack about ¼ cup of the beans in the center of each tomato disk, leaving about a ¾-inch border of tomato.

Toss the frisée with a drizzle of extra virgin olive oil and a sprinkling of salt.

For each plate, take about ¼ cup of the greens, twist it in the palm of your hand to make a compact bundle, and set the bundle on the stack of haricots verts. Sprinkle the top of each with a pinch of tomato powder.

MAKES 6 SERVINGS

**TOMATO CONFIT**

Tomatoes

Extra virgin olive oil

Kosher salt and freshly ground black pepper

Thyme sprigs

This is one of our staple preparations—tomato "petals" slow-cooked in the oven with olive oil, thyme, and salt. We make tomato confit every day and use it as a garnish in many dishes. The roasting of the tomatoes, not unlike the reduction of a stock, intensifies the flavors.

Cut out the cores from the tomatoes and cut a shallow X in the bottom of each tomato. Drop the tomatoes into a pot of boiling salted water for a few seconds to loosen the skin. This will happen very quickly with ripe tomatoes. Immediately remove the tomatoes to an ice-water bath to cool.

Peel the tomatoes and cut them into quarters through the stem. Cut away the inner pulp, seeds, and any remaining ribs to leave a smooth "tomato petal." Discard the seeds and save the trimmings to use in other recipes or for tomato powder.

Preheat the oven to 250°F. Line a baking sheet with aluminum foil. Drizzle the foil with olive oil and lightly sprinkle with salt and pepper.

Lay the tomato petals (inside of the tomato facing down) on the foil. Drizzle more oil over the tops of the tomatoes and sprinkle with salt and pepper. Top each piece of tomato with a small sprig of thyme.

Place in the oven for 1½ to 2 hours, until the tomatoes have partially dried but still have some of their juices. Discard the thyme and refrigerate the confit in a covered container, with the oil, until ready to use, or for up to 1 week.

When beans are fresh and wonderfully crisp on the outside and tender on the inside, you can truly elevate them. For the Salad of Haricots Verts, I've treated the beans as asparagus is often treated in classical French cuisine, serving them with a red wine vinaigrette. I replace the oil in the vinaigrette with cream, adding a richness that isn't usually associated with vinaigrettes, or with beans, for that matter.

Left: Roasting tomatoes for Heirloom Tomato Tart, page 66

First Course **65**

# Heirloom Tomato Tart with Niçoise Olive Tapenade, Mixed Field Greens, and Basil Vinaigrette

**TOMATOES**

¼ cup plus 2 tablespoons extra virgin olive oil

5 medium heirloom tomatoes (about 4 ounces each), peeled

Kosher salt and freshly ground black pepper

2 teaspoons thyme leaves

**TAPENADE** MAKES ABOUT ½ CUP

6 to 8 salt-packed anchovy fillets (1 ounce), bones removed, soaked in milk to cover for 1 hour, rinsed, and then soaked and rinsed two more times

½ cup (4 ounces) niçoise olives, pitted

¼ teaspoon Dijon mustard

¼ cup extra virgin olive oil

**BASIL VINAIGRETTE**

½ cup packed basil leaves

½ cup extra virgin olive oil

3 tablespoons balsamic vinegar

Kosher salt and freshly ground black pepper

½ recipe Puff Pastry (page 297)

2 cups mixed baby lettuce leaves

This is my interpretation of pizza. I love tomatoes. I love pizza. But pizza dough isn't elegant enough for a French Laundry dish. Puff pastry is. My pizzas are baked with tomatoes that have been partially dried, which prevents the dough from becoming soggy, then finished with the surprise of chilled tomatoes, topped by tapenade and a basil vinaigrette.

FOR THE TOMATOES: Preheat the oven to 250°F.

Line a baking sheet with foil and coat with 1 tablespoon of the olive oil. Cut 2 of the tomatoes into ½-inch slices (3 per tomato). Place the slices on the baking sheet and sprinkle with salt and pepper, the thyme leaves, and 2 more tablespoons of the oil. Roast the tomato slices for 45 minutes to 1 hour. The slices should have dried out slightly but should still be moist. These can be prepared a day ahead and stored, covered, in the refrigerator.

Slice the remaining 3 tomatoes into ⅛-inch slices (6 per tomato) and place them on a baking sheet lined with a kitchen towel. Season with salt and pepper and drizzle with the remaining 3 tablespoons olive oil. Cover and refrigerate for a minimum of 1 hour and up to 5 hours.

FOR THE TAPENADE: Drain the anchovies, pat them dry, and place them in a small food processor with the olives and mustard. Turn the machine on and slowly add the olive oil through the feed tube to make a purée, stopping the machine and scraping the sides as necessary. Remove the tapenade to a covered container and refrigerate until ready to serve. You will have more than you need for this recipe, but the extra can be refrigerated for up to 3 weeks.

FOR THE BASIL VINAIGRETTE: Blanch the basil leaves in boiling salted water for 1 minute. Drain the leaves and cool them under cold running water; drain well and dry on paper towels. Purée the basil in a food processor. With the machine running, slowly add the olive oil through the feed tube, blending until smooth. This can be done up to 2 days ahead; store in the refrigerator, and bring to room temperature before using.

FOR THE PUFF PASTRY: On a lightly floured surface, roll the pastry into an 8- by 12-inch rectangle about ⅛ inch thick. Place the sheet on a tray and place in the freezer (frozen puff pastry is easier to cut).

Preheat the oven to 375°F. Line a baking sheet with parchment paper.

When the pastry is frozen, cut out 3-inch rounds of pastry and place them on the baking sheet. Prick each pastry round several times with a fork, then top each round with a slice of roasted tomato. Bake for 25 to 35 minutes or until the tops and bottoms of the pastries are crisp and they are well browned on the bottom. These can be baked up to 2 hours ahead.

TO COMPLETE: If you baked the tarts ahead, reheat them in a hot oven for 5 to 10 minutes. Add the balsamic vinegar to the dressing and season with salt and pepper. Toss the baby lettuces with just enough of the vinaigrette to lightly coat the greens.

Center a pastry round on each plate. Arrange 3 overlapping slices of chilled tomato on top of each roasted tomato and spoon ¼ teaspoon of olive tapenade onto the slices. Top each tart with a portion of the dressed greens and drizzle each plate with a small amount of the remaining vinaigrette.

MAKES 6 SERVINGS

# Salad of Black Mission Figs with Roasted Sweet Peppers and Shaved Fennel

FIGS

6 large or 9 medium figs,
    preferably Black Mission

Extra virgin olive oil

Balsamic vinegar

2 tablespoons finely minced shallots

Gray salt

ROASTED PEPPERS

1 red bell pepper, roasted (see page 250),
    peeled, and cut into $1/4$-inch jullienne

1 yellow bell pepper, roasted (see page 250),
    peeled, and cut into $1/4$-inch julienne

2 tablespoons minced shallots

Extra virgin olive oil

Balsamic vinegar

Kosher salt

FENNEL SALAD

1 small fennel bulb,
    top trimmed down to the bulb

Extra virgin olive oil

Balsamic vinegar

Kosher salt

$1/4$ cup Fennel Oil (page 166)

1 tablespoon Balsamic Glaze (page 238)

$1\frac{1}{2}$ teaspoons fresh fennel buds, blanched in
    boiling salted water for 10 seconds
    and dried on paper towels (optional)

Fennel Powder (page 233)

I love the licorice flavor in plants such as fennel and tarragon. For this salad, we make a fennel oil from the fronds, and we garnish it with the wild fennel buds. In summer, I'll find a fennel patch alongside the road, where the buds are still green and haven't blossomed, and I'll cut all the tops off. We'll pick out the buds and blanch them. They're explosive. This salad is really about the Napa Valley, where we have the same problem of overabundance of figs as most people do with tomatoes.

FOR THE FIGS: Slice the figs into rounds about $1/4$ inch thick. You will need a total of 18 slices. Place them on a plate, drizzle lightly with olive oil and balsamic vinegar, and sprinkle with the shallots and gray salt. Let them marinate for 1 hour at room temperature.

MEANWHILE, FOR THE PEPPERS: Toss the roasted peppers with the shallots and olive oil, balsamic vinegar, and salt to taste. Let marinate for 1 hour.

FOR THE FENNEL SALAD: Holding the stem end of the fennel bulb in your hand, cut it on a mandoline into paper-thin slices. You will need at least $1/2$ cup. Place the shaved fennel in a bowl of cold water; it can be held for a few hours this way.

TO COMPLETE: Stir the fennel oil and balsamic glaze together. They will not emulsify, and the balsamic glaze should bead in the oil. Drain the shaved fennel and dry on a towel. Toss the fennel with olive oil, balsamic vinegar, and salt to taste.

Center a round of fig on each serving plate. Twirl a few strips of the julienned peppers around a fork, place the peppers on a fig slice, and top with another slice of fig. Repeat the process so that there are three slices of figs and two layers of peppers, then repeat with the remaining plates. Stack the fennel salad on top of the fig slices and sprinkle with the fennel buds, if using. Drizzle the fennel oil/balsamic glaze mixture around the plates and sprinkle the plates with the fennel powder.

MAKES 6 SERVINGS

## HEARTS OF PALM GROWER: JOHN MOOD

As I spoke with the restaurant's purveyors, the main thing that struck me was how many people had backed into their work—almost all of them had double lives. Charlie Akwa, a little dynamo of a woman who specializes in caviar and Mediterranean fish, first made a killing on Wall Street. Kathleen Weber, who bakes the French Laundry's bread, was a nurse and then worked in women's retail before she and her husband, Ed, built a brick oven in their backyard.

John Mood has lived a double life since he was a teenager and became infatuated with a neighbor's banana tree. The infatuation blossomed into an intense love of tropical plants. He served in Vietnam as a pilot, and after the war, he continued to fly for the army. Then he quit the army, got a job as a commercial pilot, and bought enough land in Hawaii—about thirty-five acres—to turn his hobby into a business. His wife, Pat, became his manager.

Shortly thereafter, he met an American living in Brazil who hoped to plant an experimental crop that grew abundantly in South America, a variety of palm tree called the peach palm, or *pejibaye*. It has a hard fruit, high in starch and oil, that looks like an elongated peach. It can be boiled and eaten like a sweet potato, fermented into beer, or turned into vinegar, and it has long been a staple of Peruvian Indians. But its most valuable asset is its core, the soft white shoots of underdeveloped leaves known as hearts of palm. "Vegetable ivory," Mood calls it.

Mood was happy to lend five acres to the American, and the crop flourished. John's wife got the word out that they were now growing and selling a crop that had rarely been available before in America—fresh hearts of palm.

Sales began slowly, at 30 pounds a week to local restaurants. But word of mouth spread

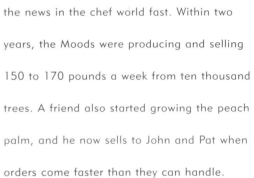

the news in the chef world fast. Within two years, the Moods were producing and selling 150 to 170 pounds a week from ten thousand trees. A friend also started growing the peach palm, and he now sells to John and Pat when orders come faster than they can handle.

The peach palm is proving to be a financially viable business. But money's not the issue, according to John, who simply likes to study fruits (not to mention a whole subsection of his hobby, the study, exploration, and growing of tropical gingers) and to search for new genuses. He's quick to tell you that he's got a decent job flying planes. —M.R.

# Hearts of Palm with Purée of Marrow Beans and Field Greens

**MARROW BEANS**

½ cup (4 ounces) dried marrow beans or Great
    Northern or other large white beans,
    soaked overnight at room temperature
    in 3 cups water

4 to 5 cups cold Vegetable Stock (page 227)

Two 2-inch pieces carrot

Two 2-inch pieces leek

One 2-inch-long onion wedge

½ small tomato

1 Bouquet Garni (page 63)

**HEARTS OF PALM**

5 pounds fresh hearts of palm stems
    (see Sources, page 315)

1 cup all-purpose flour

1 cup milk

1 cup panko (Japanese bread crumbs;
    see Sources, page 315)

Canola oil

**MARROW BEAN FILLING**

¾ cup cooked marrow beans (from above)

3 slices (2 to 3 ounces) Brioche (page 258),
    crusts trimmed

1 cup (8 ounces) mascarpone

Kosher salt and freshly ground white pepper

3 tablespoons white truffle oil

**SAUCE**

1½ cups Truffle-Infused Mushroom Stock
    (page 87) or ¾ cup truffle juice
    (see Sources, page 315) plus ¾ cup
    Mushroom Stock (page 227)

½ teaspoon sherry vinegar

2 tablespoons finely minced shallots

1 tablespoon finely minced black truffle

¾ cup cooked marrow beans (from above)

¾ cup diced hearts of palm (from above)

¼ cup tomato diamonds (see page 203)

⅓ cup Brunoise (page 155)

1 tablespoon minced chives

1 tablespoon minced Italian parsley

¼ cup white truffle oil


Chive oil (page 166), in a squeeze bottle

6 sprigs chervil

'm always searching for new foods—it's a constant quest for me. When I saw fresh hearts of palm on a trip to Hawaii, I was bowled over. Their nutty, almost artichoke flavor works beautifully with French cuisine. They're delicious raw, but poaching them until they're soft, with just a little bit of crunch, enhances their flavor.

FOR THE MARROW BEANS: Remove and discard any skins from the soaking beans that have risen to the top of the water. Drain and rinse the beans. Place the beans in a pot, add cold water to cover by at least 2 inches, and bring to a simmer. It is important that the beans do not come to a hard boil, or they will crack. More skins will float to the surface; remove them and discard. Remove the beans from the heat and drain. Rinse the beans under cold water until the water runs clear.

Place the beans in a clean medium saucepan and add enough cold vegetable stock to cover them by at least 2 inches. Add the vegetables and the bouquet garni. Bring the stock to a simmer and gently cook the beans until they are completely tender, 45 minutes to 1 hour. The beans can be cooked a day ahead and refrigerated in their liquid, along with the aromatic vegetables and bouquet garni.

FOR THE HEARTS OF PALM: Put the hearts in a large pot and cover with heavily salted water. Bring to a simmer and cook for 45 minutes.

Drain, reserving the cooking liquid, and place the hearts of palm in an ice-water bath to cool; drain again. The hearts can be cooked ahead and refrigerated in the cooled cooking liquid for up to 2 days.

Cut the hearts of palm into sections about 1½ inches long. Punch out the center of each to leave a wall about ¼ inch thick (to resemble a beef marrow bone). You need a total of 12 pieces. Cut the "punched-out" hearts of palm into ¼-inch dice. If there are not enough to make ¾ cup, use other scraps or trimmings.

FOR THE MARROW BEAN FILLING: Drain the cooked marrow beans, reserving the liquid, and discard the vegetables and bouquet garni. There will be about 1½ cups of beans; set aside ¾ cup for the sauce. Reheat the remaining marrow beans in their liquid in a saucepan until hot. Meanwhile, in a food processor, grind the brioche in three to four batches to create very, very fine bread crumbs. It is important to do this in batches to ensure even processing; if there are any large pieces of brioche, your filling will not be smooth. Then return all the crumbs to the processor and process one last time to combine. Transfer the bread crumbs to a bowl.

Drain the reheated marrow beans and discard the liquid. Place the hot marrow beans in the food processor and process, stopping often to scrape the sides of the bowl, until perfectly smooth; this could take up to 5 minutes. (If there is not adequate room in your processor to keep the beans below the top of the blade, process them in batches until completely smooth.)

Once the beans are perfectly smooth (if you've processed them in batches, return all the beans to the processor and process to blend), add a handful of the bread crumbs to the processor. As the bread crumbs are added, the mixture will take on a rough dough-like consistency and begin to pull away from the sides of the processor. At the proper consistency, the mixture will stick together when pinched but won't be too wet; you may not need to use all of the bread crumbs.

Add the mascarpone to the mixture in thirds and process to combine. As you add the mascarpone, the mixture will loosen to a smooth, thick purée. Blend in salt and white pepper to taste.

With the machine running, slowly pour in the truffle oil to create an emulsion (as if you were making mayonnaise). It is extremely important to add the oil slowly, or the emulsion may break. If the mixture begins to look grainy or broken once all the oil has been added, continue to process it until it is a silky-smooth purée. There will be about 1½ cups of purée. It can be covered and stored in the refrigerator for 1 to 2 days.

TO FILL THE HEARTS OF PALM: Stand the hearts of palm on a level work surface. Using a pastry bag with a plain medium tip, pipe the filling from the bottom of the cavities to the top, evenly distributing the purée so that there are no air pockets along the inside edges. Fill each piece to the top and use the back of a small knife to remove the excess filling from the ends. Refrigerate the filled hearts of palm for at least 3 hours to allow the purée to chill completely.

TO COMPLETE: For the sauce, place the stock or truffle juice and stock in a saucepan, add the vinegar, bring to a boil, and reduce by half. Add the shallots, black truffle, and the reserved cooked marrow beans and diced hearts of palm and heat through. Keep warm.

TO COOK THE HEARTS OF PALM: Place the flour, milk, and panko crumbs in three separate shallow bowls. Generously coat each piece of heart of palm with flour, tapping lightly to remove the excess flour. Dip in the milk, then evenly coat the hearts of palm with the panko crumbs, tapping to remove any excess crumbs.

Meanwhile, in a large skillet, heat about ⅛ inch of oil over medium-high heat. The oil should not be hot enough to burn the panko crumbs: It is ready when a few crumbs placed into the oil turn golden brown almost immediately; if they turn black, the oil is too hot. Stand the hearts of palm on end in the hot oil and brown for about 5 seconds, or until the ends are golden brown; turn each piece and brown the other end. Lay the pieces on their sides and roll them in the pan for about 10 seconds, not long enough to brown the crumbs, but long enough to remove the raw taste. Remove the pieces to paper towels to drain.

Add the tomato diamonds, brunoise, chives, parsley, and truffle oil to the sauce and gently heat through (the sauce will look thicker from all the garnishes but should still have some "movement" to it).

Place a 4-inch ring mold (see Sources, page 315) on a plate and squeeze a ring of chive oil around its interior. Spoon a layer of the sauce into the ring mold. Be careful; if you add too much of the liquid, it may break through the ring of chive oil. Lift off the ring and repeat with the remaining plates. Stand two hearts of palm side by side in the center of the sauce on each plate and garnish the top with a sprig of chervil. Serve immediately.

MAKES 6 SERVINGS

Perhaps the most important pieces of equipment in our kitchen are the chinois—also known in French kitchens as a *chinois tamis*, or Chinese sieve—and the *tamis*, sometimes referred to as a drum sieve. The first is a conical fine-mesh sieve that we pass liquids through; the second is a flat fine-mesh sieve that we press puréed solids through.

A tamis prevents lumps and ensures that every particle is the same size. We put a lot of butter (and truffle oil) in mashed potatoes, creating what is in effect an emulsion; potatoes that have been pressed through a tamis will more easily form a stable emulsion. We also press items such as foie gras or anything with veins or skin we don't want through the tamis to remove impurities.

## Tools of refinement: the chinois and tamis

The final clarifying stage of a sauce is passing it through a chinois. French Laundry chefs will pass a sauce through a chinois twenty times or more, till it is perfectly clean and all the particles that can muddy it have been caught in its mesh. We're always "cleaning" sauces with a chinois—no liquid should move from one pot or container into another except through a chinois.

We use a China cap, a coarser conical sieve, to strain bones and vegetables out of stock. For lobster stock, we crush the lobster shells in the China cap to extract as much liquid as possible, then we strain that liquid through a chinois to remove any remaining impurities.

Above all, the tamis and the chinois are tools that create perfect texture. We put our soups in a blender and then pass them through a chinois, tapping the rim rather than plunging with a ladle to move the liquid through. We pass our pea purée for the pea soup through a tamis, then we blend the purée in a blender and pass it through a chinois. The result is texture on your tongue and palate that is almost indescribable. It is the texture of luxury.

Opposite, top to bottom: Tamis, China cap, chinois

# Agnolotti

I learned to make agnolotti from the grandmother of a family I stayed with in the Piedmont region of Italy, and they're close to my heart. They're the Piedmont version of ravioli; whoever figured them out really had it over whoever invented ravioli. They're the perfect stuffed pasta, a brilliant design—a kind of self-sealing, self-defining package. They almost stuff themselves, sealing automatically when cut, and there's never any problem with air pockets. It results in the perfect ratio of pasta to stuffing, there's almost no wasted dough, and the size is consistent. I love their little pillow shape and the folds of the pasta that catch the sauce. Also, you can make a lot of them really fast. You just roll out a sheet of pasta, pipe out the filling, fold the dough over that cylinder, pinch the tube at one-inch intervals, then cut.

I love touching agnolotti dough, which is packed with egg yolks. You can incorporate thirty yolks into a kilo of flour. I roll the dough ten or fifteen times through the widest setting of the pasta machine so it develops a silkiness, a shine.

The filling can be almost anything as long as you're able to separate it into individual portions by pinching the dough: It can't be whole shrimp, but it can be a shrimp mousse. Stuffed agnolotti freeze beautifully, so you could make a whole pound of flour into dough. You prepare a filling—whatever you want—pipe it onto your pasta, and you have enough agnolotti for a month of Sundays. That's the beautiful thing about it. All you need to do is boil them up, sauce with beurre monté, mushrooms, or maybe tomato, grate some Parmesan on top, and you're done.

Following are fillings for each season, but once you master the agnolotti shape, you can do just about anything with it.

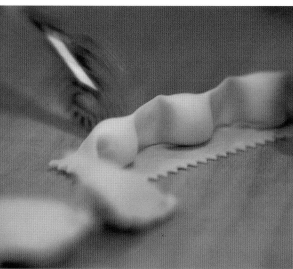

# Pasta Dough

1¾ cups (8 ounces) all-purpose flour

6 large egg yolks

1 large egg

1½ teaspoons olive oil

1 tablespoon milk

Mound the flour on a board or other surface and create a well in the center, pushing the flour to all sides to make a ring with sides about 1 inch wide. Make sure that the well is wide enough to hold all the eggs without spilling.

Pour the egg yolks, egg, oil, and milk into the well. Use your fingers to break the eggs up. Still using your fingers, begin turning the eggs in a circular motion, keeping them within the well and not allowing them to spill over the sides. This circular motion allows the eggs to gradually pull in flour from the sides of the well; it is important that the flour not be incorporated too rapidly, or your dough will be lumpy. Keep moving the eggs while slowly incorporating the flour. Using a pastry scraper, occasionally push the flour toward the eggs; the flour should be moved only enough to maintain the gradual incorporation of the flour, and the eggs should continue to be contained within the well. The mixture will thicken and eventually get too tight to keep turning with your fingers.

When the dough begins thickening and starts lifting itself from the board, begin incorporating the remaining flour with the pastry scraper by lifting the flour up and over the dough that's beginning to form and cutting it into the dough. When the remaining flour from the sides of the well has been cut into the dough, the dough will still look shaggy. Bring the dough together with the palms of your hands and form it into a ball. It will look flaky but will hold together.

Knead the dough by pressing it, bit by bit, in a forward motion with the heels of your hands rather than folding it over on itself as you would with a bread dough. Re-form the dough into a ball and repeat the process several times. The dough should feel moist but not sticky. Let the dough rest for a few minutes while you clean the work surface.

Dust the clean work surface with a little flour. Knead the dough by pushing against it in a forward motion with the heels of your hands. Form the dough into a ball again and knead it again. Keep kneading in this forward motion until the dough becomes silky-smooth. The dough is ready when you can pull your finger through it and the dough wants to snap back into place. The kneading process can take anywhere from 10 to 15 minutes. Even if you think you are finished kneading, knead it for an extra 10 minutes; you cannot overknead this dough. It is important to work the dough long enough to pass the pull test; otherwise, when it rests, it will collapse.

Double-wrap the dough in plastic wrap to ensure that it does not dry out. Let the dough rest for at least 30 minutes and up to 1 hour before rolling it through a pasta machine. The dough can be made a day ahead, wrapped, and refrigerated; bring to room temperature before proceeding.

MAKES ABOUT 14 OUNCES DOUGH

TO FORM PASTA SHEETS FOR 12 RAVIOLI: Set the rollers of the pasta machine at the widest setting. Take one third of the finished pasta dough, about 5 ounces, and cut it in half (reserve the remaining dough for another use). Keep one half wrapped in plastic warp and run the other piece through the machine. Fold the dough in half, end to end, turn it a quarter turn, and run it through the same setting again. Repeat this procedure two more times, but the last time, fold the pasta sheet lengthwise in half to give you a narrower piece of pasta and run it through the machine.

Set the openings of the rollers down one notch and run the pasta through. Do not fold it over. Decrease the opening another notch and run the dough through again. Continue the process until the sheet of pasta is quite thin (there may be a recommended setting for your machine; if not, the next-to-the-thinnest setting is usually best). Repeat with the second piece of pasta and proceed with the specific ravioli recipe.

FOR CAPELLINI: Roll out sheets of pasta (using the desired amount of dough) following the instructions for agnolotti. Run the sheets of pasta through the fine cutting blade. If the sheets of pasta stick to the machine, dust them lightly with flour. The pasta can be used immediately, or it can be dried. Lift a small handful of the noodles and drape them in a nest shape onto a tray dusted with cornmeal. Repeat with the remaining pasta, forming many small nests. Allow the pasta to dry completely in a cool, dry area. If it is damp in the kitchen, line the tray with a towel before arranging the pasta on it, and leave the pasta on the towel until it has dried completely, to prevent the formation of mold. The dried pasta can be kept for several weeks.

TO FORM SHEETS FOR AGNOLOTTI: Use ½ recipe pasta dough, divided into two or three pieces. Run the dough through a pasta machine as for ravioli, but make the sheets wider. The size will vary according to the pasta machine used, but the sheets should be at least 5 inches wide. It is important that our pasta sheet be thin enough so that you can see your fingers through it, but not so thin that it's translucent. Keep the pasta sheets covered, as they dry out quickly, and proceed with filling the agnolotti.

TO FILL AGNOLOTTI: If you are planning on using the agnolotti immediately, have a large pot of lightly salted boiling water ready. Work with one sheet of pasta at a time, keeping the remaining sheets covered. Work quickly, as fresh pasta will dry out.

Lay the pasta sheet on a lightly floured work surface with a long side facing you. Trim the edges so they are straight. Place the agnolotti filling in a pastry bag fitted with a ½-inch plain tip. Pipe a "tube" of filling across the bottom of the pasta sheet, leaving a ¾-inch border of pasta along the left, right, and bottom edges.

Pull the bottom edge of the pasta up and over the filling. Seal the agnolotti by carefully molding the pasta over the filling and pressing lightly with your index finger to seal the edge of the dough to the pasta sheet; don't drag your finger along the dough to seal, or you risk ripping the dough. When it is sealed, there should be about ½ inch of excess dough visible above the tube of filling (where you sealed it). Be certain that you are sealing tightly while pressing out any pockets of air. Seal the left and right ends of the dough.

TO SHAPE AGNOLOTTI: Starting at one end, place the thumb and forefinger of each hand together as if you were going to pinch something and, leaving about 1 inch of space between your hands and holding your fingers vertically, pinch the filling in 1-inch increments, making about ¾ inch of "pinched" area between each pocket of filling. It is important to leave this much "pinched" area between the agnolotti, or when the agnolotti are separated, they may come unsealed.

Run a crimped pastry wheel along the top edge of the folded-over dough, separating the strip of filled pockets from the remainder of the pasta sheet. Don't cut too close to the filling, or you risk breaking the seal. Separate the individual agnolotti by cutting through the center of each pinched area, rolling the pastry wheel away from you. Working quickly, place the agnolotti on a baking sheet dusted with a thin layer of cornmeal, which will help prevent sticking. Don't let the agnolotti touch each other, or they may stick together.

Repeat the same procedure on the remainder of your pasta sheets. Either cook the agnolotti immediately in the boiling water, or place the baking sheet in the freezer. Once the agnolotti are frozen, place them in airtight freezer bags and keep them frozen for up to several weeks. Cook the agnolotti while still frozen.

# Fava Bean Agnolotti with Curry Emulsion

**FAVA BEAN FILLING**

2 to 3 pounds fava beans

3/4 cup fresh bread crumbs

1/4 cup plus 1 1/2 teaspoons mascarpone

Kosher salt

1/2 recipe Pasta Dough (page 78)

**CURRY EMULSION**

2 teaspoons curry powder

2 tablespoons chopped scallions

3/4 cup plus 2 tablespoons Vegetable Stock
(page 227), Chicken Stock (page 226),
or water

1/4 cup heavy cream

1/4 cup crème fraîche

8 tablespoons (4 ounces) unsalted butter,
cut into chunks

Kosher salt and freshly ground black pepper

Eighteen 1-inch-long pieces ramps
or scallions, blanched (see Big-Pot Blanching,
page 58), chilled in ice water, drained,
and dried

Eighteen 1-inch pieces garlic sprouts or garlic
chives blanched (see Big-Pot Blanching,
page 58), chilled in ice water, drained,
and dried

Fava beans have a high starch content that results in a dense purée, perfect for filling agnolotti. Favas are so delicately flavored, I serve them with curry—just a light backdrop to accentuate their flavor—in an emulsion (a seamless combination of liquid and fat, here stock, or water, and cream).

FOR THE FAVA BEAN FILLING: Shell the fava beans and peel the skins from the beans (peeling the beans before cooking them prevents gases from being trapped between the bean and the skin that could cause discoloring). Remove the small germ at the side of each bean. You need 1 1/2 cups beans for the filling; reserve any extra beans for another use. Blanch the beans (see Big-Pot Blanching, page 58) for about 5 minutes, or until tender, and immediately transfer to ice water to chill. When they are cold, drain the beans and spread on paper towels to drain thoroughly.

Place the beans in a food processor with the bread crumbs. Blend until they come together and form a ball. Add the mascarpone and process again until the mixture is smooth. Season to taste with salt. You will have 1 to 1 1/4 cups of filling (enough to fill 48 agnolotti). Refrigerate the mixture until it is cool, or for up to 2 days.

Roll out the dough and fill the agnolotti according to the instructions on pages 78 and 79. You should have approximately 48 agnolotti.

TO COMPLETE: For the curry emulsion, toast the curry powder in a small saucepan over medium heat until it is fragrant. Stir in the scallions and heat for another minute. Add the 3/4 cup stock, the cream, and crème fraîche, bring to a simmer, and cook until the liquid is reduced to 1/2 cup. Swirl in the butter. When the butter is melted, transfer the sauce to a blender. Add the remaining 2 tablespoons stock and blend for 30 seconds to emulsify the mixture. Season with salt and pepper and strain into a wide pan.

Meanwhile, cook the agnolotti in a large pot of lightly salted boiling water until cooked through, 4 to 5 minutes.

Drain the agnolotti, add the agnolotti and ramps to the curry emulsion, and toss over low heat to coat with sauce. Divide the agnolotti and ramps among six serving dishes and garnish the top of each with 3 garlic sprouts. Serve immediately.

MAKES 6 SERVINGS

# Sweet Potato Agnolotti with Sage Cream, Brown Butter, and Prosciutto

**SWEET POTATO FILLING**

1½ pounds sweet potatoes

8 tablespoons (4 ounces) unsalted butter

2 slices bacon, frozen and cut into ¼-inch dice

Pinch of Squab Spice (page 233)
    or allspice and nutmeg

Kosher salt and freshly ground black pepper

**SAGE CREAM**

⅓ cup sage leaves (from about 4 bunches;
    use the smaller leaves for the fried sage
    leaf garnish)

1 cup crème fraîche

1 cup Beurre Monté (page 135)

Pinch of kosher salt, or to taste

Canola oil for deep-frying

48 tiny sage leaves (reserved from above)

2 tablespoons (1 ounce) unsalted butter

4 thin slices prosciutto, cut crosswise into
    fine julienne

½ recipe Pasta Dough (page 78)

For a fall agnolotti, I like a sweet potato filling; it's denser than the traditional version made from the more watery pumpkin. With the cream, butter, and prosciutto, this is a very rich and delicious dish.

FOR THE SWEET POTATO FILLING: Preheat the oven to 350°F.

Cut the ends off the potatoes and wrap the potatoes individually in aluminum foil, dividing 4 tablespoons of the butter evenly among them. Bake until they are soft, 1 to 2 hours (the time will vary, depending on the size of the potatoes).

Unwrap the cooked potatoes and cut a slit lengthwise in the skin of each. Pull the skin away from the potato and discard. Push the potatoes through a potato ricer while they are hot and place in a saucepan.

Place the diced bacon in a skillet. Cook until it is lightly browned and the fat has been rendered. Transfer the bacon pieces to paper towels to drain briefly, then add them to the potatoes.

Stir the potatoes over low heat, seasoning to taste with the squab spice and salt and pepper. Mix in the remaining 4 tablespoons butter. You will have about 1⅔ cups filling (enough to fill 48 agnolotti). Refrigerate the filling until chilled, or for up to 2 days, before filling the agnolotti.

Roll out the dough and fill the agnolotti according to the instructions on pages 78 and 79. You should have approximately 48 agnolotti.

TO COMPLETE: For the sage cream, blanch the sage leaves in boiling water for 2 minutes. Drain, cool in cold water, and drain again. Squeeze the leaves dry.

Heat the crème fraîche, beurre monté, and salt over low heat until hot; do not boil. Place the sage in a blender and process to chop it. With the motor running, pour the hot cream mixture through the top and blend thoroughly. Strain the cream into a large skillet. Check the seasoning and set aside.

In a small pot, heat oil for deep-frying to 275°F. Fry the small sage leaves briefly, just until they are crisp (their color should not change), and drain on paper towels.

Place the butter in a skillet over medium heat and cook to a nutty brown color; reduce the heat and keep warm.

Meanwhile, cook the agnolotti in a large pot of lightly salted boiling water until cooked through, 4 to 5 minutes.

Drain the cooked agnolotti and mix them gently with the sage cream sauce over low heat. Divide the agnolotti among six serving dishes and drizzle with the browned butter. Scatter some prosciutto over each serving and garnish with the fried sage leaves.

MAKES 6 SERVINGS

# Chestnut Agnolotti with Fontina and Celery Root Purée

CHESTNUT FILLING

1 generous cup peeled roasted fresh chestnuts
 (see Note) or vacuum-packed
 unsweetened chestnuts

2 bay leaves

½ cup Vegetable Stock (page 227)

½ cup water

¼ cup mascarpone

3 tablespoons (1½ ounces) unsalted butter,
 at room temperature

1 tablespoon plus 2 teaspoons white truffle oil

Kosher salt and freshly ground black pepper

½ recipe Pasta Dough (page 78)

SAUCE

½ cup sliced onions

1½ teaspoons chopped garlic

1½ tablespoons unsalted butter

1⅓ cups peeled, quartered, and sliced celery root

½ cup peeled, quartered, and sliced
 Yukon Gold potato

2 to 3 cups Vegetable Stock (page 227)

3 cups heavy cream

1 cup lightly packed shredded creamy
 Italian Fontina (2½ ounces)

Kosher salt and freshly ground white pepper

½ cup Beurre Monté (page 135)

1 teaspoon white truffle oil

Chestnut is a luxurious wintertime filling, and a great flavor combination with the Italian Fontina cheese, celery root, and truffle oil.

FOR THE CHESTNUT FILLING: Place the chestnuts, bay leaves, vegetable stock, and water in a saucepan, bring to a simmer, and cook for about 15 minutes, to reduce the liquid by half and soften the chestnuts. Strain and reserve the liquid; discard the bay leaf.

Purée the chestnuts in a food processor. With the motor running, gradually pour enough of the reserved liquid through the feed tube to form a thick purée.

Scrape the purée through a tamis (see page 73) and place it in a bowl. Mix in the mascarpone, butter, and white truffle oil. Season to taste with salt and pepper. You should have 1 to 1¼ cups of filling (enough for 48 agnolotti). Cover and refrigerate the filling until cold, or for up to 2 days, before using.

Roll out the dough and fill the agnolotti according to the instructions on pages 78 and 79. You should have approximately 48 agnolotti.

FOR THE SAUCE: Gently cook the onions and garlic in the butter in a medium saucepan over low heat for 3 to 4 minutes, or until they have softened. Add the celery root, potatoes, and enough vegetable stock to cover them completely. Simmer until the vegetables are tender, then drain, reserving the liquid.

Scrape the vegetables through a tamis and place the purée in a medium saucepan. Add the cream and simmer for 10 minutes, then whisk in the cheese until it is melted. The sauce can be made up to a day ahead and stored in the refrigerator, but do not add the cheese until ready to serve. Reheat the sauce and, if it seems too thick, whisk in enough stock or water to bring it to the desired consistency. Then whisk in the cheese until melted.

Pass the sauce through a chinois (see page 73) into a large skillet. You can use the back of a small ladle to help the liquid pass through the strainer, but do not force any solids through. Adjust the consistency with the reserved stock and season with salt and pepper.

TO COMPLETE: Cook the agnolotti in a large pot of lightly salted boiling water until cooked through, 4 to 5 minutes.

Meanwhile, stir the beurre monté and truffle oil into the sauce.

Drain the cooked agnolotti and add them to the sauce, stirring gently over low heat. Divide the agnolotti and sauce among six serving bowls and serve immediately.

MAKES 6 SERVINGS

NOTE: To peel fresh chestnuts, preheat the oven to 375°F. With a sharp paring knife, cut a slit all the way around each chestnut. Rub with a thin coating of vegetable oil to keep the shell moist and accelerate the cooking process. Place on a baking sheet and bake for 15 minutes, or until the shells begin to pull away from the chestnuts. Peel while still warm.

**POLENTA**

3/4 cup Vegetable Stock (page 227)

3/4 cup water

1/4 cup plus 3 tablespoons polenta

**RISOTTO**

1 cup Vegetable Stock (page 227),
    or more as needed

About 1 1/2 cups water

3/4 cup Arborio rice

1/2 cup mascarpone, at room temperature

8 tablespoons (4 ounces) unsalted butter,
    at room temperature

1 1/4 cups corn juice (from 7 to 8 ears; see Note)

1/2 recipe Pasta Dough (page 78; Note: If
    making extra agnolotti to freeze, you will
    need slightly less than 1 1/2 recipes dough.)

**CORN SAUCE**

2 cups corn juice (from about 12 ears; see Note)

4 tablespoons (2 ounces) unsalted butter,
    at room temperature

2/3 cup corn kernels, blanched until tender
    (see Big-Pot Blanching, page 58),
    chilled in ice water, drained, and dried

2 tablespoons finely minced summer truffle

2 tablespoons finely minced chives

1 teaspoon white truffle oil

Parmigiano-Reggiano shavings

These agnolotti contain a delicious filling that owes much of its impact to the corn juice, which is intensely flavored and also helps to blend the polenta and mascarpone-enriched risotto.

FOR THE POLENTA: Bring the vegetable stock and water to a boil in a saucepan. While whisking the liquid, pour in the polenta in a steady stream and, continuing to whisk, bring to simmer. Place the pot on a diffuser over very low heat. Cook the polenta, stirring occasionally, for about 20 minutes, or until it forms a ball as it is stirred and is fully cooked, with no raw cornmeal taste. Keep it warm over very low heat.

MEANWHILE, FOR THE RISOTTO: Bring the stock and 1 1/2 cups water to a simmer in a saucepan. Spread the rice in one layer in a wide saucepan. Add 1/2 cup of the hot liquid and stir constantly over medium heat until the liquid has evaporated. Add another 1/2 cup and continue as above, adding more liquid once the previous addition has evaporated. The rice should be fully cooked for the filling, so if it is not tender after you have used all the liquid, continue to add smaller amounts of hot water or stock until it is fully cooked. When it is cooked, it will form a sticky ball as it is stirred (it should be thicker in consistency than regular risotto when it is served as a dish).

While it is still hot, put the risotto through the fine die of a meat grinder (if you do not own a grinder, you can pass it through a food mill fitted with a fine disk). Repeat the process, so that you have ground it twice.

Place the polenta in a clean saucepan and set it over low heat. Stir in the ground risotto to combine the two mixtures. Remove from the heat and stir in the mascarpone and butter until thoroughly combined.

Place the 1 1/4 cups corn juice in a saucepan and whisk it constantly over medium heat until it has thickened and reached 180°F. Do not exceed that temperature or it may separate. Remove it from the heat and whisk it into the polenta/rice mixture. You will want to whisk vigorously at first and then beat with a spoon to be sure that all the elements are evenly blended. There should be approximately 3 cups of filling (enough for 10 dozen agnolotti), which can be used immediately or refrigerated for up to 2 days; extra filling can be frozen if you prefer. Roll out the dough and fill the agnolotti according to the directions on pages 78 and 79. You can freeze extra agnolotti, for up to a few weeks.

FOR THE CORN SAUCE: Place the corn juice in a saucepan over medium heat. Whisk constantly until it has thickened and reaches 180°F. Start the blender and pour in the hot corn liquid. With the motor running, add the butter and blend for a few seconds. Strain the sauce through a fine-mesh strainer into a saucepan.

TO COMPLETE: Cook 48 agnolotti in lightly salted boiling water for 4 to 5 minutes. Meanwhile, gently reheat the corn sauce (do not boil) and add the corn, truffle, and chives. Just before serving, add the truffle oil.

Drain the agnolotti and divide them among six serving dishes. Top with the sauce and shavings of Parmesan.

MAKES 6 SERVINGS

NOTE ON CORN JUICE: If you have a juicer, cut the kernels from the cob and follow the manufacturer's instructions. If you do not have a juicer, follow the method on page 172.

# Truffles

Fresh truffles are becoming available in more specialty stores, and they're being grown with varying degrees of success in many countries, but none matches those found in France and Italy. It's important to use enough truffles. Offering just one slice is wasteful, because you don't get its full impact. Truffles have a short season. The best black ones come from France; I buy large quantities of them in season, poach them in mushroom stock, and freeze them for when we need them. The very best white truffles are from Alba. Only use them fresh. If you need to store them, don't use rice, as some experts advise—it dries them out; instead, keep them in an airtight container wrapped with a moist towel. Truffles grow in clay-based soil and must be carefully scrubbed in warm water.

POTATO PURÉE

1¼ pounds Yukon Gold potatoes

1 cup heavy cream, warmed

10 tablespoons (5 ounces) unsalted butter,
    at room temperature, cut into 6 pieces

½ teaspoon kosher salt, or to taste

Freshly ground black pepper

MUSHROOM RAGOUT

12 ounces assorted small potatoes in a variety
    of shapes and colors (for example, 3 ounces
    each French Fingerling, Red Russian Fingerling,
    purple Peruvian, and marble potatoes)

1 teaspoon kosher salt, or to taste

1¼ cups Truffle-Infused Mushroom Stock
    (page 87) or ¾ cup Mushroom Stock
    (page 227) plus ½ cup truffle juice
    (see Sources, page 315)

¼ teaspoon white wine vinegar

6 tablespoons (3 ounces) unsalted butter,
    at room temperature, cut into 4 chunks

2 tablespoons Brunoise (page 155)

1½ tablespoons finely minced black truffle

1 tablespoon minced chives

2 tablespoons white truffle oil

Freshly ground black pepper

16 Truffle Chips (page 48)

---

This dish combines several different potato preparations—sliced small, served in a bed of mashed potatoes, with chopped truffles, a truffle sauce, and crispy truffle potato chips. The contrast of textures—creamy, firm, crunchy—makes the ordinary extraordinary.

The hardest part of this dish is the mashed potatoes; in some ways, it may be the most difficult recipe here, because there are so many small choices that have a big impact. First, you should cook the potatoes in their jackets so that the water doesn't penetrate into the meat. You must cook them in the right amount of water at the right temperature, a gentle heat, so they don't burst open; don't just throw the potatoes in a pot and boil the life out of them. Then let the excess moisture steam off after boiling and pass the potatoes through the tamis while they're still hot. Finally, you must emulsify the butter and cream into them without breaking that emulsification, knowing exactly how much butter and cream you can get into them—and then knowing how to get even more in! There's a great lesson in this recipe: how to pay attention to the details of what we think is a simple preparation.

FOR THE POTATO PURÉE: Place the Yukon Gold potatoes in a pot with enough water to cover them by at least 4 inches. Bring to a boil and boil gently until the potatoes are tender and offer no resistance when poked with a knife, 30 to 40 minutes, depending on their size. Drain the potatoes and return to the empty pot over medium heat for a minute to steam off excess moisture.

MEANWHILE, FOR THE MUSHROOM RAGOUT: Cut the assorted potatoes (do not peel them) into pieces approximately the same size so that their cooking times will be the same: Cut small round potatoes in

half and then into ¹⁄₁₆-inch half circles. Long narrow potatoes can be cut into small circles of the same thickness, and larger potatoes may need to be quartered lengthwise before they are sliced. There will be about 3 cups of sliced potatoes.

Place the potato slices in a strainer and rinse them under cold water. Place them in a pot with 1 teaspoon salt and cold water to cover by 2 inches. Bring the water to a boil and cook the potatoes for 2 to 3 minutes, or until just tender. Drain in a strainer, rinse the potatoes carefully under cold water, and set aside.

Bring the truffle-infused mushroom stock (or the mushroom stock and truffle juice) and vinegar to a simmer in a medium saucepan and let reduce for 3 to 4 minutes. Whisk in the butter, one piece at a time, then add the cooked potato slices and simmer until the stock thickens to a sauce consistency (vinegar helps prevent root vegetables such as potatoes from overcooking). Add the brunoise, black truffle, and chives and season to taste with salt and pepper. Keep warm over very low heat.

TO FINISH THE POTATO PURÉE: This recipe involves an exacting technique for achieving the perfect potato purée. Special care must be taken to maintain a low temperature while emulsifying the potatoes, butter, and cream. If the temperature becomes too high, the butter will melt as it is added and the potatoes will become oily. You will need to remain with the potatoes throughout the cooking process.

Peel the hot potatoes, pass them through a tamis (see page 73), and place the purée in a heavy pot. Stir in the salt and beat with a wooden spoon over low heat to dry them out slightly. Add the cream and butter a little at a time, alternating them and beating vigorously the entire time. The purée should be holding to the sides of the pan and will be stiffer and more difficult to mix than traditional mashed potatoes. If it does not hold, and forms a ball around the spoon, your pan may be too hot. Should this happen, remove the pan from the heat and beat in a small amount of water to return the potatoes to the proper consistency. Then lower the heat, return the pan to the heat, and continue adding the cream and butter. Serve the potatoes as soon as possible.

TO COMPLETE: Stir the white truffle oil into the ragout. Season the potato purée with additional salt if needed and pepper to taste. Spoon some purée into each serving bowl. Make a well in the center and fill with the potato ragout. Garnish each portion with 2 truffle potato chips.

MAKES 8 SERVINGS

## TRUFFLE-INFUSED MUSHROOM STOCK

4 ounces summer truffles, or winter (black) truffles
3 cups Mushroom Stock (page 227)

Fresh raw truffles are excellent if you use them right away, but poaching and freezing them allows you to buy larger quantities when they are in season and store them for future use. A great side benefit is that you're left with a wonderful truffle-infused mushroom stock. The flavor will depend on the quality of the truffle used. Don't expect robust flavors when using summer truffles. The stock will keep frozen for six months.

With a mushroom brush, nailbrush, or small scrub brush, carefully scrub the dirt from the truffles under warm water. (If it is not completely removed, it will stick to the truffles as they poach and because it is so fine, you will not be able to strain the dirt from the stock.) Place the cleaned truffles in a small pot. Strain the mushroom stock through a chinois (see page 73) over the truffles. Discard what remains in the chinois. Cover the truffles with a small plate or lid to keep them submerged in the liquid.

Heat the stock slowly to a gentle simmer and poach the truffles for 20 minutes. Remove the truffles to a small bowl and strain enough stock over to just cover. Strain the remaining stock into a separate container.

Cool in the refrigerator, then place the stock and truffles with their stock in plastic containers or resealable bags in the freezer.

MAKES ABOUT 2 1/2 CUPS (PLUS THE TRUFFLES)

# Carnaroli Risotto with Shaved White Truffles from Alba

**PART 1**

2 tablespoons canola oil

3 tablespoons minced onions (minced smaller
    than the grains of rice)

1 cup Carnaroli rice

1 cup crisp dry white wine, such as Sauvignon Blanc

2 cups Chicken Stock (page 226),
    Vegetable Stock (page 227), Mushroom Stock
    (page 227), or water, heated to a simmer
    (for risotto with white truffles, use 1 cup
    chicken stock and 1 cup water)

**PART 2**

2 to 2½ cups Chicken Stock (page 226),
    Vegetable Stock (page 227), Mushroom
    Stock (page 227), or water, heated to a
    simmer (for risotto with white truffles, use
    1¼ cups chicken stock and 1¼ cups water)

¼ teaspoon kosher salt, or to taste

5 tablespoons (2½ ounces) unsalted butter

¾ cup heavy cream, whipped to soft peaks

¼ cup freshly grated Parmigiano-Reggiano

3 tablespoons white truffle oil
    (for risotto with white truffles)

Fresh white truffle (optional)

The best rice for risotto is grown in Italy's Po Valley. You can use Arborio rice, but Carnaroli results in risotto with the creamiest consistency.

If you don't have truffles, the basic risotto could be topped with Braised Oxtails (page 162), a mushroom ragout, or a variety of accompaniments. Base the liquid used in preparing the risotto on the finished dish. For example, use chicken stock when you are serving meat, or vegetable stock for an asparagus garnish. Risotto normally requires a cook's undivided attention over a long period of time. This two-part method allows you to begin the rice preparation the day before and makes the final cooking time less than ten minutes. The dish should be served as soon as it is completed.

PART 1: Heat the oil in a deep heavy sauté pan over medium heat. Stir in the onions and cook slowly until softened and translucent but not browned. Mix in the rice and stir for 3 to 4 minutes.

Add the wine and let it simmer, without stirring, for 2 to 3 minutes. (After adding the wine, lean close to the pan and breathe in the aroma. You will be able to smell and feel the raw alcohol at the back of your nose. Breathe it in several times during the cooking process, and as the alcohol evaporates and the rice begins to toast, the raw alcohol smell will dissipate and be replaced with the smell of toasted rice.) When the liquid has been absorbed, begin stirring to "toast" the rice. The rice should not brown, but it will separate into individual grains, looking much as it did before the wine was added. Scrape the bottom of the pan to keep the rice from sticking. The alcohol smell should be completely gone. Increase the heat and add the stock; it should just cover the rice. When it boils, reduce the heat and simmer for 4 minutes. Drain the rice, discarding any remaining liquid. Spread the rice in a 9- by 13-inch pan or other similar-size container, cover, and refrigerate for several hours, or up to a day.

PART 2: Put the rice in a sauté pan, add ½ cup of the stock and the salt, and stir over high heat until the liquid begins to simmer; it should continue to simmer throughout the cooking. As the stock evaporates, add ½ cup more. Continue to cook, adding more stock as it evaporates and tasting the rice from time to time. The finished rice will be similar to al dente pasta; it should be thoroughly cooked but with a little "bite" remaining to it, never mushy. When the rice is cooked, let whatever liquid remains in the pan evaporate (you may not use all the stock called for).

Remove the risotto from the heat and, using a wooden spoon, beat in the butter a little at time, working quickly so it will "emulsify" with the rice (creating a creamy risotto) rather than melt into the risotto. Vigorously beat in the whipped cream, cheese, salt to taste, and the white truffle oil, if using. Divide among serving bowls. Place shavings of white truffle, if using, over the top of the risotto: The truffle can be shaved over the risotto at the table if you have a truffle slicer, or it can be sliced in the kitchen on a mandoline and then scattered over the risotto. Serve immediately.

PICTURED ON PAGE 2      MAKES 6 TO 8 SERVINGS

Because the white truffle is such an extraordinary gift, and because the season—roughly October through December—is so short, you want to treat it as simply as possible, as we do in this classic Piedmontese risotto. I learned the technique of folding whipped cream into risotto from Alain Ducasse. Though the cream does "melt" out of its whipped state, it coats all the individual grains more easily than it would unwhipped. Always add your fat at the end, with the pan off the heat.

# Potato Gnocchi

2 pounds russet potatoes

1 1/4 to 1 1/2 cups all-purpose flour

3 large egg yolks

2 tablespoons kosher salt, or to taste

This recipe yields more gnocchi than are needed for a single recipe, but their versatility makes them an ideal item to have on hand. Use them as a garnish or serve them as a meal. We serve small gnocchi, but they can be shaped larger if desired. Part of what makes this a great recipe is that the gnocchi freeze so well, and they go directly from the freezer into boiling water so they're always at the ready.

Preheat the oven to 350°F.

Bake the potatoes for 1 hour, or until they are completely cooked.

Split the potatoes, scoop out the flesh, and press it through a potato ricer. Place the hot potatoes on a board or counter. Make a well in the center. Place a layer of about 1/2 cup flour in the well, add the egg yolks, then add about 1/2 cup more flour and the salt. Use a dough scraper to "chop" the potatoes into the flour and eggs. This process should be done quickly (15 to 30 seconds), as overworking the dough will make the gnocchi heavy and sticky. Add more flour as necessary. The resulting dough should be homogeneous and barely sticky on the outside. Shape the dough into a ball.

Roll the ball of dough lightly in flour. Pull off a section of the dough and roll it by hand on a lightly floured surface into a "snake" about 1/2 inch thick. Cut into 1/2-inch pieces and, using your hand, roll each piece into a ball. Then roll the balls on a gnocchi paddle or over the back of a fork to create an oval shape with indentations. Test one gnocchi by placing it in a large pot of rapidly boiling lightly salted water. It is cooked as soon as it floats to the surface. Taste for seasoning and texture and add salt to the dough if necessary, or add a bit more flour if the gnocchi seems mushy. Continue forming the remaining gnocchi, placing them on a lightly floured tray until ready to cook.

Place the gnocchi in the boiling water. Use a slotted spoon or skimmer to remove them to a bowl of ice water as they rise to the surface. Once they have cooled (about 2 minutes) drain them briefly on paper towels or a kitchen towel. Lay them in a single layer on a parchment-lined baking sheet. Store in the pan in the refrigerator if they will be used shortly (up to a day), or place them in the freezer. Once they are frozen, they can be stored in well-sealed plastic bags and kept frozen for several weeks; cook them while they are still frozen. Sauté the gnocchi as directed on page 91 just before serving.

MAKES ABOUT 20 DOZEN SMALL GNOCCHI

# Warm Fruitwood-Smoked Salmon with Potato Gnocchi and Balsamic Glaze

**SALMON**

3 cups milk, or more as needed

1 pound center-cut smoked salmon fillet
(see Sources, page 315), trimmed and cut
into 6 squares 2 inches by 2 inches by ³/₄ inch

**GNOCCHI**

2 tablespoons canola oil

36 Potato Gnocchi (page 90)
(do not thaw if frozen)

³/₄ cup Chicken Stock (page 226)

Few drops white wine vinegar

4¹/₂ tablespoons (2¹/₄ ounces), salted butter,
cut into 4 pieces

1 tablespoon Brunoise (page 155)

1 tablespoon tomato diamonds (see page 203)

1 tablespoon chopped chives

Kosher salt and freshly ground black pepper

**GREENS**

¹/₂ cup assorted baby beet, arugula, and/or any
other bitter greens

³/₄ teaspoon very finely minced shallot

Lemon oil (see Sources, page 315)

Kosher salt and freshly ground black pepper

Chive Oil (page 166), in a squeeze bottle

Balsamic Glaze (page 238), in a squeeze bottle

In this dish, smoked salmon—typically served cold—is heated in milk and served warm. Take care not to let the milk get too hot—you don't want to poach the salmon or allow its color to change. The milk leaches salt from the flesh, which allows one to serve the fish warm and to keep the integrity of the smoky cured flavor without overpowering the dish with salt. As with bacon, I prefer a fruitwood smoke to a hardwood smoke for the salmon because it's sweeter.

**FOR THE SALMON:** In a saucepan just large enough to hold the salmon pieces in one layer, warm the milk to 115°F. Add the salmon. The pieces should be fully submerged in the milk. Warm the salmon for about 7 minutes over very low heat, not allowing the temperature to exceed 115°F. If the temperature begins to climb, remove the pan from the heat, or add additional cold milk to lower the temperature. If the salmon overheats, it will poach and thereby lose its beautiful translucent orange color and turn a more opaque, less vibrant color.

**MEANWHILE, FOR THE GNOCCHI:** In a large sauté pan, heat the oil over medium-high heat only until fragrant. Pour off the excess oil, leaving only enough to coat the pan. Toss in the gnocchi and cook for 1 to 2 minutes, or until golden brown on the bottom. Add the chicken stock, vinegar, and butter and let it simmer for a few minutes to reduce to a sauce-like consistency. Add the brunoise, tomato diamonds, chopped chives, and salt and pepper to taste. Remove from the heat.

**FOR THE GREENS:** In a bowl, mix the baby greens with the shallot. Lightly dress with a little lemon oil and season to taste with salt and pepper.

**TO COMPLETE:** Squeeze a ring of chive oil onto each plate. Arrange 6 gnocchi, with some of the sauce, in the center of each ring of chive oil. Place a piece of salmon on the gnocchi, twist a small bunch of greens in the palm of your hand so that they cling together, and set on top of the salmon. Squeeze dots of the balsamic glaze in a line down either side of each plate, creating spots that go from larger to smaller in size. Connect the dots with additional chive oil if you wish.

MAKES 6 SERVINGS

# Dungeness Crab Salad with Cucumber Jelly, Grainy Mustard Vinaigrette, and Frisée Lettuce

**CUCUMBER JELLY**

½ small cucumber, peeled

1¼ gelatin sheets, soaked in cold water to soften

1 cup cucumber juice (from about 1 pound
  cucumbers, unpeeled, put through a juicer
  and strained; or purchased from a health
  food store)

36 small sprigs dill

**CRAB SALAD**

½ cup heavy cream

2 teaspoons whole-grain Dijon mustard

Kosher salt and freshly ground white pepper

2½ cups (about 12 ounces) cooked Dungeness
  crabmeat (from about 2 Dungeness crabs;
  see page 50 for cooking instructions)

1 cup amaranth, baby beet greens,
  baby arugula, or other baby greens

3 tablespoons grated daikon radish

Extra virgin olive oil

Kosher salt and freshly ground white pepper

This is a wonderful chilled salad thanks to the clean and distinctive flavor of the crab. I've combined it with elements that have gone with crab forever—cucumber, fresh dill, and mustard.

FOR THE JELLY: Using a mandoline or sharp knife, cut lengthwise slices about ¹⁄₁₆ inch thick from the cucumber. Cut the slices into narrow strips about ⅛ inch wide. Cut the strips on the diagonal to make small cucumber diamonds; you will need about 2 tablespoons of diamonds.

Squeeze the gelatin to remove excess water and place it in a small metal bowl. Set the bowl over a pan of hot water and stir to dissolve the gelatin. Remove the bowl from the heat and stir in the cucumber juice, being certain that the gelatin completely dissolves.

Pour 2 to 3 tablespoons of the jelly into each of six shallow serving bowls and rotate the bowls to distribute the jelly evenly. Making certain that the dishes are level, arrange the cucumber diamonds and the dill sprigs over the jelly keeping in mind that the crab will sit in the center of each dish. Place the bowls in the refrigerator for at least 1 hour and up to several hours to set the jelly.

TO COMPLETE: In a medium bowl, whip the heavy cream until it forms a ribbon when the whisk is lifted (just before soft peaks). Whisk in the mustard and salt and white pepper to taste. Place the crabmeat in a bowl and fold in just enough of the whipped cream to bind the salad.

Toss the greens with the daikon, a drizzle of oil, and salt and white pepper to taste.

Fill a 2- to 2½-inch ring mold, about 1½ inches high (see Sources, page 315), with crab salad. Slip your hand under the filled ring and place the ring over the center of the chilled jelly in one bowl. Lift off and remove the ring and top the crab salad with a stack of the dressed greens. Repeat with the remaining bowls, and serve immediately. (If the kitchen is very warm, the gelatin may begin to melt; should this happen, return them to the refrigerator briefly to set up before serving.)

PICTURED ON PAGE 52                                      MAKES 6 SERVINGS

# Chesapeake Bay Soft-shell Crab "Sandwich"

SAUCE

2 hard-boiled egg yolks

2 tablespoons Chicken Stock (page 226), heated,
   or hot water

3 tablespoons cornichon juice

1 teaspoon Dijon mustard

½ cup canola oil

3 tablespoons minced cornichons

1 tablespoon minced shallot

1 tablespoon minced Italian parsley

2 tablespoons Brunoise (page 155)

Kosher salt and freshly ground black pepper

Canola oil for deep-frying

1 tablespoon capers, drained

6 live soft-shell crabs

Clarified Butter (page 125), for panfrying

Kosher salt and freshly ground black pepper

Flour for dusting

6 brioche Croutons (see page 238)

6 pieces Tomato Confit (page 64),
   at room temperature

¼ cup baby arugula (or regular arugula cut
   into chiffonade—long narrow strips)

This is not really a sandwich, of course, but the dish was inspired by my love of traditional soft-shell crab sandwiches heaped with tomatoes and tartar sauce. I've refashioned the ingredients of a classic tartar sauce—egg yolks, dill pickles, capers—as hard-boiled yolks, Dijon mustard, and cornichons. On top of the sauce, I put a crouton, then the crab, trimmed down to just its body and claws, then tomato confit, arugula, and fried capers.

FOR THE SAUCE: Blend the egg yolks, chicken stock, cornichon juice, and mustard in a blender. With the machine running, slowly drizzle in the oil so the mixture emulsifies. Remove the sauce to a small bowl and stir in the remaining sauce ingredients. The sauce can be refrigerated for up to 2 days; bring to room temperature before serving.

FOR THE CAPERS: In a very small pot, heat about 2 inches of canola oil to 250°F. Add the drained capers and fry slowly for 12 to 15 minutes, or until bubbles have stopped forming around the capers and they are dry and crunchy. Drain them on paper towels.

TO CLEAN THE CRABS: Using a pair of scissors, cut off the crabs' faces and discard. Cut off the two large claws where they meet the body and reserve. Cut off and discard the smaller legs and trim the sides of the body for a smooth edge. Lift off the apron, the pointed piece on the underside of each crab. Remove the lungs and any other matter beneath the apron. Rinse the six bodies and twelve claws and pat dry with paper towels.

Heat ⅛ inch of clarified butter in a large skillet over medium heat. Season the pieces of crab with salt and pepper and dredge in flour, patting off any excess. Add the crab bodies shell side down to the hot butter. The butter should be hot enough to sizzle when the crabs are added, but not so hot that it pops and spurts from the pan. Sauté the crab bodies for 2 to 3 minutes, until they are golden brown and crusty on the bottom. Turn the bodies, add the claws, and cook for 2 to 3 minutes; turn the claws after about 1 minute. Remove the crab pieces and drain on paper towels.

TO COMPLETE: Place a spoonful of sauce in the center of each serving plate. Center a crouton on the sauce and top it with a crab body. Fold a piece of tomato confit in half and place it over the crab. Arrange 2 claws over each piece of tomato and finish with a stack of baby arugula. Sprinkle the plates with the fried capers. Serve immediately.

PICTURED ON PAGE 94                               MAKES 6 SERVINGS

Above: Chesapeake Bay Soft-shell Crab "Sandwich," page 93. Opposite: Dungeness crab for Dungeness Crab Salad, page 92.

# Carpaccio of Yellowfin Tuna Niçoise

8 ounces sushi-quality yellowfin tuna fillet
    with as little sinew as possible

Extra virgin olive oil

**SALAD**

½ small yellow bell pepper

½ small red bell pepper

1 small fennel bulb

Canola oil for deep-frying

1 teaspoon capers, drained

1 cup loosely packed frisée (inner white leaves only)

¼ cup Herb Salad (recipe follows)

1 teaspoon extra virgin olive oil

¼ teaspoon balsamic vinegar

Kosher salt

3 tablespoons Tapenade (page 66)

6 quail eggs, hard-boiled (2 minutes)
    and peeled

1 tablespoon hot paprika

6 triangular-shaped brioche Croutons (page 238)

Fleur de sel

1 tablespoon Pepper Confetti (recipe follows)

This is simply another incarnation of the classic salade Niçoise, which is canned white tuna, hard-boiled eggs, olives, and whatever lettuces are around. This version uses fresh tuna, hard-boiled quail eggs rather than hen eggs, and frisée and a julienne of red and yellow peppers rather than a large salad. The olives take the form of tapenade, a very intense and concentrated preparation that adds elements of anchovy and olive oil to the dish.

FOR THE TUNA: Thinly slice the tuna fillet. Lightly oil six pieces of plastic wrap and lay the slices in 6 equal portions on the plastic wrap. Rub the top of the tuna slices with a light coating of oil and cover with more plastic wrap. Use a flat meat pounder to lightly pound the slices, then use a rolling pin to roll the tuna into paper-thin sheets.

Place a 4-inch round cutter or mold on each piece and run a sharp knife around the mold and through the wrap. The circles of tuna, still in the plastic, can be refrigerated for a few hours. (Reserve the scraps for another use, such as tuna tartare.)

FOR THE SALAD: Peel the skin from the peppers with a vegetable peeler. Cut the peppers into sections following their natural lines, and peel the edges as necessary. Trim and discard the ribs and seeds and cut the peppers into fine julienne about 1 inch long. You will need about 2 tablespoons of each color pepper.

Cut a vertical slice about ⅛ inch thick from one of the outer layers of the fennel bulb. Trim it so that you have a flat piece and cut it into a fine julienne. You will need about 2 tablespoons. (Reserve the remaining fennel for another use.)

In a very small pot, heat about 2 inches of canola oil to 250°F. Add the drained capers and fry them over low heat for 12 to 15 minutes, or until they are dry and crunchy. It's important to use a low temperature, or the capers—which are a bud—will not open. (Frying vegetables dehydrates them, or removes all the water. If the temperature is too hot, they will brown before all the moisture is removed and they will not dry out properly or get the crunchy result you seek.) Bubbles will appear around the capers as long as there is still moisture present. When the bubbles are gone, remove the capers from the oil and drain on paper towels.

TO COMPLETE: Toss the frisée with the herb salad, bell peppers, fennel, and capers. Add the olive oil, balsamic vinegar, and a pinch of salt.

Remove the top sheet of plastic wrap from one round of tuna and invert the fish onto a serving plate. Remove the second piece of wrap and rub a thin coating of olive oil over the tuna. Repeat with the remaining tuna.

Place a small quenelle (see page 274), or oval scoop (1½ teaspoons), of tapenade off to one side of each circle of tuna. Place a small mound of herb salad between the tuna and tapenade. Trim the bottom of each quail egg so that it will stand up, dip the top of the quail egg in the paprika, and nestle an egg and a crouton by the greens and tapenade on each plate. Sprinkle the tuna with fleur de sel and sprinkle the pepper confetti over the plates.

MAKES 6 SERVINGS

## PEPPER CONFETTI

Red, yellow, and green "fancy" bell peppers

This is a lovely, colorful garnish when bell peppers suit the food—in the gazpacho, say, or the blini with roasted peppers, anything Mediterranean or Provençal in style. Use "fancy" peppers as they have more flesh and will give a far superior result.

Cut off the tops and bottoms of the peppers, then cut the peppers into sections following the natural lines in the skin. Trim away the ribs and seeds. Peel off the skin, using a vegetable peeler. You will be left with smooth flat pieces of pepper about ¼ inch thick. Cut the peppers into ¹⁄₁₆-inch julienne strips.

Lay the pepper strips on the glass tray in the microwave or another microwave dish that has a smooth surface. Do not place the peppers on a plate or dish that has a textured surface, or the strips will dry unevenly and may burn in spots.

Microwave on medium-high power for 10 to 15 minutes, or until the strips are dried out. Lay the finished strips side by side and cut them into small dice. Store in an airtight container at room temperature; the confetti will keep for weeks if the pepper strips have been completely dried.

## HERB SALAD

| | |
|---|---|
| 2½ tablespoons Italian parsley leaves | 1 tablespoon tarragon leaves |
| 2½ tablespoons chervil (in small clusters) | 1 teaspoon thyme leaves (for fish dishes only) |
| 2 tablespoons chive tips (about 1 inch long) | 1 tablespoon chive or thyme flowers |

Gently mix the herbs just before serving. We not only use herbs to flavor dishes in their cooking and as garnish, we also serve them on their own in the form of an herb salad. Use small sprigs of tender herbs such as chervil, chives, parsley, cilantro, and thyme leaves. For herbs with harder stems such as thyme, use just the leaves; because when they're fresh and whole, they're powerful, so you need only a small quantity.

MAKES A SCANT ½ CUP

# Fricassée of Escargots with a Purée of Sweet Carrots, Roasted Shallots, and Herb Salad

**RED WINE SAUCE**

2 pieces marrow bone (cut 1½ inches long)

Canola oil

¼ cup chopped carrots

¼ cup chopped turnips

1 small clove garlic, crushed

1 cup dry red wine, such as Cabernet Sauvignon

3 tablespoons port

2 tablespoons minced shallots

1 tablespoon all-purpose flour

1½ cups Veal Stock (page 222)

½ cup water

2 sprigs chervil

2 sprigs Italian parsley

1 sprig tarragon

1 small bay leaf

Kosher salt and freshly ground black pepper

**COURT BOUILLON** (IF USING FRESH SNAILS)

2½ cups water

½ cup sliced carrots

½ cup sliced leeks

2 small bay leaves

¾ teaspoon black peppercorns

1 lemon

1¾ cups crisp, dry white wine, such as
 Sauvignon Blanc

**SNAILS**

36 fresh snails in the shell (about 1½ pints)
 or 36 best-quality canned large snails

3 tablespoons unsalted butter
 (if using canned snails)

2 tablespoons minced shallots
 (if using canned snails)

1½ teaspoons minced shallots

2 teaspoons tomato diamonds (see page 203)

1 tablespoon Brunoise (page 155)

½ cup Beurre Monté (page 135)

1 tablespoon water

2 teaspoons minced Italian parsley

Kosher salt

**CARROT PURÉE**

8 ounces carrots, cut into uniform pieces about
 ½ inch wide and 1 inch long (1½ cups)

About 2 cups heavy cream

Kosher salt

**ROASTED SHALLOTS**

6 medium shallots (about 6 ounces)

Canola oil

Kosher salt


6 triangular brioche Croutons (page 238)

¼ cup Herb Salad (page 97)

---

**FOR THE MARROW:** Soak the marrow bones in a bowl of ice water for 20 minutes. Drain and remove the marrow from the bones by pushing it out with your finger. If it doesn't come out easily, soak the bones briefly in warm water, just to loosen the marrow. Soak the marrow pieces in a bowl of ice water for 12 to 24 hours, changing the water every 6 to 8 hours. (It is important to change the water, because as the blood is extracted from the marrow, the water will become saturated with it and the marrow could spoil.)

**FOR THE COURT BOUILLON (IF USING FRESH SNAILS):** Place the water in a saucepan. Add the carrots, leeks, bay leaves, and peppercorns. Bring to a boil, then reduce the heat to a simmer. Cut the lemon in half, squeeze in the juice, and add the lemon halves and wine to the saucepan.

Meanwhile, rinse the fresh snails under cold running water and place them in a bowl.

After the court bouillon has returned to a simmer, pour it over the snails and place the bowl in an ice bath. Let the snails and liquid cool completely.

When the snails are cold, remove them one by one from the court bouillon, reserving it, and remove the snails from the shells: Place the tip of a paring knife or a toothpick behind the head of the snail and gently pry the snail forward. Use your fingers to carefully pull the snail from the shell while gently twisting the body. (The body follows the shape of the shell and you need to be careful not to break it.) As you remove each snail, place it in cold water; discard the shells.

Strain the court bouillon. Remove the snails from the water and place them in the bouillon. (Be careful not to put your fingers in the bouillon; as with any stock or sauce, you might add bacteria to the liquid and thereby reduce its shelf life.) Cover the snails and refrigerate for up to 4 days.

FOR CANNED SNAILS: Rinse the snails under cold running water. Melt the butter in a small skillet, add the shallots, and cook over low heat for 1 to 2 minutes, to soften the shallots. Add the snails and cook gently for about 1 to 2 minutes, or just until hot. Transfer the snails, butter, and shallots to a container and refrigerate for up to 2 days.

FOR THE CARROT PURÉE: Place the carrots in a saucepan large enough to hold them in a single layer. Pour in enough cream just to cover the carrots. Bring to a simmer over medium heat and simmer gently for 35 to 45 minutes, or until the carrots are completely tender. Adjust the heat as necessary so that the cream does not scorch.

Drain the carrots, pressing lightly on them to remove excess cream. Pass the carrots through a tamis (see page 73) and season to taste with salt. The carrots can be refrigerated in a covered container for up to a day.

FOR THE ROASTED SHALLOTS: Preheat the oven to 350°F.

Lightly coat the shallots with oil and place on a sheet of aluminum foil. Sprinkle with salt and seal the foil to make a packet. Place the packet in the oven and roast for about 1 hour, or until the shallots are tender.

Remove the shallots from the oven and let cool until they are easy to handle. Peel the shallots. Remove the outer layers and discard. Cut the centers into wedges that are smaller than the snails.

FOR THE SAUCE: Heat a film of canola oil in a medium saucepan over medium heat. Add the carrots and turnips and sauté for 2 to 3 minutes, or until lightly caramelized. Add the garlic and cook, stirring, for 1 minute. Deglaze the pan with the red wine and port, then simmer for 8 to 10 minutes, or until the liquid has evaporated and the pan is dry.

Meanwhile, drain the marrow and cut it into $\frac{1}{4}$-inch dice. There should be about $\frac{1}{3}$ cup. Place the bone marrow and shallots in a medium saucepan and cook over low heat for 2 to 3 minutes, or until the shallots are translucent. Stir in the flour and cook for another 2 minutes.

While the marrow and shallots are cooking, heat the stock and water in a small saucepan until hot. Add the hot stock and water to the carrots and turnips and simmer for a minute to incorporate the ingredients.

Whisk the carrots, turnips, and stock into the marrow and shallots. Add the chervil, parsley, tarragon, and bay leaf and simmer for 10 minutes to infuse the sauce with the flavor of the herbs. If the sauce becomes too thick, add a little water. Strain the sauce into a small saucepan.

TO COMPLETE: Preheat the oven to 350°F.

Place the minced shallots, tomato diamonds, brunoise, beurre monté, and water in an ovenproof saucepan and add the snails and roasted shallots. Place the pan in the oven and heat for about 6 minutes, or just until heated through. (Overcooking the snails will cause them to shrink and toughen.)

Meanwhile, reheat the carrot purée in a pan over low heat and season with salt to taste. Rewarm the sauce and season with salt and pepper.

When the snails are warm, remove the pan from the oven and stir in the parsley and salt to taste.

Place 2 to 3 tablespoons of sauce in each serving bowl. Form a quenelle (see page 274), a small oval scoop, of carrot purée (dip the spoon in hot water before forming each quenelle for a smoother shape), place the quenelle to one side of the center of the bowl, and lean a crouton against the quenelle, placing it in the center of the plate. Repeat with the remaining bowls.

Spoon 6 snails, along with some of the vegetable garnishes and the sauce in the pan, alongside each crouton. Sprinkle with the herb salad.

PICTURED ON PAGE 100                    MAKES **6** SERVINGS

Snails are now commercially cultivated in California, giving us a new ingredient to work with. I wanted to use them in a way that wasn't stereotypical but also wasn't so far away from traditional preparations as to be contrived or confusing. In this fricassée, they're served with roasted shallots, a red wine sauce made with bone marrow that adds a rich flavor to the dish, croutons, and a sweet carrot purée. Note that the marrow needs to be soaked for at least 12 hours.

Fricassée of Escargots, page 98

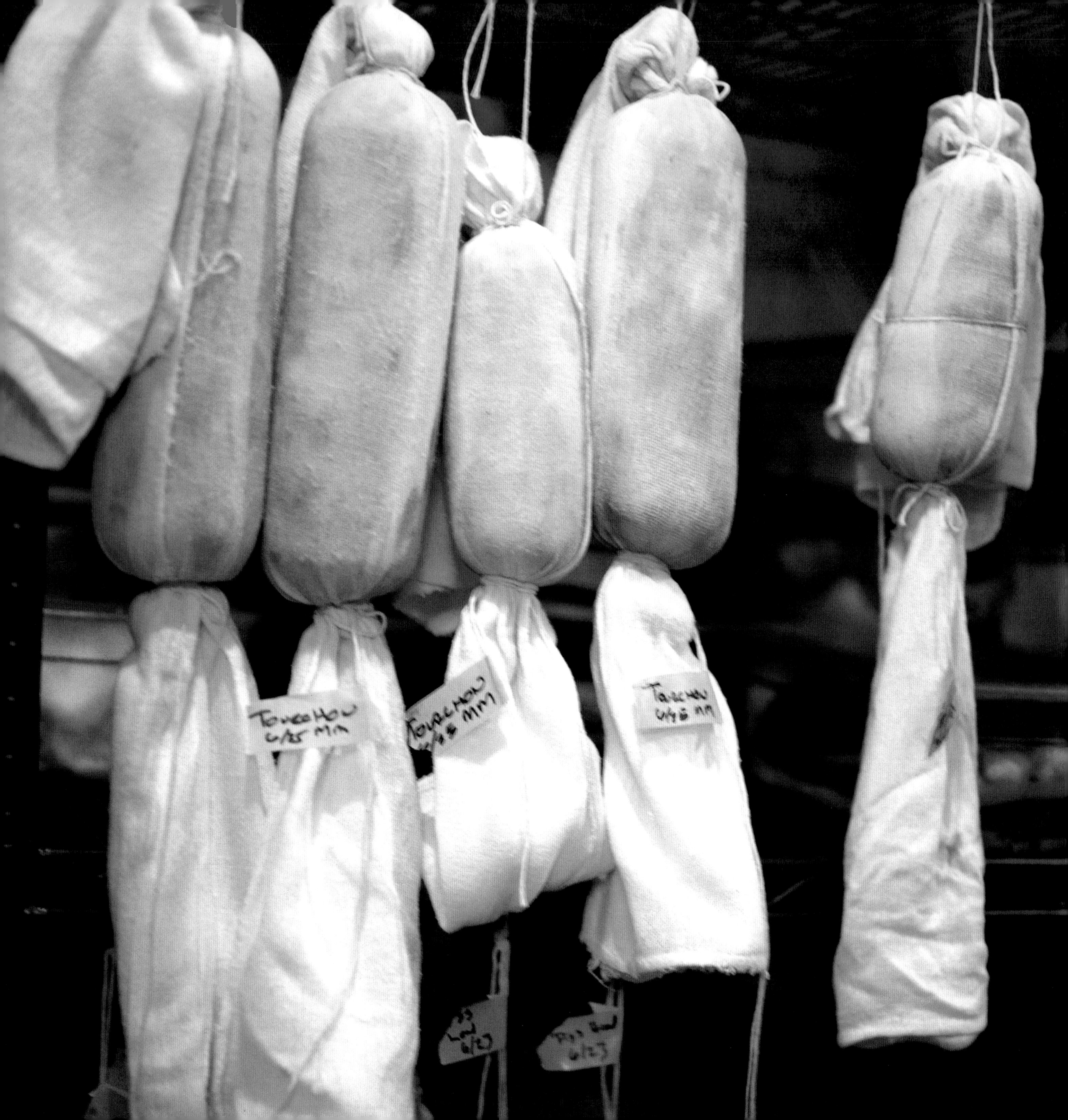

# Foie Gras

The great thing about foie gras is that it's foie gras—like the great thing about caviar is that it's caviar. You don't have to do anything to it. It's a luxury on its own, and your job is to try to make it show what it really is. Don't be afraid of it. It is probably one of the easiest things to prepare well at home, because what you will buy is the same quality as what I buy. It's available from only two companies in the United States—one in the Hudson Valley, New York; one in Sonoma County, California (see Sources, page 315)—so you're going to get a consistent product.

The only thing you really have to know about foie gras to cook it well is that it's composed almost entirely of fat. It has so much fat in it that you sauté it in a dry pan. If it gets too hot, you won't have anything left, because all the fat will have melted. I've poached it and forgotten it until someone asked, "Hey, what's this floating in the stock?"

When I left for France in 1984, there was no fresh foie gras in the United States. Nobody was raising geese or ducks for it, and it was illegal to import uncooked foie gras, so my first introduction to raw foie gras was in France. If I hadn't learned about it in France, I still wouldn't really know how to prepare it. They served it in every restaurant I worked in, so it was exciting to come back in 1985 and find it available here through Ariane Daguin's new firm, D'Artagnan.

Foie gras is something that should be left alone. It should be minimally garnished. You eat it because you like the taste and feel of foie gras. Foie gras on toast is perfect. Foie gras with a poached pear, a fig, a truffle—it's almost impossible to go wrong.

In France, I learned to marinate foie gras with nine grams of salt, one gram of sugar, and one gram of pepper per five hundred grams of foie gras. I learned how to clean it, and I learned just when to serve it and how to serve it. Foie gras should sit for a day after you cook it so that the flavors have a chance to mature together, to become whole.

Foie gras is best served cold and barely cooked. Cold, it has much more body and character to it and shows off its rich creamy texture. That's why I love the foie gras *au torchon*. Most people in America like it hot; certainly more foie gras is served hot here than served cold.

*Torchon* means "dish towel" in French, and the dish takes its name from the fact that the foie gras pieces are wrapped in a cloth (we use several layers of cheesecloth) into a thick cylinder and then quickly poached. When I serve foie gras au torchon, I always overindulge somebody with an extra-thick piece to make a point—too often people are served a minuscule slice of foie gras that's gray. That's what many people think foie gras is. My aim is to make the torchon a benchmark of what foie gras should be.

Foie gras should be bright and flesh-colored, verging on pink. It oxidizes very quickly and turns gray. A torchon can be as much as a week old, and the oxidation will be deeper, but we cut that part off before serving it. Cooks think they can't throw foie gras away because it's so expensive, and the result is that they serve bad foie gras. When that happens, people wonder what the fuss is all about and why foie gras is so expensive.

Cold foie gras—a three-quarter-inch slice of the torchon with some brioche and some pickled Bing cherries—is really the ideal way to serve it. It's one of those foods I just want to hold in my mouth and let it melt and feel it. It's a very sensual thing.

Opposite: Torchons hanging in a cooler

| TECHNIQUES | PREPARATIONS |
|---|---|

Foie gras is graded "A," "B," and "C," based on size and the amount of imperfections and bruises. I recommend using only As and Bs. An A foie gras, usually about a pound and a quarter to a pound and three quarters, which will serve four to six people, costs fifty to seventy-five dollars; so for fifty or more dollars, you can have an extraordinary experience.

The ducks raised here for foie gras are either moulard or muscovy. I use moulard foie gras rather than muscovy, because I've found that it holds up better in cooking and results in a higher yield.

CLEANING: I tell people to think of foie gras as Play-Doh. When you're cleaning it, don't be afraid you're going to make a mistake, because you can always put it back together. You cut it, you scrape it, you get as many veins out of it as possible, and then you mold it back together again. It takes some hands-on learning to know where the veins are, how to open the foie up to expose the primary vein, and then how to eliminate the secondary ones.

MARINATING: For cold preparations, marinate the foie gras with salt, sugar, and finely ground pepper (we pulverize whole peppercorns in a spice grinder). For the torchon, we use sel rose, or pink salt, which contains nitrites, to delay oxidation and help the color. If you use a wine or spirit in your marinade, cook off the alcohol first, or it will cook your foie gras. Some people like to marinate foie gras in port; if you do, use white port to avoid staining the foie gras.

SEASONING: For hot preparations, use salt and pepper. It's important to score the foie gras about a sixteenth of an inch on all surfaces to allow the salt and pepper to penetrate the liver.

TORCHON: This cylinder of foie gras, wrapped in cheesecloth and poached for about ninety seconds, is one of the best ways to prepare foie gras. The short cooking time means very little fat will cook out, giving you a high yield from what is an expensive ingredient. Second, the marinating and quick cooking—you're basically just melting pieces back together again—result in a creamy, buttery fattiness that I love. It's so lightly cooked, you're almost eating raw foie gras.

FREEZER-CURED: This is essentially the same preparation as the torchon, but instead of cooking the foie gras in water, we "cook" it in the freezer. We hang it for three months and allow dehydration (the same thing that causes freezer burn) to cure the foie gras. It works well, but it's not a method for people in a hurry.

PURÉED: Puréed foie gras is as close as we get to a terrine. Terrines are labor-intensive, with lots of cooking and weighting. For our "terrine," we simply collect our foie gras scraps, marinate them, roll them in cheesecloth, and cook them like the torchon; we then press the foie gras through a tamis to remove the veins and pipe it into small terrine molds. This is a great way to use scraps of foie gras, and for home cooks who don't want to clean the veins one by one, the method is very easy. These miniature terrines make wonderful gifts at Christmastime.

POACHED: We poach foie gras in various liquids, each with a different result. We poach foie gras in its own fat—a technique called confit—and serve it whole. This is another high-yield technique. The density of the fat and the foie are similar so the liver cooks without losing any of its fat or absorbing the cooking fat. Cooking it in fat also inhibits oxidation.

We make foie gras carpaccio by cutting thin slices of raw foie gras

Opposite, left: Lobes of moulard duck foie gras; right: rolling the torchon. Above, left: Whole Roasted Moulard Duck Foie Gras, page 110; right: torchon ready to poach.

and spooning some hot truffle juice over them just before serving, in effect, poaching the foie gras *à la minute*.

Foie gras poached whole in truffle stock results in a lower yield than a cold preparation like the torchon, but the truffle flavor is worth the exchange. Also, it's very simple to do: Score the foie gras on all sides, season it with salt and pepper, and put it in an earthenware dish, or in a pot, whatever you have. The only thing you need to be careful about is making sure you have it in a big enough vessel so that you can get it out when it's cooked, because it will be very soft and fragile, almost molten.

At the restaurant, we bring truffle stock (a mushroom stock that we've poached truffles in, see page 87) to a boil and then pour it over the foie gras, cover the baking dish, and put it in a 350°F oven for 12 to 15 minutes. We remove it from the oven and let it sit for a few minutes, then slice it and serve it with some of the broth, a little shallot, some chives or chopped parsley, and chopped truffle. That's really how simple it is. Sometimes we poach it in a straight mushroom stock instead of the truffle stock and other times we'll poach it inside a plastic bag for a really pure foie gras taste. Poaching is really that simple. While I was thinking about all this poaching of foie gras, it occurred to me that I could poach it in a bottle of Gewürztraminer. So I tried it—it's great.

ROASTED: Roasting foie gras is another exciting way to cook the entire liver. Score it, season it, sear it, and pop it in the oven for a few minutes—just don't forget about it, or no one will recognize it. Roasting is a little more tricky than poaching because the lobes can fall apart if you're not careful. After searing, we add some thyme and garlic but you

could add anything—shallots, rosemary, bay leaf, or just salt and pepper. It's delicious.

Whole roasting and poaching is good for people who love the pure taste of foie gras and don't need the crispy seared exterior of sautéed foie gras.

SAUTEED: You've got to cut foie gras to the right thickness if you're going to sauté it. This is paramount. Many chefs train their staff to cut foie gras too thin, saying, "Be careful, foie gras is really expensive." But you need the proper thickness—three quarters of an inch to 1 inch—for the three textures you want in perfectly sautéed foie gras: a crisp exterior, an almost-molten interior, and a very slim center that is firm because it's still rare.

Sautéed foie gras serves as a primary garnish in many of our dishes. It goes beautifully with squab—that's a classic pairing. But we also do a roasted lobster with the squab spice, and the foie goes amazingly well with that lobster. Monkfish, another sturdy fish that roasts beautifully, is delicious with foie gras.

The lifting of the ban on the importation into the United States of raw poultry products now allows cooks and chefs here to use fresh goose foie gras, which is a little bigger than duck foie gras and costs about 20 percent more. The goose foie gras is creamier in texture than the duck foie gras, and the taste is finer and not so forward, and thus it requires slightly more salt. The French Laundry uses goose foie gras only in cold preparations—the torchon and terrine.

# Poached Moulard Duck Foie Gras *au Torchon* with Pickled Cherries

1 Grade B moulard duck foie gras
(approximately 1¼ pounds; see page 104)

Milk to cover the foie gras

2 teaspoons kosher salt

¼ teaspoon freshly ground white pepper

¼ teaspoon sugar

½ teaspoon pink salt (see Sources, page 315)
(optional)

About 2 quarts Chicken Stock (page 226),
Veal Stock (page 222), or water

**PICKLED CHERRIES**

24 bing cherries with stems

½ cup red wine vinegar

¼ cup water

¼ cup sugar

¾ cup baby arugula

18 tiny mint leaves

Extra virgin olive oil

Gray salt and freshly ground black pepper

12 to 18 brioche Croutons (page 238)

The torchon is my favorite way to serve foie gras cold—it's almost an overindulgence. We form the torchon by placing the foie gras on cheesecloth and wrapping it into a tight cylinder, then poaching it for less than two minutes. The torchon is not difficult to make, but it must be prepared over a four-day period. Once made, it can be refrigerated for up to one week.

DAY 1: SOAKING THE FOIE GRAS: Rinse the foie gras under cold water; pat dry with paper towels. Place it in an airtight container and cover with milk. Cover and refrigerate overnight, or up to 24 hours, to draw out some of the blood.

DAY 2: CLEANING AND MARINATING THE FOIE GRAS: Remove the foie gras from the milk, rinse, and pat dry. Cover it with a damp towel and let stand at room temperature for 45 minutes. (It will be easier to work with if the foie gras is not ice-cold.)

TO CLEAN THE FOIE GRAS: Pull apart the two lobes. Keep one covered with the towel while you work on the other. Remove any membranes from the outside of the foie gras. To butterfly the large lobe: Locate the start of the primary vein at one end of the underside of the lobe. Slice through the lobe to the vein, following its path and pulling the foie gras apart to see the vein clearly. Turn your knife at a 45-degree angle and make an outward cut at each side of the vein to butterfly the foie gras. Cut far enough to open the folds and expose the interior of the liver. Use your fingers and knife to remove the primary vein.

There are smaller veins throughout the foie gras; the more you remove, the more refined the finished torchon will be. Scrape across the foie gras with a knife, working from one side of the lobe to the other, removing all the veins. (This can be a painstaking task, but the result is worth it.) Do not worry about the amount of scraping you do, but leave the outside of the foie gras intact. Think of the liver as a piece of Play-Doh. No matter how much you cut and scrape the inside, you will be able to reform the lobe.

Cut away and discard any bruised areas (if left, they will cause discoloring in the final dish). Once the foie gras is cleaned, fold over the sides and return it to an approximation of its original shape.

FOR THE SMALL LOBE: Again, with your fingers, follow the line of the primary vein on the bottom of the lobe and pull the lobe open. The vein should be close to the surface. As with the large lobe, use a knife to scrape and remove any veins and bruises. As before, form it back into its original shape.

TO MARINATE THE FOIE GRAS: Mix the kosher salt, white pepper, sugar, and pink salt, if using, together. Press the foie gras into a container in an even layer ¾ to 1 inch thick. Sprinkle and press half of the marinating mixture over and into the liver. Flip the foie gras and repeat on the other side with the remaining marinating mix. Press a piece of plastic wrap directly against the foie gras and enclose the container completely in more plastic wrap. Refrigerate for 24 hours.

DAY 3: FORMING, COOKING, AND HANGING THE TORCHON: Remove the liver from the container, place it on a piece of parchment paper, and break it up as necessary to form a loaf about 6 inches long and 3½ inches wide. Using the parchment, roll the foie gras into a log, twisting and squeezing the ends of the parchment paper to help compact the foie gras.

Unwrap the foie gras, discard the paper, and transfer the log to a piece of cheesecloth about 1 foot wide by 2 feet long, placing it along a short end of the cheesecloth. Rolling it away from you, roll it up in the cheesecloth into a tight log, again twisting the ends as you roll to force the foie gras into a compact log. If possible, have a second person hold the end of the cheesecloth flat on the work surface as you roll (see the photograph on page 104).

Loop a length of string around your index finger. With the same hand, hold one end of the cheesecloth tightly and wind the string around the end of the foie gras. Continue wrapping the string about ¼ inch into the foie gras; this will help force the foie gras to compress into a tight roll. Tie a knot around the cheesecloth. Repeat the procedure on the other end. If you have rolled and tied the torchon tightly enough, you will see bits of the foie gras being forced through the cheesecloth (see the photograph on page 105). Tie three pieces of string equally spaced around the width of the torchon. (These will be used as guides to reshape the log into its original shape after it has poached.)

Bring enough stock or water to cover the foie gras to a simmer in a wide pot. Place the torchon in the simmering liquid and poach for 90 seconds. Immediately remove the torchon to an ice-water bath to cool.

The foie gras will have lost volume (it loses fat in the poaching) and must be re-formed. Compress the torchon (still in the cheesecloth) in a thin cotton dish towel. Twist and tie the ends of the towel, returning the liver to the original density and pressing out excess fat. Tie the ends of the towel with string and hang the torchon from a shelf in the refrigerator overnight.

FOR THE PICKLED CHERRIES: If you prefer your cherries pitted, carefully remove the pits through the bottom of the cherries, keeping the stems intact. One way to accomplish this is by bending a tine of an old fork at a 90-degree angle and using it to make a hole in the bottom of the cherry to loosen and remove the pit.

Place the cherries, vinegar, water, and sugar in a saucepan and bring to a simmer. Immediately remove from the heat. Cool the cherries, then refrigerate them in the pickling liquid for a few hours, or up to several days.

DAY 4: Just before serving, remove the towel and cheesecloth from the torchon. You will see that the outside of it is gray and oxidized. Cut the ends from the log. Slice the foie gras into six ¾-inch slices. Use a round cutter (about 2¼ inches) to cut away the darkened exterior of the torchon.

Place a slice of torchon on each plate. Stack 4 cherries on the side of each slice of foie gras. Toss the arugula and mint leaves with a little olive oil. Garnish each plate with a small stack of greens and sprinkle with gray salt and pepper. Serve with the croutons on the side.

PICTURED ON PAGE 108                    MAKES 6 SERVINGS

Above: Poached Moulard Duck Foie Gras *au Torchon*, page 106. Opposite: Gewürztraminer–Poached Moulard Duck Foie Gras, page 111.

# Whole Roasted Moulard Duck Foie Gras with Apples and Black Truffles

1 Grade A moulard duck foie gras
    (approximately 1¼ pounds; see page 104)
Kosher salt and freshly ground black pepper
5 cloves garlic, unpeeled, lightly crushed
1 small bunch thyme (½ ounce)

3 Granny Smith apples, peeled, cored, cut into
    eighths, and trimmed or turned (see page 203)
1 golf ball–size black truffle, brushed of dirt under
    warm water and cut into chunks
1 teaspoon chopped chives
Gray salt

One main reason for cooking a foie gras whole is the presentation. It's very exciting to bring into your dining room an entire seared and roasted foie, and then to slice it for your guests. As with most foie gras preparations, this is very easy to make. A whole foie gras will serve six, but it's so good you might just want to make it for four to truly indulge—which is the point, I think, of foie gras.

Preheat the oven to 475°F.

Trim a 1-inch piece from the tip of the foie gras and heat it slowly in a large skillet to render about 1 tablespoon of fat. Remove the piece of cooked foie gras (it's a snack for the cook) and reserve the fat in the pan.

Score the smooth rounded side of the foie gras in a crosshatch pattern about ⅛ inch deep. Sprinkle both sides generously with kosher salt and pepper.

Heat a heavy ovenproof straight-sided sauté pan over high heat. Add the foie gras, scored side down, and sauté, moving the foie gras against the side of the pan to brown its sides, until it is well browned on the bottom, about 4 minutes; adjust the heat as necessary. Turn the foie gras over, add the garlic cloves, and brown the bottom, about 3 minutes.

Place the thyme sprigs on top of the foie gras and place it in the oven for 4 to 5 minutes. When it is done, it will still feel slightly soft to the touch, like a rare steak. Remove the foie gras from the oven and let rest in the pan for 3 to 4 minutes.

While the foie gras is cooking, reheat the rendered fat in the first skillet. Add the apple pieces and sauté over medium heat, tossing them occasionally, for about 5 minutes, or until they are cooked through and lightly browned. Add the truffle pieces and cook over low heat for another 3 to 4 minutes. Stir in the chives. Place the apples and truffles in a serving bowl.

Present the whole foie gras at the table, with the apple and truffle garnish. Then remove the foie gras from the pan and cut crosswise into slices about ½ inch thick. Arrange on serving plates, spoon a little of the fat in the skillet over each piece, and garnish with the apples and truffles. Sprinkle with fleur de sel and serve.

PICTURED ON PAGE 105                                    MAKES 6 SERVINGS

# Gewürztraminer-Poached Moulard Duck Foie Gras with Gewürztraminer Jelly

1 Grade A moulard duck foie gras
  (approximately 1¼ pounds; see page 104)

**DRY MARINADE**

2 teaspoons kosher salt

¼ teaspoon freshly ground white pepper

¼ teaspoon sugar

½ teaspoon pink salt (see Sources, page 315)
  (optional)

One 750-ml bottle Gewürztraminer

1 cup water

1½ gelatin sheets (see Sources, page 315),
  soaked in cold water to soften

Gray salt

Freshly ground black pepper

Brioche Croutons (page 238)

Because foie gras is so rich, I don't like it with the traditional sweet wines that often accompany it, such as Sauternes. I prefer a wine that introduces a counterpoint to that richness, such as a Gewürztraminer. This dish takes that appreciation a step further by poaching the foie gras in the wine, then clarifying the wine, gelling it, and serving it as an accompaniment. Once it is gelled and stirred, the white wine takes on the appearance of crushed ice, so, for a dramatic presentation, I serve the cold slices of wine-poached foie gras on shaved ice alongside a bowl of the gelled Gewürztraminer. This must be prepared over a three-day period.

DAY 1: MARINATING THE FOIE GRAS: Rinse the foie gras under cold water. Pull apart the lobes and use your fingers to remove excess fat from the bottom of the small lobe (a towel is helpful in gripping the fat).

FOR THE DRY MARINADE: Mix the ingredients together. Sprinkle them in an even layer on all sides of the two lobes. Place the foie gras in a covered container and refrigerate overnight.

DAY 2: Wrap the lobes of foie gras in separate pieces of cheesecloth. Tie each end snugly with a piece of twine, but do not squeeze the foie gras; you want to maintain the natural shape of the pieces.

Place the wrapped pieces of foie gras in a pot top side up with the Gewürztraminer and water. The liquid should come about halfway up the foie gras. Place the pot over low-to-medium heat and slowly heat the liquid until a thermometer reads 140°F. (about 4 minutes). Turn the pieces over and continue to heat until the temperature is 170°F. Turn over a final time and heat until the reading is 180°F. Remove the pot from the heat and allow the foie gras to remain in the pan for 4 minutes. (It is important to cook the foie gras gently to reduce the loss of fat, which would result in a reduced yield.)

Remove the lobes from the pot and place them in a container. Pour the poaching liquid over the foie gras, cover the container, and refrigerate overnight.

DAY 3: Remove the fat that has solidified at the top of the poaching liquid and discard. Remove the foie gras from the liquid and measure out and reserve 1 cup of the liquid for the jelly. Return the foie gras to the liquid remaining in the container and refrigerate.

Squeeze the gelatin sheets to remove the water and place in a metal bowl. Place the bowl over hot water and stir until the gelatin is dissolved. Remove the bowl from the heat and whisk into the reserved poaching liquid. Place the bowl in the refrigerator for at least 2 hours for the jelly to set.

TO COMPLETE: Remove the foie gras from the cheesecloth and use a hot knife (heated under hot water and dried) to cut it into ⅓-inch slices. Arrange the slices on a platter. Stir the jelly to break it up, spoon it into a small serving bowl, and serve with gray salt, pepper, and the croutons.

PICTURED ON PAGE 109                    MAKES 16 SLICES OF FOIE GRAS

**BEEF CHEEKS**

2 beef cheeks, (about 1¼ pounds each)

1 recipe Red Wine Marinade (page 190)

Canola oil

Kosher salt and freshly ground black pepper

Flour for dusting

2 cups Veal Stock (page 222)

2 tablespoons freshly grated horseradish

**VEAL TONGUE**

2 veal tongues (about 6 to 8 ounces each)

⅔ cup onions, cut into ½-inch mirepoix
(see page 203)

⅓ cup carrot, cut into ½-inch mirepoix
(see page 203)

⅓ cup leek (white and light green parts only),
cut into ½-inch mirepoix (see page 203)

2 cloves garlic, peeled

2 sprigs thyme

½ teaspoon kosher salt

3½ cups White Veal Stock (page 223),
Chicken Stock (page 226), or water

2 tablespoons white wine vinegar

¼ cup crème fraîche, whipped

8 baby leeks (or small scallions if leeks are
unavailable)

½ cup baby watercress, baby red oak leaf,
or mâche

2 teaspoons extra virgin olive oil

Kosher salt and freshly ground black pepper

4 pieces Tomato Confit (page 64), warmed
briefly in the oven

Dried horseradish (page 233)

"Tongue in cheek" is a collective creation. I wanted to make a braised beef cheek salad, a first course that had a lot of character and also reflected the familiar pairing of roast beef and horseradish. Beef cheek is very succulent because of its fat content. The original dish was just the braised beef cheek salad, horseradish greens, and confit of tomato. But we had already come up with a lot of paired items—the "Bacon and Eggs," "Oysters and Pearls," "Coffee and Donuts"—and Stephen Durfee, now the pastry chef, said, "Why don't we use tongue?" It's logical, not just word play: Tongue comes from the same part of the animal, and the flavors are right. This wasn't on the first menu, but it quickly became one of our signature dishes.

Both the tongues and the cheeks can be made several days in advance if stored properly: refrigerated, with the tongue submerged in its cooking liquid and the cheeks wrapped tightly in plastic.

FOR THE BEEF CHEEKS: Trim the top flap of meat from the cheeks as well as the silverskin from the bottom (there is no need to trim the piece of silverskin running through the meat). Place the pieces of meat in one layer in a tight-fitting container. Pour the marinade over and around the meat, cover, and refrigerate for at least 8 hours or overnight.

Preheat the oven to 300°F.

Remove the meat from the marinade. Strain the marinade into a pot, reserving the vegetables. Bring the marinade to a boil and skim the impurities that rise to the top. You should have about 1 cup of marinade. Remove from the heat.

Coat the bottom of a large pot with ⅛ inch of oil (use a large pot and ample oil so that the heat doesn't decrease as the meat is added) and heat over high heat. Pat the cheeks dry with paper towels, season on both sides with salt and pepper, and dust with flour, shaking off the excess. Add the meat to the pot, adjusting the heat as necessary so that the oil stays hot but the meat doesn't burn. Brown the cheeks for 2 to 3 minutes on each side, or until well browned and crusty. Remove the meat from the fat and place in a small roasting pan; the pieces should fit snugly in one layer.

Drain the fat from the pot, add the vegetables from the marinade, and sauté them over medium-high heat for 2 to 3 minutes. Place the sautéed vegetables over the meat and add the reserved marinade and the veal stock. Add water as necessary to cover the meat with liquid. Bring the liquid to a simmer on top of the stove.

Cover the meat with a parchment lid (see page 190), transfer to the oven, and cook for 3½ to 4 hours, until the meat is very tender. Let the meat rest in the liquid for 30 minutes, which will allow the meat to reabsorb part of the liquid it released during cooking.

MEANWHILE, FOR THE VEAL TONGUES: Place the tongues in an ovenproof pot and add the vegetables, garlic, thyme, salt, stock, and vinegar. Add a little water if necessary so that they just float. Bring the

liquid to a simmer (the tongues will swell, so add more water if necessary), cover with a parchment lid, and braise the tongues in the oven for about 4 hours, until very tender and the skin peels off easily.

Peel the tongues while still hot. Strain the stock into a container (discarding the solids) and add the peeled tongues. They will keep for several days in the refrigerator or you can freeze them, in the liquid.

TO CONTINUE: Remove the cheeks from the braising liquid. Wrap and refrigerate them for a few hours, until firm, or for up to 2 days. Strain the liquid (discarding the solids) into a tall narrow container (it will be easier to remove the fat that accumulates at the top) and let stand for about 20 minutes. Remove the fat that has risen to the surface and strain the braising liquid several times through a chinois (see page 73), until the chinois remains clean after straining. (Straining the braising liquid before reducing it rather than after will give you a higher yield, as any meat particles left in the liquid would absorb some of the liquid as it reduced.)

There should be about 2 cups of strained braising liquid. Set aside ½ cup to rewarm the meat before serving. Bring the remaining braising liquid to a simmer in a saucepan and reduce to about 1 cup. Add all but ¼ teaspoon of the horseradish and continue to reduce until it has a sauce consistency; there will be about ¾ cup. Strain the sauce and discard the horseradish.

Fold the reserved ¼ teaspoon horseradish into the crème fraîche and refrigerate.

Cut the root ends from the leeks and trim the tops. Tie them into a bundle with string. Cook the leeks in boiling salted water for about 3 minutes, or until they are tender. Remove the bundle to an ice-water bath to cool, and drain them when they are cold.

TO COMPLETE: Trim the edges of the cold cheeks to square them, then cut each one against the grain into 6 slices. Trim the pieces of fat from the cold tongue and cut each one starting at the base, into 4 slices, about ¼ inch thick.

Stack the slices of cheek and tongue in four portions, starting and ending with slices of cheek. Place the stacks in a pot or microwave container with the reserved braising liquid. Cover the pot and reheat over medium heat, or cover with plastic wrap and reheat in the microwave.

Toss the greens with the oil and season to taste with salt and pepper. Rewarm the leeks in the microwave or in a saucepan with a little water. Reheat the sauce.

Place a spoonful of sauce in the middle of each plate and place a portion of tongue and cheek on the sauce. Arrange 2 baby leeks on top of each and top with a piece of tomato confit. Drizzle with a little more sauce. Place a quenelle (see page 274), or small oval scoop, of the horseradish cream over the tomato and finish with the lettuces. Grind black pepper over the dish and sprinkle with dried horseradish.

MAKES **4** SERVINGS

# The Importance of **Staff Meal**

Because the South Florida restaurant business was seasonal, I left the Yacht Club and headed north in the summer to Newport, then Narragansett, Rhode Island, to look for work. My second year there, I met Roland Henin on the beach in Narragansett. He was chef at a place called the Dunes Club, a big hotel; he commanded a kitchen the size of a football field with a crew of forty cooks, and he needed someone to cook staff meal.

Henin was from Lyon, the gastronomic capital of the Western world. He was an old-school French guy, trained in the European apprentice system. There was Zeus, and there was Roland, god of cooking. He knew everything. He taught me how to peel a tomato, how to cook a green vegetable properly, things no one had taken the time to show me before. He taught me how to make stock, how to roast and braise.

The staff meal cook is a low man in the kitchen hierarchy. You cook meals from scraps for people who work in the kitchen. But the Dunes Club was a high-end kitchen and Henin was a classical French chef, so our scraps might be the butt from a tenderloin, and with that I learned how to make boeuf bourguignon. We'd have the legs left over from butchered chickens and with these I learned to make coq au vin. I turned lamb scraps into lamb navarin.

But, even more important, I learned how to make the vegetable side dishes, how to blanch a green bean, how to make a gratin of cauliflower, how not to overcook broccoli. At the yacht club, I was used to adding a chemical oxidant that kept the vegetables bright. I thought that's how everyone did it. Then Henin told me about the proper amount of water, and the proper amount of salt in that water, and how to cook and cool the vegetable. This was extraordinary to me, absolutely unique.

Henin taught me how to make a roux. Very, very, very important. How to make sauces, reduction sauces, and the clarification process that happens during reduction. The real fundamentals of cooking.

Staff meal was first about the fundamentals of cooking and how to work with by-products, using scraps to make something tasty, eye-appealing, and satisfying. But the message underlying that was "Can you be passionate about cooking at this level?" Staff meal. Only the staff sees it. If you can make great food for these people, create that habit, have that drive, that sincerity, and keep that with you and take it to another level in the staff meal, then someday you'll be a great chef. Maybe.

# Eric's Staff Lasagna

SAUCE

½ cup olive oil

1½ cups minced yellow onions

2 tablespoons minced garlic

½ cup tomato paste

8 cups cut-up peeled tomatoes

    (about 12 to 14 medium tomatoes,

    cut into rough 1-inch pieces)

¼ cup chopped oregano or ¼ cup

    plus 2 tablespoons chopped basil

FILLING

1½ pounds whole-milk ricotta

3 large eggs

½ cup chopped parsley

Kosher salt and freshly ground black pepper

1 pound lasagna noodles

½ pound mozzarella, grated

Kosher salt and freshly ground black pepper

FOR THE SAUCE: Heat the oil in a large heavy pot. Add the onions and garlic and cook gently for 4 to 5 minutes, or until translucent. Add the tomato paste and cook, stirring frequently, for 10 minutes (the tomato paste will separate from the oil and the oil will turn a vivid orange). Add the tomatoes and stir to combine.

The sauce can be completed on the stove top or in the oven. The oven method requires less attention but a longer cooking time. For the stove-top, simmer the sauce gently for 1½ to 2 hours, stirring and scraping the bottom of the pot every 10 minutes to prevent scorching.

For the oven method, preheat the oven to 325°F. Bring the tomatoes to a simmer on top of the stove, cover the pot with a parchment lid (see page 190), and place the pot in the oven for 3 to 4 hours. (The staff generally prefers the oven method; because of the indirect, even heat, the sauce requires little attention, allowing them to work on other preps for the restaurant.)

When the sauce is done, it should be thick, slightly chunky, and reduced to about 1 quart. Add the oregano and let cool to room temperature (about 1 hour) before assembling the lasagna.

MEANWHILE, FOR THE FILLING: In a large bowl, whisk together the ricotta and eggs until completely blended. Add the parsley and salt and pepper to taste and mix until well combined. Refrigerate until you are ready to assemble the lasagna.

Cook the noodles in a large pot of boiling salted water according to the package directions. Drain the noodles and allow them to cool slightly.

Preheat the oven to 350°F.

TO ASSEMBLE THE LASAGNA: Spread a thin layer (¾ to 1 cup) of sauce over the bottom of a 9- by 13-inch baking pan. Place a layer of noodles (no more than one quarter of them) in the pan, slightly overlapping them. Spread half of the ricotta mixture evenly over the noodles and top with another layer of noodles. Reserve 1 cup of the remaining sauce and spread the rest over the noodles, completely covering them. Arrange another layer of noodles on top and cover with the remaining ricotta mixture. Top with a final layer of noodles and spoon the reserved sauce over them. Toss the grated mozzarella with salt and pepper to taste (to give the cheese more flavor) and sprinkle it over the top.

Bake for 45 minutes to 1 hour, or until the mozzarella is a spotted golden grown and the lasagna is hot throughout.

MAKES ABOUT 9 SERVINGS

## Staff Dressing

1 tablespoon chopped garlic

1½ teaspoons chopped shallots

2 tablespoons plus 1 teaspoon Dijon mustard

¼ cup balsamic vinegar

1 large egg yolk

2 cups canola oil

Kosher salt and freshly ground black pepper

Place the garlic, shallots, mustard, and vinegar in a blender and blend until well combined. Add the egg yolk and blend again. With the machine running, slowly drizzle in the oil until the dressing is thick and emulsified. Season to taste with salt and pepper. You can refrigerate it in a covered container for 1 week.

MAKES ABOUT 2 CUPS

F I S H

# A passion for fish

My favorite food to work with is the most versatile: fish. Fish offers a greater variety of textures and flavors than any other protein. It also has less fat. It's the best "pedestal" for garnishes. It's visually appealing, and it makes a better final impression and impact than meat and poultry. Offal and braised foods are what I like to eat most of all, and I like to cook them too, but fish is almost alive for me when I cook it.

The quality of the fish you buy is probably the most critical factor in how good the finished dish will be. I feel very lucky to have the purveyors I do. The seafood they send me is extraordinary. I get sea bass and halibut and cod so fresh that, at the right angle, you can see a rainbow playing across the flesh. We marvel at it. I get forty black bass that are all the same size, which is critical to the dishes at the French Laundry. The scallops are still twitching, because they were practically just shucked and haven't settled down. For a cook, that's an exciting thing to see.

Unlike meat and poultry, fish is not regulated for quality and it's not inspected, which is why quality ranges are huge. How can you know when fish wasn't handled right? Was it dumped on the boat, is it bruised and beaten up? How was it caught—did it drown in a net, its gills filling with water, its flesh becoming waterlogged? Once caught, was it properly iced?

My fish purveyors are sticklers about how their fish is handled. And the handling only starts on their end. Our fish is packed in ice or seaweed and stored in our walk-in cooler in the same position it swims—not haphazardly, and not on its side. The flesh is too easily damaged. This is what I mean by treating your products with respect.

Most people now know the basics in evaluating whole fish for freshness: The fish should have clear, protuberant eyes and elastic skin and flesh (which should spring back when you touch it, not leave an imprint), and it should smell fresh. To judge a fillet, use the same criteria—color, smell, and touch.

Store whole fish in plenty of ice, making sure that the water can drain off as the ice melts; the chlorine in water can stress the flesh of the fish. Once the fish has been butchered (never more than a day ahead of cooking) or if you've bought steaks or fillets, store the fish on, but not in, ice; the water could seep into the flesh and affect the texture and cooking.

Always keep in mind how delicate fish is. Cradle it like a child.

You hear the name Ingrid a lot in the French Laundry kitchen. Ingrid, the Scallop Lady. Or Thomas will ask one of his brigade, "How are Ingrid's lobsters?" Everyone knows Ingrid, the Maine fishmonger. What they don't know, however, is that she has been a Fulbright scholar for the past three years, spending most of each year in Russia, writing and teaching English at the State University of St. Petersburg. For a brief time, in the 1970s, she was a famous author, having penned the controversial tract on human sexuality called *Combat in the Erogenous Zone*, and a few years later a novel.

"The seafood business keeps me on this earth," she says.

An intense intellectual born to Russian immigrants shortly after World War II, Ingrid moved to Maine in the late 1970s to write, but she published nothing. In the mid-1980s, dirt-poor, she began to forage wild mushrooms with hopes of selling them. She sent off a load of chanterelles to Balducci's in Manhattan.

They called her the next day and asked for twenty more pounds. Ingrid said, "You want twenty pounds, go pick them yourself." They asked, "Can you send us lobster?"

Ingrid said her friends on the island were all fishermen and many caught lobster. Balducci's said, "Good, we'll take a hundred pounds." Ingrid didn't have the cash to pay for that kind of order, so she convinced Balducci's to wire the money the next day, and bought the lobsters from the fishermen with it.

Ingrid was now a purveyor.

Ingrid explains that the waters around the archipelago in Stonington, Maine, where she lives are absolutely clean and packed with nutrients, a perfect environment for fish of all kinds. She sells only the best, and the fishermen she buys from know this and set aside their best for her.

When a trendy Manhattan restaurant recently asked her to fax what she had that week, she refused. "I'm not just selling you seafood," she explained to me. "There is a relationship happening. This isn't about product. There is a little community of souls here. I don't fax that stuff. We talk on the phone. We talk about fish, we talk about what fish is coming in. It can be a wonderful exchange of information."

Ingrid involves her chefs in that "community of souls" in Stonington. Once she sent Thomas the halibut he'd ordered, and also a videotape of the fish being caught, which he played on Rakel's video screen while it was being served.

Ingrid can step out the front door of her hillside home, gaze down at the three hundred boats in the harbor, and say to a visitor, with only slight exaggeration, "You're looking at the American seafood industry." The village itself still seems to exist in the nineteenth century. And because of the extraordinarily clean, nutrient-rich waters, that fish is some of the greatest in the world, and it provides a livelihood for writer Ingrid Bengis, who has raised fishmongering to a level approaching art.

—M.R.

# Cooking Lobster

If you take lobster out of its shell before fully cooking it, you have more control over its taste and texture. Steep the lobster just enough so that it will pull cleanly away from the shell, leaving the interior raw, so you can treat it like raw fish.

At the French Laundry, we butter-poach the lobster (see page 125), which loads the flavor of butter into the meat and cooks it so slowly and gently that the flesh remains exquisitely tender—so tender some people think it's not completely cooked. When you cook lobster violently, the meat seizes up and becomes tough, and you can't get any flavor into it. Gentle heating is the key. Butter-poached lobster is extraordinarily versatile. You can combine it with many different garnishes: beets and leeks, peas and carrots, figs, foie gras.

Sometimes we slow-roast the lobster, a technique that moves it into the realm of meat, so we treat it like a meat. We season it with squab spice, slow-roast it, and serve it with foie gras.

All our lobster dishes begin with the same initial preparation, after which the lobster may be poached in butter, roasted, or chopped for a filling. It's essential to work with the "steeped" lobsters while they are still hot; if they cool, the fat in the meat will congeal and the meat will be difficult to remove from the shell.

---

## PREPARING LOBSTER MEAT

TO STEEP THE LOBSTERS: Place the lobsters in a tight-fitting heat-proof container. Cover with cold water. Drain off the water, measure it, and place it in a large pot. Bring the water to a boil and add ½ cup of white distilled vinegar for every 8 quarts of water. Pour the boiling liquid over lobsters and let them steep for 2 minutes if using 1½-pound lobsters, 3 minutes for 2-pound lobsters. Remove the lobsters from the hot water, but do not discard the water.

One at a time, using a towel or rubber gloves to hold the hot lobster, grasp its tail and twist and pull to detach it. Twist and pull off the claws and return them to the hot water for 5 minutes. Reserve the bodies.

FOR THE TAILS: Hold each tail flat and twist the tail fan to one side; pull off and discard. Use your fingers to gently push the meat through the tail end and pull the meat out through the large opening at the other end. Discard the shell. Lay the tail meat on its back and cut lengthwise in half through the middle. Remove the vein running through the top of the meat. Lay the meat on a paper towel–lined plate or platter, cover with plastic wrap, and refrigerate.

FOR THE CLAWS: After 5 minutes, remove the claws from the hot water. Twist off each knuckle to remove it. Hold the claw in your hand and pull down to loosen the lower pincer. Push it to either side to crack it and pull it straight off. Ideally, the cartilage from inside the claw should be attached to the pincer and the claw meat should remain intact.

Still holding the claw, crack the top of the shell with the heel of a knife, about ¾ inch from the joint where the knuckle was attached. You want to go through the shell but not damage the meat. Wiggle your knife to loosen and crack the shell. If the shell does not pop off, it may be necessary to turn the claw over and repeat the procedure. Shake the claw to remove the meat (if it doesn't fall out, cut off the very tip of the shell and blow through the hole to release the meat).

FOR THE KNUCKLES: Cut off the top joint of each knuckle, the one that was attached to the lobster's body. Use scissors to cut away the shell along the smooth outside edge of the knuckle. Use your fingers to pry open the shell and remove the meat. Add knuckle and claw meat to tail meat.

FOR THE BODIES: Pull back and discard the top shell of each lobster, including the heads and antenna, and discard. Remove the tomalley, roe, lungs, and the sac behind the head. You can reserve the dark green roe for other uses, but discard the light green tomalley, feathery lungs, and sac. You will be left with bodies and legs. Rinse them thoroughly under cold water and use immediately, or freeze them to make lobster stock or consommé.

NOTE: Avoid buying frozen lobsters or bodies; you can't be assured of the quality.

# Butter-Poached Maine Lobster with Leeks, Pommes Maxim, and a Red Beet Essence

**POMMES MAXIM**

1 large (about 12 ounces) Yukon Gold potato

½ cup Clarified Butter (recipe follows)

Kosher salt

**RED BEET ESSENCE**

1 pound red beets, peeled, or 1 cup beet juice
  (from a health food store)

3 tablespoons Beurre Monté (page 135)

½ teaspoon red wine vinegar

Few drops of lemon juice

**LOBSTERS**

Three 1½- to 2-pound lobsters, "steeped"
  and meat removed (see page 124);
  reserve knuckle meat for another use

1½ cups Beurre Monté (page 135)

**LEEKS**

1½ cups thinly sliced leek rounds
  (white and pale green parts only), washed,
  blanched until tender (see Big-Pot Blanching,
  page 58), chilled in ice water, and drained

2 tablespoons tomato diamonds (see page 203)

2 teaspoons chopped chives

1 tablespoon Brunoise (page 155)

¼ cup plus 1 tablespoon Beurre Monté (page 135)

Kosher salt and freshly ground white pepper

I've been serving lobster with beets and leeks for more than a decade, and the combination has gone through many evolutions. In New York, I served it with potatoes and a fine julienne of crispy beets. In L.A., I did the Jackson Pollock thing, with splatters of reduced beet juice and a tower of mashed potatoes. In its current form—lobster with leeks, a thin sheet of pommes Maxim, which originated at Maxim's in Paris, and a red beet essence—I think I've found the perfect interpretation.

FOR THE POMMES MAXIM: Preheat the oven to 300°F. Peel the potato and slice it into paper-thin rounds on a mandoline. Toss the rounds with the clarified butter; they should be well coated. Arrange them on a Silpat-lined baking sheet (see Sources, page 315), overlapping the slices by half to form a solid sheet of potatoes, or lay them in overlapping circles in a large heavy ovenproof skillet. Sprinkle lightly with salt.

Bake the potatoes for 45 to 50 minutes, or until they are crisp and golden brown. They may not hold together completely. These can be made several hours ahead and left at room temperature.

FOR THE RED BEET ESSENCE: If using fresh beets, juice the beets (you should have a generous cup). Reduce the beet juice slowly in a small saucepan to 2 to 3 tablespoons of glaze.

TO COMPLETE: Preheat the oven to 300°F.

For the lobsters, bring the lobster pieces to room temperature. Place them in one layer in a large saucepan and add the beurre monté. They should be almost covered. Place the pan over low heat and slowly poach the lobster in the butter for 5 to 6 minutes, just to heat through.

Meanwhile, for the leeks, warm the leek rounds in a saucepan. Add the tomato diamonds, chives, brunoise, and beurre monté. Season with salt and white pepper to taste and keep warm.

Reheat the pommes Maxim in the oven for 2 to 3 minutes.

Bring the beet glaze to a simmer and whisk in the beurre monté, red wine vinegar, and lemon juice.

Place a small spoonful of the beet essence on each plate. Top with a generous tablespoon of the leek mixture, a lobster tail, and a claw. Break off a piece of the pommes Maxim and place it on top of the lobster.

PICTURED ON PAGE 130                    MAKES 6 SERVINGS

## CLARIFIED BUTTER

1 pound unsalted butter

Some foods—eggs, scallops, potatoes—cook particularly well in butter. But butter contains milk solids that separate from the butterfat and burn. Removing these solids—that is, clarifying the butter—allows you to cook with it at higher temperatures. Clarified butter can be refrigerated for several weeks or frozen almost indefinitely as long as it's in an airtight container to prevent it from absorbing freezer odors.

Place the butter in a 1-quart saucepan and melt it over low heat, without stirring. Once the butter has melted, it will have separated into three layers. Skim off and discard the foamy layer of milk solids floating on top. The clear yellow butter beneath it is the clarified butter. Carefully pour it off into a container, leaving the milky liquid behind. Keep covered and refrigerated, or frozen.

PICTURED ON PAGE 129                    MAKES ABOUT 1½ CUPS

## Maine Lobster Pancakes with Pea Shoot Salad and Ginger-Carrot Emulsion

**LOBSTER GLACE**

2 tablespoons canola oil

3 lobster bodies (reserved from lobsters),
    cut into 2-inch pieces

1 tomato, quartered

1 small carrot, cut into 1-inch pieces

2 sprigs thyme

3 to 4 cups water

**LOBSTER FILLING**

Three 1¼-pound lobsters, "steeped"
    and meat removed (about 2 cups
    [¾ pound] meat) (see page 124)

¼ cup chopped chives

1 tablespoon finely minced shallots

½ cup mascarpone

Kosher salt and freshly ground black pepper

3 to 4 tablespoons (2 ounces)
    unsalted butter, melted

8 crêpes (page 127)

**GINGER-CARROT EMULSION**

3 pounds carrots, trimmed

One 1-inch (1-ounce) slice ginger

2 tablespoons heavy cream

12 tablespoons (6 ounces) cold unsalted butter,
    cut into pieces

**PEA SHOOT SALAD**

½ cup pea shoot leaves, in ice water

Few drops of lemon oil

Pinch of minced shallots

Kosher salt and freshly ground black pepper

Carrot Powder (page 232)

---

When I hear "peas and carrots," my mind goes directly to the frozen food section of the grocery store, with its boxes of Jolly Green Giant peas and carrots. I'm not sure why anyone put the two vegetables together, but I think in most Americans' minds, it's a common pairing. So when J.B., one of my early poissonniers, and I were thinking of things to do with lobster, which we were serving with a carrot-emulsion sauce, we thought "Why not serve it with peas?" I use pea shoots to make the peas-and-carrots connection, dressed lightly with a little lemon-infused oil.

FOR THE LOBSTER GLACE: Heat the canola oil over medium-high heat in a sauté pan that will hold the shells in one layer. Add the lobster bodies and sauté for about 4 minutes, turning the shells occasionally, until the shells have turned red (be careful not to burn them). Add the tomato, carrot, thyme, and water just to cover. Simmer gently for 1¼ hours.

Strain the stock through a large strainer or China cap (see page 73), pressing firmly on the solids to extract as much liquid as possible.

Discard the bodies and strain the liquid through a chinois (see page 73). There will be 1½ to 2 cups of stock. Place the stock in a saucepan and reduce over medium heat until it has thickened to a glaze (1 to 2 tablespoons). The glaze can be refrigerated in a covered container for several days or frozen. Bring to room temperature before using for the filling.

FOR THE LOBSTER FILLING: Cut the lobster meat into small dice (do not use the claw tips, as they will detract from the texture of the filling). Mix the lobster meat with the chives, shallots, 1 tablespoon of the lobster glace, and the mascarpone. Season to taste with salt and pepper. The filling can be covered and refrigerated until you are ready to fill the crêpes.

TO FILL THE CRÊPES: Brush a baking sheet with some of the melted butter. Place the crêpes (nicest side down) on a work surface. Scoop about ¼ cup of the filling into the center of each crêpe. (A 2-ounce ice-cream scoop works well for this, but be careful not to rip the pancakes with the scoop.) One by one, fold one edge of each crêpe over the filling and then, working clockwise, continue folding the crêpe over the filling, pleating it as you go to form a round packet. Place the packets seam side down on the buttered pan. Lightly brush the tops with more butter. The filled crêpes can be refrigerated for several hours.

FOR THE GINGER-CARROT EMULSION: Run the carrots and ginger through a juicer (you can save the carrot pulp to make carrot powder). You should have 2 to 2¼ cups of juice. Place the juice in a saucepan, bring to a simmer, and remove the first layer of foam that rises to the top. Simmer for 12 to 15 minutes, or until the juice is reduced to ½ to ¾ cup and is the consistency of baby food. Do not skim again; the body is needed to yield a purée rather than a sauce. Remove from the heat and set aside. The purée can be made up to a day ahead and stored in the refrigerator.

TO COMPLETE: Preheat the oven to 350°F.

Heat the carrot purée in a saucepan. Whisk in the cream and reduce slightly, to regain the consistency it had before the cream was added. With the purée at a gentle simmer, whisk in the butter a piece at a time, adding a new piece only when the last piece is almost incorporated. Remove the sauce to a blender and blend until it is emulsified. Keep the sauce in a warm spot, but do not place it over direct heat, or it will break.

Heat the lobster pancakes in the oven for 8 to 10 minutes, or until hot throughout.

MEANWHILE, FOR THE PEA SHOOT SALAD: Drain the pea shoot leaves, then dry in a salad spinner. Toss the leaves in a bowl with the lemon oil, shallots, and salt and pepper to taste.

Place a spoonful of carrot emulsion on each serving plate. Use the back of a spoon to spread the sauce into a circle that will extend slightly beyond the edges of the pancake. Center the pancakes on the sauce and garnish the tops with the pea shoot salad. Dust each plate with a little carrot powder.

PICTURED ON PAGE 129               MAKES 8 SERVINGS

## CRÊPES

| | |
|---|---|
| Scant 1 cup (4 ounces) | 1¼ cups milk |
| all-purpose flour | 4 tablespoons (2 ounces) |
| Pinch of kosher salt | unsalted butter, melted |
| 3 large eggs, lightly beaten | 1 tablespoon minced chives |

You can make crêpes savory or sweet, depending on the dish you're serving.

Place the flour and salt in a bowl and create a well in the center of the flour. Whisk the eggs and milk together and pour into the well. Whisk the flour and egg mixture together, then whisk in the butter. Strain the batter through a fine-mesh strainer and stir in the chives.

Heat an 8½-inch nonstick crêpe pan over medium heat until hot. Spray with a non-stick spray, then use a 1-ounce ladle to pour the batter into the center of the skillet (or add 2 tablespoons of batter to the skillet). Rotate the skillet in a circular motion to cover the bottom of the pan evenly with the batter (if you hear it sizzle in the pan, your heat is too high). Cook for 30 to 45 seconds to set the batter. Then use a small narrow spatula to gently flip the crêpe. Cook for only 10 to 15 seconds more, to set the second side.

Remove the crêpe and place it with the nicer side down on a paper towel. Repeat for the remaining crêpes, spraying the pan as needed, and layering the paper towels and crêpes.

When you are ready to fill the crêpes, just lift up the towels and fill the crêpes—the best side of the crêpes will be on the outside.

MAKES 14 TO 18 CRÊPES

DESSERT CRÊPES: Omit the chives. Add 1 tablespoon of sugar to the dry ingredients. Add 1 teaspoon pure vanilla extract with the eggs.

Above: "Peas and Carrots," page 126

Opposite, left: Butter-Poached Maine Lobster with Pommes Maxim, page 125. Above: Five-Spiced Roasted Maine Lobster, page 133.

# Butter-Poached Maine Lobster with Creamy Lobster Broth and Mascarpone-Enriched Orzo

2 cups Creamy Lobster Broth (page 35)

½ cup orzo (rice-shaped pasta)

2 tablespoons mascarpone

Kosher salt

Three 1½- to 2-pound lobsters, "steeped"
    and meat removed (see page 124;
    reserve knuckle meat for another use)

1½ cups Beurre Monté (page 135)

1 tablespoon minced chives

Coral Oil (page 167), in a squeeze bottle

6 Parmesan Crisps (page 37)

We serve so much lobster at the restaurant that creating new lobster dishes is always an exciting challenge. I used to do an actual gratin with lobster and macaroni, but now I use orzo with mascarpone, the lobster on top, and Parmesan crisps—an echo of the crisp texture of a traditional gratin dish. The coral oil rings the orzo for bright color, and I finish the plate with chopped coral. This is an enormously satisfying dish to eat.

Place the lobster broth in a saucepan and bring it to a simmer. Reduce the broth to a sauce consistency; you should have 1 to 1¼ cups. Set aside in the pan.

Cook the orzo in boiling lightly salted water until just tender. Drain the cooked pasta in a strainer and rinse under cold water. Shake the strainer to remove excess water and add the orzo to the lobster broth.

TO COMPLETE: If the lobster pieces have been refrigerated, bring them to room temperature.

Heat the orzo and lobster broth to a simmer. Add the mascarpone and season with salt to taste. Let simmer for a minute, then remove the pan from the heat and keep warm.

Meanwhile, place the lobster pieces in one layer in a large saucepan. Pour in the beurre monté; the lobster should almost be covered. Heat gently to warm the lobster.

Stir the chives into the orzo. Pipe a 2-inch circle of coral oil in the center of each serving dish. Place about ⅓ cup of orzo in the center of the oil, allowing it to spread the oil out into a larger circle. Arrange a piece of lobster tail and a claw in the center of the orzo and top each serving with a Parmesan crisp.

MAKES 6 SERVINGS

# Five-Spiced Roasted Maine Lobster with Port-Poached Figs
## and Sautéed Moulard Duck Foie Gras

POACHED FIGS AND SAUCE

9 Black Mission figs

1 cup port wine

3/4 teaspoon ground coffee beans

1 tablespoon plus 1 teaspoon finely chopped
    bittersweet chocolate

1 to 2 tablespoons Beurre Monté (page 135)

2 tablespoons chopped shallots

2 tablespoons chopped chives

1 tablespoon Chicken Stock (page 226)
    or water (optional)

Kosher salt and freshly ground black pepper

LOBSTERS

Three 1 1/2- to 2-pound lobsters, "steeped"
    and meat removed (see page 124;
    reserve knuckle meat for another use)

2 tablespoons Squab Spice (page 233)

Kosher salt

1 cup Beurre Monté (page 135)

Six 3/4-inch-thick slices foie gras
    (about 1/2 ounce each)

Freshly ground black pepper

1 tablespoon chopped chives

Gray salt

During the summer, figs are in abundance, so we created a lobster dish to show them off, treating the shellfish like a meat: seasoning it with squab spice, oven-roasting it with beurre monté, and serving it with foie gras. The most beguiling element of this dish is the sauce. I knew I wanted it to be a purée of figs that had been poached in port, rather than a butter sauce; the figs and port would go well with the foie gras. But I also wanted some other elements that would give the dish some complexity and depth, so I threw in some bitter chocolate and some ground coffee beans. You don't really taste the chocolate and coffee so much as feel their bitter undertone. They counteract the sweetness of the figs, while the fruit gives the sauce its body.

FOR THE POACHED FIGS AND SAUCE: Preheat the oven to 325°F.

Remove the stems from the figs and cut a slit in the top of each fruit. Stand the figs side by side in a small ovenproof saucepan where they fit snugly. Pour in the port; it should cover the bottom two thirds of the figs. Place the pan over medium heat and bring to a boil. Cover with a parchment lid (see page 190) and place in the oven for about 1 1/2 hours, or until the figs are soft and the port is slightly reduced.

Remove the figs from the liquid. There will be 2/3 to 3/4 cup port. Place 3 of the figs in a blender with the ground coffee and chocolate. With the motor running, pour in the warm port. Blend until the mixture

is smooth and then strain it through a chinois (see page 73) into a small saucepan.

TO COMPLETE: Preheat the oven to 300°F.

For the lobsters, bring the lobster pieces to room temperature. Sprinkle the tails and claws with the squab spice and salt. Place the lobster pieces in one layer in a large ovenproof skillet. Coat them with 1/2 cup of the beurre monté, place over medium heat, and heat gently for about 2 minutes. When the beurre monté begins to simmer, place the pan in the oven for 5 minutes to finish cooking.

Meanwhile, score one side of the slices of foie gras in a crosshatch pattern about 1/16 inch deep. Season to taste with salt and pepper. Heat a skillet over high heat and sauté the foie gras, scored side down, for about 15 seconds. Turn the pieces over and continue to cook for an additional 15 seconds. Remove from the heat.

Rewarm the fig sauce and add the 1 to 2 tablespoons beurre monté, shallots, and chives. If the sauce is too thick, it can be thinned with a tablespoon of chicken stock or water. Season to taste with salt and pepper.

Spoon the fig sauce into the center of the plates. Flatten the remaining figs and center one in each pool of sauce. Top each fig with a lobster tail, then a claw, a spoonful of beurre monté, and, finally, a slice of sautéed foie gras. Sprinkle the foie gras with the chives and gray salt.

PICTURED ON PAGE 131                    MAKES 6 SERVINGS

# Beurre Monté: the Workhorse Sauce

At the French Laundry, we use an awful lot of butter without actually serving a lot of butter, because of our reliance on the substance called beurre monté. We cook in it, rest meats in it, make sauces with it. It's an extraordinary vehicle for both heat and flavor. Butter in its solid state is an emulsification of butter fat, milk solids, and water. If you melt butter, these three components separate, but beurre monté—a few drops of water and chunks of butter whisked over moderate heat—is a method of melting butter while maintaining the emulsification.

We use beurre monté in many different ways and for different reasons. Poaching lobster in it is one of its primary uses. Its flesh impregnated with the flavor of butter, this lobster reminds me of Maine lobster that you eat with drawn butter, and for me that's what lobster is all about.

Poaching lobster in beurre monté is also an easy way to cook it. Beurre monté stays between 180° and 190°F. in our kitchen (it will break, or separate, if you boil it) and therefore it's always at a perfect poaching temperature. Butter-poached lobster is meltingly tender, moist, and flavorful. And because of the gentle temperature, it's harder to overcook it; once the lobster hits the right point of doneness, it stays there for a while. Butter-poached lobster is easy to do at home: Make your beurre monté, bring it to 160° to 190°F., pop your cleaned room-temperature tails and claws into it, and let them poach for 5 to 6 minutes.

We also use beurre monté to baste meats, and this has several purposes. When we sauté beef or venison or a saddle of lamb, we typically finish cooking it in the oven. But before we do, we drain the fat out of the pan and ladle a little beurre monté over the meat. This helps to keep the meat moist, enhances the flavor, and also improves the cooking, because the even layer of fat—the beurre monté—is a heat conductor. (We always let the pan cool down a little, though; if the pan's too hot, the beurre monté will separate and the solids will burn.)

When the meats are done, they come out of the oven and are submerged in beurre monté—it's the perfect resting medium. It actually lowers the temperature of the meat, reducing what is called carryover cooking, then maintains it at a great serving temperature. But most important, the weight of the fat surrounding the meat keeps the meat juices from leaking out—they stay in the meat. So here, we use beurre monté as environmental control, and it enhances the flavor.

Almost all our canapé sauces are made *à la minute* with beurre monté. The sauce for the blini, for "Oysters and Pearls," for "Bacon and Eggs"—all are simply a spoonful of beurre monté with different flavoring ingredients.

And finally, what we don't use, we simply clarify the next day and then use this clear butter for hollandaise or for sautéing scallops, for cooking soft-shelled crabs, crêpes, potato chips. You can do that too, or simply refrigerate it and use it the same way you'd use whole butter for cooking.

## PREPARING BEURRE MONTÉ

A little bit of water helps the emulsion process: Whether you emulsify 4 tablespoons (2 ounces) or 1 pound of butter, just a tablespoon of water will do. Any amount of beurre monté can be made using the following method. Read the particular recipe through to determine the total amont of beurre monté you will need.

Bring the water to a boil in an appropriate-size saucepan. Reduce the heat to low and begin whisking the chunks of butter into the water, bit by bit, to emulsify. Once you have established the emulsion, you can continue to add pieces of butter until you have the quantity of beurre monté that you need (we make 20 pounds at a time). It is important to keep the level of heat gentle and consistent in order to maintain the emulsification. Make the beurre monté close to the time it will be used and keep it in a warm place. If you have extra beurre monté, it can be refrigerated and then reheated to use as melted butter or clarified.

Though we are enamored of beurre monté and use it all day in our kitchens, when a recipe calls for only a tablespoon or two, you can substitute whole butter.

# Pan-Roasted Maine Jumbo Scallops with Morel Mushrooms and Asparagus Purée

30 medium stalks asparagus

1 to 2 cups Vegetable Stock (page 227),
  Chicken Stock (page 226), or water

24 medium morels (about 8 ounces),
  soaked in several changes of warm water
  until clean and then rinsed

1 tablespoon unsalted butter

3 small sprigs thyme

2 cloves garlic, smashed

1 tablespoon chopped shallot

7 to 8 tablespoons Beurre Monté (page 135)

2 teaspoons minced chives

2 tablespoons Brunoise (page 155)

Kosher salt and freshly ground white pepper

1 to 2 tablespoons tomato diamonds
  (see page 203)

Canola oil

6 jumbo scallops, tough ligaments removed
  (about 2½ ounces each)

This dish uses the classic combination of morels and asparagus. The sauce is simply a purée of asparagus finished with a little beurre monté. Our scallops are briny, which I think is fundamental in a good scallop. Be careful not to overcook them; too much heat will destroy that briny quality and make them stringy.

I cherish our scallop dishes, not only because of the scallops themselves but also because of my relationship with Ingrid Bengis. Her scallops are harvested from November through May off Stonington, Maine, and Ingrid knows which fishermen shuck scallops into saltwater (as opposed to shucking them dry or into fresh water), which keeps their briny quality, and she sends them to us dry-packed (many scallops are packed in a chemical brine that plumps them and makes them too watery).

Trim away the bottom third of each asparagus spear and discard. Cut 1½-inch-long tips from the asparagus spears; reserve the stalks. Blanch the asparagus tips in boiling water (see Big-Pot Blanching, page 58) until just tender and remove to an ice water bath. Blanch the stalks until they are fully cooked and place in a second ice water bath. When the tips and spears are cold, transfer to paper towels to drain.

Purée the stalks in a blender with just enough stock or water (2 to 4 tablespoons) to allow them to turn. Pour the purée onto a tamis (see page 73) set over a bowl and let it sit for 5 to 10 minutes to allow excess liquid to drain. Discard the liquid and scrape the purée through the tamis. You should have about ⅓ cup of purée.

Trim the stems from the morels. Place them in a saucepan, add enough stock or water to cover, and simmer until tender. Drain the mushrooms and cut them into small dice.

TO COMPLETE: Heat the butter in a medium sauté pan. When it is hot, add the morels, thyme sprigs, and garlic. Cook over medium heat for about 2 minutes. Add the shallot to the pan and cook for 1 more minute. Remove the pan from the heat and discard the thyme and garlic. Add 3 to 4 tablespoons beurre monté, the chives, and brunoise. Season with salt and white pepper; keep warm.

Warm the asparagus tips with the tomato diamonds and 2 tablespoons beurre monté in a small pan over low heat. In a separate pan, warm the asparagus purée and whisk in the remaining 2 tablespoons beurre monté. Season both mixtures with salt and white pepper to taste; keep warm.

Heat ⅛ inch of canola oil in a medium skillet over medium-high heat. Pat the scallops dry on paper towels, season with salt, and place them in the pan. Cook the scallops for 1 to 2 minutes one each side, or until well browned.

Place a spoonful of the asparagus purée on each plate. Center a spoonful of the mushroom mixture over the purée and top with a scallop. Stack the asparagus tips and tomatoes over the scallops.

MAKES 6 SERVINGS

# Salmon "Chops" with Celery and Black Truffles

| | | |
|---|---|---|
| 3 medium stalks celery | Freshly ground white pepper | 18 thin slices black truffle, plus 2 tablespoons |
| Kosher salt | 2 teaspoons water | finely julienned (slivered) black truffle |
| Canola oil | 3 tablespoons (1½ ounces) unsalted butter | Six 1½-inch round brioche Croutons (page 238) |
| Six 1½- by 2- by 1-inch-thick pieces salmon | 1½ teaspoons white truffle oil | 6 sprigs chervil |
| fillet, skin on (see On Crisping Skin, page 147) | 3 tablespoons lightly whipped cream | |

The idea of doing a fish chop was inspired by David Burke, the relentlessly creative chef of New York City's Park Avenue Café. He uses swordfish, which is too big for the French Laundry, but there's a section of the salmon fillet near the head that can be cut into two chops. It's anything but practical, since you only get two from each whole salmon. Here, to replace the chop cut, use salmon fillet.

Peel the celery stalks, squaring off the rounded side of the stalks as you peel. Slice the celery lengthwise on a mandoline and cut the slices into fine julienne about 1 inch long.

Blanch the celery in boiling salted water until tender (see Big-Pot Blanching, page 58), drain it in a strainer, and place the strainer in an ice-water bath. When the celery is cold, drain, dry on paper towels, and sprinkle with salt to taste. You should have about ¼ cup of celery.

Heat about ⅛ inch of canola oil in a large skillet. Season the salmon with salt and white pepper. When the oil is hot, add the salmon fillets skin side down and cook for about 1 minute, then turn over and cook for another minute. "Kiss," or briefly cook, the sides of the pieces. Remove the cooked salmon and keep warm.

FOR THE SAUCE: Bring the water to a boil in a small saucepan. Reduce the heat to low and whisk in the butter to emulsify (see Beurre Monté, page 135). After adding the last of the butter, whisk in the white truffle oil. Remove the butter from the heat and vigorously whisk in the heavy cream to create a slight froth. Season with salt.

Spoon about 1 tablespoon of the sauce into the center of each of six bowls. Arrange three small nests of celery, equally spaced, around each pool of the sauce. Top each nest with a slice of truffle. Place a crouton in the center of the sauce and top with a piece of salmon, skin side up. Garnish each fillet with julienned truffle and a sprig of chervil. Sprinkle the dish lightly with salt.

PICTURED ON PAGE 138                              MAKES 6 SERVINGS

Above: Sautéing a Salmon "Chop," page 137. Opposite: Citrus-Marinated Salmon, page 140.

## Citrus-Marinated Salmon with a Confit of Navel Oranges, Beluga Caviar, and Pea Shoot Coulis

1 side salmon (a whole fillet, about 4 pounds),
    skin and pin bones removed

**CITRUS MARINADE**

Finely grated zest of 1 orange (about 2 teaspoons)

Finely grated zest of 1/2 lemon (about 1 teaspoon)

Finely grated zest of 1/2 lime (about 1/2 teaspoon)

Finely grated zest of 1/4 grapefruit (about 2
    teaspoons)

1/3 cup kosher salt

2 tablespoons sugar

1 tablespoon freshly ground white pepper

**ORANGE CONFIT**

4 navel oranges

1/2 cup Simple Syrup (page 271)

1/2 teaspoon white wine vinegar

**PEA SHOOT COULIS**

3 quarts (6 ounces) pea shoots

2 to 3 tablespoons Chicken Stock (page 226)
    (optional)

1 1/2 tablespoons unsalted butter

Kosher salt

Olive oil for poaching

1/3 cup finely minced chives

1 to 2 ounces beluga caviar

Citrus Powder (page 232)

As with the Warm Fruitwood-Smoked Salmon with Potato Gnocchi and Balsamic Glaze (page 91), I work a similar twist on the citrus-marinated salmon, which is cured and flavored with ground citrus zest. We poach the salmon in olive oil very, very gently, at about 110 degrees. Again, what is normally served cold, as gravlax, is served hot and yet it has even more of the qualities you look for in the cold preparation, that melting richness of cold cured salmon. I use navel oranges because they have no seeds, give the highest yield, and have the best shape. If pea shoots are unavailable, you could substitute pea tendrils or watercress, preparing them the same way.

Both of these salmon preparations are unique and embody some of the most exciting elements of cooking for me.

**NOTE:** In order to get the proper thickness needed for this dish, start with a whole fillet, or side of salmon. After trimming, you will have about two pounds of salmon left, which can be used for another dish.

Place the salmon fillet rounded side up on a cutting board. Trim the salmon of its thin fatty belly flap and any other fat, and cut off the last 2 to 3 inches of the tail end (reserve it for another use). Flip the fillet over and trim away and discard any dark flesh. You will see a line running the length of the fish; cut the salmon fillet lengthwise in half down this line. For this recipe, you will use the wider section of the fillet. Trim it into an even rectangular piece approximately 13 inches long and 3 inches wide and weighing about 1 1/4 pounds. (Use the extra salmon for tartare or another dish.)

**FOR THE CITRUS MARINADE:** Combine the marinade ingredients in a bowl, stirring with a fork to break up any clumps.

Cut a piece of aluminum foil slightly longer than the fillet. Sprinkle half of the marinade down the center of the foil and spread it into the shape of the fillet. Place the fillet on it and sprinkle the remaining marinade over the fish. Bring the sides of the foil together over the top of the fish and roll the foil down to form a packet. Turn the ends of the foil under the fish and place the packet on a baking sheet. Place a second baking sheet on the fish and weight it lightly. Marinate the salmon in the refrigerator for 3 hours (or about 1 hour for every ¼ inch of the fish fillet's thickness). Don't forget your fish; if it marinates for too long, it will be oversalted.

MEANWHILE, FOR THE ORANGE CONFIT: Using a sharp knife, slice off the peel, including all the white pith from the oranges. Working over a bowl, slice between the membranes to remove all the orange segments; discard the membranes.

Bring the simple syrup and white wine vinegar to a boil. Pour over the orange segments and let cool to room temperature (this is called a confit because the syrup stabilizes the oranges). This can be refrigerated for 1 to 2 days. You will need 32 orange sections for this; reserve any extras for another use.

FOR THE PEA SHOOT COULIS: Blanch the pea shoots in 2 to 3 batches (see Big-Pot Blanching, page 58) until the stems are completely tender, 6 to 8 minutes. As each batch becomes tender, lift the shoots to a chinois (see page 73) and submerge the chinois in ice water to chill the pea shoots, then drain them.

Place the shoots in a blender with just enough water to allow the blade to turn and blend the mixture. If you need more water, add it by the tablespoon. Scrape the purée through a tamis (see page 73); you should have ½ to ¾ cup. Place the purée in a small saucepan.

Remove the marinated fish from the foil, rinse off the marinade, and dry the fillet thoroughly. Cut the fillet crosswise into 8 pieces approximately 3 inches by 1½ inches wide. If time allows, let the fish stand at room temperature for about 30 minutes to an hour.

To determine how much oil is needed to cook the fish, stand the pieces of fish, on one of their cut sides, in a pan that will hold them in one layer and cover them with olive oil. Remove the pieces of fish and heat the oil to 110°F. Return the salmon pieces to the oil, on their sides, and heat them for about 10 minutes (it will take closer to 13 minutes if the fillets were cold). To test the cooked salmon, remove a piece and bend it slightly. It should begin to flake, but the color should still be almost the color of raw salmon. The fish can remain in the oil slightly longer without overcooking, providing the temperature does not exceed 110°F.; maintain the temperature by placing the pan on a heat diffuser or by moving the pan on and off the heat as necessary. If the temperature of the oil starts to rise, adding a little more oil to the pan will help to lower the heat quickly. When the salmon is cooked, remove the fillets from the pan and drain briefly on paper towels.

TO COMPLETE: Warm the orange sections in the syrup. Bring the pea shoot coulis to a simmer, adding a little chicken stock or water if the sauce is too thick. Once it's at a simmer, whisk in the butter and salt to taste. Pour the coulis into a sauceboat.

Place 4 warm orange sections side by side to form a rectangle in the center of each serving plate. Spread the chives on a dish and press the tops (cut side) of the salmon pieces in the chives to coat them. Set the fish chive side up over the oranges and garnish the top of each fillet with a small quenelle (see page 274), or oval scoop, of caviar. Dust each plate with a pinch of citrus powder. At the table, pour about 1 tablespoon of the coulis around each fillet.

PICTURED ON PAGE 139                    MAKES 8 SERVINGS

## Sautéed Cod with Cod Cakes and Parsley Oil

1 side cod (a whole fillet, about 2½ pounds),
    skin and any bones removed

**COD CAKES**

12 ounces Yukon Gold potatoes, peeled

1 cup crisp, dry white wine, such as
    Sauvignon Blanc

2 medium shallots, sliced

5 cloves garlic, crushed

6 sprigs thyme

12 black peppercorns

14 ounces reserved cod trimmings (from above)

1 tablespoon kosher salt

5 tablespoons (2½ ounces) unsalted butter

3 tablespoons olive oil

1 teaspoon very finely minced garlic

2 tablespoons Brunoise (page 155)

2 teaspoons finely chopped Italian parsley

**CLAMS**

6 littleneck clams, soaked in a few changes
    of cold water for several hours, drained,
    and scrubbed with a brush

1 small clove garlic, peeled

½ small shallot, peeled

1 sprig thyme

1 small bay leaf

¼ cup crisp, dry white wine, such as
    Sauvignon Blanc

1 cup heavy cream

Canola oil

Flour for dusting

Kosher salt and freshly ground white pepper

**"CHOWDER"**

¼ cup sliced celery (peeled and cut on a
    diagonal into 1/16-inch slices), blanched
    until tender (see Big-Pot Blanching,
    page 58), chilled in ice water, and drained

⅓ cup diced peeled Yukon Gold potato
    (¼-inch dice), boiled untill tender and
    drained

2 to 3 tablespoons Beurre Monté (page 135)

½ teaspoon finely minced Italian parsley

1 tablespoon Brunoise (page 155)

Parsley Oil (page 166), in a squeeze bottle

---

I love cod, because you can do so much with it. I wanted a garnish for a cod fillet that was indigenous to where that cod was from. Thus the New England chowder, and also the cod cakes, which are wonderful all by themselves—I used to serve them as a canapé. They're based on brandade, which is a traditional French dish of puréed salt cod and potatoes. These cakes are sautéed to develop a perfect crust on the outside and creaminess on the inside. I use them as the pedestal for the fillet, which is sauced with a very elegant "chowder" of celery, potatoes, and clams, and finish the dish with vivid parsley oil.

This recipe will make more cod cakes than you need, but you can store them in the freezer, ready to be used as appetizers or a first course on their own. (If you do not have 14 ounces of trimmings, just reduce the other quantities accordingly.)

FOR THE COD: Trim any darkened areas from the fillet. Cut 6 portions about 2 inches by 3 inches by 1 inch thick (2½ to 3 ounces each) from the fillet. Cut the trimmings into chunks (about 14 ounces total).

FOR THE COD CAKES: Place the potatoes in a saucepan with water to cover by at least 2 inches. Bring to a boil over high heat, reduce the heat, and simmer until tender; drain.

Meanwhile, bring the wine, shallots, garlic, thyme, and peppercorns to a boil in a large saucepan. Add the cod trimmings, cover, and steam the fish for 5 minutes, or until thoroughly cooked. Remove the pieces of fish and drain them on paper towels. Discard the cooking liquid.

Place the hot potatoes and hot fish in a bowl and break them up with a fork until evenly mixed. Add the remaining ingredients one at a time, mixing after each addition. Cover and refrigerate for about 1 hour.

Put a 14-inch piece of plastic wrap on a wet counter (this will make rolling the logs easier), place half of the cod mixture on the plastic, and form it into a 2-inch-wide log that is 7 to 8 inches long. Roll the log in the plastic and twist the ends. Tie one end and twist the other tightly to compress the mixture. Repeat to form the second log. Place in the freezer for at least several hours, or up to 2 weeks.

FOR THE CLAMS: Place the clams in a small pot with the garlic, shallot, thyme, bay leaf, and wine. Cover and bring to a boil; remove each clam as soon as it opens. Remove the clams from the shells and reserve. Strain the cooking liquid into a small saucepan and reduce to a glaze (2 to 3 tablespoons). Add the heavy cream and reduce the sauce slowly to about ⅓ to ½ cup.

TO COMPLETE: Preheat the oven to 250°F.

Cut six ¾-inch slices from one cod cake log remove the plastic wrap, and thaw them for about 15 minutes. (Keep the remaining mixture frozen for another time.) Heat ¼ inch of oil in a skillet over medium heat. Dip the cod cakes in flour, pat off any excess, and sauté for about 1½ minutes on each side, or until they are browned and hot throughout. Keep them warm on a baking sheet in the oven.

In a large skillet, heat ¼ inch of oil until hot. Season the cod with salt and white pepper and sauté until golden brown, about 3 minutes per side. Drain briefly on paper towels. Meanwhile, for the "chowder," in a saucepan, warm the celery and potato cubes with the buerre monté, parsley, brunoise, and reserved clams. Rewarm the sauce over low heat.

Pipe a ring of parsley oil in each serving dish. Fill each ring with about 1 tablespoon of the sauce, top with a cod cake, the sautéed cod, and the "chowder."

MAKES 6 SERVINGS

# Sautéed Atlantic Halibut with Summer Succotash and Rue-Scented Onion Glaze

**CIPOLLINI ONIONS AND SAUCE**

6 medium or 12 small cipollini onions
      (about 6 ounces total)

Canola oil

About 2½ cups Chicken Stock (page 226)

½ cup Veal Stock (page 222)

5 sprigs thyme

A ½-inch sprig rue

1 tablespoon honey

Pinch of kosher salt

1 tablespoon Beurre Monté (page 135)

6 tablespoons (3 ounces) unsalted butter,
      cut into 6 pieces

Freshly ground black pepper

**SUCCOTASH**

4 ears baby corn

1½ teaspoons sugar

1 cup milk

Kosher salt

18 fava beans, peeled, germ removed
      (see page 80), blanched until tender
      (see Big-Pot Blanching, page 58),
      chilled in ice water, and drained

1 teaspoon diced red bell pepper
      (peeled and cut into ¹/₁₆-inch dice),
      quickly blanched and drained

1 teaspoon diced yellow bell pepper
      (peeled and cut into ¹/₁₆-inch dice),
      quickly blanched and drained

½ teaspoon finely minced chives

1 teaspoon Brunoise (page 155)

2 to 3 tablespoons Beurre Monté (page 135)

Freshly ground black pepper to taste

**HALIBUT**

Flour for dusting

6 pieces halibut fillet, 2 inches by 2 inches
      by ¾ inches (about 3 ounces each)

Kosher salt and freshly ground white pepper

Canola oil

½ to ¾ cup Beurre Monté (page 135)

6 chive tips (about 1 inch long)

6 small sprigs chervil

One of the reasons I find fish exciting to cook is that it carries garnishes so well. Halibut is a great example. I often serve it with four different preparations of onions, sometimes even with a dusting of onion powder. I use Atlantic halibut because it has a higher fat content and a moister flesh than the Pacific. Here the garnish is succotash with an unusual glaze that originated with my favorite way to cook onions, braising them with the herb rue. Rue is a beautiful gray-green plant that isn't used often in the kitchen, but it gives a flavor to onions that's unique—kind of floral with a nutty undertone. Nothing can substitute for its flavor, but in its absence you could use thyme, rosemary, or basil.

FOR THE CIPOLLINI ONIONS: Preheat the oven to 325°F.

Trim the root ends of the onions, leaving the skin on and enough root intact to hold them together. Coat the bottom of a pan wide enough to hold the onions in one layer with ¹/₁₆ inch of canola oil. Heat the oil over medium-high heat and when it is hot, add the onions root side down. Sear the onions on the root end only until they are a dark golden brown, 3 to 4 minutes. (This initial searing will add flavor depth and character to the sauce.) Once the root ends are brown, transfer the onions to a fine strainer to drain any excess oil.

Return the onions, and any brown bits in the strainer, to the pan and add 2 cups of the chicken stock, the veal stock, thyme, rue, honey, and salt. Bring the liquid to a simmer. Cover with a parchment lid (see page 190) and braise in the oven for 45 minutes, or until the onions are meltingly tender. They should still hold their shape, but there should be no resistance when tested with a paring knife.

When the onions are tender, remove them from the pan. Peel away the skin and any tough outer layers and place the onions in a container. Strain the braising liquid through a fine strainer into a small saucepan. Reduce the liquid slowly for about 15 minutes, until about 6 tablespoons of glaze remain. The liquid should be dark and thick, but if it is too sticky (like syrup or honey), add chicken stock, a tablespoon at a time, to thin it out. Set the sauce aside in the pan.

MEANWHILE, FOR THE SUCCOTASH: Place the baby corn in a small saucepan with the sugar, milk, and a pinch of salt. Bring to a simmer and poach the corn for 10 to 12 minutes, until tender. There should be very little resistance when the corn is tested with a paring knife, but it must be able to hold its shape without falling apart when cut. Rinse the corn and cut each cob into *rondelles*, thin rounds of about 1/16 inch.

Combine the baby corn with the fava beans, red and yellow peppers, chives, and brunoise in a saucepan. Add the beurre monté and about 1 teaspoon water to moisten the vegetables and set aside.

TO COMPLETE: For the halibut, place some flour in a dish. Season both sides of the halibut with salt and pepper and lightly coat the skin side with flour, patting off any excess. Heat 1/8 inch of canola oil in a large skillet; the pan should be big enough to hold all six pieces of fish comfortably without overcrowding them. If the fillets touch each other, they will steam rather than sauté, so if your pan is not big enough, use two pans.

Place the fish skin side down in the hot oil and cook for 2 minutes, or until a crisp golden-brown crust forms. Turn the fish and cook for another minute. Halibut should be cooked only to medium, as it has a tendency to dry out. When the fish is done, turn off the heat and coat the pieces on both sides with the beurre monté. Let the fish rest for a couple of minutes, then drain the fillets on a paper towel to absorb excess butter.

Meanwhile, place the onions in a saucepan with the 1 tablespoon beurre monté and just enough chicken stock to come 1/8 inch up the sides of the pan. Heat gently to warm. Reheat the succotash over low heat and season with salt and pepper.

Set the sauce over medium heat. Whisking continuously, add the butter, a tablespoon at a time. Do not let the sauce come to a boil, or the butter will separate and become oily. The sauce is ready when it coats the back of a spoon. Adjust the seasoning with salt and pepper to taste.

Place a spoonful of sauce on each plate. Place 1 medium cipollini onion or 2 small ones on each pool of sauce and place a piece of halibut on top. Spoon the succotash over the fish. Garnish the top of each serving with a chive tip and a sprig of chervil.

MAKES 6 SERVINGS

# Black Sea Bass with Sweet Parsnips, Arrowleaf Spinach, and Saffron-Vanilla Sauce

**MUSSEL STOCK**

18 mussels, scrubbed and debearded

2 large cloves garlic, peeled

1 large shallot, peeled

4 sprigs thyme

2 bay leaves

1 cup crisp, dry white wine, preferably
   Sauvignon Blanc

**SPINACH**

Three 2-inch strips orange zest (removed with
   a vegetable peeler)

3/4 teaspoon olive oil

6 ounces spinach, washed and tough
   stems removed

Kosher salt

2 teaspoons unsalted butter

**PARSNIP PURÉE**

2 parsnips (about 5 ounces), peeled

1 cup plus 1 tablespoon heavy cream

1/2 cup water

Pinch of kosher salt

1 teaspoon unsalted butter

**SAFFRON-VANILLA SAUCE**

1/2 vanilla bean, split

Reserved 1 cup mussel stock (from above)

1/4 teaspoon saffron threads

1 1/2 teaspoons heavy cream

10 tablespoons (5 ounces) unsalted butter,
   cut into 8 pieces

**BASS**

Canola oil

Six 2- by 3-inch pieces black sea bass fillet (about
   6 ounces each), skin on (see On Crisping
   Skin, page 147)

Kosher salt and freshly ground white pepper

---

Black sea bass is an extremely versatile fish because of its neutral flavor and sturdy texture; it allows you to use your imagination in both cooking method and in the combinations of flavors you want. It's a good fish to cook with the skin on, both for the dramatic visual appeal and for the flavor. This dish is a contrast in textures: the crisp skin on the moist flesh of the fish, and the toasty exterior of the spinach balls surrounding their soft interior. The sauce uses a mussel stock, but not the cooked mussels; the mussels would be delicious served cold with Sauce Gribiche (page 214).

FOR THE MUSSEL STOCK: Place the mussels in a pot with the garlic, shallot, thyme, bay leaves, and wine. Cover the pot and bring to a boil; remove each mussel as soon as it opens. Reserve the mussels for another use. Strain the mussel stock through a chinois (see page 73).

FOR THE SPINACH: Place the strips of orange zest in a large skillet with the olive oil. Heat the oil until it is hot and the zest begins to ripple from the heat. Add the spinach and sprinkle with salt (seasoning the spinach before it wilts ensures even seasoning. Cook the spinach until it wilts, then continue to cook for another 2 to 3 minutes to evaporate the moisture. Remove the spinach from the pan and separate it into 6 parts. Take each pile of spinach, place it in a clean tea towel, and twist the towel around the spinach to squeeze out any remaining liquid and form a compact ball. Remove from the towel. Refrigerate the spinach balls until ready to complete the dish.

FOR THE PARSNIP PURÉE: Slice the parsnips lengthwise in half. Beginning at the narrow end, cut 1/2-inch pieces. When the parsnip half widens, about one third of the way up, split it lengthwise again and continue to cut. (You want to keep the pieces about the same size.)

Place the cut parsnips in a saucepan with 1 cup of the heavy cream, the water, and salt. Bring to a boil, lower the heat, and simmer gently for 25 to 30 minutes, or until the parsnips are completely soft. Strain the parsnips, reserving the cream, and scrape the parsnips through a tamis (see page 73) with a plastic scraper. Put the purée in a bowl and stir in enough of the strained cream to give them the texture of mashed potatoes. Transfer to a small saucepan and keep in a warm place.

Preheat the oven to 350°F.

FOR THE SAFFRON-VANILLA SAUCE: Scrape the seeds from the vanilla bean into a small saucepan and add the vanilla pod, mussel stock, and saffron threads. Bring the stock to a simmer, then simmer until reduced to a glaze (1 to 1½ tablespoons). Add the cream and simmer for a few more seconds. Over medium heat, whisk in the butter bit by bit (as you would for beurre monté). It is critical to maintain the sauce at the correct temperature, as it can break if it becomes too hot or cold. Strain the sauce and mix for several seconds with an immersion blender to emulsify (if you don't have an immersion blender, you can use a regular one, but rinse out the blender container with hot water before adding the sauce, so it stays warm). Keep the sauce in a warm place.

TO COMPLETE: Melt the 2 teaspoons butter in a small ovenproof skillet and roll the spinach balls around in it. Place the skillet in the oven to warm while you cook the fish.

Heat ⅛ inch of oil in a large skillet over medium-high heat. Season the fish with salt and white pepper. When the oil is hot, add the fish fillets, skin side down. Press a lid or another pan down on the fish to flatten the fillets and keep the skin in direct contact with the skillet. Cook this way for a minute, or until the fish is "set." Remove the lid and continue to cook for another 2 to 3 minutes, or until the fillets are almost cooked. Turn the fillets and "kiss" (briefly cook) the flesh side of the fish. Remove the fillets from the pan.

While the fish cooks, reheat the parsnips over low heat and stir in remaining 1 tablespoon cream and the butter.

Place a pool of sauce on each serving plate. Spoon some parsnip purée into the center of the sauce and top the purée with a spinach ball. Set the fish fillets, skin side up, on the spinach and serve.

PICTURED ON PAGE 148                    MAKES 6 SERVINGS

## ON CRISPING SKIN

I love the texture and flavor of perfectly crisped fish skin, and there's a key step in preparation that ensures proper crisping: getting as much moisture out of the skin before cooking as possible. Skin will not crisp, obviously, if there's water in it. Skin that is too moist will take a long time to crisp, and you will overcook your fish.

The way we prepare the fish is to take the blade of a knife and drag it over the skin, pressing down gently but firmly to force the water to the surface, then pulling the knife back over the skin to squeegee off the water. Repeat this pressing and scraping until you've gotten as much water out of the fish skin as possible. This will allow you to achieve crisp fish skin without overcooking the flesh.

Above: Black Sea Bass with Sweet Parsnips, Arrowleaf Spinach, and Saffron-Vanilla Sauce, page 146

Opposite and above: Pan-Roasted Striped Bass with Artichoke Ravioli, page 152

# Pan-Roasted Striped Bass with Artichoke Ravioli and Barigoule Vinaigrette

**ARTICHOKE RAVIOLI**

1 recipe Artichokes Barigoule (page 63)

1/4 teaspoon kosher salt

Pinch of freshly ground black pepper, or to taste

2 teaspoons olive oil

2 sheets Pasta Dough for ravioli (page 78)

1 large egg yolk, beaten for egg wash

Cornmeal for dusting ravioli

**VEGETABLE GARNISH**

36 carrot batons (sweet bunch carrots,
    cut 1 inch by 1/4 inch by 1/4 inch)

12 white pearl onions, peeled and trimmed
    of their root ends

12 red pearl onions, peeled and trimmed
    of their root ends

1 teaspoon sugar

2 teaspoons unsalted butter

1 teaspoon red wine vinegar

3 tablespoons tomato diamonds (see page 203)

1 tablespoon chopped Italian parsley

1/4 cup Beurre Monté (page 135)

Kosher salt and freshly ground white pepper

**BARIGOULE VINAIGRETTE**

Reserved braising liquid from Artichokes
    Barigoule (above), strained

1/2 cup chopped shallots

1/3 cup chopped garlic

3 cups dry white wine

1/2 teaspoon sherry vinegar

1/4 cup plus 1 tablespoon extra virgin olive oil

Kosher salt and freshly ground black pepper

**BASS**

Canola oil

6 thick square pieces striped bass fillet
    (about 3 ounces each), skin on
    (see On Crisping Skin, page 147)

Kosher salt and freshly ground white pepper

2 to 3 tablespoons unsalted butter

Basil Oil (page 166), in a squeeze bottle

6 sprigs chervil

There's nothing quite like the meaty quality of striped bass. You can crisp the skin well without overcooking the flesh. The vinaigrette for this dish is made from a reduction of the Artichokes Barigoule liquid, so it's intense and brilliantly flavored.

FOR THE ARTICHOKE RAVIOLI: Cut 18 slices about 1 inch long from 2 of the artichoke hearts and set aside for the garnish.

Chop enough of the remaining artichoke hearts to make a generous 3/4 cup. Mix together with the salt, pepper, and olive oil. Strain all the barigoule braising liquid and reserve.

Place a sheet of pasta dough on a lightly floured surface. Brush the surface of the dough with egg wash. Mark 12 circles in the dough with the dull side of a 2-inch round cutter, leaving at least 1/2 inch between them. Center 1 tablespoon of the artichoke filling in a mound on each circle. Line up one end of the second sheet of dough along one end of the dough and carefully drape the pasta sheet over the filling, pressing down between the mounds of artichoke. Run your fingers around each mound of filling to press out any air bubbles. Using the very tip of a paring knife, gently poke a hole in each ravioli toward the bottom of the filling (this will help any steam that builds up during cooking escape). Using a 2 1/4-inch fluted round cutter, cut out the 12 ravioli. You will need 6 ravioli for this dish; the rest can be frozen for future use.

Line a baking sheet with parchment paper, lightly dust it with cornmeal, and place the ravioli on it. If they are to be used within a few hours, cover lightly and refrigerate. For longer storage, they can be frozen on the baking sheet, then removed and stored in plastic bags; cook them while still frozen.

FOR THE VEGETABLE GARNISH: Place the carrot batons in a small saucepan, add lightly salted cold water to cover, and bring to a boil. Cook the carrots for about 3 minutes, or until they are tender; drain in a strainer and chill in an ice-water bath. Drain again, dry the carrots on paper towels, and set aside.

Place the white and red pearl onions in two separate small saucepans with water to cover by $\frac{1}{2}$ inch. Add $\frac{1}{2}$ teaspoon of the sugar and 1 teaspoon of the butter to each pan. Bring to a boil, turn down the heat, and cook for 12 to 14 minutes, until the liquid has evaporated and the onions are glazed. Be careful not to scorch the onions as the liquid reduces. At the end of cooking, add the red wine vinegar to the red pearl onions to help maintain their color. Set aside.

FOR THE BARIGOULE VINAIGRETTE: Skim any fat from the top of the strained braising liquid; you should have about 4 cups of liquid. Place the shallots, garlic, and white wine in a medium saucepan. Bring to a boil and reduce the liquid for about 15 minutes, or until the pan is almost dry. Add the barigoule liquid and cook for about 30 minutes, or until the liquid has reduced to about 1 cup.

Strain the liquid into a small saucepan and discard the shallots and garlic. Continue to reduce the liquid until it is reduced and syrupy (about $\frac{1}{3}$ cup). Strain the reduction into a blender and add the vinegar. Turn the motor on and slowly drizzle in the olive oil. Season to taste; the vinaigrette should have a nice tart flavor. Set the vinaigrette aside in a warm spot for a few hours. Any extra vinaigrette can be refrigerated and used in salads.

TO COMPLETE: For the bass, heat about $\frac{1}{8}$ inch of oil in a large skillet over medium-high heat. Season the skin side of the fish with salt and sprinkle the other side with salt and white pepper. Place the fish skin side down in the hot oil, turn down the heat to medium and cook for 2 to 3 minutes, pressing down on the pieces with a spatula to crisp the skin, until the fish is almost cooked. Turn the fish over and cook on the second side for a minute to finish the cooking. "Kiss," or cook very briefly, the sides of the fish in the hot oil just to set. Lay the fish skin side up in the pan, pour off the oil from the pan, and add the butter. Cover the pan and let the fish cook for another 30 seconds, then remove the pan from the heat and let the bass steam, still covered, for 3 to 4 minutes.

Meanwhile, cook the ravioli in lightly salted boiling water for 5 to 6 minutes, or until cooked through. Remove from the pot and drain.

Warm the reserved artichoke slices, carrots, pearl onions, tomato diamonds, parsley, and beurre monté in a small saucepan. Season to taste with salt and white pepper.

Check the consistency of the vinaigrette; if it is too thick, stir in a small amount of hot water.

Squeeze a 2-inch ring of basil oil onto the center of each plate. Fill the center of each with a spoonful of the vinaigrette. Top the vinaigrette with an inverted ravioli (rounded side down). Place a piece of fish on the ravioli and top the bass with the vegetables and sprigs of chervil.

PICTURED ON PAGES 150 AND 151                    MAKES 6 SERVINGS

# Pacific Moi with Fresh Soybeans, Scallion and Radish Salad, and Soy–Temple Orange Glaze

## RADISH SALAD

3 tablespoons finely julienned scallion
    (about 1 inch long)
3 tablespoons finely julienned
    sweet bunch carrot (about 1 inch long)
3 tablespoons finely julienned radish
    (about 1 inch long)
1 tablespoon chopped chives
Lemon oil (see Sources, page 315)

## ORANGE GLAZE

2 cups fresh orange juice
2 tablespoons (1 ounce) cold unsalted butter,
    cut into 4 pieces
1/4 teaspoon soy sauce

## SOYBEANS

1/4 cup (3 ounces) shelled fresh soybeans,
    blanched for about 8 minutes, or until tender
    (see Big-Pot Blanching, page 58), chilled in
    ice water, and drained

1 tablespoon tomato diamonds (see page 203)
2 teaspoons Brunoise (page 155)
3 tablespoons Beurre Monté (page 135)

## MOI

Canola oil
Six 3½- by 1-inch pieces moi fillet, skin on
    (see On Crisping Skin, page 147)
Kosher salt and freshly ground white pepper

On a recent trip to Hawaii, I found three exciting new foods to introduce to our kitchen. Two of them, moi and fresh green soybeans, are combined in this dish. (The third was fresh hearts of palm—see page 70.) Moi is a white fish with a lot of fat in it, which is unusual.

In putting this dish together—one of my few nods to Asian cuisine—I wanted to support the integrity of the dish by using other products indigenous to the area where the fish is caught. The fresh green soybeans we found there were amazing. Fresh soybeans come three to a pod and are a little smaller and a little fatter than fava beans, with a slightly more assertive flavor. (They may not be easy to find—sometimes you'll see them at farmers' or Asian markets.) And I finished this dish of Hawaiian items with a Polynesian-inspired orange-based glaze with soy sauce. I use temple oranges because they're very sweet and have a deep orange color, but you can use other oranges.

If you can't get moi, you might substitute pompano or pike.

FOR THE SALAD: About 1 hour before serving, place the julienned scallion, carrot, and radish in a bowl of ice water. The scallions will curl and the chilling will enable the vegetables to hold a tighter nest.

FOR THE ORANGE GLAZE: Place the orange juice in a small saucepan and reduce over medium heat to a thick glaze (about $1/3$ cup). Set aside.

FOR THE SOYBEANS: Combine the soybeans, tomato diamonds, brunoise, and beurre monté in a pan and heat over low heat. Keep warm.

TO COMPLETE: Heat the orange glaze to a simmer and whisk in the butter piece by piece. Add the soy sauce and keep the glaze warm.

Drain the iced vegetables and toss them with the chives and a small amount of lemon oil.

FOR THE MOI: Heat about $1/8$ inch of oil in a large skillet over medium heat. Season the fish with salt and white pepper. Add the moi fillets skin side down and cook for 2 to $2^{1}/2$ minutes, occasionally pressing down on the pieces with a spatula to help brown the skin. Flip the fillets and "kiss" (just briefly cook) the other side, then remove the moi from the pan.

Place 2 to 3 teaspoons of the orange glaze in the center of each plate. Place about 1 tablespoon of the soybean mixture in the center of the glaze, allowing it to spread into the glaze. Place the moi skin side up over the beans. Gently place a small pile of the crisp salad on one end of each moi fillet and serve.

MAKES 6 SERVINGS

## BRUNOISE

1 part carrots, sliced lengthwise on a mandoline into $1/16$-inch-thick strips
1 part turnips, sliced lengthwise on a mandoline into $1/16$-inch-thick strips
$1/2$ part leek greens (dark green part)

Brunoise, what we call our tiny dice of staple vegetables, is used often as a garnish at the French Laundry. Rather than making a small quantity, make a large batch and freeze it.

Cut all the vegetables into $1/16$-inch julienne strips and then cut across to make $1/16$-inch dice.

Blanch each vegetable separately in lightly salted boiling water to set the color and soften the vegetables. For small amounts of vegetables, it's easiest to place the vegetables in a strainer and submerge the strainer in the boiling water. When the vegetables are cooked, lift out the strainer and plunge it into ice water for a few seconds to chill the vegetables and set the color. Then lift out the strainer and place the vegetables on paper towels to drain.

When all the vegetables are blanched and drained, mix them together in a covered container and refrigerate for up to a day. For longer storage, spread the drained brunoise on a tray and place the tray in the freezer until frozen. Store the frozen brunoise in a well-sealed plastic bag in the freezer. You can use the brunoise directly from the freezer in recipes where it is warmed before serving.

PICTURED ON PAGE 202

Red Mullet with a *Palette d'Ail Doux* and Garlic Chips

○

PALETTES

2 large or 3 medium heads garlic, cloves
    separated and peeled (3½ ounces)

5 hard-boiled egg yolks

1½ tablespoons unsalted butter, softened

Kosher salt to taste

½ cup all-purpose flour

½ cup heavy cream

½ cup panko (Japanese bread crumbs;
    see Sources, page 315) or dry bread crumbs,
    finely ground in a blender and sifted through
    a strainer

PARSLEY COULIS

3 to 4 large bunches (12 ounces) Italian parsley

1 tablespoon Beurre Monté (page 135)

Kosher salt to taste

RED MULLET

Canola oil

12 red mullet fillets, skin on
    (see On Crisping Skin, page 147)

Kosher salt and freshly ground white pepper

PARSLEY SALAD

¼ cup small Italian parsley leaves

1 teaspoon finely minced shallot

Extra virgin olive oil

Pinch of kosher salt

About 36 Garlic Chips (recipe follows)

FOR THE PALETTES: Place the garlic in a small saucepan with cold water to cover and bring to a boil. Drain the garlic in a small strainer, cool under cold water, and repeat the process. Repeat a third time, but this time boil the garlic cloves until they are soft and there is no resistance when they are pierced with a small knife. Drain the garlic cloves, mash them slightly, and measure out ¼ cup for the palette.

Place the garlic purée, egg yolks, butter, and salt in a mini-food processor and blend until smooth. Line a small pan with plastic wrap and spread the mixture in it, in a ½-inch-thick layer. Cover and freeze for several hours, until the mixture is solid, or up to a few days.

Cut six 1½-inch disks from the frozen garlic mixture. Place the flour, cream, and crumbs in three separate dishes. Dip each disk into the flour, patting off any excess, then completely coat with cream and dredge in the crumbs, being careful to coat each round completely. Redip a second time in the cream and crumbs and return the palettes to the freezer.

FOR THE PARSLEY COULIS: Discard the tough stems from the parsley. You should have about 4 packed cups of leaves and tender stems. Blanch the parsley (see Big-Pot Blanching, page 58) until tender and remove to a bowl of ice water.

Once the parsley is cold, drain it and squeeze the excess water from the leaves. Place the parsley in a blender with just enough water to allow the mixture to turn. Blend the parsley to a purée. Spread the purée on a tamis (see page 73) and allow to sit for 5 minutes to drain any excess liquid. Discard the liquid and pass the purée through the tamis. You should have about ½ cup of purée. It can be refrigerated for up to 2 days.

TO COMPLETE: Heat about ⅛ inch of canola oil in a large nonstick skillet over medium-high heat (there should be enough oil to come about halfway up the sides of the fish). Season the red mullet with salt and white pepper, add the fillets skin side down and sauté, pressing down on the pieces of fish with a narrow spatula or small skillet to keep them flat. When the fish is almost cooked, after about 1 minute, turn the pieces to "kiss," or briefly cook, the second side. The total cooking time will be about 1½ minutes. Remove the fillets to paper towels to drain.

Add the frozen palettes to the pan and brown for about 1 minute on each side, until crisp and warmed through.

MEANWHILE, FOR THE PARSLEY SALAD: Toss the parsley leaves and shallots with a light coating of olive oil and the salt.

Place the parsley purée in a small saucepan and rewarm it. Check the consistency: It should be that of a sauce. If it is too thick, thin it with a little water; if it is too thin, simmer briefly (heat can cause the purée to change color, so cook it as little as possible). Stir in the beurre monté and season with salt to taste.

Place a spoonful of the parsley coulis on each serving plate. Center a palette on the sauce and crisscross two red mullet fillets, skin side up, over each one. Top with a stack of parsley salad and garlic chips and serve immediately.

PICTURED ON PAGE 158                    MAKES 6 SERVINGS

## GARLIC CHIPS

Garlic cloves

Cold milk

Canola oil for deep-frying

The unexpected thing about garlic chips is their crispness, something you don't normally associate with garlic. Blanching the garlic cloves in milk leaches out some of the bitterness and makes them sweeter. As chips, garlic doesn't become so forward that you're living with it for the rest of the night.

Slice the garlic cloves as thin as possible on a mandoline. Place the slices in a small saucepan and cover with cold milk. Bring the milk to a boil, then drain the garlic slices in a strainer (discard the milk) and rinse them under cold water. Return the slices to the pan and repeat the process three times, using fresh milk each time. Pat the garlic slices dry on paper towels.

Heat the oil in a deep saucepan to 300°F. Add the slices to the hot oil and fry for 12 to 15 minutes, or until the bubbles around the chips have subsided (signifying that all the moisture has evaporated) and they are a light golden brown. Drain the garlic chips on paper towels. Store airtight at room temperature for 1 to 2 days.

The red mullet is gratifying to make, and eat, over and over again. What makes

it work is not just the flavors of all the elements, but also the way they look

together—the red of the mullet against the bright green parsley coulis against the

leaves of the parsley salad, the brown of the fried palettes, the way the garlic

chips shimmer. *Palette* refers to the shape (a disk) of the *ail doux*, or sweet garlic

mixture. For me, this dish is as close to perfect as it gets.

Opposite: "Fish and Chips," page 156

# Spotted Skate Wing with Braised Red Cabbage and Mustard Sauce

**BRAISED RED CABBAGE**

3/4 pound red cabbage

3/4 cup dry red wine

1 tablespoon duck fat, unsalted butter,
   or canola oil

1/2 cup diced (1/4-inch) red onion

1/4 cup finely grated Granny Smith apple

1/4 cup White Veal Stock (page 222), Vegetable
   Stock (page 227), or water

2 teaspoons honey, preferably wildflower honey

1/2 cup finely grated peeled russet potato

Kosher salt and freshly ground black pepper

**MUSTARD SAUCE**

Canola oil

1/4 cup chopped leek

1/4 cup chopped mushrooms

3 tablespoons chopped carrot

1/2 cup Veal Stock (page 222)

1 tablespoon heavy cream

10 tablespoons (5 ounces) unsalted butter,
   cut into pieces

1 1/2 teaspoons Dijon mustard

1 1/2 teaspoons grainy mustard

1 tablespoon Brunoise (page 155)

2 teaspoons finely minced chives

Kosher salt and freshly ground black pepper

**SKATE**

1 1/2 pounds skate wing, skin removed, trimmed
   of cartilage and any red areas (have the
   fishmonger remove the skin)

Flour for dusting

Canola oil

Kosher salt

Mustard Powder (page 233)

I like skate because of its ropy texture. It's an easy fish to cook, because it doesn't fall apart when cooked at higher temperatures, and you thus have great opportunity for crispness. I use spotted, as opposed to red or gray, because it is a smaller fish, with a more compact texture.

FOR THE BRAISED RED CABBAGE: Remove the thick ribs from the cabbage and cut the leaves into chiffonade, long narrow strips about 1/4 inch wide. Place the cabbage and red wine in a large bowl, toss together, cover, and refrigerate overnight.

The next day, preheat the oven to 350°F.

In a deep ovenproof pan, warm the duck fat over medium-low heat. Add the red onion and cook gently until it begins to release its liquid, about 5 minutes. Stir in the cabbage and the marinating liquid, the apples, and stock. Cover with a parchment lid (see page 190), place in the oven, and cook for about 2 hours, until most of the liquid has evaporated.

Remove the pan from the oven, add the honey and potato, and stir well to combine. If the cabbage seems dry, add 1/4 cup of water. Re-cover with the parchment paper and return to the oven for an additional 30 to 45 minutes, or until the cabbage and potatoes are tender and have a noticeable creaminess. There will be approximately 1 1/2 cups of cabbage. Season to taste with salt and pepper. The cabbage can be stored, covered, in the refrigerator for up to 5 days.

FOR THE MUSTARD SAUCE: Heat a film of canola oil in a medium saucepan over medium heat. Add the leeks, mushrooms, and carrots and sauté, stirring often, for 2 to 3 minutes, or until the vegetables are lightly caramelized. Add the veal stock and simmer for 5 to 7 minutes, or until the liquid has reduced to a glace. Remove from the heat and set aside.

FOR THE SKATE: Cut the skate into 6 rectangular portions (about 3 ounces each). The pieces should be about 3 inches by 4 inches, but the actual size will depend on the thickness and size of the skate wing; if the piece is very thin, you may need to cut larger pieces and fold them over.

TO COMPLETE: Stir the cream into the mustard sauce and bring to a simmer. Whisk in the butter piece by piece, adding another piece only once the previous piece has been incorporated. Strain the sauce through a chinois (see page 73) into a small saucepan. Whisk in both mustards, the brunoise, and chives. Season to taste with salt and pepper and keep warm.

Reheat the red cabbage over low heat.

Heat 1/8 inch of canola oil in a large sauté pan over medium heat. Lightly dust each portion of skate with flour, patting off any excess, and place in the hot oil. Season the fish with salt and cook for 1 to 2 minutes, basting the skate occasionally with the oil, until the fish is golden brown on the first side. Turn the fillets and cook on the second side for another minute, or until the fish is opaque throughout (cooking time will vary depending on the thickness of the pieces).

Place a spoonful of the sauce on each serving plate. Top with the red cabbage and skate. Sprinkle a line of mustard powder down one side of each plate and serve immediately.

MAKES 6 SERVINGS

"SURF AND TURF"
## Sautéed Monkfish Tail with Braised Oxtails, Salsify, and Cèpes

---

**BRAISED OXTAILS**

5 pounds oxtails, cut into 1½-inch-thick pieces

1 recipe Red Wine Marinade (page 190)

Flour for dredging

Kosher salt and freshly ground black pepper

Canola oil

1 quart Veal Stock (page 222), heated

1 quart Chicken Stock (page 226), heated,
   or hot water

¼ cup Brunoise (page 155)

½ cup tomato diamonds (see page 203)

Few drops white wine vinegar

¼ cup Beurre Monté (page 135)

**SALSIFY AND CÈPES**

4 salsify (about 8 ounces), peeled

1 lemon, halved

3 cups Chicken Stock (page 226)

2 sprigs thyme

2 cloves garlic, crushed

2 tablespoons (1 ounce) unsalted butter

Canola oil

16 small cèpes (porcinis), cleaned and sliced
   about ¼ inch thick, or 16 shiitakes,
   stems removed, caps cleaned and sliced
   about ¼ inch thick

1 tablespoon Brunoise (page 155)

1 teaspoon chopped Italian parsley

1 tablespoon Beurre Monté (page 135)

**MONKFISH**

Canola oil

Kosher salt and freshly ground white pepper

8 monkfish medallions about 1 inch thick
   (about 2 ounces each)

2 tablespoons Beurre Monté (page 135)

2 tablespoons chopped Italian parsley

---

Here, the monkfish is so solid and substantial that it can support the richness of the oxtails, and the combination of fish and rich braised meat results in a very earthy dish.

Searing the meat, then slow-cooking it to extract its flavors and those of the vegetables into the braising liquid results in a "falling off the bone" tenderness and meat that melts in your mouth.

Monkfish has a high tolerance for cooking—if you inadvertently overcook it, it won't be catastrophic—and when the fish hits perfect doneness, it tends to hang there for a while, giving you some leeway in its cooking time.

FOR THE BRAISED OXTAILS: Divide the oxtails between two resealable plastic bags and add half the marinade to each of them. Seal the bags and place them in the refrigerator for 18 to 20 hours, turning them once or twice to distribute the marinade.

The next day, transfer the meat to one container and the vegetables to another. Strain the marinade through a towel-lined sieve into a saucepan. (This is the first step in the clarification process, to obtain a clean, clear sauce. Pouring it through the towel removes some of the blood and other impurities that could cloud the liquid. Do not wring out the towel; the impurities would be forced back into the liquid.) Slowly heat the marinade to a simmer. (Heating the liquid will coagulate the remaining blood proteins, but heating too quickly may pull the

impurities back into the liquid rather than separating them.) Skim and discard the impurities and other particles as they rise to the surface. Remove from the heat.

Preheat the oven to 325°F.

Place the flour in a dish. Pat the oxtails dry and dredge them in the flour just to coat. Lightly season with salt and pepper. Heat ¼ inch of oil in a large deep pot over medium heat. (The amount of oil may seem excessive, but it will keep the meat from burning and sticking to the pan. The meat will absorb only a certain amount of oil and if you don't use enough, the flour may burn and impart a bitter flavor.) Add the oxtails to the hot oil, in batches if necessary, and sear them on one side until they reach a rich deep brown color. Do not burn the flour, but allow the oxtails to brown before attempting to move them around. Then sear the meat on all sides, turning occasionally; even browning will add color and flavor to the braising liquid. Once the oxtails are completely browned, remove them from the pot. Drain the oil from the pan, leaving any little crusty particles on the bottom of the pan.

Add the reserved vegetables from the marinade to the pot. Scrape the "glaze" from the bottom of the pot and cook the vegetables, stirring occasionally, to release their moisture, 3 to 4 minutes. Then cook until the moisture has evaporated and the pot is reglazed.

Deglaze the pot by adding the clarified marinating liquid and stirring again. Reduce until most of the marinating liquid has

We do a lot of "surf-and-turf" dishes in which we pair meat and fish—lobster with foie gras, lobster with veal, scallops with cockscombs. It is important that the textures don't overwhelm each other—both the oxtails and the monkfish are meaty. The braised oxtails provides the red wine sauce that classically pairs with white fish.

evaporated. (Reglazing the pot adds yet another layer of color and intensity of flavor.) Add the hot stocks. (The veal stock is the flavor base of the braising liquid and the chicken stock or water will thin the veal stock enough for such long cooking.) Add the meat to the pot and cover with a parchment lid (see page 190). Bring the liquid back to a simmer and place in the oven to braise for 3½ to 4 hours. When the meat is cooked, it will be falling off the bone and completely tender. At this point, the oxtails can be used immediately or cooled to room temperature and then refrigerated for up to 4 days.

Remove the oxtails from the liquid, and when they are cool enough to handle, pull the meat from the bones. The yield will depend on the cut of the oxtails; some sections have a great deal more meat than others. You will need 2 cups of meat for this recipe; extra meat can be reserved for another use.

Strain the braising liquid through a China cap (see page 73) or strainer and let it sit for 10 minutes to give the fat a chance to separate and rise to the top. Remove the fat, place the remaining liquid in a medium saucepan, and simmer to reduce. When the pan seems too large for the amount of liquid, strain the sauce through a chinois (see page 73) into a smaller saucepan, without forcing any particles through the sieve. Continue to reduce the sauce until it is 1 to 1½ cups. Strain a final time into a saucepan and add the reserved 2 cups of meat. Set aside.

FOR THE SALSIFY: Place the salsify in a saucepan. Squeeze in the lemon juice and add the lemon halves along with the stock, 1 sprig of thyme, and the garlic. Simmer for 20 to 25 minutes, or until the salsify is tender, drain.

Cut the salsify pieces lengthwise in half and then cut them on the bias into 1-inch-long pieces.

TO COMPLETE: Heat the butter in a medium skillet until hot. Add the salsify pieces and the remaining sprig of thyme and cook, tossing occasionally, for about 10 minutes, until nicely browned. Remove from the heat.

Meanwhile, heat a film of oil in another medium skillet and sauté the cèpes until they are well browned. Add them to the salsify.

Heat ⅛ inch of oil in a large skillet. Season the monkfish with salt and white pepper, add to the pan, and sauté over medium-high heat for about 3 minutes, then turn the medallions to cook for an additional 2 minutes. Add the 2 tablespoons beurre monté to the pan, baste the fish, and add 1 tablespoon chopped parsley.

Meanwhile, add brunoise, tomato diamonds, vinegar, and the ¼ cup beurre monté to the oxtails and warm through. Add the brunoise, parsley, and beurre monté to the salsify and cèpes, and warm through.

Place a spoonful of the oxtails in the center of each plate. Top each with a monkfish medallion and garnish the top with the salsify and cèpes. Sprinkle with the remaining chopped parsley.

MAKES 8 SERVINGS

**Infused Oils** The important thing to know about infused oils is that you must treat the oil like the herb, spice, or vegetable with which you infused it.

For herb-infused oils, big-pot blanching (see page 58) is critical, as is shocking, or chilling, the leaves in ice water to stop the cooking—all those things that are fundamental to cooking a green vegetable are similarly important to making an herb-infused oil. It's preferable to use herb oils right away, though they can be refrigerated. Spice oils, such as curry oil, don't require refrigeration. "Hard" herbs, such as thyme and rosemary, don't have a lot of color, so we add parsley to the mixture for color. Because of these herbs' assertive flavors, the flavor of the parsley is not an issue.

We use infused oils because they are visually exciting and because they add a new dimension to the flavor of the herb, spice, or vegetable itself. For instance, I can serve a parsley salad and a parsley oil on the same plate without being repetitive in texture.

## Herb Oils

As with green vegetables, it is crucial that the water maintain a constant boil when you blanch the herbs. The more water you use, the more likely it is that the water will maintain its heat.

FOR ALL HERB OILS: Bring a large pot of salted water to a boil. Use about ¼ cup of kosher salt for every quart of water. Place the herbs in a strainer and dip them into the water for the allotted time, keeping the water at a strong boil. Remove the strainer and immediately plunge the blanched herbs into an ice-water bath to chill.

Drain the cold herbs and squeeze as dry as possible. Use scissors to cut them into small pieces (chopping some herbs causes them to oxidize and darken).

Place half the herbs in a blender with enough of the specified oil just to cover. (All of these recipes except the basil oil, which uses olive oil, call for canola oil. Depending on the dish you will be preparing, however, you may want to use olive oil for some of the others, such as the rosemary or thyme—other herbs that work in Mediterranean dishes.) Turn on the blender to medium speed and allow the herbs to blend for a minute to begin the process. If the herbs aren't turning freely, add slightly more oil so that they will. Turn the speed to high and continue to blend for another 2 minutes. If your blender has a hole at the top, remove the stopper to allow some air in. (You may see steam rise from the opening; friction is causing the purée to heat up.) Check the oil occasionally. It will become slightly warm, but it should not get too hot, or there will be some loss of color. If at any point in the recipe, the machine or mixture overheats, stop the machine, remove the herb purée, and refrigerate until cool. Clean the machine, return the cooled purée to it, and continue to blend.

Add half of the remaining herbs to the machine and blend for another 2 minutes, then add the remaining herbs and blend for 2 more minutes. Remove the purée to a container and refrigerate for at least a day to intensify the color; the purée can be stored for up to 1 week. Once strained, the oil will normally discolor in 2 days. It can be frozen for several weeks, however, with minimal loss of color and flavor.

Place a piece of cheesecloth over a container and secure with a rubber band or string. Place the purée on the cheesecloth and let the oil filter through for about an hour. Discard the cheesecloth and remaining purée—don't wring out the cheesecloth, or you may cloud the oil. Depending on the amount you are making, and the size of the container, you may need to do this in batches. Store the oil in the refrigerator (or freeze it). Put it into a small plastic squeeze bottle for garnishing dishes.

## ROSEMARY OIL

1 cup rosemary leaves

2 cups Italian parsley sprigs

About 1 cup canola oil

BLANCHING TIME: Rosemary, 30 seconds; then add the parsley and continue to blanch for another 10 seconds

MAKES ABOUT 1/4 CUP

## FENNEL OIL

2 cups fennel fronds

2 cups Italian parsley sprigs

About 3/4 cup canola oil

BLANCHING TIME: Both the fennel fronds and parsley, 10 to 15 seconds

MAKES ABOUT 1/3 CUP

## CHIVE OIL

1 packed cup chives cut into 1-inch pieces

About 1 cup canola oil

BLANCHING TIME: None; place the chives in a strainer and run hot water over them for about 2 minutes to soften and remove the chlorophyll taste

MAKES ABOUT 1/3 CUP

## PARSLEY OIL

4 cups Italian parsley sprigs

About 3/4 cup canola oil

BLANCHING TIME: 15 seconds

MAKES ABOUT 1/3 CUP

## BASIL OIL

3 packed cups basil leaves

About 3/4 cup olive oil

BLANCHING TIME: 15 seconds

MAKES ABOUT 1/3 CUP

## MINT OIL

4 packed cups mint leaves

About 3/4 cup canola oil

BLANCHING TIME: 15 seconds

MAKES ABOUT 1/3 CUP

## THYME OIL

1/4 cup thyme leaves and tender stems

3 cups Italian parsley sprigs

About 3/4 cup canola oil

BLANCHING TIME: Thyme, 30 seconds; then add the parsley and continue to blanch for another 10 seconds

MAKES ABOUT 1/3 CUP

## CURRY OIL

¼ cup curry powder

3 tablespoons coriander seed

One ½- to ¾-inch-long piece cinnamon stick

3 tablespoons mace

1¼ teaspoons cayenne

1 cup canola oil

Toast the curry powder and coriander seed in separate small pans, heating just until you get an aroma. Remove from the heat, combine with the cinnamon stick, mace, and cayenne in a coffee grinder, and grind to a powder. Remove to a small bowl and stir in some of the oil to moisten the spices. Place the spices in the blender with the remaining oil and blend. Pour into a container and let sit for a day.

Strain the oil through cheesecloth-lined fine-mesh sieve and store in an airtight container at room temperature.

MAKES ABOUT ½ CUP

## CARROT OIL

1 cup carrot juice (from about 1¼ pounds carrots)

3 tablespoons canola oil

Vegetable oils are easily made by combining any reduced vegetable juice with an equal portion of oil.

Reduce the carrot juice in a small saucepan to 3 tablespoons. Strain through a small chinois (see page 73) or fine-mesh strainer and place in a mini-blender with the oil. Blend for a minute to combine and emulsify. Transfer to a small container and store in the refrigerator.

MAKES ABOUT ⅓ CUP

## CORAL OIL

3 tablespoons lobster coral (roe)

½ cup canola oil, heated

Coral oil can be made with fresh lobster roe, or the roe can be accumulated over a period of time and kept frozen until you have enough to make the oil.

Place the lobster coral in a blender and blend for 20 to 30 seconds, or until smooth. With the machine running on low speed, drizzle in the hot oil. Increase to high speed and continue to blend for 15 to 20 minutes, stopping to scrape down the sides occasionally. The oil will continue to heat in the blender from friction and will take on a red-orange color (the coral will remain dark). The longer you run the blender, the more color the oil will take on, but be careful not to damage the blender by overheating it.

Strain the oil by pouring it through a cheesecloth-lined fine-mesh sieve into a container. Cover the oil and store it in the refrigerator.

MAKES ABOUT ¼ TO ⅓ CUP

M E A T

# The Importance of **Trussing Chicken**

Not long after I left Roland Henin's kitchen, I was hired to open a new restaurant in West Palm Beach called the Cobbley Nob. It was my first real executive chef position. I cooked classical French food.

I was very proud that I had a repertoire of fifteen different classical potato preparations. I cooked everything in clarified butter. I cooked Lobster Bohemian—lobster with cream and paprika—which was straight out of Fernand Point's book, *Ma Gastronomie*. But the Cobbley Nob, which was near the jai alai courts, died a quick death, and I learned that the quality of the food does not necessarily determine the success of a restaurant.

Fortunately, I found another job not far from there at a restaurant called Café du Parc in North Palm Beach, where the most important thing I learned was how to truss a chicken.

Is learning to truss a chicken that important? I was almost stabbed because I didn't know. The chef, Pierre, was paying me five or six dollars an hour. It was just him and me, getting ready to open the restaurant for the season. Again, a classical French chef. And there I was, this American kid who thought of himself as a chef. I'd been a chef. I'd gotten good reviews at the Cobbley Nob.

Pierre told me to truss the chickens. I wasn't going to tell him I didn't know how. I fumbled around. I tied the legs together, like at Thanksgiving—I had no idea what I was doing. Pierre watched me. He couldn't understand. He started screaming at me. How could someone who'd been a chef—I was twenty-four at this point; in France a cook learns to truss a chicken before he's old enough to drive—how could I claim to be a chef of anything, and not know how to truss chicken? He became so enraged he threw the knife at me. I don't think he was aiming for my heart, but the knife came close enough.

What that taught me—that chicken, the string, the whistling knife blade—was that if I was going to be a chef somewhere, I'd better be prepared to teach people everything they needed to know to run that kitchen. I no longer took it for granted that I knew everything. I needed to really, really study and learn all those things, how to truss a chicken, how to tie a slipknot. I knew then I couldn't call myself a chef just because I ran a kitchen. In the end, of course, the importance of trussing a chicken meant far more than actually trussing a chicken.

## TRUSSING AND ROASTING CHICKEN

Position the chicken so that its cavity faces you. Place the center of a 2-foot-long piece of butcher's string beneath the chicken's tail, the little triangle at the bottom of the cavity. Lift the string up outside each leg and pull it down between the legs, reversing the direction of each end so that they cross. Pull the string over the thighs (the drumsticks should squeeze together at this point) and the wings.

Maintaining tension on the string, turn the chicken on its side, wind the ends of the string over the neck, and tie securely.

Trussing a chicken this way will help it cook more evenly, as it should protect the thinnest part of the breast, the part that is most likely to overcook during roasting. I like to roast a chicken at a high temperature, between 425° and 450°F., because I've found the faster I cook the legs, the moister the breast will be.

Even a perfectly roasted chicken will inevitably result in a breast that's a little less moist than one you would cook separately, which is why I always want a sauce with roast chicken. The skin that sticks to the bottom of the pan and caramelizes while roasting is the very best substance for flavoring a chicken sauce or *jus*.

## Roulade of Pekin Duck Breast with Creamed Sweet White Corn and Morel Mushroom Sauce

**ROULADE OF DUCK**

1 whole boneless duck breast (about 12 ounces)
(Liberty Valley or Pekin)

Kosher salt and freshly ground black pepper

A few allspice berries

2 large outer leaves savoy cabbage or 2 large
leaves Swiss chard (with no splits or tears)

**CREAMED CORN**

5 large ears corn, shucked

4½ tablespoons (2¼ ounces) unsalted butter

Kosher salt and freshly ground black pepper

**MOREL MUSHROOM SAUCE**

4 ounces morels, preferably Oregon

3 tablespoons (1½ ounces) unsalted butter

¾ cup "Quick" Duck Sauce (page 228), warmed

1 teaspoon finely minced shallot

1 teaspoon finely minced chives

1 teaspoon finely minced Italian parsley

1 tablespoon Brunoise (page 155)

Kosher salt and freshly ground black pepper

This dish is interesting to me from a mechanical standpoint. I needed to figure out how to cook and serve duck in a way that was suitable to the style and portion size of the French Laundry. I didn't want to roast the duck breast whole and then cut it, because it tends to bleed out—all its juices go right into the sauce that has been painstakingly degreased and reduced and brought to perfection. I tried making a ragout of duck breast, but it didn't have the exactness I wanted. So I decided to try cooking it in a bag—wrapping the breast in a blanched leaf of savoy cabbage or Swiss chard and rolling it up tightly in plastic wrap. It's precise and easy to cook. The corn garnish is logical because ducks are corn-fed. And the morels are very earthy; you can almost never go wrong adding mushrooms to anything.

FOR THE ROULADE OF DUCK: Remove and discard the skin from the duck breast and cut it in half. Remove the tenderloin from the underside of each breast (reserve it for another use) and trim away any membranes, veins, and cartilage. Trim the ends of the meat to form a rectangular shape. Sprinkle the underside of each breast with salt and pepper and grind 5 to 6 small slivers of allspice over each piece (a hand-crank cheese grater works well for this if you don't have an allspice grater).

Bring a pot of salted water to a boil. Add the cabbage or Swiss chard leaves and boil gently for 3 to 4 minutes, or until tender. Gently remove the leaves to an ice-water bath to chill, then transfer to paper towels to dry.

Tear off a piece of plastic wrap about 20 inches long and lay it horizontally across a work surface. Place a leaf of cabbage or chard on a cutting board, with the inside of the leaf facing upward and the core

end toward the bottom. Carefully cut the large rib from the leaf.

Roll a duck breast lengthwise to form a cylinder. Place the cylinder of duck in the center of the widest part of the cabbage leaf. Trim the leaf so that it is the length of the breast and so that the leaf will easily wrap around the roulade once.

Roll up the duck breast in the leaf. Place the roulade in the center of the bottom of the length of plastic wrap. Roll up the roulade in the plastic, holding it in the center and rolling as tightly as possible.

Holding the roulade, twist one end of the plastic wrap several times against the duck. This will secure the shape of the roulade. Repeat on the other side, twisting in the opposite direction. You should have a perfectly shaped cylinder. Bring both ends of the wrap over to the center of the roulade and tie them in a knot pulled just tight enough to rest against the roulade. Repeat with the remaining breast and leaf and place the packets in the refrigerator. You can refrigerate them for several hours before cooking.

FOR THE CREAMED CORN: Cut the kernels from 3 ears of corn. Run them through a juicer. Or, place them in a blender with a little water (just enough to allow it to blend) and purée; remove the purée and all the liquid to a chinois (see page 73) set over a container. Allow all the corn juice to drain, pressing lightly on the corn but not forcing the purée through the strainer. You should have about ½ cup of corn juice.

Cut the kernels from the remaining 2 ears of corn. Blanch the corn in lightly salted boiling water for about 1 minute, skimming off any impurities that float to the surface. Drain the corn and cool in cold water; then drain again and dry the kernels on paper towels.

FOR THE MORELS: Trim the stems from the morels. Soak the mushrooms in warm water (if vegetables that need to be soaked are going to be cooked, use warm water, as it loosens dirt more easily than cold), changing the water two or three times. If the mushrooms are small, they can be cooked whole. Larger morels should be cut into uniform pieces.

TO COMPLETE: Heat a large saucepan of water to 190°F. Place the cold duck roulades in the water, adjusting the heat to maintain the water temperature. Poach the duck for 6 to 7 minutes for medium-rare, or 7 to 8 minutes for medium. Remove the duck and allow it to rest for 2 to 3 minutes before slicing.

While the duck cooks, make the morel mushroom sauce: Melt 1 tablespoon of the butter in a medium skillet over medium heat. Shake any excess water from the mushrooms, add to the hot butter, and sauté until the liquid has evaporated and the mushrooms are tender. If the liquid evaporates before the mushrooms are cooked, just add a tablespoon of water to the pan. Add ⅓ cup of the duck sauce to

the morels and heat through. Just before serving, add the shallots, chives, parsley, and brunoise and cook for a few seconds. Remove from the heat and swirl in the remaining 2 tablespoons of butter. Season to taste with salt and peppper.

In a heavy saucepan, whisk the corn juice over medium heat until it thickens. (The starch present in the corn—cornstarch—will cause it to thicken quickly.) Do not allow it to boil, or it may curdle. Once it thickens, turn down the heat and whisk in the butter. Add the blanched corn kernels and season with salt and pepper.

With the roulades still wrapped, cut off an end of each, using a serrated knife. Gently push the roulade out of the wrap. Slice each roulade into three equal sections.

Place a spoonful of the remaining duck sauce in the center of each of six plates. Top the sauce with the creamed corn. Stand the pieces of duck roulade on the corn and garnish the top of each with a spoonful of morels.

MAKES 6 SERVINGS

# Pan-Roasted Breast of Squab with Swiss Chard, Sautéed Duck Foie Gras, and Oven-Dried Black Figs

**SQUAB**

3 squab (see Sources, page 315)

Canola oil

Kosher salt and freshly ground black pepper

2 tablespoons Beurre Monté (page 135)

**OVEN-DRIED FIGS**

6 ripe Black Mission figs, or best quality available,

    each cut into 6 wedges

Powdered sugar for dusting

**SWISS CHARD**

1 pound Swiss chard (yellow, green, or red),

    washed and dried on paper towels

1 tablespoon unsalted butter

Kosher salt

1/3 cup Beurre Monté (page 135)

1 recipe "Quick" Squab Sauce (page 229),

    made with the reserved squab legs

    and carcasses (from above)

12 ounces fresh moulard duck foie gras,

    cut into 3/4-inch cubes

Kosher salt

Squab Spice (page 233)

2 tablespoons minced chives

Squab is difficult to cook in that you have to hit the temperature exactly right. It should be served medium-rare. When it's rare, it's tough and difficult to eat. When it starts to get over medium-rare, the meat begins to take on a livery flavor.

We oven-dry the figs left over from summer's bounty—they'll keep for a week—and serve them in this fall dish. We use a beautiful yellow Swiss chard, a variety you may be able to find at farmers' markets.

**FOR THE SQUAB:** Remove each breast half from the squab carcasses, leaving the wings attached to the breasts. Cut off the tips of the wings, leaving only the larger bottom wing bones attached to the breasts. With a paring knife, scrape the meat away from the wing bone to "french" it. Cover and refrigerate the breasts. Use the legs and carcasses to make the squab sauce.

**FOR THE OVEN-DRIED FIGS:** Preheat the oven to 350°F. Line a baking sheet with parchment. Place the fig pieces on the pan and lightly dust (using a sugar shaker or a small strainer) the figs with powdered sugar. Place in the oven and bake for 30 minutes, or until dried but still supple. The figs can be kept refrigerated in an airtight container for up to 1 week.

**FOR THE SWISS CHARD:** Cut off the stalks, pull away and discard any strings, and cut the stalks on the diagonal into 1/16-inch julienne. Cut the leaves into 2-inch pieces. You will have approximately 6 to 7 cups of trimmed leaves and stalks.

Melt 2 teaspoons of the butter in a large skillet over medium heat. Add the chard leaves, sprinkle with salt (it is important to salt the leaves before they wilt for even seasoning), and cook for 1 to 2 minutes, or until the leaves wilt. Drain on paper towels.

Melt the remaining 1 teaspoon butter in 2 tablespoons water in a second large skillet over medium heat. Add the chard stems, season with salt, and cook, stirring, for 1 to 2 minutes, or until tender. Drain.

**TO COMPLETE:** Heat 1/16 inch of canola oil in a large sauté pan over medium-high heat. Season the squab breasts with salt and pepper and place skin side down in the hot oil. Cook for about 3 minutes, or until the skin is a rich brown. Turn the meat over and cook for an additional 2 minutes, basting the meat with the oil in the pan. Drain off the fat in the pan and add the beurre monté. Continue to cook and baste the squab for about 2 more minutes, or until the meat is medium-rare. Remove the pan from the heat and allow the squab to rest for 5 minutes.

Meanwhile, combine the chard leaves and the figs with the beurre monté in a saucepan and add a splash of water. Reheat over medium-low heat. Just before serving, stir in the chard stems.

Rewarm the squab sauce.

Heat a large skillet over medium-high heat. Season the cubes of foie gras with salt. When the pan is very hot, add the foie gras and brown the pieces on all sides. This should only take about 1 to 1 1/2 minutes. Don't overcook; the pieces will continue to cook when they are removed from the heat.

Slice the squab breasts crosswise on a slight diagonal. Spoon some squab sauce into the middle of each serving plate. Top each with a portion of the chard and foie gras. Overlap the slices of squab over the chard. Sprinkle with a light dusting of squab spice, then sprinkle with the chives.

MAKES 6 SERVINGS

Roasted Guinea Fowl *en Crèpinette de Byaldi*, page 178

Ugly birds, nasty birds. They peck at you. But they're lovely to cook. I prefer guinea fowl to chicken. They're more tender than chicken and have a deeper flavor. The legs, however, are more or less useless because they're almost entirely sinew, so I use them for sauce.

## Roasted Guinea Fowl *en Crèpinette de Byaldi* with Pan Jus

**BYALDI**

¼ cup canola oil

1 cup sliced onions (halved and cut into 1- to 1½-inch-long slices)

1 red bell pepper, cored, seeded, and cut into ¼-inch julienne

1 yellow bell pepper, cored, seeded, and cut into ¼-inch julienne

1 green bell pepper, cored, seeded, and cut into ¼-inch julienne

Herb sachet—2 sprigs thyme, 2 sprigs parsley, and 1 bay leaf, tied together in a cheesecloth bundle

Kosher salt and freshly ground black pepper

1 to 1½ cups thinly sliced zucchini rounds

1 to 1½ cups thinly sliced Japanese eggplant rounds

1 to 1½ cups thinly sliced yellow squash rounds

6 small tomatoes (12 ounces), peeled and thinly sliced

1 teaspoon chopped garlic

2 teaspoons olive oil

¼ teaspoon minced thyme

One 2½-pound guinea fowl

1 large sheet caul fat, soaked overnight in cold water in the refrigerator

Kosher salt and freshly ground black pepper

Canola oil

**SAUCE**

1 cup canola oil

Reserved carcass and trimmings of the fowl, fat removed and chopped into 1-inch pieces

2½ cups water

2½ cups Chicken Stock (page 226)

½ cup carrots cut into ½-inch mirepoix (see page 203)

⅓ cup shallots cut into ½-inch mirepoix (see page 203)

1 cup onions cut into ½-inch mirepoix (see page 203)

1 cup leeks cut into ½-inch mirepoix (see page 203)

1 tablespoon extra virgin olive oil

Byaldi is a refined interpretation of ratatouille. The vegetables normally diced for a ratatouille—eggplant, zucchini, yellow squash, tomato—are sliced and layered over a stew of onions and peppers, brushed with olive oil, seasoned with salt, pepper, and thyme, and baked. The fowl is encased in this Provençal vegetable combination and wrapped in caul fat to make fragrant, self-basting packages. (If you have difficulty finding caul fat, don't let that stop you from trying this dish, if only to taste this delicious vegetable preparation.)

Byaldi goes well with most meats and seafood. It's important to use vegetables that have approximately the same diameter. Use a mandoline to cut them into very thin slices, about one sixteenth of an inch. If possible, make the byaldi the day before serving it to allow the flavors to develop.

Have the butcher cut up the guinea fowl, if you prefer; ask him to reserve the bones so you can use them for the sauce. Don't overcook the bird. The breasts and thighs should be a little pink in the center.

**FOR THE BYALDI:** Preheat the oven to 275°F.

Heat the oil in a large skillet over medium heat. Add the onions, peppers, and herb sachet, season with salt and pepper, and cook for 15 minutes, or until the vegetables are softened but not browned. Remove the sachet and spread the mixture in an even layer in a 12-inch ovenproof skillet or round baking dish.

Arrange the sliced vegetables over the onions and peppers, beginning at the outside of the pan and working toward the center, alternating and overlapping them (see the photograph on page 177).

Mix the garlic, oil, thyme, and salt and pepper to taste and sprinkle over the vegetables. Cover with aluminum foil, crimping the edges to seal, or with a tight-fitting lid and bake for 2½ hours.

Remove the lid and check the vegetables (the eggplant will take the longest to cook): They should have softened and be almost cooked. Return to the oven, uncovered, and cook for an additional 30 minutes, or until very tender. The byaldi can be served immediately or, as for this recipe, cooled to room temperature and then refrigerated until ready to use, preferably for a day or two.

FOR THE GUINEA FOWL: Using a boning knife, remove the breast in two pieces. Remove and discard the skin and trim the edges of the meat. Fold each breast crosswise in half so that the narrow end of the breast and the wide end meet. Cut a shallow slit across the width of the fold. This will ensure even cooking of the breast.

Cut off the legs and thighs and cut the legs and thighs apart. Reserve the legs and carcass for the sauce. Remove the skin from the thighs and discard; cut out and remove the bone. Trim any uneven edges and fold each thigh over into its original shape. Set the guinea fowl aside.

FOR THE SAUCE: Heat the canola oil over high heat in a heavy braising pan large enough to hold the bones in one layer. (The amount of oil is necessary for proper browning of the bones. The excess fat will be poured off later.) When the oil is very hot, add the chopped bones. Allow the bones to brown on the first side before you turn them, about 10 minutes. Turn them occasionally until they are evenly colored, about 20 minutes total.

When the bones are well browned, pour off the fat from the pan. Add ½ cup of the water to the bones and stir with a wooden spoon or spatula, scraping up the glaze from the bottom of the pan. Continue to cook until the liquid has evaporated and reglazed the pan.

Add ½ cup of the chicken stock to the pan and deglaze as above. Continue to cook until the liquid evaporates as before.

Add the vegetables to the bones and stir. The moisture from the vegetables will deglaze the pan. Continue cooking and stirring to evaporate the moisture and glaze the vegetables.

Add the remaining 2 cups chicken stock and 2 cups water to the pan. Scrape the glaze from the bottom of the pan and simmer until the liquid is reduced by about one third. Strain the sauce through a colander and then strain through a chinois (see page 73) into a small saucepan; you should have about 2 to 2½ cups of liquid. Do not force through any solids or liquid that remain in the chinois. Return the sauce to the stove and reduce to ¼ to ⅓ cup.

TO COMPLETE: Preheat the oven to 350°F.

Remove the caul fat from the water and blot dry on paper towels. Season each piece of hen with salt and pepper. Cover the entire top of each piece of fowl with a portion of the byaldi (both layers); set the remaining byaldi aside. Place one piece of guinea fowl vegetable side down on one edge of the caul fat. Roll it up securely in the caul fat, giving it a couple of turns, and trim the excess. Fold the edges of the caul fat underneath to form a tight package. Repeat with the remaining pieces.

Heat ⅛ inch of oil in a heavy ovenproof skillet over medium heat (be certain that the oil is not overly hot, or it will make holes in the caul fat). Place the packets vegetable side down in the oil and brown until they are nicely colored on the bottom, about 4 minutes. Using a narrow spatula, carefully turn the pieces and continue to cook for about 2 more minutes to brown the second side (see the photograph on page 177). Place the skillet in the oven for about 15 minutes to complete the cooking; do not overcook the fowl.

Meanwhile, reheat the remaining byaldi in the oven. Stir the olive oil into the sauce.

Divide the vegetables among four plates. Cut each piece of hen on a slight diagonal through the center. Arrange a piece of white meat and a piece of dark meat on each portion of byaldi. Drizzle some sauce over each.

MAKES 4 SERVINGS

# Salt and pepper and vinegar

The ability to salt food properly is the single most important skill in cooking. When new cooks start at the restaurant, this is one of the first things I try to convey. Salt is the primary seasoning ingredient we use. It heightens the flavor of everything across the board, no matter what you're doing—even some sweets. Without it, the flavor of meats and vegetables and fruits is a little flat, dead, *fade*, as they say in France—insipid. Salt opens up flavors, makes them sparkle.

But if you taste salt in a dish, it's too salty.

Salt's not bad for you—too much salt is bad for you. Processed food can contain enormous quantities of salt, but if you eat fresh foods and you're seasoning it yourself, salt intake should not be a problem.

The basic salt we use before and during cooking is kosher salt. We use a specific brand of kosher salt, Diamond Crystal, because of the size of the grains. We gauge the amount of salt we're using mainly by touch, and we've gotten used to the feel of the Diamond Crystal brand.

Pepper, on the other hand, should be used only in certain cases for specific tastes. Pepper on meat is a constant, but pepper on fish can be overwhelming (I'll use white, if any).

Sometimes pepper makes a dessert: marscapone sorbet with a Tellicherry pepper syrup, for instance, so that sweet, rich, and spicy elements come together. Pepper on raspberries is delicious. (Tellicherry, a common black peppercorn, is similar to Java peppercorns, but it's a little more aggressive.)

White pepper is important too, mainly in dishes that need pepper but whose appearance would be compromised by specks of black pepper.

I think people use pepper too much. It gets in the way. Salt dissolves and penetrates. Pepper doesn't.

After cooking, we use two different salts as a textural, visual, and flavor-enhancing garnish: *fleur de sel*, a pure, slightly sweet, white salt, and *sel gris*, or gray salt, which is still moist and has a lot more mineral flavors to it. They're harvested by hand along the coastal regions of western France.

Fleur de sel is expensive, but a little bit goes a long way. A little four- or six-ounce bag, for maybe ten dollars, will last a year. It's wonderful on salads. Meat benefits from fleur de sel and sel gris after cooking it. Chewing on salt sounds like an awful proposition, but when you bite down on a crystal of it on foie gras, for example, it's amazing—it just explodes with flavor.

Try tasting different salts to understand their differences, starting with fleur de sel and sel gris, then kosher salt, and lastly, table salt. See for yourself.

The other important seasoning—one that many tend to overlook—is vinegar. You don't want to taste vinegar; like salt, it's only there to help build flavors without becoming prominent itself. A lot of our *à la minute* sauces—sauces we make just before serving them—use vinegar. Many of the meat sauces have a drop or two of vinegar. Vinegar allows you to reduce the amount of salt you use.

White wine vinegar is my favorite, because it works well in just about every sauce. You wouldn't want to use a sherry or a balsamic, because they have flavors of their own. I like vinegar to have about a 6 percent acidity so I can use less of it than a vinegar with a lower acidity and therefore the flavor doesn't become prevalent. When the vinegar is a major part of the dish—in a vinegar sauce, for instance—it's important to use a good-quality vinegar.

## Roasted Rib Steak with Golden Chanterelles, Pommes Anna, and Bordelaise Sauce

◖

**CÔTE DE BOEUF**

1 double-cut rib steak (about 2 to 2½ pounds)

Kosher salt and freshly ground black pepper

Canola oil

4 tablespoons (2 ounces) unsalted butter

**BORDELAISE SAUCE**

1 cup red wine, such as Cabarnet Sauvignon

⅓ cup sliced shallots

½ cup sliced carrots

¼ cup sliced mushrooms

10 sprigs Italian parsley

2 sprigs thyme

1 bay leaf

2 tablespoons sliced garlic

6 black peppercorns

1 cup Veal Stock (page 222)

**POMMES ANNA**

10 pitted prunes

1 cup Chicken Stock (page 226)

1 tablespoon minced shallots

Gray salt

2 pounds Yukon Gold potatoes

6 tablespoons Clarified Butter (page 125), melted

Kosher salt and freshly ground black pepper

**CHANTERELLE MUSHROOMS**

1 tablespoon unsalted butter

1 generous cup (3 ounces) chanterelle
    mushrooms, washed, stems peeled,
    and cut into 1-inch pieces

Kosher salt and freshly ground black pepper

Thyme sprigs

Ask the butcher for a double-cut rib steak, or *côte de boeuf*. Request that it be trimmed of excess fat, that the bone be "frenched," or scraped clean, and that the meat be tied with string to help it hold its shape during cooking.

I season this meat—as I do any large cut of meat to be served rare to medium-rare—a day before cooking so that the salt has time to penetrate into the flesh and intensify the flavor.

Sprinkle all sides of the steak liberally with salt and pepper. Place on a plate and refrigerate for 1 day to allow the flavors to develop.

One hour before cooking, remove the meat from the refrigerator. (It is important that beef or lamb be brought to room temperature before cooking. If the meat is cold, the cooking time will be increased and the outside will be overcooked by the time the inside reaches its proper temperature.)

FOR THE BORDELAISE SAUCE: In a medium saucepan, bring the wine, vegetables, parsley, thyme, bay leaf, and garlic to a simmer, and simmer until almost all the liquid has evaporated. Add the peppercorns and veal stock and simmer for another 10 to 15 minutes, or until the stock is reduced to a sauce consistency (about ½ cup). Strain the sauce through a fine-mesh strainer into a small saucepan. This sauce can be refrigerated for 2 to 3 days.

FOR THE POMMES ANNA: Place the prunes and chicken stock in a small saucepan. The prunes should be just covered with liquid. Bring to a simmer and cook for about 20 minutes, or until the liquid has evaporated and the prunes are very soft. Remove the prunes to a cutting board and finely chop them. Add the shallots and gray salt to taste.

Preheat the oven to 450°F.

Peel the potatoes and trim into cylinders that are 1½ to 2 inches in diameter. Using a mandoline, cut the potatoes crosswise into ¹/₁₆-inch slices. Place the slices in a bowl of cold water for a minute to remove some of the starch, then drain and dry the slices on paper towels.

Put 2 tablespoons of the clarified butter in an 8-inch ovenproof nonstick skillet. Place a slice of potato in the center of the pan. Lay more potato slices around the edge of the pan, overlapping them by half, until you have completely circled the pan. Continue with another overlapping circle of potatoes inside the first. When the entire bottom of the pan is covered, sprinkle a little kosher salt and pepper over the potatoes and repeat the process to form a second layer. Spread half of the prune mixture over the potatoes, leaving a $1/2$-inch border all around. Work carefully to avoid moving the potatoes around too much. Make another two layers of potatoes, seasoning the first layer with salt and pepper, and spread the remaining prune mixture over them, again leaving a border. Cover the prunes with a final two layers of seasoned potatoes.

Pour the remaining $1/4$ cup clarified butter over the potatoes and place the skillet over medium-low heat. Once the butter begins to bubble, cook for 3 to 4 minutes, shaking the pan occasionally to be sure that the potatoes are not sticking. Use a spoon to gently shape the top and sides of the potato cake, keeping the prune filling from leaking out. Transfer the pan to the oven and bake for about 30 minutes, or until the potatoes are well browned and crisp. Invert the potato cake onto a board or serving platter. The potato cake can be made a few hours ahead and set aside at room temperature in the skillet. Reheat in a 450°F. oven for about 10 minutes, or until sizzling hot.

FOR THE STEAK: While the potatoes are cooking, pat the meat dry (it won't sear well if it is wet) and wrap the bone in aluminum foil to prevent it from burning.

Heat $1/8$ inch of canola oil in a heavy ovenproof pan over high heat. Add the steak and sear it for 4 to 5 minutes, or until it is dark brown and crusty on the bottom. Flip the steak and brown the second side for 2 to 3 minutes.

Pour off most of the oil and add the butter to the pan. Place the pan in the oven and roast for about 5 minutes. Baste the meat with the butter and pan juices, turn the steak over, and sprinkle with salt. Continue to cook, basting every 5 minutes, for a total of about 20 to 25 minutes, or until a meat thermometer reads 115°F. for rare meat. Another way to determine if the meat is cooked is to pierce the meat in the center with a cold knife or metal skewer and leave it there for 45 seconds. Hold the tip to your lip; if it is warm, the meat is done. Remove from the oven and let the meat rest in the pan for 10 minutes.

MEANWHILE, FOR THE CHANTERELLE MUSHROOMS: Heat the butter in a skillet over medium heat. Add the mushrooms, season with salt and pepper, and cook for about 5 minutes, or until the mushrooms are tender and slightly "toasty" around the edges and any liquid has evaporated.

TO COMPLETE: Rewarm the sauce over low heat. Remove the string from the steak. Slice the meat against the grain into $1/4$-inch slices. Overlap the slices on the serving plates and place a wedge of the potatoes Anna alongside. (There will be enough potatoes for seconds.) Arrange the chanterelle mushrooms over the steak and spoon some sauce over the top. Garnish with thyme sprigs.

PICTURED ON PAGE 185          MAKES 2 TO 3 GENEROUS SERVINGS

Sometimes we bring a whole pheasant to the table, or a whole roasted foie gras, or a large cut of beef such as this steak, which we serve with crispy potatoes, layered with prunes, and a classic bordelaise sauce. This is an important step to us because it involves the diner in the cooking process.

Above: "Yabba Dabba Do," page 182

**Braising and the Virtue of the Process** I love dishes that are succulent, that have a lot of character, complexity, and depth by virtue of a long cooking process, things like the veal breast or the short ribs in the pot-au-feu. The technique is what satisfies. What I love about these braised items is that they're not just sauté-and-serve. The process behind them requires thought on the part of the cook, and technique, to create something more than what you started with. A filet mignon is a filet mignon—there's little difference between the raw meat and the cooked meat. But short ribs, veal breast—they become completely different entities after they're cooked. They transcend themselves, developing a full, complex, satisfying taste and aroma.

The process of braising short ribs—it could be any kind of braise—is an exquisite thing. First, we make the marinade by cooking the alcohol out of the wine, then adding the aromatics: carrots, onions, herbs. When the mixture cools, we pour it over the meat and let it sit for a day.

The next step is to separate those three elements—marinade, aromatic vegetables, and meat—and work separately with each. First, we strain the marinating liquid, then bring it to a boil. The albumin (proteins) in the meat juices that leached into the marinade solidify and form a clarifying raft, which is removed, leaving a clear mixture. As always, we're searching for the cleanest, brightest possible flavors.

Next, we brown the aromatic vegetables, to develop some of the caramel richness of their sugars. Then we dust the meat with flour and brown it on all sides. That aroma of the browning ribs has a depth to it that is like no other aroma for me. When the meat is browned, we add the browned vegetables and the clarified marinade, then finish the braising liquid with some veal stock. Then we cook the ribs in the oven for five to six hours.

When the short ribs are cooked, we remove them, very gently because they're so succulent and tender they're falling apart, from the cooking liquid. We strain out the aromatics and reduce the liquid to a sauce consistency, skimming it often. Finally, we strain it again and serve the dish.

Braised dishes like the short ribs get better with age. After a day or two, their flavors have had a chance to mature together. These are the kinds of things I like to make at home in the winter and eat over several days.

What we're doing here is taking cheaper, tougher cuts of meat and transforming them into beautiful, tender, exquisite dishes that are far more satisfying than filet mignon or rack of lamb. Again, to me, these dishes are what cooking is all about.

"Pot-au-Feu," page 188

**MARROW BONES**

8 pieces marrow bone (cut 1½ inches long)

About 1 cup all-purpose flour

Kosher salt

Canola oil

**BRAISED SHORT RIBS**

2 pieces prime boneless short ribs (about 1 inch
   thick and 1¾ pounds each) or 3½ pounds
   boneless short ribs or 8 pieces bone-in
   short ribs (about 7 to 8 ounces each)

1 recipe Red Wine Marinade (page 190)

Canola oil

Kosher salt and freshly ground black pepper

Flour for dusting

2 to 3 cups Veal Stock (page 222)

2 to 3 cups Chicken Stock (page 226)

**ROOT VEGETABLES**

2 medium sweet bunch carrots

2 small parsnips

2 small turnips, cut into ¼-inch dice

2 tablespoons sugar

8 baby leeks or small scallions, tough outer layer
   removed and trimmed

16 white pearl onions, peeled

16 red pearl onions, peeled

½ teaspoon red wine vinegar

½ cup tomato diamonds (see page 203)

3 tablespoons chopped Italian parsley

1 pound caul fat (only for boneless short ribs),
   soaked in cold water for 30 minutes (optional)

Canola oil

Gray salt

1 tablespoon finely chopped chives

We use the extraordinary short ribs from Dawson-Baker in Kentucky. The recipe will work with bone-in short ribs as well. Marrow is a traditional element of pot-au-feu, but we flour and pan-roast it so that it's crunchy on the outside and succulent on the inside, adding a whole new dimension to the dish.

I wrap the short ribs in caul fat to create tighter, more compact pieces of meat, but caul fat can be difficult to find. Try ethnic markets or specialty butchers if you would like to use it, but eliminating it will not affect the flavor of the dish much. If you've never used it, though, do try to find some and experiment. Caul fat helps the meat keep its shape, and it bastes the meat as the fat renders.

Begin preparing the short ribs and the marrow the day before you plan to serve this dish.

FOR THE MARROW: Soak the marrow bones in a bowl of ice water for 20 minutes. Drain and remove the marrow from the bones by pushing it out with your finger. If it doesn't come out easily, soak the bones briefly in warm water, just enough to loosen the marrow. Soak the marrow pieces in a bowl of ice water for 12 to 24 hours, changing the water every 6 to 8 hours. (It is important to change the water because as the blood is extracted from the marrow, the water will become saturated with blood and the marrow could spoil.)

FOR THE SHORT RIBS: If you have two large pieces of boneless short ribs, trim the excess fat from the meat (leaving the silverskin attached) and cut each piece against the grain into two pieces. If you have smaller boneless short ribs, there is no need to split them in half. Bone-in short ribs usually don't require any trimming. Place the meat in a well-sealed plastic bag with the marinade and refrigerate for 8 to 24 hours, turning the bag once or twice.

Preheat the oven to 275°F. Remove the meat from the marinade. Strain the marinade into a saucepan and reserve the vegetables. Bring the marinade to a simmer and "clarify" the liquid by skimming off the impurities that rise to the top. Remove from the heat.

Heat ⅛ inch of canola oil in a large skillet over high heat. Season both sides of each piece of meat with salt and pepper and dust with flour, patting off the excess. Place the meat in the hot oil and cook for 2 to 3 minutes on all sides, until well browned (adjusting the heat as necessary). Remove the meat to a heavy ovenproof pot or casserole that holds the pieces in one layer.

Pour off the excess oil from the pan, return to the heat, and sauté the reserved vegetables for a few minutes, or until they begin to caramelize. Spread the vegetables over the meat in an even layer and add the marinade and 2 cups each of veal and chicken stock. The meat should be covered with liquid; if it is not, add more veal and chicken stock as necessary.

Bring the liquid to a simmer on the stove. Cover with a parchment paper lid (see page 190), transfer to the oven, and braise for 5 to 6 hours for boneless short ribs or 3 to 4 hours for ribs with bones, or until the meat is very tender.

Remove the meat from the pot and strain the liquid into a tall narrow container. Discard the vegetables. Once the meat has cooled slightly, cover it and refrigerate it; it can be stored for up to 2 days.

Skim the fat that rises to the top of the braising liquid and strain the liquid several times through a chinois (see page 73) until the chinois remains clean. Reserve one third of the braising liquid for reheating the short ribs and vegetable garnish before serving. Transfer the remaining braising liquid to a saucepan and reduce until it is a sauce consistency (about 2 cups).

FOR THE ROOT VEGETABLES: Cut the vegetables into pieces of about the same size: Starting at the narrow end of each carrot, cut it in an oblique cut (see page 203): First, cut off a diagonal piece about ⅓ inch long, with the knife blade pointing away from you at a 45-degree angle. Roll the carrot a quarter turn and cut another piece at the same angle. Repeat the process until the carrot widens. Slice the wider part of the carrot lengthwise in half and continue to turn and cut the carrot. If the pieces become too large, cut the carrot lengthwise in half again to keep the finished pieces equal in size. Use the same method to cut the parsnips. Keep them separate.

Blanch the carrots, parsnips, and turnips together in boiling salted water sweetened with the sugar until completely tender. Remove the vegetables with a slotted spoon or skimmer and chill in ice water; drain when cold and set aside.

Add the leeks to the boiling water and blanch until tender. Remove to another ice-water bath. Repeat with the white pearl onions and finally the red pearl onions, adding the red wine vinegar, which will help the onions keep their red color, to the boiling water. When the vegetables are cold, drain and dry them on paper towels.

TO COMPLETE: If using boneless short ribs, trim the sides to even them. Cut each piece of rib into rectangular pieces about 1½ inches by 2½ inches. (The size will depend largely on the form of your meat.) If you are wrapping the meat in caul fat, dry the caul fat well. Wrap each piece of meat in caul fat, rolling it over to encase it in a double layer of caul fat; you should still see the meat through the fat.

In a skillet that will hold the ribs comfortably in one layer, heat ⅛ inch of oil over medium-high heat. The oil should be hot but not smoking. Place the ribs in the pan and cook until golden brown on all six sides, about 30 seconds per side. If you have used caul fat, it will be almost completely rendered but should still form a translucent "seal" around the short ribs. Transfer the browned ribs to a pot where they fit in one layer.

Place enough of the braising liquid to just cover the cooked vegetables in a saucepan and set aside. Add the remaining braising liquid to the pot with the ribs. The ribs should be floating in liquid; if necessary, add veal stock. Bring the liquid to a simmer. Remove from the heat and cover the meat with a lid or parchment paper lid (see page 190). Keep in a warm spot or in a 300°F. oven until ready to serve, or for up to 45 minutes.

Add the cooked carrots, parsnips, turnips, red and white pearl onions, and the tomato diamonds to the reserved braising liquid in the saucepan and heat gently to warm. Add the chopped parsley.

Meanwhile, cook the bone marrow: This step should be done at the last minute before serving. Drain and dry the pieces of bone marrow and trim the ends of each to create a flat surface. Place the flour in a small container or on a plate. Season the bone marrow on all sides with kosher salt. Generously coat each piece in the flour and lightly top off any excess. Heat ⅛ inch of oil in a large nonstick skillet over medium heat until hot. (If the oil is too hot, the flour will burn before the marrow has a chance to crisp; if the oil is too cold, the marrow will melt before the outside is crisp—and you'll be left with a ring of flour and no marrow. Working with half the marrow pieces at a time, stand each piece of marrow in the pan and cook until the ends are golden brown, 30 to 45 seconds per end. Lay the pieces of marrow on their sides and roll them to brown lightly on all sides, 2 to 3 minutes. The outside should be crispy but the inside should still have a gelatinous consistency. Remove from the pan and keep in a warm place.

Using a slotted spoon, arrange an equal amount of the vegetables on each serving plate. Place the leeks in the vegetable braising liquid to warm for a minute.

Place the short ribs on top of the vegetables and spoon the sauce over the sides, so that it lightly coats the meat and drizzles onto the vegetables. Lay a piece of bone marrow over the top of each rib. Sprinkle gray salt and then the chopped chives over the bone marrow. Top each with a baby leek.

PICTURED ON PAGE 187                                           MAKES 8 SERVINGS

## PARCHMENT PAPER LIDS

Very rarely will you see a pot with its lid on it in my kitchen. I prefer parchment paper lids, because they allow some evaporation as well as a long cooking time, and they also protect the surface of the meat from becoming caramelized as it cooks. It's like having a lid and not having a lid at the same time.

To make a parchment lid, cut or tear a square of parchment bigger than the pot to be covered. Fold two opposite corners together to form a triangle, then fold this triangle in half into a smaller triangle; it will have two short sides and one long side. Position the triangle so that one of the short sides faces you. Fold this bottom edge up, making a narrow triangle, and crease it, maintaining the point of the triangle, as if you were making a paper airplane. Fold this "wing" over again, maintaining the point, and continue folding in this manner until you get to the other side—about five or six folds in all. You should finish with a very slender triangle.

To measure the size, place the tip over the center of the pot to be covered, mark the edge of the pot with your thumb, and cut the end off here. Then cut a quarter inch off the tip. Unfold your triangle. It will be a circle the size of your pot, with a steam hole in the center. Place this paper lid in the pot so that it rests gently on the food you're cooking.

## MARINATING MEATS USING WINES OR SPIRITS

If you're marinating anything with alcohol, cook the alcohol off first. Alcohol doesn't tenderize; cooking tenderizes. Alcohol in a marinade in effect cooks the exterior of the meat, preventing the meat from fully absorbing the flavors in the marinade.

Raw alcohol itself doesn't do anything good to meat. So put your wine or spirits in a pan, add your aromatics, cook off the alcohol, let it cool, and then pour it over your meat. This way you have the richness of the fruit of the wine or Cognac or whatever you're using, but you don't have that chemical reaction of "burning" the meat with alcohol or its harsh raw flavor.

I don't know if there's a place for raw alcohol, as opposed to wine that is cooked in some way, in the preparation of haute cuisine. And if you're serious about eating, if you're serious about food and wine, you should consider the fact that raw alcohol in food will overwhelm the wine you're serving with that food.

### RED WINE MARINADE

| | |
|---|---|
| One 750-ml bottle red wine | ½ cup onions cut into 1-inch mirepoix |
| ½ cup carrots cut into 1-inch | (see page 203) |
| mirepoix (see page 203) | 3 cloves garlic, smashed |
| ⅔ cup leeks cut into 1-inch mirepoix | 10 sprigs Italian parsley |
| (white and pale green parts | 2 sprigs thyme |
| only, see page 203) | 1 bay leaf |

This marinade, used in several dishes, can also be made with white wine when appropriate—with veal, for example. Use a wine that is acceptable for drinking, such as a Cabernet Sauvignon or Sauvignon Blanc. Always cook off all the alcohol first, or the alcohol will begin to cook your meat (see above).

Place all the ingredients in a wide pot and bring to a boil. Tilt the pan away from the burner and carefully ignite the wine with a match. Allow the alcohol to burn off, then light it again. If there are no flames, the alcohol is gone. Cool the marinade, then pour over the meat and marinate for 8 to 24 hours.

MAKES A GENEROUS QUART

Braised Breast of Veal with Yellow Corn Polenta Cakes, page 192

# Braised Breast of Veal with Yellow Corn Polenta Cakes, Glazed Vegetables, and Sweet Garlic

VEAL

1 Bobby veal breast (about 5 pounds)

Kosher salt and freshly ground black pepper

Canola oil

2 tablespoons Dijon mustard

1/2 cup panko (Japanese bread crumbs;
   see Sources, page 315) or dry bread
   crumbs, finely ground in a blender
   and sifted through a fine strainer

BRAISING LIQUID

1 1/2 cups leeks cut into 1-inch mirepoix
   (see page 203)

1 cup carrots cut into 1-inch mirepoix
   (see page 203)

1 cup onions cut into 1-inch mirepoix
   (see page 203)

1/2 large head garlic, cut in half, root end and
   loose skin removed

1 bay leaf

4 sprigs thyme

1/2 cup Italian parsley sprigs

5 cups Chicken Stock (page 226), water,
   or a combination

3 cups Veal Stock (page 222)

POLENTA

2 1/2 cups Chicken Stock (page 226)

3 cups water

1/2 teaspoon minced garlic

1 1/2 cups polenta

8 tablespoons (4 ounces) unsalted butter, at room
   temperature

2 tablespoons mascarpone

2 tablespoons minced chives

Kosher salt and freshly ground black pepper

Flour for dusting

SAUCE

1 cup reduced braising liquid (from above)

2 tablespoons finely minced shallots

1 tablespoon finely minced Italian parsley

1/4 cup Beurre Monté (page 135)

Kosher salt and freshly ground black pepper

VEGETABLE GARNISH

Thirty-two 1-inch pieces carrot, turned (see page
   203) or cut into 1/4-inch-thick batons

24 batons celery root (1 inch by 1/4 inch)

24 fluted ovals of turnip (see page 203)

32 parisienne balls of beet (see page 203)

8 cloves garlic, peeled

2 teaspoons unsalted butter

Pinch of sugar

1 tablespoon canola oil

1/3 cup Beurre Monté (page 135)

1 teaspoon finely minced chives


2 teaspoons finely minced chives

A week before the French Laundry opened, I cooked this in my oven at home for the original crew, and we sat out on the back deck and ate together. It was the last time we did that, so this is a meaningful recipe to me, an original French Laundry dish.

The veal breast (ask your butcher for a Bobby veal breast; from a very young animal, it's smaller than a regular breast) is braised, then cooled; the bones are removed and the breast is folded over to double its thickness, cut into serving portions (I cut it into rounds), and sautéed to reheat. It's served on a polenta cake with root vegetables and a sauce made from the braising liquid.

This recipe must be started a day ahead.

TO BRAISE THE VEAL: Preheat the oven to 325°F.

Trim the bottom of the veal breast of excess connective tissue. Season both sides of the breast with salt and pepper. In a heavy ovenproof pot large enough to contain the veal breast and the braising liquid, heat 1/8 inch of oil over medium heat until it is so hot that you hear it "pop." Place the veal breast skin side down in the pot and sear until it is crispy and a rich golden brown. Turn the breast and sear the other side the same way (the second side won't brown as evenly as the first side because of the curvature of the ribs). Remove the meat and drain off any excess fat that has accumulated in the pot.

Add the leeks, carrots, onions, garlic, bay leaf, thyme, and parsley to the pot. Cook for 3 to 4 minutes, so the vegetables begin to caramelize. Return the meat to the pot, bone side down, add the chicken and veal stocks, and cover with a parchment lid (see page 190). Bring the liquid to a simmer on top of the stove, then transfer to the oven and cook for 3 1/2 to 4 hours, or until you can slide out the rib bones without any resistance.

Using two large spatulas, carefully remove the meat from the pan.

(Lift from underneath the meat, or it may fall apart because it is so tender.) Place the veal on a cutting board, bone side up. While the meat is still hot, use your fingers and a knife to remove all the gummy pieces of connective tissue, being careful not to remove too much meat with it. Pull out the rib bones. Remove all the cartilage that runs the length of the side of the breast. This white, soft cartilage will be larger at the top of the breast and get smaller as you approach the bottom of the breast; you will need to feel under the surface, because not all the pieces of cartilage are visible.

Season the top side of the breast with salt and pepper. Fold the breast in half and season both sides. Place the veal breast on a parchment-lined baking sheet. Cover the meat with another piece of parchment and lay another baking sheet on top. Place a light weight on the baking sheet and refrigerate overnight to flatten the meat. (The weighted veal breast should be about ¾ inch high.)

Strain the braising liquid through a China cap (see page 73) and then through a chinois (see page 73), without pressing on anything that remains in the strainer. (Pushing through any solids or thick and pasty liquid would cloud your finished sauce.) Cool down the strained liquid (There should be about 3 quarts) in a container set over ice. Once cool, cover and refrigerate overnight.

The next day, remove any fat that may have solidified on top of the braising liquid. (The liquid will probably have gelled from the gelatin in the meat.) Place the braising liquid in a pan, heat slowly to a simmer, and reduce the liquid until it is a deep red brown, thick, and glossy; you should have about 2 cups. Set aside 1 cup of sauce for this dish. (The remaining sauce can be frozen for future use.)

FOR THE POLENTA: Bring the chicken stock, water, and garlic to a boil in a saucepan. Whisking constantly, pour in the polenta. Return the liquid to a simmer and cook the polenta over very low heat, stirring occasionally, for 25 to 35 minutes, or until the polenta is thick and smooth.

When the polenta is cooked, stir in the butter, mascarpone, chives, and salt and pepper to taste. Spread the polenta in a 9- by 13-inch baking pan. Let it cool to room temperature, then cover the surface with plastic wrap and refrigerate. (This recipe makes extra polenta, but it will keep for a few days for another meal.)

FOR THE VEGETABLE GARNISH: Place the carrots, celery root, and turnips in a pot of lightly salted cold water, bring to a boil, and cook until tender. Meanwhile, cook the beets the same way in a small pot (so they don't discolor the other vegetables). Remove the blanched carrots, celery, and turnips to a bowl of ice water to cool. Chill the beets separately in another bowl of ice water (the beets should be kept separate until ready to serve so they don't discolor the other vegetables).

Put the garlic in a small saucepan of cold water and bring to a boil. Drain the garlic in a strainer and rinse under cold running water. Repeat the procedure two times, but the last time, boil the garlic cloves until they are tender.

TO COMPLETE: With a 2-inch round cutter (or similar size), cut 8 rounds from the polenta. Use the same cutter to cut 8 rounds from the veal breast. Brush the pieces of veal breast with the mustard and dredge them in the crumbs.

Heat about ⅛ inch of canola oil in each of two ovenproof skillets over medium heat. Coat the pieces of polenta with flour, patting off any excess. Add the veal breast to one skillet and the polenta to the other. Cook for 2 to 3 minutes on each side, or until evenly browned and hot. (Shake the pan containing the veal; when the meat moves freely, it is ready to turn.) If the meat or polenta browns before the centers are hot, the skillets can be placed in a 350°F. oven to finish cooking.

Meanwhile, drain the vegetables. Melt the butter with the sugar in a small skillet. When the butter is hot, add the garlic cloves and sauté for 2 to 3 minutes over low heat, until golden brown. Set aside.

Heat the canola oil in a medium skillet. When it is hot, sauté the blanched carrots, celery root, and turnips over medium heat until they have colored slightly. Drain the oil from the skillet, lower the heat, and add the beurre monté and the chives. Keep the vegetables warm over low heat; do not boil.

Warm the sauce in a small saucepan. Stir in the shallots, parsley, and beurre monté. Season to taste with salt and pepper.

Center a pool of sauce on each serving plate, top with a round of polenta, and cover with a piece of veal breast. Stir the beets into the warm vegetable garnish and spoon the vegetables and garlic cloves over the veal. Sprinkle with the chives.

PICTURED ON PAGE 191                     MAKES 8 SERVINGS

The first day I was in the French Laundry kitchen, I watched Thomas Keller seam out tuna—that is, remove the sticky silver membranes between the layers of pure flesh—to make tartare. I asked, "Why are you doing that?"

Thomas halted to stare at me. Then he peeled one of the membranes off his board, extended it like a dangling mixture of silverskin and saliva, and said, "Eat it." I figured he couldn't be serious. "Go ahead," he said.

I took it, I chewed it, and I swallowed it.

Thomas said, "Sometimes you have to experience the really bad in order to avoid it." Then he went back to his cutting.

In 1989, Keith Martin, a stockbroker in downtown Pittsburgh, came home from his office and told his wife, Mary, that he was going to become a farmer. The whole family thought Keith was crazy.

"The first time I walked into Edgar Miller's barn," Keith explains, referring to one of his brokerage clients, "it didn't smell bad to me. It smelled good. Something locked into me and I knew I was in the right place."

So at the age of thirty-one, he quit his job, cashed in his small pension, and used it to by a flock of ewes and yearlings and one fence. He raised lamb the way he believed was right, using no processed feed, no antibiotics, letting the animals grow in the best possible conditions. He couldn't compete with the big growers at the livestock auctions. So he tried to sell his lamb on his own, picking up a restaurant here, a specialty grocer there, going broke fast. Then Thomas Keller, who'd heard about Keith from a Pittsburgh food writer, called and asked to try his lamb.

"It's the most extraordinary lamb," Thomas says. "The fat content is perfect. It really tastes like lamb. Some people don't like it because they're not used to what good lamb tastes like. I feel lucky to have found Keith. He loves what he does so much, it really shows up in the product." Keith will send Keller lamb sweetbreads and hanger steak and kidney. He'll bone out thirty lamb cheeks, painstaking work. He'll send brains and other, more obscure innards. "All kinds of goofy stuff," says Keith.

From the moment of conception, Keith's lambs grow at their natural rate.

"There's a glow about them when they're in good order," Keith says of his flock. "There's a sheen to their coats. See how tight and crinkly that wool is. Look how pink the flesh is when you part the wool."

When I ask him what makes the meat taste so good, Keith says, "It's what they eat." And he runs off to what looks like bales of hay stacked at the far end of the barn. Keith yanks out a handful of dried grass—alfalfa and clover he grew, cut, and baled the previous summer. Keith rushes me. He says, "Taste this."

I take it, I chew it, and I swallow it. Keith eats some, too, and nods at me, smiling.

Keith does not give his lamb antibiotics, and because they are susceptible to respiratory infection, he must take special care of them in the winter. He will lie down in their bedding, feel the dryness of the hay they live on, breathe the air that they breathe to make sure they're completely comfortable.

Once, when their bedding was foul, he called the hired man in charge of spreading fresh hay. He brought the man into the pen area and said, "Lie down." The hired man looked at the hay, which was soaked with urine and excrement. "Go on," Keith said. The man did, and when he stood, his clothes were soaked with urine. After that, the man kept the bedding fresh.

Sometimes you have to experience the really bad in order to avoid it. —M.R.

Flageolets and leg of lamb is a classic dish; I've simply added a few more elements, notably fresh beans. Beans are one of the gifts of summer; I love their freshness and variety. We grow many kinds of beans in the garden at the French Laundry. Here we use pole beans, fresh soybeans, and dried beans. I use the term *cassoulet*—the name of a classical French peasant stew of beans and meat—because we cook the dried beans very slowly with aromatics to develop that creaminess that makes a cassoulet so special. The important step is to make the fresh beans as creamy in texture as the dried beans, which I do with the butter in the sauce.

# Double Rib Lamb Chops with Cassoulet of Summer Beans and Rosemary

**CASSOULET OF BEANS**

2 tablespoons dried marrow beans
(or other white beans), soaked overnight
at room temperature in 1 cup water

2 tablespoons dried cranberry beans, soaked
overnight at room temperature in 1 cup water

½ cup Chicken Stock (page 226)

Two 2-inch sections leek

Two 2-inch sections carrot

Two 2-inch-long onion wedges

1 recipe "Quick" Lamb Sauce (page 228)

1 teaspoon unsalted butter

10 large green beans, blanched until tender
(see Big-Pot Blanching, page 58), chilled in
ice water, drained, and cut on the bias into
1-inch pieces

10 large yellow wax beans, blanched until tender
(see Big-Pot Blanching, page 58), chilled in
ice water, drained, and cut on the bias into
1-inch pieces

¼ cup peeled fava beans, germs removed
(see page 80), blanched until tender
(see Big-Pot Blanching, page 58), chilled in
ice water, and drained

¼ cup fresh soybeans (see Sources, page 315),
blanched until tender (see Big-Pot Blanching,
page 58), chilled in ice water, and drained

2 tablespoons tomato diamonds (see page 203)

2 teaspoons Brunoise (page 155)

Kosher salt and freshly ground black pepper

**LAMB**

6 double-cut rib lamb chops, trimmed
of excess fat and silverskin and bones
frenched (about 4 to 5 ounces each)

Kosher salt and freshly ground black pepper

Canola oil

2 tablespoons (1 ounce) unsalted butter

3 cloves garlic, split and crushed

6 sprigs thyme

1 sprig rosemary, leaves only

Rosemary Oil (page 166)

TO COOK THE DRIED BEANS: Remove and discard any bean skins that have risen to the top of the water. Drain and rinse the beans and place them in two separate small pots. Add cold water to cover by 2 inches and bring to a boil. Remove and discard any beans that come to the surface. Drain the beans and run under cold water to cool.

Return the beans to the pots and cover each with half the chicken stock and enough water to cover the beans by 1 inch. Add a piece of leek, carrot, and onion to each pot and slowly bring to a simmer. Any beans that have not hydrated and any loose skins will come to the top; skim them off and discard. Simmer the beans for about 1 hour, or until they are tender. The beans can be cooked up to a day ahead and refrigerated in their cooking liquid.

FOR THE LAMB: Loop a piece of kitchen twine around the bone of a lamb chop just above the meat, wrap both ends of the twine around the meat, bring them back to the bone, and tie the twine around the bone to give a uniform shape to the chop. Cut off the excess twine and repeat with the remaining chops. Wrap the bones in aluminum foil to protect them from burning, season the chops with salt and pepper, and let rest at room temperature for an hour.

TO COMPLETE: Preheat the oven to 375°F.

Heat ⅛ inch of canola oil in a large skillet over medium-high heat. Add the lamb chops and sauté for about 3 minutes to brown on the bottom. Turn the chops and continue to cook for another 3 minutes. Place the chops on their sides and rotate them to brown the sides, another 1 to 2 minutes. The chops should be well browned but still slightly rare.

Remove most of the fat from the pan and add the butter, basting the lamb chops with the butter as it melts. Top the lamb with the garlic cloves and sprigs of thyme. Place the pan in the oven for about 4 minutes, or until the meat is medium-rare; an instant-read thermometer should register 115° to 120°F. Remove the pan from the oven and let the meat rest for 3 to 4 minutes.

While the lamb is cooking, drain the cooked beans and combine the beans and about half of the lamb sauce in a saucepan. Bring to a simmer, skim the sauce, and warm through, about 1 to 2 minutes. Stir in the butter, then add the green and yellow beans, the fava beans, soybeans, tomato diamonds, brunoise, and salt and pepper to taste.

Meanwhile, place the remaining lamb sauce in a small pot and simmer over low heat for 3 to 4 minutes to reduce the glaze (about ¼ cup).

Place a portion of the warm ragout on each plate. Stand a lamb chop on its side with the bone facing up over the beans. Scatter a few rosemary leaves over the ragout and drizzle a few drops of rosemary oil over the beans and the lamb.

MAKES 6 SERVINGS

## Bellwether Farm Baby Lamb—Five Cuts Served with Provençal Vegetables, Braised Cipollini Onions, and Thyme Oil

I value this dish as a chef because it's a learning experience for my staff. It gives them an understanding of how to break down an entire four-legged animal and where the individual parts come from. These things are important for any chef to know.

The exciting part about this elaborate preparation is cooking the entire animal in different ways: braising the neck, forequarters, and breast; Frenching the rack; stuffing the saddle; and boning out the leg, marinating it with salt, pepper, thyme, garlic, and mustard, tying it up, and roasting it. Then, making a stock from the liquid you've braised the neck and breast in, making a quick sauce from that stock with the bones left over from the rack and the saddle and the leg. The different aromas that emerge when you're doing all this are phenomenal.

And then the small miracle: to put the animal back together, presenting the parts of the entire lamb on a single plate. This, to me, is what cooking is all about.

We use the Callahan family's Bellwether Farm baby lamb, but any fresh baby lamb can be used. Here is how it is prepared at the French Laundry.

Butcher 1 dressed baby lamb (22 to 25 pounds) to yield: 1 neck, 2 pieces of breast (trimming the rib bones 2 inches from the eye), 2 shoulders, 1 saddle (split and deboned), 1 rack (split), 2 legs, and 4 shanks. Save the bones for the sauce and the trimmings for a *farce* (stuffing).

**FOR THE SADDLE:** Make a *farce* with the lamb trimmings. Remove the silverskin from the loin and tenderloin and season the pieces of meat. Spread the *farce* on the inside (the bone side) of the sirloin, place the tenderloin over it, and wrap the pieces three times in caul fat. Tie the pieces to maintain their shape.

**FOR THE RACK:** French the bones, tie the racks to maintain their shape, and season with salt and pepper.

**FOR THE LEGS:** Debone and butterfly the legs and rub with a mixture of minced garlic, extra virgin olive oil, Dijon mustard, chopped thyme, and gray salt. Reform the legs and tie them.

For the shanks, shoulders, breasts, and neck: Braise in lamb stock in the oven for about 3½ hours, or until tender. Cool the lamb pieces in the stock for an hour, then remove them and strain the stock. Reserve the breasts and remove the meat from the shanks, shoulders, and neck.

**TO MAKE RILLETTES:** Reduce some of the lamb braising liquid to a glaze (straining several times). Shred the meat and add it to the glaze, along with some butter, extra virgin olive oil, brunoise, salt, and pepper. Roll the rillettes in plastic wrap to form a log 1¼ inches in diameter. Refrigerate.

When the log is chilled, cut into ½-inch rounds. Just before serving, coat the rillettes with panko (Japanese bread crumbs) and sauté in clarified butter.

**FOR THE BREAST:** Follow the cleaning, weighting, and cooking instructions for veal breast (see page 192), brushing them with Dijon mustard and coating them with bread crumbs mixed with minced parsley and garlic before cooking.

**FOR THE SAUCE:** Make a "quick" sauce (see page 228) with the lamb bones and remaining braising liquid.

**TO COOK:** Preheat the oven to 350°F.

Sauté the legs in canola oil to brown; add butter, garlic, and thyme to the pan and place in the oven for 30 to 35 minutes. Cook the saddle and rack in the same way and place in the oven for about 10 minutes. Cook the meat until it is medium. There is no fat in a baby lamb, so it is cooked longer than an older lamb; if it is undercooked, it will be tough. Sauté the kidney at the last minute (it should be cooked until just pink).

**TO COMPLETE:** Slice all the meats. Place a ring of thyme-infused oil in the center of each plate. Fill the ring with sauce. Place a base of the lamb breast on the sauce. Top the breast with a braised cipollini onion and Provençal vegetables. Arrange the other cuts of lamb around the vegetables, ending with a piece of the kidney. Garnish with thyme leaves.

PICTURED ON PAGE 200                    MAKES 14 TO 20 SERVINGS

# Venison Chop with Pan-Roasted Butternut Squash and Braised Shallots

**BRAISED SHALLOTS**

2 large (2 ounces each) shallots, unpeeled

6 sprigs thyme

2 tablespoons olive oil

2 teaspoons Brunoise (page 155)

1 tablespoon tomato diamonds (see page 203)

1/4 cup Beurre Monté (page 135)

Six 3-ounce venison chops (see Sources, page 315), cut 1 1/4 inches thick, bones frenched

Kosher salt and freshly ground black pepper

Canola oil

**BUTTERNUT SQUASH**

1 butternut squash (with a neck at least 4 inches long)

Kosher salt and freshly ground black pepper

3 cups Chicken Stock (page 226) or water

Canola oil

3/4 cup "Quick" Venison Sauce (page 228)

6 small pieces crisp cooked bacon

6 sprigs chervil

I like venison because it's low in fat and high in protein. You can find high-quality venison year-round, but its association with winter lingers, so we serve it with autumn or winter vegetables and fruits: quinces, squashes, beets. Don't cook it past medium-rare, because the lean meat dries out quickly.

FOR THE SHALLOTS: Preheat the oven to 350°F.

Place the shallots and thyme sprigs on a square of aluminum foil, drizzle with the olive oil, and enclose in the foil. Bake for 30 minutes, or until the shallots are soft. Peel the shallots, cut off the root end, and cut into small wedges. Place the shallots in a small saucepan.

FOR THE VENISON: Loop a piece of kitchen twine around the bone of a venison chop just above the meat, wrap both ends of the twine around the meat, bring them back to the bone, and tie the twine around the bone to give a uniform shape to the chop. Cut off the excess twine and repeat with the remaining chops.

FOR THE SQUASH: Cut off the neck of the squash and peel it (reserve the remaining squash for another use). Cut six 1/2-inch-thick rounds from the neck of the squash. With a 2- to 2 1/2-inch cutter, cut a round from each slice. Score one side of each round in a diamond pattern.

Season to taste with salt and pepper. Bring the chicken stock or water (lightly salt the water) to a boil and blanch the squash rounds until tender. Drain the slices.

TO COMPLETE: Season the venison chops. Heat 1/8 inch of canola oil in a large heavy sauté pan. When the oil is hot, add the chops and cook on the first side for 2 to 3 minutes to brown. The pan should be hot enough that when you shake the pan after about 10 seconds, the chops move freely. Don't move the chops until they move on their own. Turn the chops and brown the second side for 2 to 3 minutes for medium-rare, basting the chops several times with the oil in the pan.

Meanwhile, in a second large sauté pan, heat 1/8 inch of canola oil. Add the butternut squash, scored side down, and sauté until slightly browned on the bottom. Turn and continue cooking until the squash is heated through.

Add the brunoise, tomato diamonds, and beurre monté to the shallots and heat through. Warm the venison sauce.

Place a spoonful of venison sauce on each plate and top with a round of squash and a venison chop. Divide the shallots among the chops, set a piece of bacon on each bone, and garnish each with a sprig of chervil.

MAKES 6 SERVINGS

For about three months in the spring and early summer, we get three or four baby lambs a week. Twenty-two to twenty-five pounds, never fed anything other than mother's milk. Because they're so special, we've composed a single course that features various parts of the animal on a single plate.

Above, right: Bellwether Farm Baby Lamb, page 198

# Vegetable cuts

OBLIQUE CUTS

BATONS

PARISIENNE BALLS

TOMATO DIAMONDS

JULIENNE

BRUNOISE

MINCE/DICE

FLUTED OVAL

DICE

TURNED

LARGE MIREPOIX

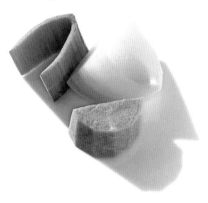

SMALL MIREPOIX

### OBLIQUE CUT

This cut is used on elongated vegetables such as carrots and parsnips. Starting at the narrow end of each vegetable, cut a diagonal piece about ⅓ inch long, with the knife blade pointing away from you at a 45-degree angle. Roll the vegetable a quarter turn and cut another piece at the same angle. Repeat the process until the vegetable widens. Slice in half lengthwise and continue to turn and cut. If the pieces become too large, cut lengthwise again to keep pieces equal in size.

### BATONS

Using a mandoline or sharp knife, cut vegetables into sheets of the desired thickness. Trim to desired length. Cut crosswise to form batons of an even thickness and width.

### PARISIENNE BALLS

Scoop very small balls using a #12 melon baller.

### TOMATO DIAMONDS

Peel and quarter a tomato. Place skin side down, cut away the interior, and trim the ribs to create an even sheet. Turn pieces over and cut into ¼-inch strips. Cut strips on the diagonal into diamond shapes.

### JULIENNE

Trim the vegetable into the desired length. Using a mandoline, slice the vegetable into thin sheets. Overlap the sheets to form a line of the vegetable. Finely slice the sheets to form a julienne.

### BRUNOISE

Small dice of approximately ¹⁄₁₆ inch.

### MINCE/DICE

*To mince:* Using a mandoline or sharp knife, cut the vegetables into thin slices. Chop finely.

*To dice an onion or shallot:* Peel and cut the vegetable in half through the root end. Place cut side down on a cutting board. Slice vertically in ⅛-inch slices, cutting forward from within ½ inch of the root end, leaving the onion or shallot intact. Repeat with horizontal slices. Cut vertical slices across the onion or shallot to form the dice.

### DICE

Slice batons into the desired thickness, leaving the pieces as long as possible. Cut across into squares to form the dice. (The dice shown here is ¼ inch.)

### FLUTED OVAL

Scoop using a fluted, oblong vegetable scoop.

### TURNED

Cut the vegetables into pieces slightly larger than the desired size of the shaped vegetable. Using a paring knife, cut from top to bottom to "whittle" a football shape.

### MIREPOIX (LARGE AND SMALL)

Cut the vegetables into pieces of the same approximate size. The longer the vegetables will be cooked, the larger the pieces of mirepoix. Large mirepoix is primarily used in stocks and small mirepoix in the making of sauces.

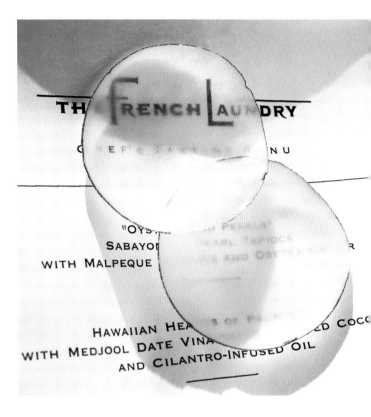

### PAPER-THIN (ABOVE)

Using a mandoline, cut slices as thinly as possible from the fruit or vegetable.

# The Importance of **Rabbits**

From 1980 to 1983, I worked in the kitchen of a small restaurant near Catskill, New York, on a patch of the Hudson River Valley so remote it didn't have an address. The sixty-seat restaurant was owned by René and Paulette Macary (she remains its proprietor today). La Rive, named thus because it sat on a wide running creek, was a fruitful training ground, and New York State had extraordinary livestock. Beautiful veal came down from Utica. I found a man who raised spectacular pigeons. I began to ask these farmers for unusual items to experiment with, things like pigs' ears, cockscombs, duck testicles.

One day, I asked my rabbit purveyor to show me how to kill, skin, and eviscerate a rabbit. I had never done this, and I figured if I was going to cook rabbit, I should know it from its live state through the slaughtering, skinning, and butchering, and then the cooking. The guy showed up with twelve live rabbits. He hit one over the head with a club, knocked it out, slit its throat, pinned it to a board, skinned it—the whole bit. Then he left.

I don't know what else I expected, but there I was out in the grass behind the restaurant, just me and eleven cute bunnies, all of which were on the menu that week and had to find their way into a braising pan.

I clutched at the first rabbit. I had a hard time killing it. It screamed. Rabbits scream and this one screamed loudly. Then it broke its leg trying to get away. It was terrible.

The next ten rabbits didn't scream and I was quick with the kill, but that first screaming rabbit not only gave me a lesson in butchering, it also taught me about waste. Because killing those rabbits had been such an awful experience, I would not squander them. I would use all my powers as a chef to ensure that those rabbits were beautiful. It's very easy to go to a grocery store and buy meat, then accidentally overcook it and throw it away. A cook sautéing a rabbit loin, working the line on a Saturday night, a million pans going, plates going out the door, who took that loin a little too far, doesn't hesitate, just dumps it in the garbage and fires another. Would that cook, I wonder, have let his attention stray from that loin had he killed the rabbit himself? No. Should a cook squander anything, ever?

It was a simple lesson.

# Saddle of Rabbit in Applewood-Smoked Bacon with Caramelized Fennel and Fennel Oil

**CARAMELIZED FENNEL**

3 fennel bulbs (about 7 ounces each)

2 sprigs thyme

2 pieces star anise

1 teaspoon fennel seeds

1 bay leaf

¼ cup kosher salt

Canola oil

**RABBIT**

3 "super" rabbit saddles (see Sources, page 315)

18 thin slices bacon, preferably applewood-smoked

Kosher salt and freshly ground black pepper

Canola oil

½ cup "Quick" Rabbit Sauce (page 228)

Fennel Oil (page 166), in a squeeze bottle

6 sprigs fennel

I love using rabbit, which we get from co-ops in Oregon. It tastes neither like chicken nor like wild hare. It's moist and incredibly tender. It's like fish in that it's a good vehicle for tastes. Here it carries the bacon and fennel flavors beautifully.

Serve rabbit no more than five to ten minutes after cooking it, as it has a tendency to become mealy if it rests too long.

For this recipe, we do not use the legs. D'Artagnan sells what they call a "super" saddle, the saddle with the ribs attached, including the kidney—the three parts of the rabbit you'll need for this dish.

FOR THE CARAMELIZED FENNEL: Trim the tops and root ends from the fennel bulbs and cut an X into the root end of each. Place the fennel in a pot, cover with cold water, and add the remaining ingredients except the oil. Bring the water to a boil, cover the pot, and simmer for about 45 minutes, or until the fennel is tender to the core when tested with a knife. Drain the fennel and refrigerate.

When the fennel bulbs are cold, cut 2 center-cut slices, about ½ inch each, from each bulb.

FOR THE RABBIT: Remove the kidneys and peel off the outer membranes. Set aside.

Separate the racks from the saddles, but leave the last rib attached to the saddle. Using kitchen shears or a sharp heavy knife, split each rack lengthwise in half to form two individual racks.

To bone the saddles, use a sharp boning knife and remove the loins and tenderloins. Trim the flaps (flanks) attached to the saddle to 1 inch wide. Season the loins and tenderloins with salt and pepper and replace the tenderloins on each loin. Fold the flaps around the meat to form a compact cylinder. Arrange 6 slices of bacon on a work surface,

overlapping them so they form a rectangle as wide as the length of one loin. Repeat to make two more rectangles. Season each piece of meat, lay it across the bacon slices, and roll the rabbit loin up in the bacon. Tie each cylinder with butcher's twine at ¾-inch intervals.

To french the bones of the rabbit racks, scrape the ends of the bones with a knife to release the fat and reveal the end of the bones. Using a towel to grip the fat, pull it away from the bones in one piece. Trim away any reamaining fat. Season the meat with salt and pepper.

TO COMPLETE: Preheat the oven to 350°F.

TO COOK THE RABBIT: Heat about ⅛ inch of canola oil in a large skillet over medium-high heat. Sauté the saddles, rolling them around from time to time, for about 5 minutes, or until they are evenly browned. Transfer them to a baking pan and place in the oven for about 5 minutes, or until cooked to medium, while you finish the dish.

Pour off any bacon fat remaining in the skillet and add the racks to the skillet. Sauté them, turning to brown on all sides, until they are cooked to medium, 3 to 4 minutes. During the last minute of cooking, add the kidneys and sauté briefly.

Meanwhile, heat ⅛ inch of canola oil in a second large skillet. Add the fennel slices and sauté them until they are slightly caramelized, about 2 minutes per side.

Warm the sauce.

Cut each saddle and rack into two pieces. Cut each kidney in half.

Squeeze a ring of fennel oil onto each plate and spoon the sauce into the center to fill the rings. Center a slice of fennel on the sauce. Arrange a piece of saddle, rack, and kidney on top, and garnish each portion of rabbit with a fennel sprig.

MAKES 6 SERVINGS

# The Importance of **Offal**

Roland Henin taught me how to cook tripe. This was another critical step for me. At La Rive, I had become interested in offal, the innards that were in abundance in the rural Hudson Valley in the early 1980s—brains, kidneys, liver, testicles, stomach, lungs. The owners of La Rive, who were French, loved offal because in France it is cooked beautifully, but it was rarely used in American restaurants at the time.

Not long after I arrived at La Rive, Henin began teaching at the Culinary Institute of America, an hour south of where I was. He visited me occasionally on weekends, and every now and then I'd sit in on one of his classes. When I couldn't figure something out, or the food didn't behave the way I thought it would, I could ask Henin, because he was right there.

It was at La Rive that Henin taught me that the true test of a chef is how well he can cook offal. Because of the killing of the rabbits, I knew that to waste anything was about as close to sin as a chef gets. Furthermore, having failed to learn to truss a chicken early enough, I did not want to fall short in failing to learn to cook offal. At La Rive, I cooked alone and could therefore make mistakes without being humiliated, as so many young cooks are, by the chef. When you're belittled for making a mistake, you're less likely to take chances and to learn.

Once you've determined not to waste offal, you must learn to cook it. Often, these items are smelly, composed of fibrous cells, or have an overly powerful taste, all of which must be accounted for in the cooking process. With tripe, the stomach of a ruminant animal, you must wash it for a long time, scraping it and cleaning it, until it has no odor, membrane, or fat. Then you should cook it in layers in a packed pot, stuffing plenty of aromatics between each layer so that the tripe is thoroughly flavored throughout, and you must cook it gently, for a long time.

It's easy to cook a filet mignon, or to sauté a piece of trout, serve it with browned butter à la meunière, and call yourself a chef. But that's not really cooking. That's heating. Preparing tripe, however, is a transcendental act: to take what is normally thrown away and, with skill and knowledge, turn it into something exquisite.

## HOW TO COOK TRIPE

The first thing to do with tripe is to clean it thoroughly by rinsing it well and scraping off excess membrane. When it has been well cleaned, it will have very little odor. Choose a cooking vessel that is small enough to allow you to make many layers of tripe. Layer plenty of aromatic vegetables between the layers of tripe—carrots, onions, some parsley if you wish, and turnip, which adds a sweetness to the tripe. Pack the tripe down to compress it; the packing is critical in flavoring the tripe evenly throughout. Cover the tripe with white wine and veal stock—you shouldn't need much liquid if you've packed it well. Bring this to a simmer on the stove top, then cover it tightly and place it in a 275°F. oven for at least 5 hours (I've never been able to overcook tripe). For garnish, braise some onions, glaze some carrots—the preparation becomes almost like a blanquette. Remove the cooked tripe from the cooking liquid, strain the liquid, reduce it, add some cream, season it, and add a little mustard. Cut the tripe into portion-sized squares, return it to the sauce, and serve with the vegetables and with noodles. It's terrific.

## Sautéed Calf's Liver, Vidalia and Red Onion Confit, Onion Rings, and Vinegar Sauce

**RED WINE VINEGAR SAUCE**

2 tablespoons canola oil

1 cup sliced button mushrooms

½ cup sliced sweet bunch carrots

½ cup sliced shallots

8 sprigs Italian parsley

2 sprigs thyme

1 cup red wine vinegar

4 cups Veal Stock (page 222), heated

**ONIONS**

2 cups sliced red onions

2 cups sliced Vidalia or Maui onions

2 tablespoons (1 ounce) plus 1 teaspoon
  unsalted butter

Kosher salt

1 teaspoon honey

Freshly ground black pepper

12 red pearl onions, peeled and an X cut
  into the root ends

12 white pearl onions, peeled and an X cut
  into the root ends

1 teaspoon sugar

**ONION RINGS**

Canola oil for deep-frying

¼ cup plus 2 tablespoons Tempura Batter Mix
  (recipe follows)

¼ cup sparkling water

Twelve ½-inch slices Vidalia or Maui onion

**LIVER**

Canola oil

6 calf's liver steaks, cut 1 inch thick
  (3 to 3½ ounces each)

Flour for dusting

Kosher salt and freshly ground black pepper

2 tablespoons (1 ounce) unsalted butter

2 tablespoons chopped chives

This is your classic blueplate special. I like to cook the calf's liver as a "steak," rather than in thin slices, so that I have better control over the cooking and I can achieve various textures and flavors in one piece of meat—the seared crust, the medium interior, and the rare center. Onions and liver are a well-known pair, of course, but I use three different onion preparations—creamy slow-cooked onions, glazed onions, and crunchy onion rings in tempura batter—resulting in different textures and varying levels of sweetness.

FOR THE RED WINE VINEGAR SAUCE: Heat the oil in a medium saucepan over medium-high heat and sauté the mushrooms, carrots, and shallots, stirring occasionally, for 2 minutes. Add the parsley and thyme and continue cooking for 2 minutes, or until the vegetables caramelize. Add the vinegar and simmer for about 20 minutes, or until the pan is almost dry.

Strain the hot stock over the vegetables. (Heating the stock before adding it allows it to return to a boil more quickly, which in turn keeps the fat from emulsifying in the cold liquid and creates a clearer sauce.)

Simmer the sauce until it is reduced to about 1 cup. Strain the sauce through a chinois (see page 73) into a saucepan and set aside.

FOR THE ONIONS: Preheat the oven to 300°F.

Place the sliced red and white onions in two separate ovenproof saucepans. Cover the onions with cold water and bring to a boil. As soon as the water boils, drain the onions in strainers (keeping them separate) and rinse under cold running water, then repeat the process. (This blanching will sweeten the onions and eliminate excess acid.)

Drain the onions, squeeze dry, and return them to the pans. Place 1 tablespoon of butter and a little salt in each. Heat the onions on the stove top to melt the butter, then cover each pan with a parchment lid (see page 190) and place in the oven for 1 hour, or until soft.

Remove the pans from the oven and stir the honey and some pepper into the white onions. Set both pans of onions aside.

Meanwhile, trim the pearl onions as necessary so that they are uniform in size and will cook evenly. Place them in two separate small saucepans. Add 1 cup of water, ½ teaspoon of the remaining butter, and ½ teaspoon of the sugar to each pan of onions. The water should just cover the onions. Bring the water to a simmer and cook over medium heat for 20 to 25 minutes, or until the water has evaporated and the onions are tender and glazed but not browned.

TO COMPLETE: For the onion rings, heat oil for deep-frying to 325°F. in a small deep pot. Mix the tempura mix with the sparkling water. Add an ice cube to the batter to keep it cold.

Dip a few of the rings into the batter, carefully add them to the hot oil, and fry for 4 to 5 minutes, or until golden brown and crisp. Remove to paper towels to drain. Repeat with the remaining onion rings.

Meanwhile, reheat the cooked white, red, and pearl onions and the sauce.

FOR THE LIVER: Heat ¼ inch of canola oil in a large skillet over high heat. Dust the liver with flour and season with salt and pepper. Add the liver to the pan and reduce the heat to medium. Cook for 4 to 5 minutes, turning and searing on all sides, until the liver feels somewhat firm to the touch, like a steak cooked to medium. Drain the liver briefly on paper towels; place 1 teaspoon of butter on each piece, allowing it to melt over the liver.

Spoon some sauce into the center of each serving dish. Arrange small mounds of the red and white sliced onions side by side in the center of the sauce. Top the onions with the liver and sprinkle with the chopped chives. Garnish each piece with two each of the red and white pearl onions and two onion rings.

MAKES **6** SERVINGS

### TEMPURA BATTER MIX

³/₄ cup cornstarch

3 cups cake flour

2 teaspoons baking soda

1 teaspoon kosher salt

Combine all the ingredients. Store indefinitely in an airtight container. Mix the batter when needed in proportions of 3 parts tempura mix to 2 parts sparkling water. This batter can be used with a variety of vegetables and seafood.

# Roasted Sweetbreads with Applewood-Smoked Bacon, Braised Belgian Endive, and Black Truffle Sauce

SWEETBREADS

1½ pounds sweetbreads

Canola oil

Kosher salt and freshly ground black pepper

¾ cup carrots cut into ½-inch mirepoix
   (see page 203)

¾ cup leeks (white and light green parts only)
   cut into ½-inch mirepoix (see page 203)

¾ cup onions cut into ½-inch mirepoix
   (see page 203)

8 sprigs Italian parsley

4 sprigs thyme

2 fresh bay leaves or 1 dried bay leaf

¾ cup dry vermouth

4 cups cold White Veal Stock (page 223),
   Chicken Stock (page 226), or water

Five to six ¼-inch-thick slices slab bacon, frozen

¼ cup canola oil

4 tablespoons (2 ounces) unsalted butter

BRAISED ENDIVE

6 Belgian endive (1 inch to 1½ inches in diameter)

Kosher salt

Canola oil

3 to 4 cups Chicken Stock (page 226)

TRUFFLE SAUCE

¾ cup Veal Stock (page 222)

1 tablespoon chopped black truffle
   (from a whole truffle, pieces, or peelings)

Few drops of white wine vinegar

1 teaspoon white truffle oil

Kosher salt and freshly ground black pepper

TRUFFLE GARNISH

30 thin slices black truffle (from a 1- to
   1½-ounce truffle)

½ teaspoon minced chives

Few drops of white truffle oil

Gray salt to taste

Sweetbreads have a wonderful texture and a flavor that's almost neutral, so you can play with a lot of garnishes. Here it's larded with bacon, to infuse the meat with that flavor, and paired with truffles and slow-cooked endive.

Preparing sweetbreads is a two- to three-day process; these are soaked and then blanched in water, then cleaned, braised in stock, and finally sautéed. Sweetbreads come in two parts. The "heart" lobe, or top rounded portion (*noix*, or "nut," in French), has a thin layer of membrane and very little sinew. The "throat" lobe, or bottom part (*gorge*) is made up of two pieces, with more membrane and sinew. If possible, specify "heart" sweetbreads to your butcher, though the recipe can be made using both sections.

FOR THE SWEETBREADS: Soak the sweetbreads in water to cover for at least 6 hours, or overnight, changing the water at least two or three times.

Fill a large pot with lightly salted water and bring to a boil (using a large volume of water will help to maintain the boil when the sweetbreads are added). Add the sweetbreads, reduce the heat slightly, and simmer for 2 minutes. Drain the sweetbreads, place them in ice water to cool, and drain again. Remove any excess membrane or fat from the sweetbreads. Place them on a towel-lined baking sheet and cover with another towel, another baking sheet, and a light weight. The sweetbreads should compress to about ¾ inch thick but should not be severely flattened. Refrigerate overnight.

Heat ⅛ inch of oil in a large deep heavy sauté pan. Lightly season the sweetbreads with salt and pepper and place them smooth side down in the hot oil. Sauté the pieces for about 5 minutes, or until they are golden brown. Turn them and cook for an additional 2 minutes. Pour off half the fat from the pan. Add the vegetables, parsley, thyme, and bay leaves, immediately pour in the vermouth and stock, and bring to a simmer. Simmer for 5 minutes.

Remove the sweetbreads from the cooking liquid and strain the liquid into a tall narrow container, discarding the solids (or use them in a stock). Let the cooking liquid sit for 5 to 6 minutes to allow the fat to rise to the top. Remove the fat, return the sweetbreads to the liquid, and refrigerate until ready to finish the dish, or up to 2 days.

FOR THE BRAISED ENDIVE: If the endives are thicker than 1½ inches, remove enough outer leaves to reduce them to that size. Cut off the bottom of each endive so that it will stand upright. Cut out and remove the conical core from the root end of each, following the shape of the endive so that the walls of the endive will be about the same thickness and the endives will cook evenly. Pack the inside of each endive with kosher salt, sprinkle a little additional salt over the outside, and stand them up on a tray. Let them sit for 30 minutes, then rinse them to remove the salt.

Heat ¼ inch of oil in a pot large enough to hold the endive in one layer. Add the endive and lightly brown on all sides. Add chicken stock to cover, cover with a parchment lid (see page 190), and simmer for 30

to 40 minutes, or until the endive is fully cooked. Set aside in the liquid until ready to serve.

FOR THE TRUFFLE SAUCE: Combine the veal stock, truffles, and vinegar in a small saucepan (you shouldn't taste the vinegar; use it as you would use salt to enhance the other flavors). Reduce the sauce for 3 to 4 minutes, or until it coats the back of a spoon. Remove from the heat.

TO COOK THE SWEETBREADS: Cut the frozen bacon into 54 lardons, or strips, about 3 inches long by ¼ inch wide (it is easier to cut bacon while it is frozen). Place them in a saucepan, cover with cold water, and bring to a boil. Immediately drain the lardons in a strainer and rinse with cold water. (This quick blanching process removes excess saltiness and keeps the lardons from shrinking excessively when they are cooked.)

Trim the sweetbreads into 6 brick shapes approximately 2 inches by 3 inches. (Save the trimmings for another use, such as a *farce*, or stuffing.) Use a larding needle to insert the lardons into the sweetbreads, from top to bottom, leaving equal space (about ½ inch) between each lardon; use 9 lardons per sweetbread. Trim the ends of the lardons with scissors, leaving ½ inch to ¾ inch at each end. (If you do not have a larding needle, the lardons can be added to the skillet and cooked with the sweetbreads.) Season both sides of the sweetbreads with salt and pepper.

TO COMPLETE: Preheat the oven to 350°F.

Heat a large ovenproof skillet over medium heat. Add the ¼ cup canola oil, let it heat slightly, and then add the butter. When the fat begins bubbling, add the sweetbreads, rounder side down, to the pan. Cook for a minute, or until the bacon begins releasing its fat. (The darker brown bacon fat will add color to the finished sweetbreads.) Using a spoon, baste the sweetbreads with the fat for a minute or so, until the tops have a little color. Place the uncovered pan in the oven and cook for 10 to 15 minutes, basting the sweetbreads occasionally with the rendered fat. After the first 5 minutes, turn the sweetbreads over.

Meanwhile, in a small bowl, toss the truffle garnish ingredients together.

Remove the endive from the cooking liquid and cut each endive lengthwise in half, return them to the pan, and heat. One endive at a time, remove both halves and drain off any excess liquid. Overlap and twist the halves around your finger to form a turban shape.

Reheat the sauce and stir in the truffle oil. Season to taste with salt and pepper.

Place a spoonful of truffle sauce in the center of each plate. Place an endive "turban" in each pool of sauce. Use a paper towel to blot excess fat from the sweetbreads and place one on each turban. Stack 5 slices of truffle on each sweetbread.

MAKES 6 SERVINGS

These two separate preparations are both elaborate and each is enormously satisfying in its own way. The first uses the succulent fatty meat in a pig's head, wrapped around cooked pig's tongue, pig's ear, and sweetbreads, rolled tightly into a cylinder, and oven-poached all day. After it's cooled, it's sliced into medallions, sautéed, and served with a gribiche sauce. The pig's foot, or trotter, a classic French country preparation, is also stuffed and cooked over an extended period.

### BRAISED STUFFED PIG'S HEAD
### WITH SAUCE GRIBICHE

Cut off the ears and reserve. Split the skin and meat down the center of the head, beginning at the top and working around the snout and to the back of the head to split the skull down the middle. Then, beginning on one side of the head, run the knife along the contour of the head, following the bone structure, to remove the skin and the attached meat. Be careful to remove the piece of meat on the temple, behind the eye, first and then the cheeks; you want these pieces of meat to stay attached to the skin. Follow the line from the jawbone to the snout. Repeat on the other side. Remove the tongue and set it aside.

Lay out the piece of pig, skin side down. At the back of the top of the head is a flap of meat that is very fatty. Trim off the fat until you reach the meat. Run a knife along the skin and remove the skin from the meat and remaining fat (much as you would skin a fish fillet). You can roll up the skin and tie it in a bundle; it adds a great deal of gelatin if added to stocks. Trim away and discard the excess bits of skin, the gums, and the ear canal. Trim off the top of the fat until only the very white fat remains. Score the fat in a crosshatch pattern. Trim the excess fat from the inside. Butterfly the meat of the cheek and crosshatch the interior. Pound the piece flat and season with salt and pepper. Dice some of the pig's ear and set aside.

Braise the tongue as you would veal tongue (see page 112).

Arrange batons of cooked tongue, sweetbreads, and diced pig's ear over the meat. Roll the head in plastic wrap to shape it (as you would the torchon; see page 107), then remove the piece, roll it, and tie it in cheesecloth. Place the pig's head in a pot, cover with stock (chicken or white veal), and add aromatics (carrots, onions, leeks, bay leaves, thyme sprigs, and parsley stems). Cover the pot in foil and place in a 300°F. oven for 6 hours.

Drain the cooked meat, rewrap it in cheesecloth, and hang it for 1 day in the cooler.

Slice the pig's head into medallions. Brush with Dijon mustard, dredge in fresh bread crumbs, and sauté the pieces in oil. Serve on a bed of the gribiche sauce, garnished with chopped egg white and a halved egg yolk of a hard-boiled pheasant egg and fresh tarragon.

### SAUCE GRIBICHE

1 heaping tablespoon finely minced shallots

1½ teaspoons finely minced capers

1½ teaspoons finely minced cornichon

½ teaspoon Dijon mustard

1 tablespoon Banyuls vinegar or sherry, white wine, or red wine vinegar

¼ cup extra virgin olive oil

1 heaping tablespoon finely chopped hard-boiled egg white

1 tablespoon finely chopped hard-boiled egg yolk

¼ teaspoon finely minced tarragon

1 teaspoon finely minced Italian parsley

½ teaspoon finely minced chives

This wonderful sauce will serve four. The ingredients in the sauce have a high degree of acid, so the proportion of oil is higher than usual.

Place all the ingredients in a mixing bowl and stir together. The sauce can be refrigerated in a covered container for a few days.

MAKES ABOUT $^1/_2$ CUP

### PIG'S FEET WITH FRENCH GREEN LENTILS

Try to buy pig's feet, or trotters, that are long, with half or all of the shank attached. The shank will provide more meat and skin, for a nicer wrapper.

TO COOK THE PIG'S FEET: Split the trotters lengthwise. Place a bed of mirepoix (see page 203) and aromatics (carrots, onions, leeks, bay leaves, thyme sprigs, and parsley stems) in the bottom of a rondeau, or deep straight-sided braising pan. Place the trotters skin side down over the mirepoix. Sprinkle the top with more mirepoix and aromatics. Add chicken stock to cover by 2 inches. Cover the pot with a lid and bring to a simmer over medium heat.

Transfer the pot to a 300°F. oven and cook for about 6 hours, or until the meat is falling away from the bones. Remove from the oven and cool for an hour to make them easier to handle.

Remove the trotters from the liquid, debone them, and discard the bones. Remove the meat, shred it, and reserve. Remove any sinew still attached to the pig's skin. The skins will become the wrappers, so scrape them with a knife to make it a uniform thickness. Refrigerate both the skin and the meat to chill. Strain the cooking liquid and reserve.

FOR THE FARCE: Dice some sweetbreads and season them. Dredge them in flour and cook in $^1/_8$ inch of hot oil in a rondeau until they are crispy and golden brown. Drain the sweetbreads and wipe out the pot. Add some chicken stock (twice the volume of sweetbreads). Bring the liquid to a boil and add the sweetbreads, some minced shallots, a few drops of white wine vinegar, and some butter.

Simmer to reduce the liquid until it thickens and coats the sweetbreads. Add a vegetable brunoise, some chopped chives, and the reserved meat. (If the sauce begins to break, add more stock.) If desired, finish with white truffle oil. Transfer the stuffing to a bowl and let it cool to room temperature.

TO STUFF THE TROTTERS: Remove the skin from the refrigerator. If it is too stiff to work with, place it in the microwave briefly to make it pliable, or let stand at room temperature until softened. For each trotter, place a piece of caul fat (soaked and drained) on a work surface; it should be large enough to wrap around the stuffed trotter three times. Place the skin (outside down) on the caul fat and season the inside of the skin. Place the *farce* down the middle of the skin and roll it up in the skin. Roll up the stuffed trotter in the caul fat.

Heat $^1/_8$ inch of oil in an ovenproof sauté pan over medium heat until hot but not smoking.

Add the trotters and brown on the first side. Turn the trotters over and place in a 300°F. oven for about 10 minutes, turning occasionally. (They need to heat evenly, or they may burst.)

Serve the trotters on a ragout of green lentils garnished with lardons of smoked bacon.

PICTURED ON PAGES 216 AND 217        MAKES 4 SERVINGS
                                     WITH SHANK,
                                     2 SERVINGS WITHOUT

Opposite: Braised stuffed pig's heads in cheesecloth. Left: Pig's Feet with French Green Lentils, page 215; above: Braised Stuffed Pig's Head, page 214.

# Stocks and Sauces

You can't have a good sauce if you start with a bad stock. Too many people take stocks for granted. In many restaurants the stock pot is like a garbage can; they throw in all kinds of trimmings. They slather the bones with tomato paste and roast them until they burn.

The ideology of a stock is important. The idea is to remove through extended gentle heat the flavor and gelatin of the bones and meat while continually removing the impurities: the blood, fat, bone, and vegetable particles released in the cooking process. You need to cook your bones and meat in the proper amount of liquid, adding the proper amount of vegetables. I like sweet things in my stock: carrot, onion, tomato, and also some garlic. I don't use celery, because it makes the stock a little bitter. Every step of the way, you remove impurities. Everything follows from this.

## Stocks

When we make veal stock, we wash the bones. Next, we blanch them. Any blood on the surface of the bones or in the meat will coagulate, and these impurities will float in the stock. We pour off the blanching water, rinse the bones again, and clean them. (If we had the time and space, we would blanch the bones twice, but it's impractical.)

We then return the bones to the clean pot, add the appropriate amount of water, and bring it up to a gentle heat. It's always important to have a gradual temperature change and to cook the stock at a low temperature. You don't want to cook stock over too-high heat for three reasons: flavor, clarity, and yield.

First, boiling bones and vegetables—cooking them over high heat—will release all their fats and impurities, and the violence of the boiling water will emulsify them into the stock. These impurities, emulsified into clear liquid, will cloud the stock. And if the bones and vegetables are cooked too violently, or too long, they will break down particle by particle. These millions of particles will act like little sponges, soaking up your good stock, so that when you strain it, a lot of stock will be caught in your China cap and wind up in the garbage, reducing your total yield.

After the stock has cooked for the specified time and been strained, the final step is to reduce it slowly. Reduction brings the stock to the proper consistency. By setting your pot half off the burner, you'll create a natural convection current that pushes the impurities to one side of the pot so you can skim them away—a kind of natural clarification process.

To increase yield and use all the flavor in veal bones, we make a *remouillage*, a second, weaker stock from the same bones. We add this to the first stock and reduce it all to about a quarter of its original volume.

We also make a white veal stock without tomatoes (we do not make a *remouillage* for this stock) that is only cooked for four hours, yielding a clear, gelatinous stock that we use to cook sweetbreads, tongue, trotters—things we don't want to darken. Because it's so gelatinous, anything cooled and stored in the stock remains very fresh. Furthermore, the item being cooled imparts more of its own flavor to the stock. After cooking with it, we add leftover white veal stock to our brown stock.

While the veal stock needs a long, slow simmering time, our chicken stock is quick. We use the same method, but we cook the bones (twenty pounds in about 4 gallons of water) for forty-five minutes for a very light flavor, one that won't overpower a vegetable soup or a risotto or become too assertive in a quick sauce.

With vegetable stock, it's important to understand that there is a point at which the vegetables will have imparted all their flavor to the water and will begin to disintegrate and absorb liquid, potentially decreasing your yield. As with our mushrooms when we make mushroom stock, we grind our vegetables and cook them for only 45 minutes.

We add chicken feet and duck feet to our chicken and duck stock, respectively, and calves' feet to all meat stocks. The feet contain gelatin, adding viscosity to the stock without reduction.

Although we don't roast the veal bones, we do roast venison, lamb, and duck bones for our stocks to create a more pronounced flavor. These stocks are going to be used only in finished sauces for venison, lamb, and duck dishes. Because roasting adds impurities to these stocks, it's important to be careful to bring them up to heat gently and be diligent in the skimming and straining.

## VEAL STOCK

10 pounds veal bones, necks, and
    backs

1 calf's foot, split (optional)

24 quarts cold water

Scant 2 cups (1 pound) tomato paste

**AROMATICS**

2½ cups (12 ounces) carrots cut
    into 1-inch mirepoix
    (see page 203)

4 cups (1 pound) leeks cut into
    1-inch mirepoix (see page 203)
    (white and some light green
    parts only)

1½ cups (8 ounces) onions cut into
    1-inch mirepoix (see page 203)

1 head garlic, halved, broken into
    pieces, root end and excess skin
    removed

1½ ounces Italian parsley sprigs

½ ounce thyme sprigs

2 bay leaves

1 pound tomatoes, cut into 1-inch
    pieces (2½ cups)

At the French Laundry, veal stock is used as a base for a number of different sauces. Unlike most recipes for veal stock, ours does not contain a step for roasting the bones. The depth of color comes from the tomatoes and tomato paste and the final reduction process. The stock is neutral and clean-flavored, with the presence of veal, but not an overwhelming flavor of it.

You will need a stockpot with a minimum capacity of twenty quarts. If necessary, the recipe can be split between two smaller pots or cut in half.

Although making veal stock is a time-consuming procedure, it can be done over several days. The first day, blanch the bones and prepare Veal #1; the second day, continue by making Veal #2; and the third day, combine the liquids to produce the final stock.

1. The blanching of bones for clarification (1 to 1½ hours).
2. Veal #1—The initial extraction of flavor from bones and aromatics to obtain a first liquid (5 to 6 hours).
3. Veal #2, or *remouillage*—The second extraction of flavor to obtain a second liquid (5 to 6 hours). *Remouillage* is the French term for the "remoistening," or second extraction from the bones.
4. "Marriage" of Veal #1 and Veal #2 and further reduction to concentrate color and consistency (8 to 9 hours).

TO BLANCH THE BONES: Blanching is an essential first step in the making of a clear, clean stock. Rinse the veal bones in cold water and put the bones and calf's foot, if using, in a stockpot with at least a 20-quart capacity. (If you do not have a stockpot large enough, split the recipe between two pots.) Fill the pot with cold water, adding twice as much water as you have bones. Bring to a simmer slowly; this coagulates the blood proteins and brings other impurities to the surface. As the liquid is being brought to a simmer, move the bones around from time to time, but do not stir, which would create too much movement and disperse the impurities. Skim off the scum that rises to the surface. As soon as the liquid comes to a simmer, remove the pot from the heat. (If the bones continue to blanch any longer than is necessary to coagulate blood proteins and draw out other impurities, more flavor will be extracted into a liquid that you will end up discarding rather than into the liquid that will become your stock.)

Drain the bones in a large colander and rinse with cold water to stop the cooking process and remove any scum. It is important that the bones be rinsed while they are hot; if they are allowed to cool first, the impurities will cling to the bones and go into your stock. Rinse out the stockpot to remove any impurities on the bottom and sides of the pot.

FOR VEAL #1: Return the rinsed bones to the clean stockpot. Add 12 quarts of the cold water to the pot. Slowly bring the water to a simmer. This will take 1 to 1½ hours. Skim continuously! (It is easier to skim before the aromatics are added, and the more you skim, the better your chances are for a clear stock.)

Once the liquid is at a simmer, skim and then stir in the tomato paste. Add the aromatics and the tomatoes. Bring the liquid back to a simmer and simmer for 4 hours: Skim, skim, skim.

Strain the liquid, first through a China cap (see page 73) or colander, then through a chinois (see page 73) into a second container, reserving the bones and aromatics. Do not press on the solids in the strainer or force through any liquid that does not pass on its own. You should have approximately 8 to 10 quarts of liquid. Rapidly cool it by filling a sink with ice water, placing the container in the sink, and stirring the liquid occasionally until there are no traces of steam and the liquid is cool. Once it is cool, refrigerate.

FOR VEAL #2: Return the bones and aromatics to the clean stockpot. Fill with the remaining 12 quarts cold water. Slowly bring the liquid to a simmer, skimming often. Simmer for another 4 hours, skimming frequently.

Strain the liquid twice, as for Veal #1. You should have approximately 8 to 10 quarts of liquid. Rapidly cool it down as directed for Veal #1. If you will not be finishing the stock within a few hours, refrigerate the liquid.

FOR THE "MARRIAGE" OF VEAL #1 AND VEAL #2: Clean the stockpot and add Veal #1 and Veal #2. Slowly bring the liquid to a simmer. This may take 1 to 1½ hours. Simmer for 6 to 8 hours, or until the stock reduces to approximately 2 quarts. It should have a rich brown color and a sauce-like consistency. Store in the refrigerator for several days, or freeze in several containers for longer storage.

MAKES ABOUT 2 QUARTS

## WHITE VEAL STOCK

| | |
|---|---|
| 10 pounds veal bones, necks, and backs | 3 cups (1 pound) onions cut into 1-inch mirepoix (see page 203) |
| 1 calf's foot, split (optional) | ½ ounce Italian parsley sprigs |
| 10 quarts cold water | 2 bay leaves |
| AROMATICS | 5 sprigs thyme |
| 4 cups (1 pound) leeks cut into 1-inch mirepoix (see page 203) (white and some light green parts only) | |

Rinse the veal bones in cold water and place the bones and calf's foot, if using, in a 16-quart stockpot. Add enough cold water to come three quarters of the way up the sides of the pot; there should be at least twice as much water as there are bones. Slowly bring the water to a simmer; this may take 1 to 1½ hours. As the liquid is being brought to a simmer, move the bones around from time to time, but do not stir, which would create too much movement and disperse the impurities. Skim off the scum that

rises to the surface. As soon as the liquid comes to a simmer, remove it from the heat. (If the bones continue to blanch any longer than is necessary to coagulate blood proteins and draw out other impurities, more flavor will be extracted into a liquid that you will end up discarding rather than into the liquid that will become your stock.)

Drain the bones in a large colander. Rinse the bones well, until there is no film left on them; they should feel smooth to the touch and the water should run clear. It is very important that the bones be rinsed thoroughly to remove any impurities, which would not only cloud the stock but make the finished stock gray.

Clean the pot and return the bones to it. Add the cold water and slowly bring the water to a simmer, skimming frequently. Once it is at a simmer, add the aromatics and continue to simmer for 4 hours, skimming frequently to remove any impurities. The stock will have a noticeable clarity.

Turn off the heat and allow the stock to rest for 10 minutes; this allows any particles left in the stock to settle at the bottom of the pot. Set a chinois (see page 73) or fine-mesh strainer over a container large enough to hold at least 4 quarts. Use a ladle to remove the stock from the pot and strain it into the container. (It is important to ladle the stock rather than pouring it, as the force of pouring it out all at once would force impurities through the strainer.) Discard any stock toward the bottom of the pot that is cloudy with impurities.

Fill a sink with ice water and place the container in it to cool down the stock rapidly. Stir occasionally until there are no traces of steam. Refrigerate the stock for 1 to 2 days, or freeze in several containers for longer storage.

MAKES 3 QUARTS

### LAMB STOCK

10 pounds lamb bones, cut into
    small pieces

½ cup canola oil

1 calf's foot, split (optional)

10 quarts cold water

**AROMATICS**

2½ cups (12 ounces) carrots cut
    into 1-inch mirepoix
    (see page 203)

4 cups (1 pound) leeks cut into
    1-inch mirepoix (see page 203)
    (white and some light green
    parts only)

1½ cups (8 ounces) onions cut into
    1-inch mirepoix (see page 203)

1 head garlic, halved, broken into
    pieces, root end and excess skin
    removed

1½ ounces Italian parsley sprigs

½ ounce thyme sprigs

2 bay leaves (1 pound)

Scant 2 cups tomato paste

1 pound tomatoes, cut into 1-inch
    pieces (2½ cups)

TO ROAST THE BONES: Preheat the oven to 400°F.

Place the lamb bones in a roasting pan that is large enough to hold them in one layer. (If they are crowded, they will steam and not brown evenly; use two pans if necessary.) The optional calf's foot is not roasted, as that would decrease the extraction of gelatin.

Coat the bones with the oil; using oil speeds the roasting process. Roast for about 1½ hours, stirring occasionally to ensure even browning. Once the bones are a rich deep brown color, remove them from the roasting pan and place them in one large stockpot or two smaller ones.

TO DEGLAZE THE ROASTING PAN: Add just enough water to barely cover the bottom of the roasting pan. Place the pan over medium heat and use a wooden spatula to scrape up the glaze and bits of meat on the bottom of the pan. Add this to the stockpot.

FOR THE EXTRACTION: Add the calf's foot, if using, and the cold water to the pot. Bring the liquid slowly to a simmer, skimming off any scum as soon as you see it. (It is easier to skim before the vegetables are added.) Once the liquid is at a simmer, add the aromatics, tomato paste, and tomatoes and simmer the stock for 5 hours.

LADLE THE STOCK INTO A CONTAINER: First ladle from the top, rather than dipping deep, then tilt the pot to continue ladling the liquid; remove and discard the bones as you go. Do not be tempted to pour the stock through a colander; it would make the stock cloudy. Then strain the stock through a chinois (see page 73) or fine-mesh strainer. Do not force through any meat or liquid remaining in the strainer.

You should have 3 to 4 quarts of lamb stock. If necessary, return the strained stock to the heat and reduce to 3 quarts. Refrigerate for 1 to 2 days, or freeze in several containers for longer storage.

MAKES 3 QUARTS

## DUCK STOCK

| | |
|---|---|
| 5 pounds duck bones, cut into 2- to 3-inch pieces | 1½ cups (8 ounces) onions cut into 1-inch pieces |
| ½ cup canola oil | 1 ounce Italian parsley sprigs |
| 1 pound duck feet (optional) | |
| 6 quarts cold water | ¾ cup tomato paste |
| AROMATICS | 1 pound tomatoes, cut into 1-inch pieces (2½ cups) |
| 1¾ cups (8 ounces) carrots cut into 1-inch mirepoix (see page 203) | |
| 2 cups (8 ounces) leeks cut into 1-inch mirepoix (see page 203) (white and some light green parts only) | |

Compared to the fairly neutral chicken and veal stocks, which are used as a base for sauces, this duck stock is more concentrated and flavorful. The bones are roasted to make the duck flavor more pronounced.

TO ROAST THE BONES: Preheat the oven to 425°F.

Rinse the duck bones well to remove any traces of blood. Using a towel, dry the bones well (wet bones would steam rather than roast). Place the bones in a roasting pan that is large enough to hold them in one layer. (If they are crowded, they will steam and not brown evenly.) The optional duck feet are not roasted, as that would decrease the extraction of gelatin.

Coat the bones with the oil; using oil speeds the roasting process. Roast the bones for about 1½ hours. During the roasting process, water and fat will leach from the bones; remove it as it accumulates, or you risk the bones steaming rather than roasting. Once the bones are a rich deep red-brown (not black), remove them from the roasting pan and place in a 12-quart stockpot.

TO DEGLAZE THE ROASTING PAN: Place the roasting pan over medium heat to concentrate any remaining liquid. (It is important to have a "glaze" before you "deglaze.") Once the liquid has reduced to a glaze, add just enough water to barely cover the bottom of the roasting pan. Use a wooden spatula to scrape up the glaze and combine it with the liquid. Add this to the stockpot.

Add the duck feet, if using, and the cold water to the pot. Bring the liquid slowly to a simmer, skimming off any scum as soon as you see it. (It is easier to skim before the vegetables are added.) Once the liquid is at a simmer, add the aromatics, tomato paste, and tomatoes and simmer the stock for 4 hours.

Strain the stock three times to ensure that any impurities are removed: First strain it through a colander and discard the bones and aromatics. Next strain through a China cap (see page 73), and finally through a chinois (see page 73). Do not force any solids or thickened liquids through the strainers, as they would cloud the finished stock. You should have approximately 3 quarts of stock.

FOR THE FINAL REDUCTION: The stock should be a deep red-brown color, with a consistency you can feel between your fingers and with a pronounced duck flavor. If the stock appears red in color and is watery, further reduction is necessary to concentrate the color, consistency, and flavor. For use in any of these recipes, slowly reduce the stock to 2 cups. Refrigerate the stock for 1 to 2 days, or freeze in one or two containers for longer storage.

MAKES 2 CUPS

## VENISON STOCK

| | |
|---|---|
| 10 pounds venison bones | 1½ cups (8 ounces) onions |
| ½ cup canola oil | cut into 1-inch mirepoix (see |
| 14 quarts cold water | page 203) |
| AROMATICS | 1½ ounces Italian parsley sprigs |
| 1 head garlic, halved, broken into | ½ ounce thyme sprigs |
| pieces, root end and excess | 2 bay leaves |
| skin removed | |
| 2½ cups (12 ounces) carrots | 1 pound tomatoes, cut into 1-inch |
| cut into 1-inch mirepoix (see | pieces (2½ cups) |
| page 203) | Scant 2 cups tomato paste |
| 4 cups (1 pound) leeks cut into | |
| 1-inch mirepoix (see page 203) | |
| (white and some light green | |
| parts only) | |

You will need a very large stockpot—at least twenty-four quarts—for this recipe. If you do not have one, make it in two pots, or cut the recipe in half.

TO ROAST THE BONES: Preheat the oven to 425°F.

Place the bones in a single layer in a large roasting pan and drizzle with the oil. Roast, turning the bones occasionally, for about 1 hour 45 minutes, or until they are well browned. Remove the bones to a very large stockpot.

TO DEGLAZE THE ROASTING PAN: Add about a cup of water to the pan, place the pan over medium heat, and scrape the bottom with a wooden spatula to loosen the glazed juices. Add to the stockpot.

Add the cold water to the pot and slowly bring to a simmer. Add the aromatics, tomatoes, and tomato paste to the pot and simmer for 5 hours.

LADLE THE STOCK INTO A CONTAINER: First ladle from the top, rather than dipping deep, then tilt the pot to continue ladling the liquid; remove and discard the bones as you go. Do not be tempted to pour the stock through a colander; it would make the stock cloudy. Then strain the stock through a chinois (see page 73) or fine-mesh strainer. Do not force through any meat or liquid remaining in the strainer. You should have about 4 quarts of venison stock.

Chill the stock and remove the fat that will solidify on the top. Then reduce the stock to 3 quarts and strain. Refrigerate for 1 to 2 days, or freeze in several containers for longer use.

MAKES 3 QUARTS

## CHICKEN STOCK

| | |
|---|---|
| 5 pounds chicken bones, necks, | 2 heaping cups (8 ounces) leeks cut |
| and backs | into 1-inch mirepoix (see page |
| 1 pound chicken feet (optional) | 203) (white and some light |
| 4 quarts cold water | green parts only) |
| 2 quarts ice cubes | 1½ cups (8 ounces) onions cut into |
| AROMATICS | 1-inch mirepoix (see page 203) |
| 1¾ cups (8 ounces) carrots cut into | 1 bay leaf |
| 1-inch mirepoix (see page 203) | |

This light, clean-flavored chicken stock is suitable for a variety of uses. As a base for a quick sauce or a braising liquid, it will take on the flavors of the individual dish. I like its light, almost neutral, taste. But for a stock with more chicken flavor, reduce the water by one third or increase the amount of bones used. For a more flavorful soup base, gently reduce it to the color and flavor intensity desired, the pot pulled to the side of the flame or burner so you can skim any residue that collects at the side of the pot.

Rinse the bones, necks, backs, and optional chicken feet thoroughly under cold water to remove all the visible blood. Remove any organs that may still be attached to the bones. (The rinsing of bones and removal of any organs is an essential first step in the clarification of the stock, as blood proteins are removed that would coagulate when heated and there will therefore be less chance that impurities will cloud your stock.)

Place all the bones and the feet, if using, in a 14- to 16-quart stockpot. Cover with the cold water. Slowly bring the liquid to a simmer, beginning to skim as soon as any impurities rise to the top. (It is important to keep skimming, because as the stock comes to a simmer, impurities could otherwise be pulled back into the liquid and emulsify and cloud the finished stock.)

Once the liquid is at a simmer, add the ice and then remove the fat. (The ice will chill and thicken the fat and turn it opaque, making it easier to remove.) Skim off as much of the impurities as possible. (Once the vegetables are added, skimming will be more difficult.)

Add the aromatics and slowly bring the liquid back to a simmer, skimming frequently. Simmer for another 30 to 40 minutes, skimming often. Turn off the heat and allow the stock to rest for 10 minutes; this allows any particles left in the stock to settle at the bottom of the pot.

Set a chinois (see page 73) or fine-mesh strainer over a container large enough to hold at least 6 quarts. Use a ladle to remove the stock from the pot and strain it into the container. (It is important to ladle the stock rather than pouring it, as the force of pouring it out all at once would force impurities through the strainer.) Discard any stock toward the bottom of the pot that is cloudy with impurities.

Fill a sink with ice water and place the container in it to cool the stock rapidly. Stir occasionally until there are no traces of steam. Refrigerate for 1 to 2 days, or freeze in several containers for longer storage.

MAKES ABOUT 6 QUARTS

## MUSHROOM STOCK

| | |
|---|---|
| 1 pound button mushrooms, washed and sliced | ½ cup Italian parsley sprigs |
| 1 cup sliced carrots | ¼ cup canola oil |
| 1 cup sliced leeks | ½ teaspoon curry powder |
| 1 cup sliced onions | 1 bay leaf |
| | 1 large sprig thyme |
| | 4 quarts water |

This stock can be made with any mushroom and used in soups or sauces. As with any stock, it freezes well. We grind the vegetables in a meat grinder to expose more surface area for quick cooking and purer flavor. This recipe calls for a food processor, which more home kitchens are likely to have, as an alternative. The curry powder brings out the mushroom flavor.

Finely grind the mushrooms, carrots, leeks, onions, and parsley separately in a food processor, pulsing and scraping down the sides as necessary for an even cut.

Heat the oil in a stockpot. Add the vegetables and curry powder. Cook for 2 minutes, stirring occasionally, then add the bay leaf, thyme, and 2 quarts of the water. Bring to a simmer and simmer for 45 minutes.

Strain the stock through a chinois (see page 73), pressing down on the solids, and return the vegetables to the stockpot. Set the stock aside; you should have about 6 cups. Refill the stockpot with the remaining 2 quarts water and return to a simmer. Cook for another 45 minutes. Strain as before.

Combine the two batches of stock in a pot. Bring to a boil and reduce until you have 3 cups. Refrigerate for up to 2 days, or freeze for up to 6 months.

MAKES 3 CUPS

## VEGETABLE STOCK

| | |
|---|---|
| 1½ pounds leeks (1 large bunch; white part only), well washed and coarsely chopped (about 4½ cups) | 1 small fennel bulb, trimmed and coarsely chopped |
| | ¼ cup canola oil |
| 1 pound carrots, peeled and coarsely chopped (about 3 cups) | 2 bay leaves |
| | 2 sprigs thyme |
| 1½ pounds (about 2) Spanish onions, coarsely chopped (about 4½ cups) | 2 ounces (1 large bunch) Italian parsley |
| | 3 to 4 quarts water |

Vegetable stock loses its flavor quickly. Make it as close to the time of use as possible, make it in small quantities or freeze it immediately.

Chop all the vegetables in a food processor.

Cook the vegetables in the canola oil in a medium stockpot over low heat for 5 to 8 minutes, or until softened. Add the bay leaves, thyme, and parsley, and enough water to cover. Bring to a gentle simmer, skimming frequently, and cook for 45 minutes. Strain through a chinois (see page 73). Refrigerate for 1 to 2 days, or freeze in several containers for longer storage.

MAKES 3 TO 4 QUARTS

½ cup canola oil

1½ pounds bones, chopped into 1-inch pieces

3 cups water

2½ cups strained Chicken Stock (page 226) or water

1 cup (5 to 6 ounces) onions cut into ½-inch mirepoix (see page 203)

1 cup (4 ounces) leeks cut into ½-inch mirepoix (see page 203) (white and light green parts only)

1 cup (5 ounces) diced carrots cut into ½-inch mirepoix (see page 203)

2 cups strained Veal Stock (page 222) or 1 cup strained Veal Stock plus 1 cup strained stock made with the same bones as "quick" sauce (venison, duck, or lamb)

Ideally, a great sauce is made from stock using the bones of the meat that is featured in the dish. The French Laundry doesn't have the space to store a dozen different stocks—nor do most home freezers. This method uses chicken and veal stock (two stocks you should keep on hand) as a base for building different flavored sauces that impart the flavor of the meat or bird being served yet require only a small amount of bones. (For example, it would be difficult to acquire enough squab bones to make a proper stock.)

The "quick" sauces mirror the stock-making process in many ways, but the quick sauces are flavored by caramelizing the vegetables, browning the bones, and then by repeated deglazing, reduction, and clarification. Listen for the sounds: When the bones are placed in the oil, you should hear a violent sizzle, which tells you your oil is hot enough. Once the liquid is added, the sizzling will quiet. As the liquid evaporates, a glaze will form on the bottom of the pan, which tells you that it's time to deglaze again. Each time a glaze is formed, you will hear sizzling, and each time you deglaze, the pot will become quiet.

We use some chicken stock and water as well as veal stock for these; if straight veal stock were used, it would reduce too much and become too gelatinous, and the flavor would be too concentrated. The chicken stock allows us to cook the bones long enough to extract their flavor without the stock becoming too reduced. If you have a stock already made from the same kind of bones you're making the quick sauce with (e.g., if you're making a quick lamb sauce and have lamb stock on hand), replace half the veal stock with that stock.

Again, the proper amount of reduction over gentle heat, with the pot pulled to the side of the flame, and continual skimming to remove impurities are paramount. And when the sauces are done, we strain them many times to remove as many impurities as possible. A single sauce may be strained as many as twenty times, the chinois washed between each straining, until the sauce passes through the chinois without leaving any particles. Initially we rap the rim of the chinois to speed the straining and then progress to a swirling motion, but we never pump the sauce with a ladle; the goal is to remove the particles, not push them through.

You can make a "quick" sauce with the bones of squab, venison, lamb, or whatever meat you are preparing.

Heat the canola oil over high heat in a wide heavy pot large enough to hold the bones in one layer. When it just begins to smoke, add the bones. Sear the bones, without stirring, for about 10 minutes. They should be well browned before they are moved, or they will give off their juices and begin to steam rather than brown. Turn the bones and cook for about 10 minutes longer, or until they are evenly colored. (Well-roasted bones will give the sauce its flavor.)

FOR THE FIRST DEGLAZING: Add the 1 cup water to the pot. Listen as the liquid goes into the pot: You will hear it sizzling as it hits the hot pot; then, as it reduces, it will become quiet. Stirring with a wooden spoon, scrape up any glazed juices clinging to the bottom of the pot and cook until the liquid has evaporated and the pot is reglazed and sizzling again. (The oil still in the pot will be removed later.)

FOR THE SECOND DEGLAZING: When the water has evaporated, deglaze the pot with ½ cup of the chicken stock as above. This time, as the stock boils down, the color of the bones and liquid will become deeper and the natural gelatin present in the stock will glaze the bones.

FOR THE THIRD DEGLAZING: Add the vegetables. The water in the vegetables provides the liquid for deglazing. Cook as above until the moisture has evaporated and the vegetables are lightly caramelized.

FOR THE FOURTH DEGLAZING: Add the remaining 2 cups chicken stock, the veal stock, and the remaining 2 cups of water. Deglaze the pot, scraping up the glazed juices from the bottom, then transfer the stock and bones to a smaller, narrower pot so that it will be easier to skim.

Bring to a simmer (with the pot set partially off the burner to force the impurities to the side of the pot) and ladle off the oil as it rises to the top. Simmer for 30 to 45 minutes, skimming often, until the stock has reduced to the level of the bones.

Strain the sauce through a China cap (see page 73) and then again through a chinois (see page 73). Do not force any of the solids through the strainer, or they will cloud your sauce. You should have about 2 cups of liquid.

Pour the liquid into a small pot, reduce to about 1 cup, and strain.

MAKES ABOUT 3/4 CUP

### VARIATIONS

The ingredients for all of the variations are added during or after the addition of the vegetables, during the third deglazing.

SQUAB SAUCE: Add ½ teaspoon Squab Spice (page 233) with the vegetables.

VENISON SAUCE: After the vegetables are lightly caramelized, add 2 cups huckleberries (fresh or frozen). The huckleberries will begin to release their juices; let them evaporate and reglaze the pot, then continue with the recipe.

LAMB SAUCE: After the vegetables are lightly caramelized, add ¼ ounce thyme sprigs, 1 cup chopped tomatoes, and 2 medium cloves garlic, crushed, and cook until the juices of the tomato as well as those released from the vegetables evaporate to form another glaze.

VINEGAR SAUCE: After the vegetables are lightly caramelized, deglaze the pot with ¾ cup Banyuls, sherry, white wine, or red wine vinegar, allowing the liquid to evaporate and reglaze the pot before continuing (use a high-quality vinegar for the best-tasting sauce).

SWEET-AND-SOUR-SAUCE: After the vegetables are lightly caramelized, deglaze the pot with ¾ cup Banyuls, sherry, white wine, or red wine vinegar and ¼ cup plus 2 tablespoons of sugar or honey and allow the liquid to evaporate and reglaze the pot before continuing (use a high-quality vinegar for the best-tasting sauce).

MAKES ABOUT 3/4 CUP

**Powders** are primarily a visual device, to make a dish look more appealing. They're typically a by-product related to the dish—tomato powder for a tomato salad, beet powder when we're serving beets. But some of our powders have a more pronounced effect on the finished dish. The squab spice is used both as a spice and as a powder: It seasons the squab sauce and then interacts with the sauce again on the plate in the final presentation; also, it's very volatile, so when it hits a hot plate, the oils in the spices add an exciting aromatic dimension to the dish. The dried horseradish, not ground to powder, adds a distinct flavor and crunch.

During a typical dinner service, I will have squab spice, mushroom powder, dried horseradish, paprika, carrot powder, yellow and black mustard, beet powder, red onion powder, pepper, and fennel powder at my station. Powders are fun.

At the French Laundry, we make these powders by putting the pulp or purée of a given vegetable on a baking sheet and setting it above the ovens, where the temperature happens to be perfect for drying it. It would be difficult for you to try to re-create this effect at home, so we've come up with a way of simulating the effect using a microwave oven. Microwave ovens vary in power, so you may need to adjust the cooking times accordingly.

NOTE: If when you are grinding a vegetable or fruit powder, it seems damp and won't grind properly, return it to the microwave. Microwave at low power for 1 to 2 minutes at a time, until it is completely dry, and then regrind.

All of the powders will keep at room temperature for several days or longer, but they begin to lose flavor and color after a few days.

### CARROT POWDER

½ cup very finely chopped carrots (chopped in a food processor; or use
    the pulp left after juicing carrots in a juicer)

Squeeze the carrots in a towel or blot on paper towels to remove excess moisture. Line a microwave tray with a piece of parchment paper and spread the carrots on it in a thin, even layer. Microwave on low power for about 40 minutes, or until the carrots are completely dried out. Let cool to room temperature.

Grind the carrots to a powder in a coffee or spice grinder. Store in a covered plastic container.

MAKES ABOUT 1 TABLESPOON

### CITRUS POWDER

¼ cup julienned orange zest

¼ cup julienned lime zest

¼ cup julienned lemon zest

Use a zester to remove the zests of the fruits in a fine julienne.

Place each zest in a separate small pan, cover with cold water, and bring to a boil. Once the water is at a boil, drain the zest and return to the

pan. Repeat the blanching process two more times. Dry the zests on paper towels. Line a microwave tray with a piece of parchment paper and spread all the zest evenly on it in one layer, without mixing the different zests. Microwave at medium power for 8 to 10 minutes, or until the zests are dried out. If one type of zest dries before the others, remove it.

Once the zests are dried, grind them all together in a coffee grinder for several minutes, or until as fine as possible. Sift the zest through a fine-mesh strainer, stirring it with a spoon, to obtain a finer powder. Store in a sealed plastic container.

MAKES 1 GENEROUS TABLESPOON

### MUSHROOM POWDER

5 shiitake mushrooms (1 ounce), stems removed

Using a very sharp knife, cut the shiitake mushrooms into paper-thin slices. Line a microwave tray with a piece of parchment paper and lay the mushroom slices on it in a single layer. Microwave on medium power for about 10 minutes, or until the mushrooms look shriveled and about half of their original size. If the mushrooms are not crisp, return to the microwave briefly; they should be fully dried but should not brown.

Cool the slices for a few minutes, then grind in a coffee grinder or spice grinder until the powder resembles coarsely ground black pepper. Do not grind the powder too fine or it will not be noticeable on the plate. Store in a covered plastic container.

MAKES ABOUT 1 TABLESPOON

### ONION POWDER

½ cup finely minced red onion (minced by hand or in the food processor)

Line a microwave tray with a piece of parchment paper and spread the onions on it in a thin, even layer. Microwave on medium power for about 20 minutes, or until the onions are completely dried out. Let cool to room temperature.

Grind the onions in a coffee or spice grinder until they resemble the flakes of kosher salt. Store in a covered plastic container.

MAKES ABOUT 1 TABLESPOON

### TOMATO POWDER

1/2 cup finely chopped tomato pulp (from a peeled and seeded tomato)

Squeeze the tomato pulp in a towel to extract any excess moisture. Line a microwave tray with a piece of parchment paper and spread the tomatoes on it in a thin, even layer. Microwave on low power for 30 to 40 minutes, or until the pulp is completely dried out but maintains its color. Let cool to room temperature.

Grind the dried pulp in a coffee or spice grinder until as fine as possible. There may be some pieces that do not break up, so when you feel the powder is as fine as it will get, sift it through a fine-mesh strainer, stirring with a spoon. Store in a covered plastic container.

MAKES ABOUT 1 TABLESPOON

### BEET POWDER

1/2 cup finely chopped beet (chopped in a food processor; or use the pulp left after juicing beets in a juicer)

Blot the beet pulp with paper towels to extract excess moisture. Line a microwave tray with a piece of parchment paper and spread the beets on it in a thin, even layer. Microwave on low power for 30 to 40 minutes, or until the beets are completely dried out but still maintain their color. Let the beets cool to room temperature. Grind the beets to a powder in a coffee or spice grinder. Store in a covered plastic container.

MAKES ABOUT 1 TABLESPOON

### MUSTARD POWDER

1 tablespoon black mustard seeds
1 tablespoon yellow mustard seeds

Grind the mustard seeds together to a fine powder in a coffee or spice grinder. Sift through a fine-mesh strainer, stirring with a spoon. Store in a covered plastic container.

MAKES ABOUT 1 TABLESPOON

### FENNEL POWDER

2 tablespoons fennel seeds

Toast the fennel seeds in a small skillet over low heat until fragrant.

Grind the seeds to a fine powder in a coffee or spice grinder. Sift through a fine-mesh strainer, stirring with a spoon. Store in a covered plastic container.

MAKES ABOUT 1 TABLESPOON

### DRIED HORSERADISH

1/4 cup shredded fresh horseradish

Drain the horseradish on paper towels to extract excess moisture. Line a microwave tray with a piece of parchment paper and spread the horseradish on it in a thin, even layer; try to spread the shreds apart as much as possible. Microwave on low power for 12 to 15 minutes, or until the horseradish is completely dry. Let cool to room temperature, then store in a covered plastic container.

MAKES ABOUT 1 GENEROUS TABLESPOON

### SQUAB SPICE

1/4 stick cinnamon, broken into small pieces
1 tablespoon coriander seeds
1 1/2 teaspoons cloves
2 tablespoons quatre épices (four-spice powder; see Sources, page 315)
2 tablespoons black peppercorns

Toast the cinnamon, coriander, cloves, and quatre-épices in a small skillet over low heat until fragrant.

Finely grind the toasted spices with the black pepper in a spice or coffee grinder. Sift through a fine-mesh strainer, stirring with a spoon. Store in a sealed container at room temperature or in the freezer. (The squab spice begins to lose some of its intensity after a few days; freeze for longer storage and use directly from the freezer.)

MAKES ABOUT 1/3 CUP

CHEESE

# The Composed Cheese Course

When I opened the French Laundry, it was clear we didn't have the space to roll a cheese cart around the room. But I like cheese and wanted to serve it. Traditional French service includes cheese, some dried and fresh fruit, some bread. I thought "Why not put this all together on individual plates to begin with?" So when the restaurant opened, I offered two composed cheese plates, one of them the Brie with balsamic vinegar and Tellicherry pepper. Today the cheese course has its own station in the kitchen, requiring its own chef.

I'm a fan of all cheeses, even Cheddars. We get an amazing Cheddar from a farmhouse in Wisconsin. Cheese has really come a long way in America. Proper French cheese service was a novelty as recently as the late 1970s. And now we've got countless American cheese makers creating excellent cheeses. It makes me happy; it's as if we're finally putting together all the pieces of what European and French cuisine is all about.

Whipped Brie de Meaux en Feuilleté, page 238

## Whipped Brie de Meaux en Feuilleté with Tellicherry Pepper and Baby Mâche

---

12 ounces ripe Brie, chilled

Extra virgin olive oil

12 thin slices baguette

Balsamic Glaze or Port Wine Glaze (recipe follows),

in a squeeze bottle

Freshly ground Tellicherry pepper (see page 180)

1 cup baby mâche

Fleur de sel

---

This is a very simple, elegant way to serve a familiar cheese and was, in fact, how I began composed cheese courses. Not only did I want to compose a cheese course, but I also wanted to manipulate the cheese into an elegant form. Brie is creamy and cream whips—therefore, I figured, I could whip Brie, and it worked. Be sure to use a very good, ripe, creamy Brie in this dish. Whipping makes it light and luxurious, even surprising. You recognize the flavor of Brie, but here, because the cheese is light and airy, that flavor is pleasantly out of context and feels new, especially paired with the spicy pepper and delicate greens.

Remove the rind from the Brie; you will have about 8 ounces of trimmed Brie. Put the cold cheese in a mixer with the paddle attachment and beat at medium speed, scraping down the sides from time to time, for about 10 minutes, until the cheese is very white and creamy.

Place a film of oil in a large skillet and rub each side of bread on both sides in the oil. Place over medium heat and cook on each side until golden brown, 1 to 2 minutes. Remove from the heat.

Squeeze the balsamic or port glaze in an X or other design on one side of each plate. Form a quenelle (see page 274), or small oval scoop, of the Brie (about 1 tablespoon) and place it in the center of one plate. Sprinkle with pepper and angle a crouton on top. Angle another quenelle of Brie over the crouton, sprinkle with pepper, and top with a second crouton. Repeat with the remaining Brie and croutons.

Toss the mâche with a small amount of olive oil. Place a small pile of mâche at the side of each serving of cheese and sprinkle the greens with fleur de sel.

MAKES 6 SERVINGS

### BALSAMIC GLAZE OR PORT WINE GLAZE

---

2 cups balsamic vinegar or port wine

We use glazes often in the cheese course, always sparingly, because they are so intense. When making a vinegar or wine glaze, reduce it slowly, almost as if you were letting it evaporate. If you boil it too hard, the acid will remain and make the glaze too sharp. Reducing it slowly and gently results in a much softer tasting glaze. It's easiest to control the heat with the aid of a heat diffuser.

Heat the vinegar or port in a heavy saucepan over medium heat until steam rises from the liquid. Place the saucepan on a heat diffuser and let the liquid reduce very slowly (it shouldn't simmer) for 2 to 3 hours, until it has reduced and thickened to a syrupy glaze. There should be approximately ½ cup of balsamic glaze or ¼ cup of port glaze. Keep the glaze in a squeeze bottle at room temperature for garnishing plates; if the glaze is too thick, warm the bottle in hot water to loosen the glaze.

PICTURED ON PAGE 237

MAKES ABOUT ½ CUP
USING VINEGAR,
¼ CUP USING PORT

### CROUTONS

---

Baguette or other bread, cut into thin slices,

or Brioche (page 258) rounds or triangles,

cut ¼ inch thick

Extra virgin olive oil

Kosher salt

Preheat the oven to 300°F.

FOR CROUTONS FOR CHEESE COURSES AND OTHER DISHES: Place the slices of bread on a baking sheet and drizzle or brush with a little olive oil. Sprinkle lightly with kosher salt. Bake for 10 to 15 minutes, or until an even golden brown.

FOR BRIOCHE CROUTONS FOR FOIE GRAS: Arrange the croutons (without any oil) on a baking sheet and bake for 10 to 15 minutes, or until an even golden brown.

Store all croutons in airtight containers.

## Ashed Chevreaux with Slow-Roasted Yellow and Red Beets and Red Beet Vinaigrette

1 cup red beet juice (from about 1 pound beets;
      or purchased from a health food store)

1 teaspoon red wine vinegar

1 to 2 yellow beets at least 2¼ inches in diameter (enough to yield
      twelve ⅛-inch slices), scrubbed

1 to 2 red beets (enough to yield thirty-six 1-inch-long batons;
      see page 203), scrubbed

2 tablespoons canola oil

Extra virgin olive oil

Kosher salt

6 ounces ashed Chevreaux or other ashed goat cheese,
      at room temperature, cut into 6 wedges or portions

½ cup baby beet greens

Beet Powder (page 233)

FOR THE BEET GLAZE: Heat the beet juice to a simmer in a small saucepan and cook until there are large bubbles forming at the top. Add the red wine vinegar and reduce until the liquid has a syrupy consistency. Pour into a small squeeze bottle.

Preheat the oven to 300°F.

Wrap the yellow beets and red beets separately in aluminum foil, adding 1 tablespoon of the canola oil to each. Roast for 1½ to 2 hours, or until they are tender.

Peel the cooked beets. Cut the yellow beets into twelve ⅛-inch slices, then cut them with a cutter into 2-inch rounds. Cut the red beets into 36 batons about 1 inch long by ¼ inch thick. Season all the beets with a little olive oil and salt.

TO COMPLETE: Pipe some beet glaze in dots of decreasing size down one side of each plate. Place a round of yellow beet in the center of each plate. Top each with 6 red beet batons laid side by side and another slice of yellow beet. Lay a wedge of cheese over each slice.

Toss the beet greens with a little olive oil and salt. Stack a small pile of greens on each round wedge of cheese and sprinkle the plates with beet powder.

PICTURED ON PAGE 240                    MAKES 6 SERVINGS

## Chaource with Red Plums, Clove-Scented Oil, and Lola Rossa

CLOVE OIL

1 tablespoon cloves

½ cup canola oil

PLUMS

6 red plums

1 teaspoon minced summer savory

Kosher salt

½ cup lola rossa (or other greens)

2 teaspoons minced chives

Extra virgin olive oil

Kosher salt

6 ounces Chaource, Camembert, or Explorateur,
      cut into 6 wedges, at room temperature

Chaource is a double-cream cow's milk cheese (double cream contains 50 to 60 percent fat), very luscious. This is a late-summer dish, when plums are harvested. If you can't find Chaource, you might try using a good Camembert or even Explorateur.

FOR THE CLOVE OIL: Toast the cloves in a small skillet over medium heat until fragrant. Finely grind the cloves in a spice grinder or coffee mill. Mix with the oil, place in a squeeze bottle, and let the flavor infuse for a day before using.

FOR THE PLUMS: Separate the flesh from the pit by cutting the flesh off in two vertical slices, one on each side of the pit. Cut the pieces crosswise into ⅛-inch slices (the pieces will be half-circles). Toss them with the summer savory, a little of the clove oil, and salt to taste.

Place a 2-inch ring mold (see Sources, page 315) on one serving plate. Layer one sixth of the slices of plum in the ring, overlapping the pieces and working in a circular pattern, with the skin side of the plum facing out. (There will be a hole in the middle.) Lift off the ring and repeat with the remaining plates.

TO COMPLETE: Toss the lola rossa with the chives, a little olive oil, and salt to taste. Arrange small "bouquets" of lettuce leaves and stand them in the holes in the center of the plums. Stand a wedge of cheese at the side of each bouquet. Squeeze a small amount of clove oil around the edges of the plums, letting it drizzle down onto the plate.

PICTURED ON PAGE 241                    MAKES 6 SERVINGS

Beets with goat cheese—that's a perfect combination. I think beets are

underappreciated; here, with their sweetness playing off the acidity of

the goat cheese, they're just wonderful. I'm partial to this ashed Chevreaux—

it's rolled in wood ashes, which add color and depth to the cheese—but

you can use almost any goat cheese.

Opposite, left: Ashed Chevreaux with Slow-Roasted Yellow and Red Beets, page 239. Above: Chaource with Red Plums, page 239.

# Corsu Vecchiu with Spiced Carrot Salad and Golden Raisin Purée

**SPICE MIX**

1½ teaspoons coriander seeds

1 tablespoon black peppercorns

One 1-inch-long piece cinnamon stick
    or 1½ teaspoons ground cinnamon

¾ teaspoon cloves

¾ cup carrot juice (from about 1¼ pounds
    carrots; or purchased from a
    health food store)

½ cup golden raisins

Juice of ½ lemon

One 8-ounce wedge Corsu Vecchiu or Gruyère,
    Emmenthal, Mahón, or Petite Basque,
    rind trimmed

¾ cup shredded sweet bunch carrots

2 teaspoons Brunoise (page 155)

Kosher salt

6 sprigs chervil

Carrot Powder (page 232)

Corsu Vecchiu is a semi-hard Spanish sheep's milk cheese, about the consistency of Gruyère, that has a nuttiness I like. It works very well with spices, so we created a sweet carrot salad that we season with a spice mix and added a golden raisin purée that links the carrots and cheese nicely. If you can find it, Mahón, another Spanish cheese, would work well in this dish.

Cutting the cheese into thin slices for serving allows more air to circulate around it; oxygen brings out the flavor of cheese, as does the proper temperature. The perfect temperature for cheese is 65° to 70°F.

FOR THE SPICE MIX: Heat the spices together in a small pan until fragrant. Place in a spice grinder and grind to a powder. You will have about 2½ tablespoons spice mix. Store in an airtight container for up to a week or in the freezer for longer.

Strain the carrot juice into a small saucepan, bring to a boil, and boil for about 1 minute. Skim off the scum that has risen to the top, strain the juice again, and simmer for about 10 minutes longer, or until reduced to 1½ to 2 tablespoons. Add a pinch of the spice mix and set aside.

Place the raisins in a saucepan. Cover completely with water, add the lemon juice, and simmer for 2 to 3 minutes, just until they plump. Turn off the heat and let the raisins sit in the liquid for a few minutes.

Place the raisins in a blender with enough of the cooking liquid to allow them to turn and blend to a purée. Strain the purée through a fine-mesh strainer.

Cut the cheese into 30 thin triangles. Arrange 5 triangles in a fan shape, then repeat to make portions.

TO COMPLETE: Combine the shredded carrots with the carrot reduction and the brunoise in a small bowl. Season with salt to taste.

Place about 1 tablespoon of raisin purée in the center of each plate. Top each with a haystack of carrot salad. Set a fan of cheese on top of each carrot salad and top the cheese with a sprig of chervil. Sprinkle a line of carrot powder down the side of each plate.

PICTURED ON PAGE 244    MAKES 6 SERVINGS

# Tête de Moine with Sauerkraut and Toasted Caraway Seed Vinaigrette

SAUERKRAUT

1 pound cabbage

5⅓ cups Champagne vinegar

5⅓ cups crisp, dry white wine, such as
    Sauvignon Blanc

¾ cup sugar

¾ cup kosher salt

CARAWAY SEED VINAIGRETTE

MAKES ½ CUP

⅓ cup chopped onions

½ teaspoon caraway seeds

Freshly ground black pepper

1 tablespoon sherry vinegar

¾ teaspoon dry mustard

½ teaspoon kosher salt, or to taste

¾ teaspoon sugar

1 tablespoon white wine vinegar

¼ cup plus 2 tablespoons olive oil

1 wheel tête de moine (you will use only a small
    portion of the wheel for this recipe),
    top trimmed, at room temperature
    or an 8-ounce piece, cut into 6 wedges,
    at room temperature

6 triangular rye bread Croutons (see page 238)

Tête de moine ("monk's head" in French) is a hard cheese from Switzerland. A special cutter is used to shave it into very long thin ruffles that are folded into a flower shape. It's buttery, if you can imagine a hard cheese being buttery, but there's also a sharpness to it. I pair it with sauerkraut—cabbage that we've marinated and cooked in white wine and vinegar.

If you don't have the special cutter designed for making the rosettes, the dish can be prepared by cutting the cheese into triangles and fanning it, as in the recipe for Corsu Vecchiu with Spiced Carrot Salad (page 242). As the cheese ages, it becomes more crumbly, and if it gets too brittle, it will be difficult to cut properly.

Begin the sauerkraut five days before you plan to serve the dish.

FOR THE SAUERKRAUT: Remove the core and thick ribs from the cabbage and cut it into fine chiffonade, long narrow strips about ⅛ inch wide (you will have about 4 cups of cabbage). Put the cabbage in a bowl or other container.

Combine 1⅓ cups each of the Champagne vinegar and white wine and 3 tablespoons each of the sugar and salt in a saucepan and bring to a boil. Remove from the heat and let cool to room temperature.

Pour the liquid over the cabbage, cover, and refrigerate for 24 hours. Drain the cabbage in a strainer and rinse with cold water. Repeat the marinating process three more times.

On the fifth day, preheat the oven to 275°F.

Drain and rinse the cabbage and place it in a baking dish. Cover the dish with a lid or aluminum foil and bake for 2 to 3 hours, or until the cabbage is tender but not mushy. Drain any excess liquid from the sauerkraut and refrigerate it until chilled. The sauerkraut will keep for up to 2 weeks.

FOR THE CARAWAY SEED VINAIGRETTE: Place the onions in a saucepan, add cold water to cover, and bring to a simmer. Cook for about 10 minutes, or until the onions are very tender. Drain the onions and place them in a blender.

Meanwhile, toast the caraway seeds in a small skillet over medium heat until fragrant. Set aside.

In a small bowl, mix together the sherry vinegar, mustard, salt, and sugar. Stir in the white wine vinegar. Add the mixture to the blender and purée for about 2 minutes, scraping the sides of the container as necessary, until the mixture has the consistency of syrup. If it is thicker, add a small amount of water to thin. With the blender on, drizzle in the oil.

Add the caraway seeds to the blender and blend to grind the seeds. Strain the dressing and adjust the seasoning with salt if necessary and pepper to taste. Store the dressing in the refrigerator for up to 1 week.

TO COMPLETE: If using a cheese cutter, form rosettes of cheese by turning the cutter about one and a half times around the cheese for each rosette.

Place a spoonful of vinaigrette in the center of each serving plate. Place a spoonful of sauerkraut to one side of the vinaigrette and prop a crouton against it, setting the crouton in the middle of the plate. Place a rosette or wedge of cheese on the other side of each crouton.

PICTURED ON PAGE 245                    MAKES 6 SERVINGS

Above: Corsu Vecchiu with Spiced Carrot Salad, page 242. Opposite: Tête de moine, for Tête de Moine with Sauerkraut, page 243.

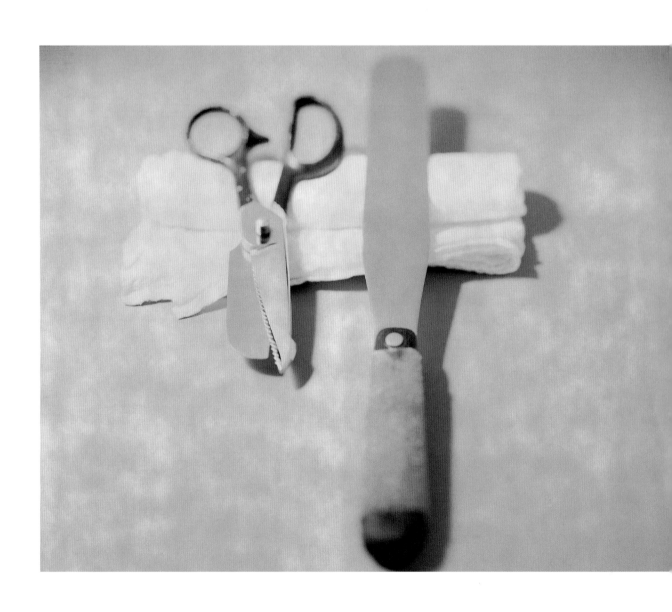

# The Importance of France

After my mother died, I determined to own my own restaurant. René and Paulette would not sell me an interest in La Rive, so I went to New York City and worked as a *poissonnier* (fish cook) at The Polo Restaurant, an exciting, dynamic kitchen with talented young French chefs. Here I saw composed plates for the first time. All the sauces were reductions, and it was my first experience working within a traditional French brigade system.

That job eventually launched me to Paris, where I worked in half a dozen two- and three-star restaurants for a full year. It was in France that I concluded my self-styled apprenticeship.

In these great French kitchens—Taillevent, Guy Savoy, and Pré Catalan among them—what I learned once again was respect for food, but here it had a new depth and dimension. This was a society that reinforced and amplified everything I'd begun to learn on my own.

And it turned out that was a lot. Just short of thirty years old, I found that I was well grounded in my profession. Now I could focus on details: I could learn the foie gras torchon. I could learn how to extract chlorophyll from green vegetables so that I could make a fish terrine with a chlorophyll-based mousse that stayed a beautiful green after I cooked it. I learned how a breast of lamb—a country-style one-pot item—could be prepared and served in a way that was satisfying and worthy of a Michelin-starred restaurant. I learned how to work with chocolate.

When I returned to America after a year, I began what was in effect my search for my own La Rive, for the kind of three-star restaurant that I had seen in the gorgeous landscapes of France. The moment I beheld the French Laundry, in the spring of 1992, I knew I'd come to the end of the journey. Or the beginning, depending on how you look at it.

## WORKING WITH CHLOROPHYLL

Chlorophylls are the pigments in green vegetables and herbs. Though extracted chlorophyll can be flavored, the reason for extracting it is to color food or a sauce green, particularly things you want to cook, such as a fish mousse, since chlorophyll stays green through cooking. At the French Laundry, we add it to herb sauces for heightened visual impact, and to cream—say, a parsley cream for fish or a watercress cream for veal.

To extract chlorophyll, push your greens through a grinder (I use two parts spinach and one part each parsley and watercress, though flavor is not an issue here); place a collar of foil around the die so you don't get spattered with green. You can also pulse the greens in a food processor, but don't purée them. Add at least four times as much water to your ground greens and let them soak in the refrigerator overnight. Strain the liquid through a China cap into a pan, squeezing as much moisture as possible from the greens. Bring the liquid to a simmer, stirring continuously. You will see the chlorophyll separating from the water as it heats. As soon as the water and chlorophyll have clearly separated, shock the mixture by adding ice, just enough ice to cool it down but not so much that you're left with a lot of ice cubes in the pot. Strain the liquid through a strainer lined with a kitchen towel or a cloth napkin. Let the liquid drain overnight.

The next day, you should find in your cloth pure chlorophyll; it will look like an artist's oil paint squeezed straight from the tube. Remove it to a jar until ready to use. It must be used within a day or two, or it will begin to spoil.

## THE ATTORNEY CHEESEMAKER: CINDY CALLAHAN

"If I ever get depressed," says Cindy Callahan, "I go sit on a stump and watch my lambs."

Cindy, a former attorney, sits in the dining room of her ranch house in Valley Ford, Sonoma County. Her son Brett pops into the open kitchen, retrieves something from the fridge, says, "Hi," and departs. Mainstream middle-class living, it would seem, except for the fact that Cindy is cradling a lamb, feeding it milk out of a large beer bottle. It's lambing season and winter rains have been pounding the entire coast of California. Some lambs are too weak to nurse outdoors, so Cindy has brought them inside till the weather improves and the babies are stronger.

"Sheep are not very smart, they just eat and tend their young," Cindy says. "But there's something very calming about them."

When Cindy and her late husband left San Francisco for the bucolic hills of Sonoma, Cindy bought some sheep, more or less as a hobby. Soon she had more lamb than the family could use. So she called Chez Panisse, the Berkeley restaurant famous for supporting small farmers, and they began to buy lamb. Cindy read about certain cultures that raised baby lamb and she began selling these to California restaurants. But it wasn't until a friend visiting the farm raved about the splendors of sheep's milk yogurt that the Callahans began to wonder if they didn't have something even more valuable and creatively

satisfying than lamb raised for its meat. They had as a by-product gallons and gallons of sheep's milk.

When they learned that one of their favorite cheeses, Roquefort, was made from sheep's milk, they knew they had to start making cheese. After a trip to Italy in 1992 to learn about cheese making, they began fashioning what they hoped would be the main product of Bellwether Farm. Son Brett tends the sheep, son Liam makes the cheese.

Cindy says that they make cheese for the same reason vintners make wine. "Why do people make wine?" she says. "There's the science of it, but above that, there's the creativity of it." The Callahans' cheese is handmade and varies slightly from season to season. In the summer, the milk tends to be higher in protein; in winter, higher in fat. These factors influence the resulting cheese.

They produce from six hundred to eight hundred pounds of cheese a week from the milk from their sheep and from Jersey cows. They make three different cheeses from each milk, and they make ricotta from the whey, or liquids, left over from each milk.

"I like sheep's milk cheeses because the flavors are so complex," says Cindy.

In 1986, Cindy had bought her lambs mainly to keep the grass short. Within a decade, the Callahans had built the first sheep dairy in the state and they now have a thriving business in handmade cheeses. —M.R.

# Pecorino Toscano with Roasted Sweet Peppers and Arugula Coulis

ARUGULA COULIS

1 cup kosher salt

1½ cups (6 ounces) arugula

1½ tablespoons extra virgin olive oil

ROASTED PEPPERS

¼ cup julienned (¼ inch thick) roasted red
    peppers

¼ cup julienned (¼ inch thick) roasted yellow
    peppers

1½ tablespoons extra virgin olive oil

2 teaspoons balsamic vinegar

2 teaspoons minced chives

Kosher salt

One 4- to 6-ounce wedge pecorino Toscano
    or other pecorino, rind removed

½ cup baby arugula

Extra virgin olive oil

Kosher salt

Balsamic Glaze (page 238), in a squeeze bottle

6 Croutons (see page 238)

We serve this Italian-style sheep's milk cheese in an Italian style: on crostini with roasted bell peppers and a purée of arugula. We use the Callahans' artisan cheese, but you could use any pecorino.

FOR THE ARUGULA COULIS: Bring a gallon of water to a boil in a large pot, then add the salt and bring to a rolling boil. (The water needs to be boiling rapidly to maintain the boil once the arugula is added.) Add the arugula and cook for 5 to 10 minutes, until the stems are tender. Drain the arugula and place in an ice-water bath to chill.

Remove the arugula from the water and squeeze out the excess water. Place the arugula in a blender with just enough water to allow it to blend and blend to a purée. Spread the purée on a tamis (see page 73) and allow to sit for 5 minutes to drain any excess liquid. Discard the liquid and pass the purée through the tamis and then return it to the blender. Add the olive oil and blend well. Remove to a container. Refrigerate until you are ready to use it, or for up to a few hours.

FOR THE ROASTED PEPPERS: An hour before serving, toss the peppers together in a small bowl with the oil, vinegar, chives, and salt to taste. Set aside.

Using a mandoline, cut the pecorino into thin triangular slices; you will need a total of 30 slices. Fan the slices in 6 groups of 5 slices each.

TO COMPLETE: Toss the baby arugula with olive oil and salt to taste.

Squeeze a ring of balsamic glaze dots onto the center of each plate: To do so, squeeze the bottle until a bead of glaze starts to come out the top. Hold the bottle at about a 75-degree angle, with the tip of the bottle touching the plate, and, maintaining a slight pressure on the bottle, drag the tip around the plate to form the dotted line. (This takes a little practice; just adjust the angle of the bottle and the pressure exerted until you achieve the desired effect.)

Place a spoonful of arugula coulis in the center of each ring of glaze. Top each with a portion of the roasted peppers, a crouton, and a fan of cheese. Garnish each fan of cheese with a stack of baby arugula salad.

MAKES 6 SERVINGS

## ROASTED PEPPERS

Bell Peppers

Olive Oil

I'm amazed that I can dislike a vegetable in its raw form yet manipulate it into something I love. I don't like raw peppers, but this simple preparation is one of my very favorites. The peppers keep for weeks in the refrigerator.

Preheat the oven to 350°F. Line a baking sheet with foil. Cut the peppers lengthwise in half. Trim and discard the white ribs and seeds. Brush the peppers with olive oil and place cut side down on the baking sheet. Bake for 15 to 20 minutes, or until they have softened and the skin has loosened from the flesh. Place in a covered container for several minutes to steam and loosen the skin further. When the peppers are cool enough to handle, peel off the skin and discard any remaining seeds or ribs.

# Parmigiano-Reggiano Custards with Romaine Lettuce, Anchovy Dressing, and Parmesan Crisps

**ANCHOVY DRESSING** MAKES 2 CUPS

1½ tablespoons chopped garlic

1½ tablespoons chopped shallots

¼ cup balsamic vinegar

2 tablespoons Dijon mustard

1 teaspoon fresh lemon juice

2 salt-packed anchovy fillets, deboned,
    soaked in milk to cover for 30 minutes,
    drained, and patted dry

1 large egg yolk

1 cup extra virgin olive oil

1 cup canola oil

Freshly ground white pepper

**CUSTARDS**

⅔ cup heavy cream

⅔ cup milk

3½ ounces Parmigiano-Reggiano,
    cut into ½-inch pieces

2 large eggs

1 large egg yolk

Kosher salt and freshly ground white pepper

3 cups chiffonade, or long narrow strips,
    romaine lettuce (cut from the "hearts,"
    or small inner leaves)

2 tablespoons freshly grated Parmigiano-Reggiano

Freshly ground black pepper

12 Croutons (from a baguette),
    about ¼ inch thick (page 238)

Twelve 1-inch (or the diameter of the molds)
    Parmesan Crisps (page 37)

Parmigiano-Reggiano shavings for garnish
    (made with a vegetable peeler)

Balsamic Glaze (page 238), in a squeeze bottle

I frequently return to classical preparations and look for a way to reinterpret them, using the standard elements but surprising you with them. Here those elements include a Parmesan custard set on croutons, a chiffonade of romaine, and a Parmesan crisp, with a classic Caesar dressing.

FOR THE ANCHOVY DRESSING: Pureé the garlic, shallots, vinegar, mustard, lemon juice, and anchovies in a blender until smooth. Transfer to a mixer with the paddle attachment and beat in the egg yolk. With the machine running, slowly drizzle in the oils. Season with white pepper. Cover and refrigerate. There will be more dressing than you need for this recipe, but the extra can be stored in the refrigerator for up to 3 days.

FOR THE CUSTARDS: Place the cream, milk, and Parmigiano-Reggiano in a saucepan and bring to a simmer. Turn off the heat, cover the pan, and let the flavors infuse for 45 minutes.

Preheat the oven to 250°F.

Whisk the eggs and yolk together in a medium bowl. Reheat the cream mixture until it is hot. While whisking, gradually strain the cream and milk onto the eggs to temper them. Season with salt and white pepper.

Ladle 2 tablespoons of the custard mixture into each of twelve 1- to 2-ounce aluminum foil baking molds, timbale molds, or other small molds. Place the molds in a roasting pan and add hot water to come about halfway up the sides of the molds. If you are using foil cups and they float, place a baking sheet or pan over them to hold them down. Cover the roasting pan with aluminum foil and bake for 30 minutes, or until the custards are just set; the edges should look set, but the very centers may not be. Remove the molds from the water bath and refrigerate the custards for at least 2 hours and up to 2 days.

TO COMPLETE: Toss the romaine with the Parmigiano-Reggiano and just enough dressing to lightly coat the lettuce. Season with pepper to taste.

Place a spoonful of dressing on each plate. Run a small paring knife around the edge of each custard, dip the molds briefly into hot water, and unmold each custard onto a crouton. Center one crouton in each pool of dressing. Lay a Parmesan crisp over each custard and top with a stack of the salad. Place shavings of cheese over the romaine and garnish each plate with a ring or a small pool of the balsamic glaze.

PICTURED ON PAGE 253                MAKES 12 SERVINGS

Above, left: Roquefort Trifle, page 256. Opposite: "Caesar Salad," page 251.

Perail de bribes is a wonderful soft
French sheep's milk cheese with
a thick-as-honey interior. It's ripened
in small disks that are a perfect
size for two people.

Opposite: "Soup and Sandwich," page 258. Above: Perail de Bribes with Frisée aux Lardons, page 257.

# Roquefort Trifle with French Butter Pear Relish

**PEAR PURÉE**

6 allspice berries

15 black peppercorns

1 1/4 cups water

3 tablespoons sugar

2 2/3 cups (6 ounces) dried pear halves,
    cut into 1/4-inch dice

**PEAR RELISH**

3/4 cup peeled and diced (1/16 inch) ripe French
    Butter, Bosc, or other firm pears

3 tablespoons diced (1/16 inch) red onion

1 1/2 tablespoons peeled and diced (1/16 inch)
    red bell pepper

3 tablespoons sugar

3 tablespoons red wine vinegar

**ROQUEFORT MOUSSE**

4 ounces Roquefort

3/4 cup milk

1 gelatin sheet, soaked in cold water to soften

1/4 cup plus 2 tablespoons heavy cream

**DACQUOISE**

1 1/4 cups (4 ounces) walnuts

1/2 cup (2 ounces) all-purpose flour

8 tablespoons (4 ounces) unsalted butter,
    well softened

2 large egg whites

1/2 teaspoon kosher salt

Roquefort, pears, and walnuts—I take this traditional combination, tastes we know go well together, and manipulate it into something elegant and unusual, without losing that reference point. For the finished dish, a Roquefort mousse, a purée of dried pears, and a walnut cookie, or dacquoise, are served like an English trifle. This is best presented in small crystal bowls or glasses with about a four-ounce capacity.

FOR THE PEAR PURÉE: Wrap the allspice berries and peppercorns in a piece of cheesecloth and tie the bundle with a piece of string to form a sachet. Combine the water, sugar, and sachet in a small saucepan and bring to a simmer. Add the diced pears, cover with a parchment lid (see page 190), and continue to simmer gently for 20 to 30 minutes, or until the pears are plump and very soft; there will be some liquid remaining.

Remove the sachet and purée the pears with the remaining cooking liquid in a blender until very smooth. Transfer the purée to a container (there will be 1 to 1 1/2 cups of puree) and store in the refrigerator until ready to serve. The pear purée will keep for a few weeks.

FOR THE PEAR RELISH: Combine all the relish ingredients in a saucepan and cook over very low heat for 20 to 30 minutes, or until all the liquid has evaporated and the ingredients are tender. You should have about 1/3 cup of relish. Store, covered, in the refrigerator for up to 2 days.

FOR THE ROQUEFORT MOUSSE: Crumble the Roquefort cheese into a bowl and let sit at room temperature until the pieces have softened.

Heat the milk in a saucepan until it is hot to the touch and pour it over the cheese. Allow the cheese and milk to sit for a few minutes, then scrape into a blender and blend for about 10 seconds to combine. Pour the mixture back into the saucepan and rewarm it slightly, just so it's hot enough to melt the gelatin. Squeeze excess water from the gelatin and whisk it into the warm liquid to dissolve. Strain through a chinois (see page 73) into a bowl and place in the refrigerator to cool.

Using a whisk, whip the cream in a metal bowl until it just begins to form soft peaks; it should still be pourable. Fold the cream into the Roquefort mixture, one third at a time. You should have about 1 1/2 cups of mousse.

TO COMPLETE: Spoon 2 to 3 tablespoons of pear purée into the bottom of each serving dish or glass. (The amount you use is a matter of taste as well as the size and shape of your dishes. Wide bowls will need more purée than narrower glasses.) Smooth the top of the purée and top each with about ¼ cup of the Roquefort mousse. Refrigerate for at least 3 hours to set, or for up to a day.

FOR THE DACQUOISE: Preheat the oven to 325°F. Line a 12- by 16-inch baking sheet with a Silpat (see Sources, page 315).

Place the walnuts and flour in the thoroughly dry bowl of a food processor fitted with a metal blade. Pulse the mixture carefully until the nuts are finely ground and powdery in texture; do not overprocess, or the nuts may become oily and pasty.

Whisk the butter in a bowl until it resembles mayonnaise in consistency. Fold the nut and flour mixture into the butter. It will be somewhat dry at first but will come together.

In a second bowl, whisk the egg whites until foamy. Add the salt and continue to whisk until the egg whites are blended but not yet holding peaks. Fold half the whites into the nut mixture to combine, then fold in the rest (it will resemble muffin batter).

Use an offset spatula to spread the dacquoise batter in a layer $\frac{1}{16}$ to $\frac{1}{8}$ inch thick over the Silpat liner. The dacquoise must be marked into circles the same size as the top of the trifles. Measure the diameter of the top of the finished trifles and use a cutter of the same size to mark circles in the dacquoise. Mark several more than needed; you may need extras because of their fragile nature.

Place the pan in the oven for 20 to 30 minutes, reversing the pan after 10 minutes to ensure even cooking. The finished dacquoises are medium brown and firm to the touch. Remove from the oven and, while they are still hot, place the cutter on the premarked circles and rotate it back and forth between your fingers to recut the disks. Let them cool, then store the dacquoises in an airtight container.

Just before serving, set a dacquoise over each trifle and garnish with a quenelle (see page 274), or small oval scoop, of the pear relish.

PICTURED ON PAGE 252                          MAKES 6 SERVINGS

## Perail de Brebis with Frisée aux Lardons

Three ⅛-inch-thick slices bacon, frozen and cut into ⅛-inch cubes

3 tablespoons Dijon mustard

1½ tablespoons sherry vinegar

¼ cup extra virgin olive oil

Six 1¾-inch rounds Brioche (page 258), cut ⅔ inch thick

2 tablespoons (1 ounce) unsalted butter

6 quail eggs

¾ cup frisée lettuce

1 teaspoon minced chives

12 small wedges Perail de Brebis or other soft sheep's milk cheese

Freshly ground black pepper

Preheat the oven to 350°F.

Place the pieces of bacon in a small skillet over low heat and cook until browned. Remove the bacon to drain on paper towels.

Whisk the mustard and vinegar together in a small bowl. Stir in the olive oil with a spoon. The dressing should be "broken" in appearance rather than emulsified.

Use a 1-inch round cutter to make a hole in the center of each bread round. Melt the butter in a large nonstick ovenproof skillet over medium heat. When the butter is frothy, add the rounds of brioche. When the bottoms are golden brown, remove the pan from the burner, flip the brioche rounds over, and break a quail egg into each hole. Return the skillet to the burner and cook until the bottoms are golden brown. If the egg whites still look uncooked, place the skillet in the oven for 30 seconds or so, just to set the whites.

TO COMPLETE: Toss the frisée with the chives and just enough dressing to lightly coat the greens. Place a small mound of frisée on each plate and sprinkle with the bacon. Arrange 2 wedges of cheese alongside each pile of greens. Set a warm brioche round next to the lettuce and cheese; sprinkle black pepper over the plate.

PICTURED ON PAGE 255                          MAKES 6 SERVINGS

# Grilled Farmhouse Cheddar, Early Girl Tomato Consommé, and Butter-Fried Chips

### TOMATO CONSOMMÉ

18 to 24 very ripe Early Girl tomatoes
(about 6 pounds) (or the most flavorful
variety available), cored and halved

1 dried chipotle pepper, soaked in hot water
for about 30 minutes to soften, and drained

6 each red, yellow, and green cherry tomatoes,
such as Sweet 100, Golden Jubilee,
and Green Grape

Salt to taste

### POTATO CHIPS

1½ cups Clarified Butter (page 125)

1½ cups canola oil

2 each very small purple Peruvian, baby
red-skinned, and very small
Yukon Gold potatoes

Kosher salt

### GRILLED CHEESE SANDWICH

3 ounces white Cheddar cheese,
cut into paper-thin slices

12 crustless 2-inch squares Brioche (recipe
follows), ¼ inch thick

¼ cup Clarified Butter (page 125), melted

Grilled cheese—Kraft Singles and Wonder Bread—taken to another level with slices of brioche and a beautiful farmhouse Cheddar. Serve it with tomato soup just as Mom did when you were a kid—a dish straight out of an American childhood, refined into haute cuisine. Note that the tomatoes for the consommé need to drain overnight.

FOR THE TOMATO CONSOMMÉ: Place the halved tomatoes in a food processor with the chipotle pepper and pulse until the tomatoes are finely chopped. Line a bowl with a clean, damp cotton dish towel or a triple layer of cheesecloth. Pour the chopped tomatoes and pepper into the towel. Bring up the edges of the towel around the tomatoes and tie with a piece of string to form a pouch. Discard the liquid in the bowl. Hang the bag of tomatoes from a rack in the refrigerator, suspended over the bowl, and let drain overnight. (Or hang it from a wooden spoon set over a deep container.)

The next day, there should be about 2 cups of tomato water, or consommé. Strain it and chill for at least 1 hour, or up to 1 day.

Blanch the cherry tomatoes in lightly salted water for a few seconds to loosen the skin. Remove the tomatoes with a slotted spoon and plunge them into an ice water bath to cool. Remove the tomatoes and peel them with a small paring knife. These can be held at room temperature for a few hours before serving.

FOR THE POTATO CHIPS: Heat the clarified butter and oil in a small deep saucepan to 300°F. Meanwhile, cut the unpeeled potatoes on a mandoline into paper-thin slices. Deep-fry them in batches, for 2 to 3 minutes, or until they are crisp and the oil around the chips is no longer bubbling. (The moisture in the potatoes causes the bubbles and once

they stop, the chips will be crisp.) Transfer to paper towels to drain.

TO COMPLETE: For the grilled cheese sandwich, divide the cheese evenly among six pieces of the brioche. Top with the remaining slices of bread to form sandwiches. Brush each sandwich on both sides with the clarified butter.

Heat a nonstick skillet over medium heat. Cook the sandwiches, turning once, until the brioche is golden brown and the cheese has melted. Cut each sandwich in half on the diagonal to form two triangles.

Place one of each color cherry tomato in each of six demitasse cups. Season the consommé with salt and fill the cups with the chilled tomato consommé. Place each cup on a serving dish and arrange a grilled cheese sandwich and a portion of the potato chips alongside. Sprinkle the chips with kosher salt.

PICTURED ON PAGE 254                    MAKES 6 SERVINGS

## BRIOCHE

⅓ cup very warm water (110° to
115°F.)

One ¼-ounce package active dry
yeast (not quick-rising)

2⅓ cups (10½ ounces) cake flour

2 cups (10 ounces) all-purpose flour

⅓ cup sugar

2½ teaspoons fine sea salt

6 large eggs, at room temperature

20 tablespoons (10 ounces) unsalted
butter, at room temperature, cut
into 1-inch cubes, plus butter
for the pans

Chef Jean-Louis Palladin makes some of the best brioche I've ever had; this is his recipe, and it's the one we use at the restaurant. Start this a day before you want to make it, as it has to rest overnight.

Combine the water and yeast in a small bowl. Let set for 10 minutes, then stir until the yeast is completely dissolved. Set aside.

Sift together the flours, sugar, and salt into the bowl of a mixer fitted with the dough hook. Add the eggs and beat for 1 minute at low speed, scraping down the sides with a rubber spatula as needed. Slowly add the dissolved yeast and continue beating at low speed for 5 minutes. Stop the machine, scrape any dough off the dough hook, and beat for another 5 minutes. Add the butter cubes, about one quarter of them at a time, beating for about 1 minute after each addition. Once all the butter has been added, beat for 10 to 15 minutes more.

Place the dough in a large floured mixing bowl and cover with plastic wrap. Set aside in a warm place until doubled in size, about 3 hours.

Turn the dough out onto a generously floured work surface and gently work the air bubbles out by folding the dough over several times while lightly pressing down on it. Return the dough to the bowl, cover with plastic wrap, and refrigerate overnight.

Generously butter two 8½- by 4½- by 3-inch loaf pans. Turn the dough out onto a floured work surface. With floured hands, divide the dough in half and shape it into two rectangles to fit the loaf pans. Place the dough in the pans and let the dough rise uncovered in a warm place until it is about ½ inch above the top of the pans, about 3 hours.

Preheat the oven to 350°F. Bake the brioche until it is well browned on top and sounds hollow when tapped on the bottom, 35 to 40 minutes. Remove from the oven and immediately turn the brioche out onto a wire rack.

If using immediately, let the breads cool for 10 minutes, then slice and serve. If serving within a few hours, promptly wrap the hot bread in aluminum foil and store at room temperature until ready to use. If freezing, immediately wrap the hot bread in foil and promptly freeze; when ready to use, reheat (without thawing, and still wrapped in foil) in a 250°F. oven until heated through, 20 to 25 minutes. The bread can be kept frozen for up to 1 month.

If using the brioche for croutons, let the loaf sit at room temperature, uncovered, to dry for a day.

MAKES 2 LOAVES

DESSERT

# Cappuccino Semifreddo with Cinnamon-Sugar Doughnuts

**CAPPUCCINO SEMIFREDDO**

2 large eggs, separated

3 large egg yolks

³/₄ cup sugar

¹/₂ vanilla bean, split

2 tablespoons espresso extract (see Note)

¹/₂ cup heavy cream

**CINNAMON-SUGAR DOUGHNUTS**

**PART 1**

¹/₄ cup plus 1 tablespoon water,
    at room temperature

¹/₄ ounce compressed fresh yeast

¹/₂ cup all-purpose flour

**PART 2**

¹/₄ ounce compressed fresh yeast

2 tablespoons milk, at room temperature

1 cup plus 2 tablespoons all-purpose flour,
    or more as needed

3 tablespoons sugar

1 teaspoon kosher salt

¹/₄ cup egg yolks (about 3 large yolks)

2 tablespoons (1 ounce) unsalted butter, melted
    and cooled

Canola oil for deep-frying

Cinnamon sugar: ¹/₂ cup sugar mixed with
    1¹/₄ teaspoons ground cinnamon

¹/₂ cup milk

This may be another of those had-to-be-sad-to-see-it creations, like the salmon cornet. I was working in L.A., miserable and poor. I had a James Beard Foundation dinner coming up and had no idea what I was going to serve. Across from my apartment was an S and K doughnut shop. I'd go there once a week for a glazed old-fashioned doughnut and a cup of coffee. I liked the glazed old-fashioned because it was so heavy—it felt like you were getting a lot for your money. And there it was: Coffee and Doughnuts. I tried it for the first time at the Beard House and it worked.

An element of surprise here is that the semifreddo, a partially frozen mousse, is cold beneath hot, frothy steamed milk. The doughnuts are delicious traditional deep-fried treats, coated with cinnamon sugar. It's a great do-ahead recipe; not only can the semifreddo be kept frozen, but the uncooked doughnuts can also stay frozen for up to three days. This dessert always seems to make people smile.

FOR THE CAPPUCCINO SEMIFREDDO: Place the egg yolks and ¹/₄ cup plus 2 tablespoons of sugar in the bowl of a mixer fitted with the whisk attachment. Scrape the seeds from the vanilla bean into the bowl. Whip for about 12 minutes at medium speed, or until the mixture has lightened and tripled in volume. Beat in the espresso extract. Transfer the mixture to a bowl placed in a larger bowl of ice water to maintain its consistency.

In a mixer bowl or a metal bowl, whip the heavy cream with 3 tablespoons of the sugar until it holds its shape when the whisk or beater is lifted. Fold the whipped cream into the yolk mixture and return the bowl to the ice.

Whip the egg whites in a mixer bowl or metal bowl until they are frothy. While whipping, add in the remaining 3 tablespoons of sugar and whip the egg whites just until they hold soft peaks, being careful not to overwhip them. Fold the beaten egg whites into the egg yolk mixture until they are completely combined.

Spoon the semifreddo into six 8- to 10-ounce coffee cups, leaving at least ¹/₂ inch at the top for the steamed milk. Gently tap the cups against the counter to level the mixture. Cover the cups with plastic wrap and place them in the freezer until frozen, at least 6 to 8 hours, or overnight. These will keep for up to 3 days in the freezer; after that time, they will start to deflate.

Preceding page: "Coffee and Doughnuts"

FOR THE CINNAMON-SUGAR DOUGHNUTS: PART 1: Place the water in the bowl of a mixer. Crumble the yeast into the water; mix and crush the yeast with a spoon to dissolve. Add the flour to the bowl and, using the dough hook, mix slowly until the ingredients are thoroughly blended.

Transfer this sponge to a bowl, cover, and let proof at room temperature for 1 to 2 hours, until it has doubled; or place the bowl in the refrigerator to proof overnight.

PART 2: Crumble the yeast into the milk in a small bowl, stirring to dissolve. Place ¾ cup of the flour, the sugar, and salt in the bowl of a mixer fitted with the dough hook. Mixing on low speed, pour in the milk and yeast mixture, followed by the egg yolks and butter. Mix for a minute to combine.

Add the proofed sponge and the remaining ¼ cup plus 2 tablespoons flour. Continue to beat at low speed until combined. Turn up the speed slightly and knead the dough for 4 to 5 minutes, or until it has formed a ball and cleans the sides of the bowl. If the dough seems wet, it may be necessary to add 1 to 2 more tablespoons flour. Cover the bowl and let the dough proof overnight in the refrigerator.

TO SHAPE THE DOUGHNUTS: Place the chilled dough on a lightly floured surface and roll it out to a ½-inch thickness. Cut out the doughnuts using a 2-inch doughnut cutter, or a 2-inch biscuit cutter (in which case, you will also need a ¾-inch cutter to make the hole). Place the doughnuts and doughnut holes on a baking sheet lined with parchment paper. Cover the doughnuts with a sheet of plastic wrap that has been sprayed with nonstick spray.

At this point, the doughnuts can be frozen for several days, refrigerated, or allowed to rise at room temperature. If they're frozen, defrost them and then allow them to rise at room temperature for 1 to 1½ hours. They can be refrigerated for several hours or overnight, to rise slowly. When you remove them from the refrigerator, uncover them and let them finish proofing in a warm place for 20 to 30 minutes. If they have not been refrigerated or frozen, they should rise at room temperature in about 15 minutes. Once proofed, they will have risen to approximately ¾ inch.

TO COOK THE DOUGHNUTS: In a deep heavy saucepan large enough to hold half the doughnuts and holes at a time, heat canola oil for deep-frying to 325°F. Add half the doughnuts and holes to the oil and cook for approximately 30 seconds on the first side. Flip the doughnuts and fry for 1 minute on the second side, then turn back to the first side to cook for an additional 30 seconds, or until a deep golden brown. Remove the doughnuts, drain them briefly on paper towels, and toss them in a bowl with the cinnamon sugar. Repeat with the remaining doughnuts.

TO COMPLETE: Remove the semifreddo from the freezer a few minutes before serving to soften slightly. Steam the milk using a cappuccino machine or frothing machine. Place a cup of semifreddo and a doughnut on each of six plates. Top each doughnut with a doughnut hole. Spoon the steamed milk over the semifreddo and serve immediately.

MAKES 6 SERVINGS

NOTE: Coffee extract is available to culinary professionals. An alternative is to fill a jar of instant espresso with boiling water. This will dissolve the granules and create espresso extract, which can be stored indefinitely in the refrigerator. Or you can make a smaller quantity, using equal amounts of espresso powder and boiling water.

# Cream of Blueberry Soup with Yogurt Charlottes

**YOGURT CHARLOTTES**

2/3 cup heavy cream

1/4 cup sugar

1 gelatin sheet, soaked in cold water to soften

1 cup plain whole-milk yogurt

**CRÈME ANGLAISE**

1/2 vanilla bean, split

1 cup heavy cream

1 cup milk

1/2 cup sugar

5 large egg yolks

**TELLICHERRY PEPPER SYRUP**

1 cup water

3/4 cup sugar

6 Tellicherry peppercorns (see page 180), lightly crushed (with the bottom of a heavy pan or a meat pounder)

1 pint raspberries

1 pint small strawberries, hulled

1 small sprig mint

**DACQUOISE**

1 cup (3 ounces) sliced blanched almonds, finely ground in a coffee mill

1 cup sugar

2 tablespoons cornstarch

1/3 cup egg whites (2 to 3 egg whites)

**BLUEBERRY SOUP**

1 cup dry crisp, white wine, such as Sauvignon Blanc

Julienned zest (removed with a zester) and juice of 1 lemon

1 1/2 pints blueberries

1/2 cup sugar

2 egg cartons or a baking pan filled with a 1/2-inch layer of salt or crumpled foil (to support the molds)

The blueberry soup is fantastic all by itself, but I like the charlotte because it is a unique way to use yogurt, which replaces the traditional milk or cream. We use as little gelatin as possible to keep the delicacy of the yogurt intact.

The charlottes are formed in 4-ounce "hemisphere"-shaped stainless steel molds (see Sources, page 315). They should be made a day or two ahead.

FOR THE YOGURT CHARLOTTES: Combine 1/3 cup of the cream with the sugar in a small saucepan and bring to a simmer over medium heat, stirring until the sugar is dissolved. Pour the cream into a bowl. Squeeze the excess water from the gelatin sheet and stir it into the hot cream until it has dissolved. Stir in the yogurt and allow the mixture to cool to room temperature.

In a medium bowl, lightly whip the remaining 1/3 cup cream just until it begins to hold its shape. Stir the cooled yogurt mixture into the cream.

Place 6 hemisphere molds in the egg cartons, or nestle them in the foil or salt to keep them from tilting. Divide the charlotte mixture among the molds. Cover and refrigerate for at least 1 and up to 2 days.

FOR THE CRÈME ANGLAISE: Scrape the seeds from the vanilla bean into a medium saucepan; add the pod, cream, milk, and half the sugar. Bring to a simmer, stirring to dissolve the sugar.

Meanwhile, in a medium bowl, whisk the egg yolks with the remaining sugar until they have thickened and lightened to a pale yellow. Whisk one third of the hot cream mixture into the yolks to temper them and return the mixture to the saucepan. Stir with a wooden spoon over low heat until the custard thickens and coats the back of the spoon. Pour the custard into a metal bowl set in an ice-water bath to cool. When the custard is cool, strain it, cover, and place in the refrigerator to chill.

FOR THE TELLICHERRY PEPPER SYRUP: Combine all the ingredients in a saucepan and bring to just under a simmer (a bubble or two is all right, but if the mixture begins to boil, the syrup will be cloudy). Cook for 45 minutes, allowing the flavors to infuse. Strain the syrup; discard the fruit and seasonings. There will be 1 to 1½ cups of syrup; it can be refrigerated in a covered container for up to 1 month.

FOR THE DACQUOISE: Preheat the oven to 300°F. Line two baking sheets with parchment paper. Blend the almonds, ⅔ cup of the sugar, and the cornstarch together in a food processor until the nuts are very finely ground.

In a mixer bowl, whip the egg whites at medium speed for 2 to 3 minutes until they start to hold their shape. Slowly add the remaining ⅓ cup sugar and continue to beat until the meringue holds its shape and is silky and shiny (like shaving cream). Thoroughly fold the dry ingredients into the meringue.

Using an offset spatula, spread half the batter in a very thin layer (about ⅛ inch thick) onto each baking pan. Bake for 10 minutes. If the dacquoises seem to be baking unevenly, reverse their positions after 5 minutes. Remove from the oven (leave the oven on). Using a 2¾-inch cutter (or a cutter with the same diameter as the charlotte molds), cut at least 6 rounds. Using a 2-inch cutter, cut at least 18 rounds and then, with a knife, cut each of these rounds in half. If the meringue sticks to the cutter or knife, dampen a cloth with some canola oil and rub the cutter or knife as necessary. You will have more than you need, but you may have some breakage.

Return the dacquoises to the oven for another 10 to 15 minutes. Test by breaking off a scrap and letting it cool for a minute. If it crisps, remove the rest from the oven; otherwise, continue cooking them a little longer. Check the dacquoises often, as the two pans may finish cooking at different times. When they are done and still warm, recut them if necessary, using the same cutters. Carefully remove the dacquoises from the pan with a small offset spatula and store in an airtight container. They are best used within a day, as humidity may cause them to soften.

FOR THE BLUEBERRY SOUP: Bring the wine to a boil in a small saucepan and skim off any residue that comes to the top. Add the lemon zest and juice and simmer until the liquid is reduced to ¼ cup. Strain the reduced liquid (discarding the lemon zest) into a medium saucepan. Stir in the blueberries and cook over medium-low heat until they burst.

Add 1 cup of the pepper syrup and the sugar and simmer gently for 15 minutes. Pour half the mixture into a blender (it is best to do this in parts because the mixture is hot and the steam could cause the lid to blow off). If you have a hole in the top of the blender, remove the small cap to release the steam. Pulse several times, then blend the mixture until it is smooth. Strain the soup base into a large measuring cup and repeat with the remainder of the mixture, adding it to the measuring cup. Stir in cold water to bring the quantity of soup base to 4 cups. Place in a bowl set in an ice-water bath and chill thoroughly.

Stir 1⅓ cups of cold crème anglaise into the soup base. You will have approximately 5⅓ cups of soup; you need only 3 cups of soup for this recipe, but the remaining soup will keep for several days, covered, in the refrigerator.

TO COMPLETE: Dip each mold briefly into hot water, hold a dacquoise round directly against the charlotte, and invert the charlotte to unmold. (It will be easy to handle the charlotte as it sits on the cookie.) Place one charlotte in the center of each serving bowl. Gently press 6 dacquoise halves around each charlotte. Place the cold soup in a pitcher or other container with a spout and carefully pour the soup around the charlottes; serve immediately.

PICTURED ON PAGE 266                                                     MAKES 6 SERVINGS

Opposite: Cream of Blueberry Soup, page 264. Above: Poached peaches for serving with verjus sorbet, page 269.

# Cream of Walnut Soup

**WALNUT CREAM**

1¼ cups (5 ounces) walnuts, toasted,
    excess skin rubbed off, and chopped

2 cups heavy cream

¼ cup milk

¼ vanilla bean, split

**PEAR PURÉE**

1 large pear

1½ cups Poaching Liquid (page 269)

Walnut oil

Our walnut soup began as a walnut sauce for a walnut bread pudding, and indeed the soup can be used as a sauce. But it tastes so good we decided to serve it as a soup. The pear purée adds the perfect sweetness to the subtle bitterness of the toasted walnuts. This is rich and should be served in small portions. At the restaurant, it's served as a canapé dessert soup, playing off our custom of serving canapé soups to begin the meal.

Walnut soup is best when eaten shortly after it is made, but, if necessary, it can be refrigerated for a couple of days.

FOR THE WALNUT CREAM: Place the walnuts, cream, and milk in a saucepan. Scrape the seeds from the vanilla bean into the pan and add the pod. Bring to a simmer, then reduce the heat to keep the liquid just below a simmer and heat for 30 to 45 minutes to let the flavors infuse. Strain the infused liquid into another saucepan and discard the walnuts and vanilla pod. You should have about 1½ cups of walnut cream.

MEANWHILE, FOR THE PEAR PURÉE: Peel the pear, core, and cut it into 8 wedges. Put the wedges in a saucepan with the poaching liquid. Cover them with a parchment lid (see page 190) and bring the liquid to a simmer. Cook for about 15 minutes, or until the pear wedges are completely softened and there is no resistance when they are tested with the tip of a sharp knife. Transfer the pears and ⅓ cup of the poaching liquid to a blender.

Reheat the walnut cream. Purée the pears, then, with the motor running, pour the hot walnut cream into the blender to combine (the cream must be hot when it is added to the purée, or the soup may break). There will be about 2 cups soup.

Strain the soup through a fine-mesh strainer into a saucepan and reheat gently over low heat. Serve warm in demitasse cups, sprinkled with a few drops of walnut oil.

MAKES 8 SMALL SERVINGS

# Verjus Sorbet with Poached Peaches

One 750-ml bottle verjus (see Sources, page 315)

1 cup corn syrup

1 cup Poaching Liquid (recipe follows)

3 tablespoons honey

2 large ripe but firm peaches

Verjus is a flavoring ingredient—much like vinegar—that was popular in the Middle Ages, but has only in this decade become more well known in the United States. The word derives from *vertjus*, or "green juice," and refers to the juice of unripe grapes. It's a fruity, acidic liquid that lends itself naturally to sorbets. You can use a variety of fruits in this dessert, but because the sorbet is very tart, the fruit should be very sweet.

FOR THE SORBET: In a bowl, combine the verjus and corn syrup. Place in the refrigerator until cold.

Freeze the sorbet base in an ice-cream machine. Remove the sorbet to a covered container and store in the freezer. This is best eaten within a day, but it can be held in the freezer for a few days. It makes about 1 quart, so you will have extra sorbet.

FOR THE PEACHES: Bring the poaching liquid and honey to a simmer in a small saucepan.

Meanwhile, blanch the peaches in boiling water just to loosen the skins. Remove the peaches, chill them in a bowl of ice water, and peel. Stand a peach on a cutting board with the stem end pointing up and cut 3 slices from the peach by making equal vertical cuts around the pit (in a triangular shape). Repeat with the remaining peach. Cut a round from each slice with a ¾-inch cutter (or whatever size you have).

When the poaching liquid is simmering, add the peach rounds, cover with a piece of paper towel (to keep the peach rounds submerged),

and reduce the heat so that the peaches poach at just under a simmer in the syrup. After 45 minutes to 1 hour, the peaches should be cooked through but not mushy. Remove the pot from the heat and let the peaches cool in the syrup.

Remove the peaches to a container. Reduce the poaching liquid to about ½ cup and let cool to room temperature. Add the syrup to the peaches and refrigerate them to chill, or for up to 2 days.

TO COMPLETE: Place a peach round on each serving plate and top with a small scoop of sorbet.

PICTURED ON PAGE 267                    MAKES 6 SERVINGS

## POACHING LIQUID

One 750-ml bottle crisp, dry white wine, such as Sauvignon Blanc

3 cups water

1 cup sugar

Juice of 1 lemon

Bring the wine to a boil in a saucepan. Skim off any foam that has risen to the top, then add the water and sugar. Return the liquid to a boil and stir until the sugar has dissolved. Remove the pan from the heat and stir in the lemon juice. Store in a covered container in the refrigerator for up to several weeks.

MAKES ABOUT 6 CUPS

## "Salad" du Printemps
### Rhubarb Confit with Navel Oranges, Candied Fennel, and Mascarpone Sorbet

**RHUBARB CONFIT**

¾ cup sugar

¼ cup plus 2 tablespoons water

2 stalks rhubarb

**CANDIED FENNEL**

1 small fennel bulb

½ lemon

Pinch of salt

2 cups water

1 cup sugar

**MASCARPONE SORBET**

1 pound mascarpone, at room temperature

2¼ cups Simple Syrup (see Note), cold

¼ cup fresh lemon juice

**PIROUETTE COOKIES** MAKES 12 TO 24

2 tablespoons (1 ounce) unsalted butter,
    at room temperature

¼ cup powdered sugar

4 tablespoons plus 2 teaspoons
    all-purpose flour, sifted

1 large egg white

¼ teaspoon vanilla extract

½ cup navel orange sections
    (use small navel oranges)

½ cup parisienne balls (see page 203) of
    strawberry

Fennel Oil (page 166), in a squeeze bottle

Powdered sugar, in a shaker

FOR THE RHUBARB CONFIT: Bring the sugar and water to a simmer in a small saucepan. Meanwhile, cut off the ends of the rhubarb, discarding any leaves, and use a paring knife to strip away the strings that run the length of the stalks.

Add the trimmings to the saucepan and simmer for about 2 minutes to infuse the syrup. Strain and discard the trimmings. Return the hot syrup to the saucepan and place over low heat.

Slice the rhubarb crosswise into ¼-inch slices. There should be about 1 cup. Add the pieces to the syrup and poach for 5 to 7 minutes, or until the slices are tender but haven't lost their shape. Place the rhubarb and its syrup in a container and cool to room temperature, then cover and refrigerate the confit for a few hours, or up to a week.

FOR THE CANDIED FENNEL: Trim away the top of the fennel and any tough or bruised outside layers. You'll need solid sheets of fennel: Cut ⅜-inch-thick slices of fennel vertically through the root end, working your way around the fennel to cut the best slices.

Fill a small saucepan with water, squeeze in the juice of the lemon half, and add the salt. Add the slices of fennel to the pan and bring to a boil. Reduce the heat and simmer for 10 minutes, or until the fennel is tender and there is no resistance when the slices are pierced with the tip of a knife; drain.

Bring the 2 cups of water and the sugar to a boil in a small saucepan,
stirring occasionally until the sugar dissolves. Add the fennel and cook gently over low heat until the fennel is translucent, about 1 hour. Remove the fennel and syrup to a container and allow it to cool to room temperature. Cover and refrigerate the fennel for a few hours to chill; it will keep for up to a month.

FOR THE MASCARPONE SORBET: Mix the mascarpone and syrup in a bowl, then place the mixture in a blender and pulse a few times to blend thoroughly. Freeze the mixture in an ice-cream machine; when it is almost frozen, add the lemon juice and complete the freezing. Remove to a covered container and store in the freezer. The sorbet is best the day it is made, but it can be stored for up to 3 days.

FOR THE PIROUETTE COOKIES: Preheat the oven to 350°F. Place the butter in a bowl and sift the powdered sugar over it. Mix with a wooden spoon to cream the mixture. Stir in half the flour. Mix in the egg white and then the remaining flour. Add the vanilla extract and beat the mixture until well blended and creamy.

Cut a narrow stencil 6½ inches by ¾ inch (a manila file folder works well for this). Place a Silpat (see Sources, page 315) on the counter. Place the stencil in one corner of the Silpat and, holding it flat against the Silpat, scoop some of the batter onto the back of an offset spatula and spread it in an even layer over the stencil. It should be thin but not transparent. Run the spatula over the top of the entire stencil to remove any excess batter. Repeat with the remaining batter, spacing the cookies about 1½ inches apart.

Place the Silpat on a baking sheet and bake on the top rack of the oven for 5 to 6 minutes, or until the cookies are set and light golden brown. Pull out the oven rack with the baking sheet on it, leave the door open and work from the oven rack shelf. Should the cookies harden before they are rolled, close the oven door and rewarm them briefly to soften. Remove a cookie from the pan and immediately wrap it in a spiral around a ¼-inch dowel or a wooden spoon handle of the same diameter; it will stiffen almost immediately. Slide the cookie off the dowel and continue to form the cookies. Store in an airtight container for 1 to 2 days (you'll need only 6 cookies for this dessert).

TO COMPLETE: Remove a piece of candied fennel from the syrup, drain, and cut it into strips about ¼ inch wide. Cut the fennel strips on the diagonal into ¼-inch diamonds. Continue to cut enough fennel to make 3 tablespoons of fennel diamonds. (Reserve any remaining fennel to garnish another dessert or for another use.)

Remove ⅓ cup rhubarb from the poaching liquid; reserve the rest for another use. Arrange equal portions of the oranges, strawberries, fennel diamonds, and rhubarb on each of six plates. Drizzle with a little of the rhubarb poaching liquid and the fennel syrup. Squeeze a few drops of fennel oil around each fruit salad. Place a quenelle (see page 274), or small scoop, of mascarpone sorbet atop each salad. Dust 6 pirouette cookies with powdered sugar and set one on top of each quenelle of sorbet. Serve immediately.

MAKES 6 SERVINGS

NOTE: Simple syrup is used in several of these dessert recipes. You can make a batch and store it covered in the refrigerator for several weeks. Using ½ cup each sugar and water will give you about ¾ cup syrup. Bring equal parts of sugar and water to a boil in a heavy saucepan, stirring to dissolve the sugar. Remove from the heat, let cool to room temperature, and then refrigerate.

I love rhubarb, and here I make

a "salad" with it, using candied fennel

and an incredible mascarpone sorbet;

the latter is straight from Alain Ducasse.

It's a beautiful, refreshing dessert.

## Nectarine Salad with Green Tomato Confiture and Hazelnut Sabayon

GREEN TOMATO CONFITURE

Julienned zest and juice of 1 lemon (see Note)

Julienned zest and juice of 1 lime

Julienned zest and juice of 1 orange

4 medium green tomatoes (1 pound 10 ounces)

⅓ cup water

⅓ cup diced dried peaches (¼-inch dice)

⅓ cup golden raisins

1¼ cups plus 2 tablespoons packed
   light brown sugar

One 1-inch piece ginger

1 tablespoon sherry vinegar

DACQUOISE

1 cup (3 ounces) sliced blanched almonds,
   finely ground in a coffee mill

1 cup sugar

2 tablespoons cornstarch

⅓ cup egg whites (2 to 3 egg whites)

6 nectarines

HAZELNUT SABAYON

½ cup heavy cream

2 large egg yolks

3 tablespoons sugar

1½ teaspoons hazelnut oil

Powdered sugar, in a shaker

We serve this dessert—whole nectarines sliced and "rebuilt"—topped with a confiture of green tomatoes and dacquoise, which can be made weeks ahead and kept in the refrigerator. The dacquoise recipe will make more cookies than you need, but it is difficult to make the batter in a smaller quantity.

FOR THE GREEN TOMATO CONFITURE: Combine the citrus zests in a small saucepan, add cold water to cover, and bring to a boil. Drain in a strainer and rinse under cold water. Set aside.

Blister the skin of the tomatoes over a gas flame, under a broiler, or using a blowtorch, turning the tomatoes for even blistering. Remove the skins by rubbing the tomatoes with a new pot scrubber (no soap) under cold water.

Cut the tomatoes into ¼-inch dice (about 4 cups) and place them in a saucepan with the citrus zests and the remaining ingredients. Cover with a parchment lid (see page 190) and simmer for about 1½ hours, or until the tomatoes are translucent and fully cooked and the liquid is reduced and syrupy (but not quite as thick as honey).

FOR THE DACQUOISE: Preheat the oven to 300°F. Line two baking sheets with parchment paper.

Blend the almonds, ⅔ cup of the sugar, and the cornstarch together in a food processor until the nuts are very finely ground.

In a mixer bowl, whip the egg whites at medium speed until they start to hold their shape, then slowly add the remaining ⅓ cup sugar. Continue to whip until the meringue holds stiff peaks and is silky and shiny (like shaving cream). Thoroughly fold the dry ingredients into the meringue.

Using an offset spatula, spread half the batter in a very thin layer onto one parchment-lined baking sheet. Bake for 10 minutes, then remove from the oven and use a 2½-inch round cutter (or whatever size you will use in assembling the finished dish) to cut 8 circles in the dacquoises. Return to the oven for another 15 to 20 minutes: Test by breaking off a scrap piece and letting it cool for a minute. If it crisps, remove the rest from the oven; otherwise, continue cooking them for a little longer. When the daquoises are done and still warm, recut them using the same cutter, if necessary. Remove the cookies from the sheet with a small offset spatula.

Meanwhile, place the remaining batter in a pastry bag with a #2 (¼-inch) plain tip and pipe into 4- to 5-inch sticks on the second parchment-lined baking sheet. Hold the tip slightly above the pan as you pipe the daquoise, rather than against it, so that the batter can fall and hold a rounded shape. Bake for 30 minutes. Test as above and remove from the sheet when done.

Store the dacquoises in an airtight container until ready to assemble the dessert. They are best used within a day, as humidity may cause them to soften.

FOR THE NECTARINE STACKS: Cut the flesh of the nectarines away from the pits, slicing it off in two vertical slices, one on each side of the pit. Cut the pieces crosswise into paper-thin slices (half-rounds). Place a dacquoise round in the bottom of a 2½-inch ring mold. Overlap the slices of one nectarine around the inside of the mold, skin side out, stacking them until you have used the whole nectarine or reached the top of the mold. There will be a hole in the center. Form 5 more stacks (you will be able to move them once they are made, because they have a solid base).

FOR THE HAZELNUT SABAYON: Pour about 1½ inches of water into a pot that is slightly smaller than the metal bowl of a mixer and heat just until hot.

Meanwhile, in a medium bowl, whip the cream to medium peaks. Set aside. Place the egg yolks and sugar in the metal mixer bowl, and whisk over the hot water until the sugar has dissolved and the mixture has thickened to the ribbon stage (when the whisk is lifted, the mixture will hold some shape as it falls back into the bowl).

Place the bowl on the mixer stand and whip until the mixture has cooled. Mix in the oil. Remove the bowl from the machine and whisk in about one quarter of the cream to lighten the mixture. Fold in the remaining whipped cream.

Spoon about 2 tablespoons of sabayon onto the center of each plate. Center a nectarine stack in the sauce and top each with a quenelle (see page 274), or small scoop, of tomato confiture. Sprinkle 6 dacquoise sticks with powdered sugar and rest them on the confiture.

MAKES 6 SERVINGS

NOTE: Use a zester to remove the citrus zests in julienned strips.

# Strawberry Sorbet Shortcakes with Sweetened Crème Fraîche Sauce

**STRAWBERRY SORBET** MAKES 1 QUART

2½ pounds strawberries, preferably organic,
    rinsed and hulled

¼ cup honey, or to taste

1 cup superfine sugar

Pinch of kosher salt

**BISCUITS** MAKES 8 OR 9

1½ cups all-purpose flour, plus a little extra
    for cutting the biscuits

½ teaspoon kosher salt

1½ teaspoons sugar

½ teaspoon baking powder

¼ teaspoon baking soda

4 tablespoons (2 ounces) unsalted cold butter,
    cut into chunks

About ½ cup buttermilk

2 tablespoons milk

**CRÈME FRAÎCHE SAUCE** MAKES ¾ CUP

¾ cup crème fraîche

1 tablespoon plus 1½ teaspoons sugar, or to taste

¼ vanilla bean, split

¾ cup chopped strawberries, drained

Sugar to taste

Powdered sugar, in a shaker

All the components of this dessert can be made ahead. The uncooked biscuits can be frozen and baked directly from the freezer. Or, since the biscuit doubles easily, you may want to make a double batch and freeze half the unbaked biscuits for another time.

FOR THE STRAWBERRY SORBET: Purée the strawberries in a blender and strain through a fine-mesh sieve into a bowl. You should have about 4 cups. Add the honey, superfine sugar, and salt. Freeze in an ice-cream machine, then transfer to a container and place in the freezer.

FOR THE BISCUITS: Sift the dry ingredients into a bowl. Add the butter and rub the butter and flour through your fingertips until they are completely combined and the butter is in small beads. Make a well in the center of the flour mixture and pour in ½ cup buttermilk and the milk. Use a dough scraper to incorporate the milk and flour, pulling the flour from the edges toward the center. If the dough seems too dry, add a little more buttermilk. The finished dough should feel damp, but not wet, and be a "shaggy mess," not a solid mass.

Turn the dough out onto parchment and let rest for 10 to 15 minutes.

Preheat the oven to 500°F. Stack two baking sheets (for more even heat distribution) and place a piece of parchment on top.

Place the dough on a lightly floured work surface and roll out ½ inch thick. Dip a 2-inch biscuit cutter in flour and cut out rounds. Place the rounds 2 inches apart on the baking sheet.

Bake for 8 to 10 minutes, or until golden brown. Transfer to a rack to cool.

FOR THE CRÈME FRAÎCHE SAUCE: Combine the crème fraîche and sugar in a small saucepan. Scrape the seeds from the vanilla bean into the crème fraîche, add the pod, and bring to a simmer, whisking constantly until the sugar is dissolved. Remove the sauce from the heat and strain through a fine-mesh strainer. Keep the sauce warm, or cover and refrigerate until ready to serve.

Sweeten the drained chopped strawberries with sugar to taste.

TO COMPLETE: Rewarm the crème fraîche sauce over low heat.

Cut the biscuits into neat rounds with a 1½-inch biscuit cutter and split them in half. Dust the tops with powdered sugar.

Put a spoonful of sauce on each plate. Top with the bottoms of the biscuits. Spoon the chopped berries over the biscuits and cover each with a quenelle (see below), or small scoop, of sorbet. Set the tops of the biscuits on the sorbet and serve.

PICTURED ON PAGE 277                   SERVES 8

## HOW TO MAKE A ONE-SPOON QUENELLE

Quenelles are typically made with two spoons, but the edgeless oval created by drawing a spoon through something smooth like ice cream or mousse is a more elegant shape. To make a one-spoon quenelle, you need a cup of very hot water, a spoon (whose bowl will determine the size of the quenelle), and whatever you're "quenelling." Dip the spoon in the water so it's hot. Hold the spoon with the rounded bottom up, place the far edge of the spoon into the mixture, with the near edge close to the surface but not touching, and drag the spoon toward you. The mixture you're scraping should curl with the shape of the spoon. As you drag, twist your wrist up until the quenelle folds over itself into an egg shape. For the best shape, drag only once through the mixture; dip and clean your spoon for each new quenelle. It takes some practice.

PICTURED ON PAGE 295

# Strawberry and Champagne Terrine

STRAWBERRY LAYER

2 pints (1½ pounds) strawberries,
    preferably organically grown

2 to 4 tablespoons superfine sugar

3½ gelatin sheets, soaked in cold water to soften

3 tablespoons Champagne

Pinch of kosher salt

CHAMPAGNE LAYER

1¼ cups Champagne

3 gelatin sheets (see Sources, page 315),
    soaked in cold water to soften

3½ tablespoons superfine sugar

⅓ cup crème fraîche, whipped

Small mint leaves

Jellies appear often in our desserts and elsewhere in the meal—such as the jelly made out of Gewürztraminer for the foie gras. In desserts, a jelly can take the place of a syrup. We made Champagne jelly to accompany a kir sorbet for a Kir Royale dessert. Here, we serve a Champagne jelly with puréed and gelled strawberries. It's a good flavor combination, healthful and light, and, served as a terrine, a simple fresh dessert. The jelly should be set but still wobbly for an elegant texture.

Organically grown strawberries have the sweetest flavor, which is intensified by drying them overnight. Although the terrine will keep for several days, the Champagne layer, which is clear the day it is made, will redden and the intense color of the strawberry layer will fade after the first day.

FOR THE STRAWBERRY LAYER: Refrigerate a few strawberries for the garnish. Hull the remaining berries and let sit at room temperature overnight to dry them slightly and intensify the flavor.

The following day, purée the strawberries and strain the purée through a chinois (see page 73) using a small ladle to help move it through the strainer. Measure out 1¼ cups of purée. Add sugar to taste; the purée should be on the sweet side, but the amount will vary according to the quality of the strawberries.

Squeeze the excess water from the gelatin and place the sheets in a small saucepan with the Champagne. Warm gently, stirring to dissolve the gelatin. Mix it into the strawberry purée. Add the salt.

Place 6 tablespoons of the strawberry purée in the bottom of a small metal bread pan or mold about 6 inches by 3 inches, with a 2-cup capacity (choose a pan with the straightest sides to keep the layers the same thickness; if your pan flares at the top, use a little extra for each layer as necessary to compensate, keeping the layers the same thickness). Allow the purée to level out and fill the bottom of the mold evenly. Refrigerate the mold to allow the purée to set completely.

FOR THE CHAMPAGNE LAYER: While the first layer sets, boil the Champagne for a minute to remove the alcohol, skimming off any scum that rises to the top. Measure out 1 cup of the Champagne (discard the rest). Wring out the gelatin sheets and place them in a bowl. Stir the hot Champagne into the gelatin, then stir in the sugar to dissolve. Let the Champagne mixture cool to room temperature.

When the strawberry layer is set, top it with 6 tablespoons of the Champagne mixture and refrigerate until set. Continue the layering process until you have three layers of strawberry and two of Champagne. If you used a straight-sided pan, there will be a little extra of each mixture. Should either of the mixtures set up before you are finished, gently heat them over a saucepan of warm water just until they soften.

TO COMPLETE: Using a #12 melon baller, cut small parisienne balls (see page 203) from the reserved strawberries for garnish.

Quickly dip the mold into hot water to loosen the terrine. Unmold onto a cutting surface. Using a hot knife (dipped in hot water and wiped between each slice), cut the terrine into ½-inch slices and place in the serving dishes. Garnish each dish with a few strawberry balls, a quenelle (see page 274), or small oval scoop, of whipped crème fraîche, and some small mint leaves.

PICTURED ON PAGE 276    MAKES 12 SERVINGS

In adapting the classic American strawberry shortcake—strawberries, cream, biscuit—into a French Laundry dessert, the challenge was to intensify the flavors of the various components, primarily the strawberries. We make a strawberry sorbet, which is simply puréed strawberries with honey and sugar; the addition of lemon juice heightens the flavor of the strawberries even further.

Opposite, right: Strawberry and Champagne Terrine, page 275. Above: Strawberry Sorbet Shortcakes, page 274.

## Poached-Banana Ice Cream with White Chocolate—Banana Crêpes and Chocolate Sauce

**BANANA ICE CREAM** MAKES 1 QUART

6 large bananas, peeled

2 to 2½ cups cream

2 to 2½ cups milk

1 cup sugar

½ vanilla bean, split

10 large egg yolks

Pinch of kosher salt

**CRÊPE FILLING**

Banana purée (reserved from above)

About 9 ounces white chocolate, finely chopped

¼ teaspoon kosher salt

Few drops of lemon juice

6 Dessert Crêpes (page 127)

**CHOCOLATE SAUCE**

8 ounces bittersweet chocolate, finely chopped

1 cup heavy cream

1 tablespoon light corn syrup

1½ to 2 cups sweetened whipped cream

36 to 42 candied morello cherries
or maraschino cherries

---

Here's our nod to the old drive-in days and a dessert I loved as a kid. All the components for this dessert can be made ahead, and in fact the crêpes must be assembled and frozen before serving. Once sliced, the crêpes resemble slices of banana, so when you make the crêpes, be sure to allow them to brown and spot slightly to give them the look of a banana peel.

FOR THE BANANA ICE CREAM: Place the bananas, 2 cups of the cream, 2 cups of the milk, and ½ cup of the sugar in a large saucepan. Scrape the seeds from the vanilla bean into the pan and add the pod. Cover the bananas with a piece of paper towel (to keep them submerged) and heat slowly for 10 to 15 minutes. Do not simmer the mixture; keep it just under that point, so that the bananas poach in the hot liquid. Pierce the bananas with a knife; they should be soft but not mushy. Remove the paper towel and vanilla bean and discard.

Remove the bananas from the pan and drain them well. Strain the poaching liquid through a chinois (see page 73). There should be 4 cups of liquid; if not, add the difference in additional cream and/or milk. Place the bananas and any bits of banana left in the strainer in a food processor and blend well, then scrape the purée through a tamis (see page 73). You should have about 2 cups of banana purée. Reserve this to use for the crêpe filling.

Place the strained poaching liquid in a large saucepan and bring to a simmer.

Meanwhile, place the egg yolks in a bowl. Whisk in the remaining ½ cup sugar and the salt and whisk until the yolks have thickened slightly and lightened in color.

Whisk about one third of the hot cream into the yolks to temper them, then return the mixture to the saucepan. Cook the custard over low heat, stirring constantly with a wooden spoon, until it has thickened and coats the back of the spoon. Immediately pour the custard into a bowl set in an ice-water bath, and stir occasionally until the custard has cooled.

Strain the custard and refrigerate until it is very cold (for the creamiest texture, refrigerate overnight).

Freeze the ice cream in an ice-cream machine. Remove to a covered container and place in the freezer. The ice cream is best the day it is made, but it can be kept for 2 days before serving.

FOR THE CRÊPE FILLING: The most precise way to make the filling is to weigh the banana purée and combine it with half its weight in white chocolate. Follow that formula if you have more or less than 2 cups of purée; for 2 cups, use 9 ounces of chocolate. It is important that the purée and the melted chocolate are the same temperature when they are combined.

Place the white chocolate in a metal bowl, set it over a saucepan of hot water, and heat gently, stirring, until melted and smooth.

Meanwhile, warm the banana purée (a microwave works well for this).

Transfer the purée to a food processor, add the warm melted white chocolate, and process to blend. Add the salt and lemon juice and process just to combine. Refrigerate the purée for several hours, or up to 2 days, to firm.

Trim the edges of the crêpes to square them. Spoon one sixth of the cooled filling across the lower third of a crêpe, shaping it into a rectangle approximately 5 inches by 2 inches. Turn up the bottom of the crêpe to encase the filling and gently roll up the crêpe into a cylinder. Roll the filled crêpe up in plastic wrap and twist the ends of the wrap to help mold the shape. Repeat with the remaining crêpes and filling. Place the finished crêpes in the freezer for at least a few hours or up to 2 weeks. (Each frozen crêpe will serve 2 to 3 people, depending on its length after trimming.)

FOR THE CHOCOLATE SAUCE: Place the chocolate in a bowl. Bring the cream and corn syrup to a boil. Pour the hot liquid over the chocolate and allow it to sit for a few minutes to melt the chocolate, then stir until smooth. The sauce can be refrigerated for several days.

TO COMPLETE: Remove the banana crêpes from the freezer. Unwrap, trim the ends, and cut each one into ⅜-inch slices. Place 3 slices in a row across the center of each plate. Let them sit at room temperature for about 5 minutes to thaw slightly.

Meanwhile, warm the chocolate sauce and pour it in a squeeze bottle. Place the whipped cream in a pastry bag fitted with a star tip.

Pipe chocolate sauce around the crêpe slices. Top each slice of crêpe with a small scoop of the banana ice cream. Pipe a rosette of whipped cream onto each scoop of ice cream. Garnish each rosette with a cherry and serve immediately.

MAKES 12 SERVINGS

# Oven-Roasted Maui Pineapple with Fried Pastry Cream and Whipped Crème Fraîche

**FRIED PASTRY CREAM**

1 cup milk

¼ cup sugar

⅓ cup plus ½ cup all-purpose flour

3 large egg yolks

Small pinch of salt

¼ teaspoon vanilla extract

½ cup milk

½ cup panko (Japanese bread crumbs, see Sources, page 315) or dried bread crumbs, finely ground in a blender and sifted through a strainer

Canola oil for deep-frying

**PINEAPPLE**

1 ripe pineapple

1 vanilla bean, split

2 tablespoons (1 ounce) unsalted butter

**CARAMEL SAUCE**

6 tablespoons (3 ounces) unsalted butter, at room temperature

⅓ cup sugar

½ cup crème fraîche, whipped

FOR THE PASTRY CREAM: Line a small loaf pan (6 to 7 inches by 3 inches, measured across the bottom) with plastic wrap. Whisk the milk, sugar, ⅓ cup of the flour, the egg yolks, and salt together in a large saucepan. Bring to a boil, whisking constantly until the mixture thickens. Continue cooking for another 2 to 3 minutes, to cook the flour completely. Add the vanilla extract and remove from the heat.

Pour the pastry cream into the loaf pan. Smooth the surface with an offset spatula; the pastry cream should be about ¾ inch thick. Cover the pastry cream with plastic wrap, pressing it directly against the surface of the cream to prevent a skin from forming, and refrigerate for a couple of hours, or until firm.

Cut the pastry cream into eight 1¼-inch rounds. Return the pastry cream to the refrigerator.

TO CUT THE PINEAPPLE: You should visualize a rack of lamb or other meat when trimming the pineapple to resemble one. You will be cutting two "racks," one from each side of the pineapple. Each rack will have 4 "bones." The roasted "racks" are presented whole at the table, then cut into 8 individual "chops."

Cut off the top and bottom of the pineapple. Cut 8 small green tips from the top and reserve for garnish. Cut the pineapple lengthwise in half and lay the halves on a cutting board, skin side down.

Cut a V-shaped wedge in each pineapple half to remove the core by cutting at a 45-degree angle from the outer edge of the core on one side and moving downward toward the center of the pineapple. Leave a thin layer of pineapple at the bottom; do not cut all the way to the skin or you risk splitting the skin. Repeat on the opposite side to complete the V and

remove and discard the core. Repeat with the remaining pineapple half.

Work with one pineapple half at a time. If you are right-handed, it will be easier to trim away the pineapple flesh from the right to form the "bones" (if you are left-handed work from the other side). Cut away almost all of the fruit from the right half of the pineapple, leaving only a small layer of fruit on the skin. Trim the outer edge of the skin to make a flap about 4 inches wide, with a straight edge.

TO CUT THE "BONES": Make 8 parallel cuts about ¾ inch apart in the trimmed skin, cutting with a sharp knife in a downward motion from the remaining pineapple flesh toward the outer edge. Do not use a sawing motion, as it might tear the flesh. Then snap the skin downward and break off the first "bone"; leave the second, break the third, and so on. You will be left with 4 "bones."

TO TRIM THE "EYE": The remaining pineapple flesh is the "eye," or "meaty" portion, of your rack. Trim away some of the skin still encircling the fruit to round the pineapple so it resembles the shape of chops. Repeat with the second piece of pineapple.

TO COOK THE "RACKS": Preheat the oven to 400°F.

Scrape the vanilla seeds from the pod and reserve the seeds for the caramel sauce. Melt the butter in a heavy ovenproof skillet that will hold the pineapple pieces in one layer and add the pineapple, fruit side down. Cook over medium heat for about 8 minutes, or until browned, rotating the racks to brown the fruit all around the edges. (If the butter starts to burn at any point, remove the pineapple and replace with new butter.)

Turn the pineapple fruit side up, add the vanilla pod, and place the skillet in the oven. Bake, basting occasionally with the pan juices, for

Here is another way we mimic in our dessert course what we serve earlier in the meal, in this case the salmon "chops" (page 137). The pineapple bakes for a very long time, so the sugars in the fruit develop great complexity. We serve the pineapple on a base of fried pastry cream.

10 minutes. Turn the pineapple fruit side down and bake, basting occasionally, for 30 minutes. Turn the pineapple fruit side up and bake, continuing to baste, for 10 to 15 minutes, or until the fruit is soft and a rich brown color.

Transfer the pineapple to a plate and reduce the oven temperature to 350°F. Clean the skillet. (The pineapple can also be prepared to this point several hours ahead and finished just before serving.)

TO COMPLETE: For the caramel sauce, in a small bowl, combine the reserved vanilla seeds with the butter and blend well. Heat the sugar in the skillet over medium heat until it caramelizes. Stir in the vanilla/butter mixture. Return the pineapple to the pan, fruit side down, baste with the caramel syrup, and return to the oven for 5 to 10 minutes, to warm through.

MEANWHILE, COOK THE PASTRY CREAM: Place the remaining ½ cup flour, the milk, and panko in three small bowls. Heat the oil in a deep heavy saucepan to 325°F. Coat each round of pastry cream with flour, patting off any excess, dip in the milk, turning to coat, and coat with the panko crumbs. Repeat with the milk and panko. Deep-fry until browned on both sides, 1 to 2 minutes in all. Remove to paper towels to drain.

To serve, turn the pineapple "racks" fruit side up and present in the skillet at the table. Remove to a cutting board and cut into individual "chops." Place a spoonful of caramel sauce in the center of each serving plate. Top with a round of fried pastry cream. Garnish each pineapple chop with a quenelle (see page 274), or small oval scoop, of crème fraîche and a small green tip from the pineapple top. Serve warm.

MAKES 8 SERVINGS

# Vanilla Bean—Roasted Figs with Wildflower Honey—Vanilla Ice Cream

**HONEY-VANILLA ICE CREAM**

MAKES 1 QUART

2 cups milk

2 cups cream

1/4 cup sugar

10 large egg yolks

1/2 cup wildflower honey

**ROASTED FIGS**

18 ripe figs (Black Mission, Brown Turkey,
    Adriatic green, or a combination)

4 vanilla beans, split and cut into 2-inch pieces

3 tablespoons (1 1/2 ounces) unsalted butter

1 1/2 teaspoons sugar

If you like figs, this is an almost unbeatable combination—hot fruit, roasted briefly with vanilla beans, and cold ice cream. Simple.

FOR THE HONEY-VANILLA ICE CREAM: In a saucepan, combine the milk, cream, and 2 tablespoons of the sugar and bring to a simmer.

Meanwhile, in a mixer or other metal bowl, whisk the egg yolks and the remaining 2 tablespoons sugar until thickened and lightened in color. Gradually whisk in one third of the warm milk mixture to temper the egg yolks. Return the mixture to the saucepan and stir over medium heat until the custard has thickened and coats the back of a wooden spoon. Pour the custard into a bowl set in an ice-water bath and stir in the honey to combine. Let the mixture cool to room temperature, then strain it into a container and refrigerate at least 5 hours, or overnight (for the creamiest texture).

Freeze the cold custard in an ice-cream machine. Remove to a covered container and freeze for several hours, or until hardened.

FOR THE ROASTED FIGS: Preheat the oven to 400°F.

Wash and dry the figs. Slice off and discard the tops. Make a small slit in the center of the top of each fig and insert a section of vanilla bean.

Melt the butter over medium heat in an ovenproof skillet large enough for all the figs to stand in one layer. Stir in the sugar to dissolve. Stand the figs in the butter and add any remaining vanilla beans to the pan. Place the pan in the oven for 10 minutes to heat the figs. The figs can be served warm or at room temperature.

TO COMPLETE: Place a scoop or quenelle (see page 274) of ice cream into each of six bowls. Arrange 3 of the figs (still with the vanilla beans) around each scoop. Drizzle the syrup remaining in the pan around the plates. Serve immediately.

MAKES 6 SERVINGS

# Velouté of Bittersweet Chocolate with Cinnamon-Stick Ice Cream

**CHOCOLATE VELOUTÉ**

3 large eggs, separated

⅓ cup plus ¼ cup sugar

⅔ cup milk

¼ cup unsweetened cocoa

2 tablespoons all-purpose flour

Pinch of kosher salt

1 gelatin sheet, soaked in cold water to soften

1 ounce bittersweet chocolate,
　　finely chopped

**COOKIES**

½ cup plus 2 tablespoons all-purpose flour

¼ cup whole-wheat pastry flour

¼ teaspoon baking soda

¼ teaspoon ground cinnamon

⅛ teaspoon kosher salt

6 tablespoons (3 ounces) unsalted butter

3 packed tablespoons light brown sugar

3 tablespoons granulated sugar

1½ teaspoons honey

**CINNAMON-STICK ICE CREAM**

MAKES 1 QUART

2 cups heavy cream

2 cups milk

One 3-inch cinnamon stick, split lengthwise

¾ cup sugar

10 large egg yolks

Chocolate Sauce (page 280)

Powdered sugar, in a shaker

Here a seductive disk of molten chocolate sits atop a frozen platform of cinnamon ice cream—for that hot-cold surprise—in a pool of chocolate sauce.

FOR THE CHOCOLATE VELOUTÉ: Place six 2- to 2½-inch ring molds (see Sources, page 315) on a parchment-lined baking sheet or line six 4-ounce soufflé molds or ramekins with plastic wrap.

The meringue should be folded into the chocolate mixture as soon as the chocolate mixture is completed; try to time the meringue and chocolate mixture so that they are ready at the same time.

Place the egg whites and ⅓ cup of the sugar in a metal mixer bowl and set it over a pan of gently simmering water. Whisk the mixture for 2 to 3 minutes, or until it is hot and foamy and the sugar has dissolved.

Transfer the bowl to the mixer fitted with the whisk attachment and whip at medium speed for about 5 minutes, or until the meringue is cool to the touch, fluffy, and holds soft peaks.

Meanwhile, place the milk in a medium saucepan and sift the ¼ cup sugar, cocoa, flour, and salt into it. Whisk to combine, then whisk in the egg yolks. Place the pan over medium heat and cook, whisking, until it has thickened to the consistency of pudding. Continue to cook and whisk for an additional 1 to 2 minutes, or until it is thick and glossy. Squeeze the soaked gelatin sheet dry and add it to the chocolate mixture, whisking to combine. Remove from the heat and whisk in the chopped chocolate until it is melted. Transfer the chocolate mixture to a bowl. Whisk a spoonful of the meringue into the chocolate mixture to lighten it. Fold in the remaining meringue.

Transfer the mixture to a pastry bag fitted with a large plain tip. Divide the velouté among the prepared molds by piping it into their centers and allowing it to spread and fill the molds; the mixture should be approximately ¾ inch high. Cover the veloutés and freeze them for several hours, or until completely frozen. They can be frozen for up to 2 weeks.

FOR THE COOKIES: Whisk both flours, the baking soda, cinnamon, and salt together.

In a mixer fitted with the paddle, beat together the butter, sugars, and honey. Add the dry ingredients and mix until well combined.

Place the cookie dough on a Silpat, (see Sources, page 315), pat it down slightly, and cover with a sheet of parchment paper. Roll the dough into a thin sheet approximately ¹⁄₁₆ to ⅛ inch thick. Place the Silpat on a baking sheet and place in the freezer for at least an hour, or until frozen; the dough can be kept frozen for several weeks.

When you are ready to bake the cookies, preheat the oven to 350°F.

Remove the sheet of dough from the freezer; pull away and discard the parchment paper. Place the Silpat on a baking sheet and bake for 8 to 10 minutes, or until the cookies are set but not crisp.

Remove the pan from the oven and, using a round cutter, cut out rounds about ½ to ¾ inch larger than the chocolate veloutés. You will have about 8 to 10 cookies. (Leave the trimmings on the pan, and eat them as a treat later.) Return the pan to the oven for 3 to 4 minutes, or until the cookies are a rich golden brown; do not allow the cookies to become too brown, because they will be baked again. Cool the cookies on the pan for about 10 minutes, then carefully remove them to an airtight container. They can be stored for up to a week.

FOR THE CINNAMON-STICK ICE CREAM: Combine the cream, milk, and cinnamon stick in a saucepan, bring to a simmer, cover, and remove from the heat. Let infuse for 30 minutes.

Remove the cinnamon stick from the cream mixture and add half the sugar. Return to a simmer, stirring to dissolve the sugar.

Meanwhile, in a medium bowl, whisk the egg yolks with the remaining sugar until they have thickened slightly and lightened in color. Gradually whisk in one third of the hot liquid to temper the yolks. Return the mixture to the saucepan and heat, stirring constantly with a wooden spoon, until the custard thickens and coats the back of the spoon. Pour the custard into a bowl set over ice water and stir occasionally until the custard has cooled.

Strain the cooled custard into a container, cover, and refrigerate for at least a few hours, until cold, or overnight (for the creamiest texture).

Freeze the ice cream in an ice-cream machine. Line a pan with plastic wrap, transfer the ice cream to the pan, and spread it into a ¾-inch layer. Cover the ice cream and place in the freezer for at least 2 hours, or up to 2 days.

When the ice cream is frozen, cut it into disks that are the same size as the chocolate veloutés. Return to the freezer.

TO COMPLETE: Preheat the oven to 400° F.

Remove the veloutés from the freezer. Push them gently from the top to release them from the ring molds, or remove them from the soufflé molds and peel off and discard the plastic wrap. Center each velouté on a cookie and place on a baking sheet. Place in the oven and bake for 14 minutes. The veloutés should look set but still be soft in the center. To test, insert a metal skewer into the center of a velouté for a few seconds, then touch it to your lip; it should feel warm. If the center is still cold, return the veloutés to the oven. Don't overbake; an overcooked velouté will begin to crack.

Place a spoonful of chocolate sauce on each serving plate. Center an ice-cream disk in the sauce and top with a cookie and velouté. Dust the top of each dessert with powdered sugar. Serve immediately (after about 3 minutes, they will begin to lose their shape).

MAKES 6 SERVINGS

Above: Île Flottante, page 290

# ÎLE FLOTTANTE
## Slow-Baked Meringues with Crème Anglaise and Bittersweet Chocolate

**MERINGUES**

5 large egg whites

1 cup sugar

**CHOCOLATE MOUSSE**

3 ounces bittersweet chocolate, finely chopped

3/4 cup heavy cream

1/2 cup meringue (reserved from above)

**CRÈME ANGLAISE** MAKES 2 CUPS

1/2 vanilla bean, split

1 cup milk

1 cup heavy cream

5 large egg yolks

1/3 cup sugar

**CHOCOLATE TUILES**

MAKES 4 DOZEN

2 tablespoons (1 ounce) unsalted butter,
    at room temperature

1/4 cup powdered sugar

3 tablespoons all-purpose flour

5 teaspoons unsweetened cocoa powder

1 large egg white

Block of bittersweet chocolate
    for chocolate shavings

Mint Oil (page 166), in a squeeze bottle

Fleur de sel

This is a classical French preparation, further enhanced and refined. The meringue is very finely textured (before it's cooked it should look exactly like shaving cream) and we put a surprise inside—a chocolate ganache. To take it to the next level, we set a "salad" of chocolate shavings on top, and, as a salad typically requires some sort of dressing, we drizzle mint oil on the chocolate and finish it with some crystals of fleur de sel, which enhance the sweetness.

FOR THE MERINGUES: Preheat the oven to 250°F. Spray six 4-ounce soufflé molds or foil cups (about 3 inches wide) with nonstick spray.

Combine the egg whites and sugar in a metal mixer bowl. Set the bowl over a saucepan of simmering water and whisk gently until the whites are warm and the sugar is completely dissolved. Remove the bowl from the heat and place it on the mixer stand. Use the whisk attachment to beat the whites until soft peaks form.

Reserve 1/2 cup of the meringue for the mousse. Fill a pastry bag fitted with a large plain tip with the remaining meringue. Pipe the meringue into the centers of the 6 molds, allowing the filling to move outward from the center as you pipe to fill them. Smooth the tops of the meringues and place the molds in a deep baking pan. Pour in enough hot water to come halfway up the sides of the cups. If you are using foil cups and they float in the water, place a baking sheet or pan over them to hold them down.

Cover the baking dish with foil and bake for 20 minutes, or until the meringues are set but still moist. Remove the molds from the baking dish and refrigerate for 1 hour, or until firm.

FOR THE CHOCOLATE MOUSSE: Place the chocolate in a medium bowl. Bring 1/2 cup of the cream to a simmer and pour over the chocolate. Let sit for a minute, then stir until the chocolate has melted and the mixture is smooth. Let cool to room temperature.

Beat the remaining ¼ cup cream to soft peaks. Fold the reserved meringue, and then the whipped cream, into the chocolate mixture.

TO FILL THE MERINGUES: Leaving the baked meringues in the cups, gently scoop out the center of each to make a rounded cavity, leaving a ½- to ¾-inch wall of meringue. (A one-ounce ice-cream scoop works well for this.) Using a spoon or pastry bag, fill the cavities with the mousse; you will have some extra mousse. Return the meringues to the refrigerator to chill for at least 1 hour to set, or for up to a day.

FOR THE CRÈME ANGLAISE: Scrape the seeds from the vanilla bean into a saucepan, add the pod, milk, and cream, and bring to a simmer. Turn off the heat and let cool to room temperature to infuse the flavors.

Add half the sugar to the milk mixture and bring to a simmer, stirring to dissolve the sugar.

Meanwhile, whisk the egg yolks and the remaining sugar in a bowl to blend. Gradually whisk in one third of the hot milk mixture to temper the yolks and then return the mixture to the saucepan. Stir the custard with a wooden spoon over low heat until it thickens and coats the back of a wooden spoon. Immediately pour into a bowl set in an ice-water bath and stir it occasionally until cool. Strain the sauce and refrigerate until ready to serve; it can be made a few days ahead.

FOR THE CHOCOLATE TUILES: Preheat the oven to 350°F.

In a bowl, cream the butter and sugar. Sift the flour and cocoa together. Beat half the cocoa mixture into the butter mixture, add the egg white, and then add the remaining cocoa mixture.

Cut out a hollow round stencil with a 2¼-inch diameter. The top of a plastic container works well for this.

Place a Silpat (see Sources, page 315) on the counter. Place the stencil in one corner of the Silpat and holding it flat against the Silpat, scoop some of the batter onto the back of an offset spatula and spread it in an even layer over the stencil. Run the spatula over the top to remove any excess batter. Repeat to fill the Silpat. You will need only 6 tuiles for the recipe; extra batter can be frozen.

Place the filled Silpat on a baking sheet and bake for 8 minutes, or until the tuiles are set. Let the tuiles cool to room temperature, then remove them from the Silpat using a small narrow spatula. Store the cookies in an airtight container until ready to assemble the dessert.

FOR THE CHOCOLATE "SALAD": You will need about a tablespoon of shavings for each dessert. If you have a large block of chocolate, pull the blade of a large chef's knife over the top of the block of chocolate toward you at about a 45-degree angle to create shavings of chocolate. Adjust the angle of the blade as necessary. If you have a smaller piece, use a vegetable peeler to peel off shavings. If the shavings are too brittle and the pieces are too small, let the chocolate warm up very slightly in a warm spot. Keep the shavings in a cool place.

TO COMPLETE: Invert the meringues onto a paper towel and unmold them. (The towel will absorb any excess liquid.) Dip a 2¼-inch cutter in hot water, center it over a meringue, and cut down from the top to even the sides. Repeat with the remaining meringues.

Spoon some crème anglaise onto each plate. Place a meringue in the center of the sauce and lay a chocolate tuile over the top. Squeeze dots of the mint oil over the custard. Stack some chocolate shavings on each tuile, drizzle the chocolate "salad" with mint oil, and sprinkle with fleur de sel.

PICTURED ON PAGE 288                    MAKES 6 SERVINGS

PEARS

8 ripe but firm Comice pears, peeled and cored

1 recipe Poaching Liquid (page 269)

CHESTNUT CREAM

6 ounces vacuum-packed unsweetened chestnuts
or peeled roasted fresh chestnuts
(see Note, page 82)

1 cup heavy cream

¼ vanilla bean, split

¼ cup pear poaching liquid, reserved from above

Pinch of kosher salt

PEAR CHIPS

1 Bosc pear

1 cup sugar

2 cups water

4 to 8 sheets filo dough

1½ cups Clarified Butter (page 125), melted

½ cup sugar

1 recipe Crème Anglaise (page 290)

Powdered sugar, in a shaker

This is pastry chef Stephen Durfee's interpretation of a traditional strudel. One of the elements I like most in this dish is the crystallized fruit chip, a technique I learned in France from chef Michel Trama.

The main components of the dish, the poached pears, the chestnut cream, and the pear chips, can all be prepared a day ahead (the cream must be made in advance), and the strudels can be assembled a few hours before they are baked.

FOR THE PEARS: Slice off the bottoms of the pears so that they will stand upright. Cut off the necks of the pears at the point where the fruit begins to round. Using a 2-inch ring mold or round cutter, push straight down on the pears to cut out cylinders. Use an apple corer to remove the cores from the cylinders.

Place the pears in a saucepan with enough poaching liquid to cover them. Cover with a parchment paper lid (see page 190) and bring the liquid to a simmer. Poach the pears over low heat for 1 to 1½ hours, or until there is no resistance when they are pierced with the tip of a sharp knife. (The time will vary depending on the ripeness of your pears.)

Remove from the heat. Transfer about ¼ cup of the syrup to a measuring cup and set aside for the chestnut cream. The pears can be poached up to a day ahead; place them, along with their syrup, in a container and cool to room temperature, then cover and refrigerate.

FOR THE CHESTNUT CREAM: Combine the chestnuts and cream in a saucepan. Scrape the seeds from the vanilla bean into the pan and add the pod. Bring the cream to a simmer over low heat and cook the chestnuts for about 45 minutes, or until they are very soft.

Remove the pan from the heat and discard the vanilla bean. Pour the chestnuts and cream into the bowl of a food processor. Blend for about 3 minutes, or until smooth. There may be a few bits of chestnut that will not be incorporated; they will be removed later. Scrape down the sides of the bowl and with the motor running, add the reserved pear poaching liquid a little at a time until the mixture is creamy but still has enough body to hold some shape. You may not need all the liquid. The cream will be very soft while it is still hot, but it will thicken dramatically as it cools.

Scrape the chestnut cream through a tamis (see page 73) set over a bowl. Season with the salt. This will make about 1 cup of chestnut cream. Place the cream in a container, cover, and refrigerate overnight.

FOR THE PEAR CHIPS: On a mandoline, slice the unpeeled Bosc pear lengthwise as thin as possible; the slices should be almost transparent. Bring the sugar and water to a boil in a medium saucepan, stirring to dissolve the sugar. Turn the heat to low and, one by one, drop the pear slices into the hot syrup. Cook until they are translucent, about 8 to 10 minutes. Turn off the heat and let the pear slices cool in the syrup.

Preheat the oven to 275°F. Line a baking sheet with a Silpat (see Sources, page 315).

Remove the pear slices from the syrup, quickly blot the slices on paper towels to remove any excess syrup, and lay them on the baking sheet. Dry the pear chips in the oven for about 30 minutes. To test, remove a chip from the pan and let cool. It should be crisp; if not, continue to bake the slices for a little longer. Let cool, then store the chips in an airtight container. These chips can be made a day ahead. You'll only need 8 for this recipe; enjoy the rest as a snack.

TO ASSEMBLE THE PEAR STRUDELS: Remove the pear cylinders from the poaching liquid, lay them on paper towels, and cover them with a second layer of paper towels. Allow to drain thoroughly, about 30 minutes.

Meanwhile, transfer the poaching liquid to a saucepan, bring to a simmer, and reduce until it is thickened to a syrup consistency. Pour the reduced syrup into a squeeze bottle and set it aside at room temperature.

When you are ready to assemble the strudels, have the poached pear cylinders, filo, clarified butter, sugar, and a pastry brush ready. Lay the stack of filo dough on a work surface and cover with plastic wrap and then a damp towel to keep the leaves from drying out as you work. Remove one sheet of filo and place it with a long side in front of you.

Brush the entire sheet with clarified butter and sprinkle lightly with sugar. Cover with a second sheet of filo, brush with the clarified butter, and sprinkle with sugar again. Repeat the process until you have used 4 sheets of filo.

Trim off any dried edges of filo. Lay a pear cylinder across the bottom right of the filo stack, leaving a ⅛-inch border on the right. Cut a vertical strip of filo using a sharp knife, leaving a ⅛-inch border of filo to the left of the pear as well. Roll up the cylinder in the strip, wrapping the filo around it. Brush the wrapped strudel on all sides with more clarified butter, particularly at the seam to seal it well. Repeat this process with the remaining pear cylinders, stacking more filo if necessary. Place the rolled pears seam side down on a baking sheet and cover lightly with plastic wrap. The pears can be prepared to this point and refrigerated for a few hours, until ready to bake.

TO COMPLETE: Preheat the oven to 350°F. Line a baking sheet with a Silpat.

Place the pear strudels seam side down on the baking sheet and bake for 30 to 40 minutes, or until the filo is a rich golden brown.

Pour ¼ cup of the crème anglaise into a squeeze bottle.

Lay a hot pear strudel on each serving dish. Place two small quenelles (see page 274), or oval scoops, of chestnut cream to the right of the strudel, one leaning against the other. Nestle a pear chip between the chestnut cream and the strudel. Squeeze a series of dots of crème anglaise to the left of each strudel. Squeeze a small dot of pear syrup into the center of each dot of crème anglaise. Dust the strudels with powdered sugar. Serve the remaining crème anglaise in a sauceboat.

MAKES 8 SERVINGS

# Lemon Sabayon—Pine Nut Tart with Honeyed Mascarpone Cream

Butter and flour for the tart pan

1/3 recipe Pine Nut Crust (recipe follows)

**LEMON SABAYON**

2 large eggs, cold

2 large egg yolks, cold

3/4 cup sugar

1/2 cup fresh lemon juice

6 tablespoons (3 ounces) cold unsalted butter,
cut into 6 pieces

**HONEYED MASCARPONE CREAM**

1/2 cup heavy cream

3 tablespoons mascarpone cheese

1 tablespoon honey

This tart is best served at room temperature, within a few hours of assembling, but if necessary, it can be refrigerated and served cold.

FOR THE CRUST: Preheat the oven to 350°F. Generously butter and flour a 9-inch fluted tart pan with a removable bottom and refrigerate it while the oven preheats.

Remove the tart pan from the refrigerator. Use your fingertips to press the chilled dough evenly over the bottom and up the sides of the pan. Trim off any excess dough.

Bake the crust for 10 to 15 minutes, then rotate the shell and continue baking for another 10 to 15 minutes, or until the shell is golden brown. Remove the shell from the oven and let it cool while you make the filling. There may be some cracks in the shell; they will not affect the tart.

FOR THE LEMON SABAYON: Bring about 1½ inches of water to a boil in a pot that is slightly smaller than the diameter of the mixing bowl you will be using for the sabayon. Meanwhile, in a large metal bowl, whisk the eggs, yolks, and sugar for about 1 minute, or until the mixture is smooth.

Set the bowl over the pot and, using a large whisk, whip the mixture while you turn the bowl, for even heating. After about 2 minutes, when the eggs are foamy and have thickened, add one third of the lemon juice. Continue to whisk vigorously and when the mixture thickens again, add another one third of the lemon juice. Whisk until the mixture thickens again, then add the remaining lemon juice. Continue whisking vigorously, still turning the bowl, until the mixture is thickened, light in color, and the whisk leaves a trail in the bottom of the bowl. The total cooking time should be approximately 8 to 10 minutes.

Turn off the heat but leave the bowl over the water as you add the butter: Whisk in the butter a piece at a time. The sabayon may loosen slightly, but it will thicken and set as it cools. Pour the warm sabayon into the tart shell and place the pan on a baking sheet.

Preheat the broiler. While the sabayon is still warm, place the tart under the broiler. Leaving the door open, brown the top of the sabayon, rotating the tart if necessary for even color; do not leave the oven—this will happen in a few seconds. Remove the tart from the broiler and let it sit at least 1 hour before serving. Serve at room temperature or cold.

FOR THE HONEYED MASCARPONE CREAM: In a bowl set over ice, whip the cream until it is frothy. Add the mascarpone and honey and continue to whisk for about 2 minutes, or until the cream is thick and creamy. Keep refrigerated until serving.

TO COMPLETE: Serve the slices of the tart with the mascarpone cream on the side.

MAKES 8 SERVINGS

## PINE NUT CRUST

2 cups (10 ounces) pine nuts

1/3 cup sugar

3 cups all-purpose flour

16 tablespoons (8 ounces) unsalted
butter, at room temperature

1 large egg

1 teaspoon vanilla extract

Since the recipe uses only one egg, it would be difficult to cut down, but the extra dough can be frozen for future use.

Place the pine nuts in a food processor and pulse a few times. Add the sugar and flour and continue to pulse until the nuts are finely ground. Place the mixture in a mixing bowl (the dough can be mixed by hand or in a mixer fitted with the paddle).

Add the softened butter, the egg, and vanilla extract and mix to incorporate all the ingredients. Divide the dough into three parts. Wrap each piece in plastic wrap and refrigerate for at least 10 minutes before using. The dough can be frozen for future use.

MAKES ENOUGH DOUGH FOR THREE 9-INCH TARTS

This is an elegant dessert that
is very easy, can be done ahead
of time, and tastes absolutely
exquisite. The lemon sabayon is
a lot like a lemon curd; the difference
is you cook the eggs over hot water
until you develop those nice big trails
and ribbons, then add the butter, which
helps it set up as it cools to room
temperature. The honey in the
mascarpone cream perfectly balances
the lemon in the tart, a flavor
combination I didn't have to look any
further for than a cup of hot tea.

## "CANDIED APPLE"
## Crème de Farine with Poached Apples and Ice Cream

POACHED APPLES

5 large Golden Delicious apples

4 cups Poaching Liquid (page 269)

1 cinnamon stick

"CANDIED APPLE" ICE CREAM

4 cups apple juice (from about 8 Golden Delicious
    apples; or store-bought)

2 cups milk

2 cups heavy cream

3/4 cup sugar

1/4 vanilla bean, split

10 large egg yolks

CINNAMON TWIST COOKIES

4 ounces Puff Pastry (recipe follows)

1 large egg, beaten for egg glaze

Cinnamon sugar: 3 tablespoons sugar
    mixed with 1/4 teaspoon ground cinnamon

CRÈME DE FARINE

3 1/2 cups water

1/2 cinnamon stick

1 star anise

2 allspice berries

1/2 teaspoon salt

2/3 cup uncooked farina, such as Cream of Wheat
    (10-minute cooking)

1/4 cup sugar

2/3 cup mascarpone

2 tablespoons (1 ounce) unsalted butter,
    at room temperature

1/4 cup milk

1/4 cup all-purpose flour

1 cup panko (Japanese bread crumbs; see
    Sources, page 315) or dried bread crumbs,
    finely ground in a blender and sifted through
    a medium-mesh sieve

About 3 cups canola oil, for deep-frying

Pastry chef Stephen Durfee created this "Cream of Wheat" dish after noticing that some Cream of Wheat that he'd cooked for his four-year-old son firmed up in the pan into a perfect disk, and he thought it would make a perfect base for a dessert. This is a terrific dessert because you've got the hot Cream of Wheat and the cold ice cream, and you've got a variety of textures, the crispy exterior of the Cream of Wheat disk, the luxurious, creamy ice cream, and the crunchy cookies, finished with a sauce of the reduced apple-poaching liquid.

FOR THE POACHED APPLES: Cut two 3/4-inch rings from the center of each apple (you will have one extra). Remove the apple cores with an apple corer or small cutter. Cut each slice into an even round with a 2 1/4-inch cutter. Place the rings in a saucepan and add the poaching liquid. Cover the apples with a parchment lid (see page 190), bring to just under a simmer over low heat, and poach the apple rings for 25 to 35 minutes, or until they are tender and translucent. Remove the apple rings and drain them on paper towels. The rings can be poached a day ahead and refrigerated in a covered plastic container.

Add the cinnamon stick to the poaching liquid and simmer to reduce the liquid to about 1 1/4 cups. Strain the syrup into a covered container and refrigerate for at least 3 hours, or up to several days.

FOR THE "CANDIED APPLE" ICE CREAM: Boil the apple juice in a saucepan, skimming as necessary, until it is reduced to about 1 cup. When the liquid is reduced to the proper consistency, you will see small bubbles breaking across the entire surface. Remove from the heat and let cool while you make the custard.

Combine the milk, cream, and half the sugar in a large saucepan, scrape the seeds from the vanilla bean in the pan, and add the pod. Bring to a boil, stirring to dissolve the sugar.

Meanwhile, in a bowl, whisk the yolks with the remaining sugar until the mixture thickens and lightens in color. While whisking the yolks, gradually pour one third of the hot cream mixture into the yolks to temper them. Return the mixture to the saucepan and cook over low heat, stirring constantly with a wooden spoon, until the custard has thickened and coats the back of the spoon.

Pour the custard through a chinois (see page 73) into a metal bowl set in an ice-water bath. Add the reduced apple juice and cool, stirring occasionally. When the custard has cooled, it can be refrigerated overnight before freezing (which will result in the creamiest texture) or frozen immediately.

Freeze the ice cream in an ice-cream machine, then transfer it to an airtight container and place it in the freezer to harden. The ice cream is best eaten within a day but can be made several days ahead.

FOR THE CINNAMON TWIST COOKIES: On a lightly floured surface, roll the puff pastry into a square approximately 6 inches by 6 inches. Lightly brush the bottom half of the dough with the egg glaze and sprinkle it with the cinnamon sugar. Fold the top half of the dough over and roll the dough into a rectangle about 10 inches by 8 inches and $\frac{1}{8}$ inch thick. Place the dough on a parchment-lined baking sheet and chill for about an hour, or until it is very firm.

Preheat the oven to 375°F. Stack two baking sheets and line the top one with a piece of parchment (two pans stacked together will result in more even heat when baking).

Cut the dough crosswise into $\frac{1}{4}$-inch strips. Starting in the center of each strip and working toward the ends, twist the dough in opposite directions to form spiral-shaped cookies. Place the cookies on the doubled baking sheets and press the ends down flat against the parchment so they will hold their shape and not unwind as they bake.

Bake for 20 to 30 minutes, or until the cookies are golden brown and crisp. Cool slightly, then remove from the pan and cut off the flattened ends. They can be stored in an airtight container for a couple of days.

FOR THE CRÈME DE FARINE: Line a 9-inch square baking pan with plastic wrap. Bring the water, cinnamon stick, star anise, and allspice to a boil in a heavy medium saucepan. Simmer for 1 minute, then remove from the heat. Cover and allow the spices to steep for 5 minutes.

Strain the liquid, measure out 3 cups, and return it to the saucepan. Add the salt and bring to a boil. Whisking constantly, pour in the farina and cook over low heat, stirring constantly, for 6 to 8 minutes, or until it is thickened. Whisk in the sugar, mascarpone, and butter and pour into the baking pan. Press a piece of plastic wrap onto the surface to prevent a skin from forming and chill the crème de farine for at least 3 hours, or up to 3 days.

TO COMPLETE: If they've been refrigerated, bring the apple rings to room temperature.

Place the milk, flour, and crumbs in three separate bowls. Heat the oil to 350°F. in a pan for deep-frying. With a $2\frac{1}{4}$-inch cutter, cut out 9 rounds from the chilled farina. Dredge each disk in the flour, patting off any excess, dip into the milk, and coat in the crumbs. Fry the cakes, 3 at a time, for 2 to 3 minutes, or until golden brown, turning them over halfway through the cooking. Transfer the cooked farina to paper towels to drain. Be certain that the oil regains the proper temperature before adding the next batch.

Spoon some syrup into the center of each serving plate. Top each pool of syrup with a hot farina cake, an apple ring, and a quenelle (see page 274), or scoop, of apple ice cream. Lean a cookie against each dessert and serve immediately.

PICTURED ON PAGE 299                    MAKES 9 SERVINGS

## PUFF PASTRY

| DÉTREMPE | |
|---|---|
| 2¾ cups (12 ounces) all-purpose flour | 1 cup water |
| 1 cup plus 3 tablespoons (4 ounces) cake flour | 1 teaspoon white wine vinegar |
| 1 tablespoon kosher salt | BEURRAGE |
| 1 tablespoon sugar | 1 pound cold unsalted butter |
| 8 tablespoons (4 ounces) cold unsalted butter, cut into small pieces | ¼ cup plus 3 tablespoons (2 ounces) all-purpose flour |
| | Flour for dusting |

It's important to adhere to the allotted resting time when making puff pastry. As you work, the dough will become more elastic as the gluten develops and the butter warms. Resting the dough in the refrigerator between rolling the "turns" allows the gluten to relax and the butter to firm. The more you make, the better—it freezes well and you can use it for many other dishes.

FOR THE DÉTREMPE: Sift both flours, the salt, and sugar into a large mixing bowl. Add the butter and with your fingers, rub it into the dry ingredients for several minutes, until it is well incorporated and the pieces of butter are about the size of gravel. Add the water and vinegar and mix with your hands and a rubber spatula just until the dough comes together. It should still be a shaggy mass. Pat the dough into an 8-inch square on a piece of parchment paper, cover with a piece of plastic wrap, and refrigerate while you make the beurrage.

FOR THE BEURRAGE: Place the butter on a cold surface, such as a marble slab, and pound it with a rolling pin to make it malleable. Fold it over itself once or twice and pound it again. Sprinkle the flour over the butter and use a plastic dough scraper to cut the flour into the butter. Then use the heel of your hand to knead the mixture for about 30 seconds to combine; the butter should have the same consistency as the détrempe. Form the beurrage into a 6-inch square.

Clean the work surface and dust it with flour. Lay the détrempe on the surface and mark a diamond shape in it, starting at the center of each side. Dust the dough lightly with flour. Roll out the edges (the triangles) of the dough so the points extend about 5 inches, leaving the center mound thicker than the edges.

Lay the beurrage on the diamond, adjusting its size to fit the dough as necessary. Fold the dough flaps over the beurrage, stretching them and overlapping them as necessary to totally encase the butter and form a square package. Seal the edges by pressing lightly with the rolling pin. Dust with flour.

Gently press the package into a rectangle approximately 8 inches by 10 inches. Place on a tray and clean the work surface. If it is warm and the butter seems soft, refrigerate it for 30 minutes before continuing.

FOR THE FIRST DOUBLE TURNS: Place the dough on the work surface with a short side facing you. Press down on the dough with the rolling pin, working from the top to the bottom to set its shape. Roll the dough, using even pressure, into a rectangle approximately 10 inches by 20 inches. It is important to keep the edges of the pastry straight as you roll, or you will not get even folds and the pastry will not rise as it should. As you roll, sprinkle the work surface with flour as necessary to prevent sticking (use a brush to dust off excess flour) and always be careful that the butter does not start to leak out from the sides. If it does, seal the hole and refrigerate the dough for several minutes before continuing.

Fold over both short ends of the dough to meet in the center, then fold one side over the other to form four layers. Turn the dough 90 degrees to the left, so that the fold is on your left, and roll and fold the puff pastry the same way a second time. Wrap the dough in plastic and refrigerate it for 1 hour.

FOR THE SECOND DOUBLE TURNS: Place the chilled dough on the work surface with the fold to the left and roll and fold two more double turns as you did before. Wrap the dough and refrigerate again for at least 30 minutes.

FOR THE FINAL DOUBLE TURNS: Repeat the rolling and folding process two more times for a total of six turns. The puff pastry is ready to use. It can be cut into smaller pieces, wrapped well, and kept for a day in the refrigerator or frozen for longer storage.

MAKES ABOUT 2 POUNDS DOUGH

Left: "Candied Apple," page 296; right: "Coffee and Doughnuts," page 262; Chocolate Fondant, page 300

## Chocolate Fondant with Coffee Cream and Chocolate Dentelles

CHOCOLATE FONDANT

5½ ounces bittersweet chocolate, chopped

1 large egg, separated

¼ cup sugar

7 tablespoons (3½ ounces) unsalted butter,
    well softened

⅔ cup heavy cream

2 tablespoons very hot strong brewed coffee

2 large egg yolks, at room temperature

¼ cup currants, soaked in hot water for about 30
    minutes, or until plump, drained, and dried

¼ cup toasted sliced, blanched almonds,
    finely chopped

GANACHE

2 ounces bittersweet chocolate, finely chopped

¼ cup heavy cream

CHOCOLATE DENTELLES

MAKES 4 DOZEN

1 cup toasted sliced blanched almonds

1 tablespoon unsweetened cocoa powder

2 tablespoons milk

2 tablespoons corn syrup

¼ cup sugar

6 tablespoons (3 ounces) unsalted butter

SABLÉ COOKIES

MAKES 8 DOZEN

14 tablespoons (7 ounces) unsalted butter,
    at room temperature

⅔ cup sugar

1 large egg yolk

2½ cups all-purpose flour

½ recipe Crème Anglaise (page 291)

1½ teaspoons coffee extract
    (see page 263), or to taste

This is a beautiful chocolate dessert featuring a chocolate fondant, which, as I make it, is like a mousse only lighter, creamier, more refined. It's also less stable than a mousse and will break down if it's left out for too long. Although the techniques used in this recipe are not difficult, it's imperative that the ingredients for the fondant be at the proper temperatures. If not, the mixture will separate and you will not be able to recombine it. Dentelle, "lace" in French, refers here to the lace cookie, halved and resting on top of each fondant.

FOR THE CHOCOLATE FONDANT: Place 6 ring molds (2 inches wide by 2 inches high; see Sources, page 315) on a parchment-lined baking sheet. At the end of the recipe, you will need to use a blowtorch to release the fondant from the molds; if you do not have a blowtorch, line the inside of each ring mold with a strip of clear acetate (available at artists' supplies stores) or with parchment paper to enable you to lift off the ring before serving.

Place the chocolate in a metal bowl, set it over a saucepan of hot water, and heat gently, stirring, until melted and smooth. Keep hot over the hot water.

In another metal bowl, whisk the egg white until it begins to hold a shape, then gradually whisk in the sugar. Continue to whip until the meringue holds a shape, 4 to 5 minutes.

Place the softened butter in a bowl and whisk until it is smooth and creamy.

Place the cream in a medium bowl and whip it to soft peaks.

Add the hot coffee to the chocolate and stir to combine. (Both the coffee and the chocolate must be hot, or the mixture will seize.) Remove the bowl from the heat and let the chocolate cool slightly, just enough so that when you add the butter, it will combine with rather than melt into the chocolate; the chocolate should still be quite warm.

Working quickly, whisk the egg yolks and then the butter into the chocolate. With a spatula, fold in the meringue and then the heavy cream. Add the currants and almonds, mixing just to combine.

Transfer the fondant mixture to a pastry bag (without a tip) and pipe into the ring molds. (Piping rather than spooning the mixture helps prevent air pockets in the fondant.) The mixture should come to the top of the molds. Using an offset spatula, smooth the tops level with the rims of the molds. Refrigerate the fondants for at least 4 hours to firm. The fondants can be prepared to this point and refrigerated for up to 5 days, then glazed on the day they will be served; or they can be refrigerated just to firm, glazed, and then refrigerated for up to 5 days.

FOR THE GANACHE: Put the chocolate in a small bowl. Heat the heavy cream to just under a boil and pour it over the chocolate. Let sit for a minute to melt the chocolate, then stir to combine the ganache.

Remove the fondants from the refrigerator and cover the top of each one with a spoonful of glaze, smoothing it to the rim of the mold. Refrigerate the fondants for at least 1 hour before serving (see above).

FOR THE CHOCOLATE DENTELLES: Pulse the nuts and cocoa in a food processor to break up the nuts, then process until the nuts are in small pieces about the size of fine gravel. Remove to a bowl.

Place the milk, corn syrup, sugar, and butter in a saucepan. Bring to a boil, stirring occasionally, and cook until the mixture reaches a temperature of 220°F.

Stir the nuts and cocoa into the hot milk mixture. Stir for a few seconds to combine, then remove from the heat. Pour half the dentelle mixture onto a large sheet of parchment paper, cover with another sheet, and roll out as thin as possible. Lift the parchment sheets onto a baking sheet and place in the freezer (the batter must be frozen before you can remove the top sheet of parchment). Repeat with the remaining dentelle batter. Each sheet of batter makes about 24 cookies; they can be kept in the freezer for several weeks. For smaller batches, just cut through the parchment paper once the batter is frozen and store in smaller quantities.

TO BAKE THE DENTELLES: Preheat the oven to 350°F.

Remove a sheet of batter from the freezer and pull off and discard the top sheet of parchment paper. Place the batter, still on the bottom sheet of parchment, on a baking sheet and bake for about 12 minutes. To test for doneness, cut off a small piece of the cookie and let cool slightly;

it should harden in a few seconds. Remove the pan from the oven and let cool slightly.

Cut out the dentelles with a 2½-inch round cutter, then cut each disk in half. If the cookies harden before you can cut them, return them to the oven to resoften. Let the dentelles cool, then store them in an airtight container for up to 2 days.

FOR THE SABLÉ COOKIES: This recipe will make about 8 dozen cookies. Although extra baked cookies can be frozen, for better results, freeze the uncooked dough and then bake when desired. The frozen dough will keep for several weeks.

In a mixer fitted with the paddle attachment, cream the butter and sugar until smooth. Add the egg yolk and beat well, then mix in the flour until combined. Remove the dough from the mixer and divide it into quarters. One at a time, place each portion on a large piece of parchment paper, cover with another sheet, and roll into a thin sheet, about ¹/₁₆ inch thick. Place the parchment-wrapped dough on a baking sheet and place in the freezer for 30 minutes or so to harden completely.

To bake the sablés, preheat the oven to 350°F.

Remove a sheet of sablé dough from the freezer, peel off the top sheet of parchment, and use it to line a baking sheet. Place the sheet of cookies on a cutting board or work surface. Using a 2-inch cutter, cut the dough into rounds. (Or, if your ring molds are slightly larger or smaller, cut out rounds the same diameter as the molds.) Place the cookies ½ inch apart on the baking sheet and bake for 12 minutes, or until golden brown. Remove the cookies from the oven and let cool. Store them in an airtight container for up to 5 days.

Mix the crème anglaise with the coffee extract and refrigerate.

TO COMPLETE: Place each fondant on a sablé cookie. Briefly run a blowtorch around the mold just to release the fondant and remove the ring; or, if you used acetate, just lift off the ring. Place a spoonful of crème anglaise on each serving plate and top with the fondant. Press 2 pieces of the chocolate dentelles into the top of each dessert to garnish.

PICTURED ON PAGE 299                            MAKES 6 SERVINGS

# Chocolate Cakes with Red Beet Ice Cream and Toasted Walnut Sauce

**RED BEET ICE CREAM**

2 pounds red beets, peeled and quartered

2 cups heavy cream

2 cups milk

¾ cup sugar

8 large egg yolks

**WALNUT SYRUP AND CANDIED**

**WALNUTS**

2 cups Poaching Liquid (page 269)

8 ounces walnut halves, toasted and
    excess skins rubbed off

½ teaspoon kosher salt

**CHOCOLATE CAKES**

8 ounces bittersweet chocolate,
    such as Valhrona Equitorial, chopped

8 tablespoons (4 ounces) unsalted butter

3 large eggs

2 teaspoons sugar

¼ cup heavy cream, whipped to soft peaks

**BEET CHIPS**

Canola oil for deep-frying

Flour for dusting

2 to 3 small red beets, sliced paper-thin
    on a mandoline (about 60 slices)

Kosher salt

Powdered sugar, in a shaker

This dessert has its origins in a cake my mother used to make for me. She put grated beets in it, which resulted in a deep, dark color. When I decided to create a dessert using beet ice cream, I knew I should serve it with this kind of chocolate cake. I've added more flavor and textural contrast in the form of toasted candied walnuts.

FOR THE RED BEET ICE CREAM: Put the beets through a vegetable juicer, reserving the pulp; you should have about 2 cups of juice. Place the juice in a saucepan and reduce over low heat, skimming as necessary, to about ¼ cup. Strain the liquid into a container, cover, and place in the refrigerator.

In a saucepan, combine the reserved beet pulp with the cream and milk. Bring to a simmer, cover, and remove from the heat for 30 minutes.

Strain the liquid and measure out 3 cups (discard any extra). Return it to the saucepan, add half the sugar and bring to a simmer, stirring to dissolve the sugar.

Meanwhile, in a bowl, whisk the egg yolks with the remaining sugar until they have thickened slightly and lightened in color. Gradually whisk about one third of the hot liquid into the yolks to temper them.

Return the mixture to the saucepan and heat, stirring with a wooden spoon, until the custard has thickened and coats the back of the spoon. Pour the custard into a bowl set in an ice-water bath and let cool.

Strain the cooled custard into a container, cover, and refrigerate for a few hours, until cold, or overnight (for the creamiest texture).

Stir the reduced beet juice into the custard and freeze in an ice-cream machine. Remove the ice cream to a covered container and store in the freezer for at least 2 hours, or up to 2 days.

FOR THE WALNUT SYRUP AND CANDIED WALNUTS: Bring the poaching liquid to a boil in a medium saucepan and add the walnuts. Lower the heat and simmer until the syrup is reduced to ⅔ cup.

Preheat the oven to 250°F. Line a baking sheet with parchment paper.

Strain the walnut syrup into a container, cover, and refrigerate. Spread the walnuts on the baking sheet and sprinkle with the salt. Toast in the oven for about 30 minutes. To test, remove a walnut and let cool—it should be crunchy; if not, continue baking the walnuts for a little longer. Let cool on the baking sheet. You will need 20 walnuts for this dessert; extra nuts can be kept in an airtight container at room temperature, or in a plastic bag in the freezer.

FOR THE CHOCOLATE CAKES: Preheat the oven to 350°F. Spray ten 4-ounce soufflé molds or foil cups with nonstick spray.

Melt the chocolate with the butter in a bowl set over a pot of hot water. Stir to combine, remove the bowl from the heat, and let the mixture cool to room temperature. (Keep the water hot over low heat.)

Whisk the eggs with the sugar in a metal mixer bowl over the hot water until the sugar is dissolved. Place the bowl on the mixer stand and whip until the eggs are cool and have tripled in volume. Fold in the cooled melted chocolate and then the whipped cream.

Spoon the batter (about 2 ounces each) into the prepared molds, place the molds in a baking pan, and add hot water to come about one third of the way up the sides of the molds. Bake for 10 minutes. Lay a piece of aluminum foil loosely over the pan and continue to bake the cakes for another 15 to 20 minutes, or until the tops are set but still slightly shiny. Remove the cakes from the water bath and let cool at room temperature for several hours; do not refrigerate.

FOR THE BEET CHIPS: Heat the oil to 275°F. in a deep heavy pot. Flour the beet chips, a few at a time, and place them in the hot oil. As they fry, tiny bubbles will form around the beets, indicating moisture in the chips. As soon as the moisture has evaporated (at which point, the chips will be crisp), the chips will sink to the bottom of the pot. Remove them as they do, drain on paper towels, and sprinkle with salt. Keep the chips at room temperature until serving.

TO COMPLETE: Spoon some of the walnut syrup onto each serving plate. Unmold the cakes and center one, upside down, in each pool of the syrup (dip the molds in hot water to loosen the cakes if necessary). Arrange 2 candied walnuts on opposite sides of each cake and place a scoop or quenelle (see page 274) of red beet ice cream between them. Stack a small pile of beet chips over the ice cream and sprinkle the chips with powdered sugar.

MAKES 10 SERVINGS

## Beginning and ending

After you arrive at the French Laundry and begin to peruse the menu, a waiter in a white collarless shirt and ankle-length apron will bend to offer you what looks like a miniature sugar cone with a scoop of pink ice cream and say, "Salmon tartare with red onion crème fraîche in a savory tuile."

Some diners, whole tables even, stare for a long time at this salmon ice-cream cone, glancing up to see if anyone else is eating it, and how. The first brave soul will tip the small cone sideways, nibble at the edge of the pink orb, and look up, noncommittal. "Oh." Another tiny bite. "Mmm." And then another, capturing a bit of cone and some of the onion crème fraîche inside. "Mmm. This is really good." Genuine surprise. Others will regard the cone, shrug, then decapitate it with a smile. But everyone always stops to look.

All meals proceed in various ways from that moment, and after the meal, some people wander back to look at the kitchen and watch Keller, towering over his expediting station, called the pass. During service, when you stand in the broad kitchen entryway, Keller won't pay much attention; he'll more likely be studying the tickets lined on the cloth before him. He'll say, "Ordering four tastings. Ordering two tastings and two regular, agnolotti and crab salad, one salmon, one scallop, one veal, one lamb."

The kitchen is clean, cool, and bright. The pans are a uniform brushed silver. The air is calm and quiet, the brigade gliding across the carpet below their feet, bending at right angles over white china to construct dish after perfect dish. Visitors stand to the side and watch. A mother and son wander down the breezeway after their dinner and halt at the kitchen's entrance. The young man is grinning hard, his eyes wide. He is a cook himself at a well-known San Francisco restaurant. "It's so quiet," he says. The mother whispers, "It's like a watchmaker's shop." —M.R.

Jellies are often served in France. They're very delicate and very elegant.

Of course, we needed to add a little bit of America, so we serve them with

peanut butter truffles. The jellies are easy to make, but it's important that

you find pure apple pectin, the key to their delicate texture.

Opposite and above: Truffles and jellies for "Peanut Butter and Jellies," page 308

### PEANUT BUTTER TRUFFLES

4 ounces milk chocolate, chopped

1 pound natural peanut butter (scant 2 cups)

¼ cup sugar

2 teaspoons kosher salt

12 tablespoons (6 ounces) unsalted butter,
    at room temperature

1 pound bittersweet or milk chocolate

About ⅓ cup unsweetened cocoa powder

### YUZU JELLIES

1 cup apple juice

½ cup plus 2 tablespoons yuzu juice

¼ cup plus 2 tablespoons water

2¼ cups plus 3½ tablespoons sugar

½ cup light corn syrup

2 tablespoons apple pectin powder
    (see Sources, page 315)

Granulated or superfine sugar for dusting

### CONCORD GRAPE JELLIES

3 pounds Concord grapes or 2 cups
    unsweetened Concord grape juice

2¼ cups plus 3½ tablespoons sugar

½ cup light corn syrup

2 tablespoons apple pectin powder
    (see Sources, page 315)

Granulated or superfine sugar for dusting

## PEANUT BUTTER TRUFFLES

FOR THE TRUFFLE FILLING: Place the chocolate in a metal bowl, set it over a saucepan of hot water, and heat gently, stirring, until melted and smooth. Remove from the heat and let cool to room temperature.

Place the peanut butter, sugar, and salt in a food processor and blend for 3 minutes. Add the chocolate and process until well blended. Scrape down the sides of the bowl and add the softened butter; process until combined. Remove the truffle mixture to a container, cover, and refrigerate until firm. The filling (at any stage) can be kept for up to a week.

To shape the truffles, use a #100 ice-cream scoop to scoop up balls of the filling and place them on a parchment-lined pan. Or, using about 2 teaspoons of the mixture for each truffle, roll into balls between the palms of your hands. (This will make about 3 dozen truffles, but they can be made larger or smaller.) The truffles should be chilled before dipping; refrigerate for at least 1 hour.

Melt the bittersweet chocolate in a metal bowl set over a pot of warm water, stirring until smooth. Remove the bowl from the heat and let it sit for about 20 minutes, stirring occasionally, until the chocolate is at room temperature.

Line a baking sheet with a piece of parchment paper. Remove the truffles from the refrigerator. Lift them up one at a time, dip them in the melted chocolate, and place on the parchment-lined pan to set. Should the bowl of chocolate become too cool at any point, return the bowl to the pot of hot water just to soften. When all the truffles are dipped and the chocolate is set, dip them a second time in the remaining chocolate. Refrigerate the dipped truffles to harden the chocolate. This will only take a few minutes, but they can be refrigerated for several days.

TO COMPLETE: Remove the truffles from the refrigerator and, leaving them on the baking sheet, sift the cocoa over the top. Shake the pan back and forth to roll the truffles in the cocoa. You may not use all the cocoa; they should have a light dusting rather than a heavy coating. The truffles can be served immediately or can be refrigerated in a covered container for several days.

PICTURED ON PAGE 306                    MAKES ABOUT 3 DOZEN TRUFFLES

## YUZU JELLIES

Yuzu, a lemon-like Japanese citrus fruit, is not available here fresh, but you can buy it as juice and as zest in Japanese markets. We use it because it's unfamiliar and therefore has an exotic appeal. Also, it's more intense than lemon, and you need less of it. But you can substitute lemon juice if you wish.

Line a 9- by 13-inch baking pan with plastic wrap and set it aside. Combine the apple juice, yuzu juice, water, 2¼ cups of the sugar, and the corn syrup in a large saucepan.

Bring the mixture to a simmer over medium heat, whisking to dissolve the sugar. Using a fine-mesh skimmer, skim off the foam and sediment that rises to the top. Continue to skim until the liquid is clear, about 10 minutes. Keep warm over low heat.

Combine the apple pectin and the remaining 3½ tablespoons sugar in a medium bowl. Add half the hot liquid, whisking constantly to dissolve the sugar and pectin; continue to whisk until there are no lumps. Return this mixture to the saucepan.

Bring to a simmer and cook, whisking constantly, for 5 to 10 minutes, until the jelly has thickened and reached a temperature of 219°F. Immediately pour the jelly into the prepared pan. Smooth into an even layer, working quickly, before it begins to set. Let the jellies sit at room temperature for at least 1 hour, or until completely set.

TO COMPLETE: Cut the jellies into 1-inch squares and roll them in a bowl of sugar to coat them completely. Store the jellies at room temperature.

PICTURED ON PAGE 307         MAKES ABOUT 100 JELLIES

## CONCORD GRAPE JELLIES

If using grapes, remove them from the stems and place them in a large resealable plastic bag; push down on the grapes to squeeze out as much of the juice as possible. Let the grapes and juice steep with the skins for about 2 hours or longer at room temperature, so that the juice will extract as much color and flavor from the skins as possible.

Strain the grape juice through a chinois (see page 73), pressing on the skins with a small ladle. Measure out 2 cups of juice.

Line a 9- by 13-inch baking pan with plastic wrap and set it aside. Combine the grape juice, 2¼ cups of the sugar, and the corn syrup in a large saucepan.

Place the pan over medium heat and bring the mixture to a simmer, whisking to dissolve the sugar. With a fine-mesh skimmer, skim off the foam and sediment that rises to the top; continue to skim until the liquid is clear, about 10 minutes. Keep warm over low heat.

Combine the apple pectin with the remaining 3½ tablespoons sugar in a medium bowl. Add half the hot liquid, whisking constantly to dissolve the sugar and pectin; continue to whisk until there are no lumps. Return this mixture to the saucepan.

Bring to a simmer and cook, whisking constantly, for 5 to 10 minutes, or until the jelly has thickened and reached a temperature of 219°F. Immediately pour the jelly into the prepared pan. Using an offset spatula, smooth the jelly into an even layer, working quickly, before it begins to set. Let it sit at room temperature for at least 1 hour, or until completely set.

TO COMPLETE: Cut the jellies into 1-inch squares and roll them in a bowl of sugar to coat them completely. Store the jellies at room temperature.

PICTURED ON PAGE 307         MAKES ABOUT 100 JELLIES

# DON AND SALLY SCHMITT AND THE BIRTH OF THE FRENCH LAUNDRY

It's fitting that Don and Sally conclude this book because they are the ultimate purveyors. They purveyed a restaurant.

Don Schmitt, as one Yountville resident put it, had built the town with his own hands, transforming it from a beer-soaked backwater into a thriving municipality and serving for many years as its mayor. When he and Sally, a housewife-turned-chef, took over the French Laundry, the building was decrepit and unlivable, abandoned, but known to all of Yountville as the French Laundry because it had once been, during the 1920s, a French steam laundry. The Schmitt family would build it into a one-seating, fixed-menu, handmade restaurant that was a harbinger of what was to become known as Californian cuisine.

In 1992, Don and Sally didn't so much sell the restaurant as pass it on to Keller, going to great lengths to integrate Keller into the community. They had put their lives and soul into this place and if it were to fail in Keller's hands, a part of them would die, too.

The Schmitts, the restaurant itself, and all those connected with it seemed directed by an unspoken, intuitive worldview that embraces people, the earth, and what grows on it, that shuns waste and adores luxury.

Over the Mayacamas, along mountainous roads through moss-covered forest into Mendocino County, a hundred miles from the French Laundry, lies a minuscule town called Philo and a small apple orchard. When Don and Sally bought the orchard, it was virtually dead, the site of their present house a cardboard shanty for migrant workers, livestock running through it.

The orchard is now two thousand trees strong, both new and ancient, heirloom and common, all organic. The apples have become a business, retail and wholesale, and the source of numerous products: cider, cider vinegar, cider syrup, apple balsamic vinegar, juice, and chutneys of apple, apricot, quince, green tomato, and persimmon. Don and his son-in-law are working on a selection of hard ciders. Sally runs a cooking school on the farm along with a small bed and breakfast. All of it under the name the Apple Farm.

The Schmitts have chosen this place because they sense it will be the next Napa Valley, and, just as they were instrumental in transforming Yountville in the late sixties from a bar-and-trailer-home town into a vibrant community in the heart of wine country, their visionary hope is that this new spot in Mendocino called the Anderson Valley—with its young vineyards, orchards, and rich farming land—will become the new California destination. —M.R.

# Sally Schmitt's Cranberry and Apple Kuchen with Hot Cream Sauce

KUCHEN

6 tablespoons (3 ounces) unsalted butter, at room
    temperature, plus butter for the baking pan

3/4 cup sugar

1 large egg

1½ cups all-purpose flour

2 teaspoons baking powder

¼ teaspoon kosher salt

¼ teaspoon freshly grated nutmeg

½ cup milk or light cream

3 to 4 Gravenstein or Golden Delicious apples

1 cup cranberries or firm blueberries

Cinnamon sugar: 1 tablespoon sugar mixed with
    ¼ teaspoon ground cinnamon

HOT CREAM SAUCE

2 cups heavy cream

½ cup sugar

8 tablespoons (4 ounces) unsalted butter

This was always a favorite at the original French Laundry. It's simple and delicious. The hot cream sauce, cream cooked with sugar, can be used with a variety of other desserts.

FOR THE KUCHEN: Preheat the oven to 350°F. Butter a 9-inch round cake pan.

In a mixer bowl or by hand in a large bowl, beat the butter, sugar, and egg together until the mixture is fluffy and lightened in texture.

In a separate bowl, combine the flour, baking powder, salt, and nutmeg. Add the dry ingredients and the milk alternately to the butter mixture. Do not overbeat; mix just until the ingredients are combined.

Peel and core the apples. Slice them into ¼-inch wedges.

Spoon the batter into the pan. Press the apple slices, about ¼ inch apart and core side down, into the batter, working in a circular pattern around the outside edge (like the spokes of a wheel). Arrange most of the cranberries in a ring inside the apples and sprinkle the remainder around the edges of the kuchen. Sprinkle the kuchen with the cinnamon sugar.

Bake for 40 to 50 minutes, or until a cake tester or skewer inserted in the center of the kuchen comes out clean. Set on a rack to cool briefly, or let cool to room temperature.

FOR THE HOT CREAM SAUCE: Combine the cream, sugar, and butter in a medium saucepan and bring to a boil. Reduce the heat (to reduce the chances of scorching or boiling over) and let the sauce simmer for 5 to 8 minutes, to reduce and thicken slightly. Serve the hot sauce with the kuchen.

MAKES 8 SERVINGS

The staff, April 9, 1999

# Sources

EQUIPMENT

The equipment used most often for these recipes includes: food processor, blender, KitchenAid or other heavy-duty mixer, large stockpot (over 16 quarts), heavy sheet pans, Silpat (flexible silicon-coated nonstick fabric sold in sizes to fit commercial baking sheets), chinois (fine-meshed conical strainer), tamis (large flat sieve), heat diffuser, juicer, Japanese mandoline (Benriner), plastic bowl scraper, coffee grinder or spice mill, scale, instant-read thermometer, deep-fry thermometer, palette knife and small offset palette knife, graduated round cutters, pastry bag and tips, and small plastic squeeze bottles.

Special equipment used in specific recipes includes: small blowtorch, mini food processor, ice-cream maker, meat grinder attachment for KitchenAid or other heavy-duty mixer, pasta machine, fluted pastry wheel, scalloped oval melon baller or scoop, parisienne baller, larding needle, sugar shaker, oval ice-cream scoop, gnocchi paddle, juicer, ring molds in assorted sizes, 4-ounce hemisphere molds, cornet molds, egg cutter, and truffle shaver.

Note: Ring molds can be purchased from a variety of stores listed in this section or they can be made using cans readily available in the grocery store. Remove both the tops and bottoms of appropriately sized cans, making sure that the edges are smooth. Wash the cans well before using.

All sources below ship to customers.

**Culinary Institute of America at Greystone**
tel: 888-424-2433; fax: 877-967-2433

**J.B. Prince Company, Inc.**
tel: 800-473-0577; 212-683-3553

**Sur La Table**
tel: 800-243-9852
Web site: www.surlatable.com

**Williams-Sonoma**
tel: 800-541-1262
Web site: www.williams-sonoma.com

It is essential to use high-quality cookware, such as Bourgeat or Le Creuset. Le Creuset is available in cookware stores and kitchenware departments. For Bourgeat's high-quality French copper, stainless steel, and nonstick cookware, which is used in many restaurant kitchens, contact:

**Bourgeat**
tel: 800-469-0188
Web site: www.bourgeat.fr
E-mail: bourgeat@aol.com (reference: *The French Laundry Cookbook*)

INGREDIENTS

Most specialty food stores carry or can order most items used in these recipes. The following sources will ship directly to you.

For wildflower honey, Banyuls vinegar, Carnaroli rice, pink and gray salt, fleur de sel, marrow beans, salt-packed anchovies, candied Morello cherries, vacuum-packed unsweetened chestnuts, verjus, white truffle oil, lemon oil, gelatin sheets, white rock salt, and apple pectin:

**Culinary Institute of America at Greystone**
see Equipment

**Dean & DeLuca**
tel: 800-221-7714; 212-226-6800
fax: 800-781-4050
Web site: www.dean-deluca.com

**Williams-Sonoma**
see Equipment

For fresh truffles, white truffle oil, truffle juice, bottarga di muggine, and caviar:

**Urbani Truffles USA**
tel: 800-281-2330; 718-392-5050
fax: 718-391-1704; also
tel: 213-933-8202; fax: 213-933-4235
Web site: www.urbani.com
E-mail: urbaniusa@aol.com

For fruitwood smoked salmon:

**Max & Me Atlantic Smoked Salmon**
tel: 800-503-3663
fax: 215-297-0391

For moulard duck foie gras, squab, quail, guinea hen, venison, and rabbit "super" saddles:

**D'Artagnan**
tel: 800-DARTAGN (800-327-8246);
973-344-0565
fax: 973-465-1870
Web site: www.dartagnan.com

For specialty produce such as hearts of palm stems:

**George Cornille & Sons Produce**
tel: 312-226-1015; fax: 312-226-3016

Panko crumbs, quail eggs, fresh soybeans, garlic chives, yuzu juice, and black sesame seeds are available at Asian grocery stores and markets.

Veal tongues, beef cheeks, pigs' heads, pigs' feet, sweetbreads, and caul fat are available at ethnic butcher shops.

# List of recipes

# index

Page numbers in italics refer to photographs.

marrow bones:
  braised prime beef short ribs with root
    vegetables and sautéed, 188–90
  in fricassée of escargots with a purée of
    sweet carrots, roasted shallots, and
    herb salad, 98–99, 100
Martin, Keith, 8, 194–95, *194*
mascarpone:
  in crème de farine with poached apples
    and ice cream, 296–97
  -enriched orzo, butter-poached Maine
    lobster with creamy lobster broth and,
    132
  in fava bean agnolotti with curry
    emulsion, 80
  honeyed, cream, 294
  in Maine lobster pancakes with pea
    shoot salad and ginger-carrot
    emulsion, 126–27
  sorbet, rhubarb confit with navel
    oranges, candied fennel, and, 270–71
  in white corn agnolotti with summer
    truffles, 83
Maxim's, 125
mayonnaise, 42
meringues, slow-baked, with crème Anglaise
  and bittersweet chocolate, 290–91
Miller, Edgar, 195
mince/dice vegetable cuts, *202, 203*
mint:
  eggplant and, 15
  oil, 166
mirepoix vegetable cuts, *202, 203*
moi, Pacific, with fresh soybeans, scallion
  and radish salad, and soy–temple
  orange glaze, 154–55, *154*
monkfish tail, sautéed, with braised oxtails,
  salsify, and cèpes, 162–63
Mood, John, 8, 68–69
Mood, Pat, 68–69
morel mushrooms:
  pan-roasted Maine jumbo scallops with
    asparagus purée and, 136
  sauce, roulade of Pekin duck breast with
    creamed sweet white corn and,
    172–73
moulard duck foie gras:
  five-spiced roasted Maine lobster with
    port-poached figs and sautéed, 133
  Gewürztraminer-poached, with
    Gewürztraminer jelly, 111
  pan-roasted breast of squab with Swiss
    chard, oven-dried black figs, and
    sautéed, 174
  poached, *au torchon* with pickled
    cherries, 106–7
  whole roasted, with apples and black
    truffles, 110
mousse:
  chocolate, in slow-baked meringue with
    crème Anglaise and bittersweet
    chocolate, 290–91
  goat cheese, Parmigiano-Reggiano crisps
    with, 49
  in Roquefort trifle with French butter
    pear relish, 256–57
  shrimp, 74
mozzarella, in Eric's staff lasagna, 116
mullet, red, with a *palette d'ail doux* and
  garlic chips, 156–57
mushroom ragout:
  Carnaroli risotto with, 88

in tasting of potatoes with black truffles,
  86–87
mushrooms:
  powder, 232
  purveyors of, 28–29
  sauce for agnolotti, 74
  stock, 220, 227
  wild, 28–29
  *see also* cèpes; chanterelles; morel;
    mushroom ragout
mussels:
  in sauce gribiche, 146
  stock, in black sea bass with sweet
    parsnips, arrowleaf spinach, and
    saffron-vanilla sauce, 146–47
mustard powder, 233
mustard sauce, spotted skate wings with
  braised red cabbage and, 161

## N
Napa Valley, Calif., 3–4, 28
nectarine salad with green tomato confiture
  and hazelnut sabayon, 272–73
Niçoise yellowfin tuna, carpaccio of, 96–97

## O
oblique vegetable cuts, *202, 203*
offal, 209
oils, 11, 165–67
  basil, 166
  carrot, 167
  chive, 166
  clove-scented, 239
  coral, 167
  curry, 165, 167
  fennel, 166
  infusing, 165–67
  mint, 166
  parsley, 166
  rosemary, 165, 166
  thyme, 165, 166
  truffle, 73
  *see also* white truffle oil
olive tapenade, Niçoise, heirloom tomato
  tart with mixed field greens, basil
  vinaigrette, and, 66
onion(s), 11
  Bellwether farm baby lamb—five cuts
    served with Provençal vegetables,
    thyme oil, and braised cipollini, 198
  glaze, rue-scented, sautéed Atlantic
    halibut with summer succotash and,
    144–45
  preparations for, 15
  rings, 210–11
  in salad of globe artichokes with garden
    herbs and gazpacho, 62
  sweet red, crème fraîche, salmon tartare
    with, 6–7
  Vidalia and red, confit, 210–11
onion powder, 232
orange(s), navel:
  citrus-marinated salmon with beluga
    caviar, pea shoot coulis, and confit of,
    140–41
  rhubarb confit with candied fennel,
    mascarpone sorbet, and, 270–71
orzo, butter-poached Maine lobster with
  creamy lobster broth and
  mascarpone-enriched, 132
osetra caviar, sabayon of pearl tapioca with
  Malpeque oysters and, *21,* 23

oven-roasted Maui pineapple with fried
  pastry cream and whipped crème
  fraîche ("pineapple chop"),
  282–83
oxtails, 2
  Carnaroli risotto with braised, 88
  sautéed monkfish tail with salsify, cèpes,
    and braised, 162–63
oysters:
  in cauliflower panna cotta with beluga
    caviar, 22
  Malpeque, sabayon of pearl tapioca with
    osetra caviar and, 23
  pickled, with English cucumber
    "capellini" and dill, 24
  shopping for, 21
  shucking, 22
"oysters and pearls" (sabayon of pearl
  tapioca with Malpeque oysters and
  osetra caviar), 21, 23, 135

## P
Pacific moi with fresh soybeans, scallion
  and radish salad, and soy–temple
  orange glaze, 154–55, *154*
*palette d'ail doux,* red mullet with garlic
  chips and, 156
palettes, 159
Palladin, Jean-Louis, 258
Palm Beach Yacht Club, 42, 115
pancakes, Maine lobster, with pea shoot
  salad and ginger-carrot emulsion,
  126–27
panko (Japanese bread crumbs), 156
  in crème de farine with poached apples
    and ice cream, 296–97
  in oven-roasted Maui pineapple with
    fried pastry cream and whipped
    crème fraîche, 282–83
  in red mullet with a *palette d'ail doux*
    and garlic chips, 156–57
panna cotta, cauliflower, with beluga
  caviar, 22
pan-roasted:
  breast of squab with Swiss chard,
    sautéed duck foie gras and oven-dried
    black figs, 174
  Maine jumbo scallops with morel
    mushrooms and asparagus
    purée, 136
  striped bass with artichoke ravioli
    and barigoule vinaigrette,
    *151,* 152–53
paper-thin vegetable cuts, 203, *203*
parchment paper lids, 190
Parisienne ball vegetable cuts,
  *202, 203*
Park Avenue Café, 137
Parmesan crisps, 37
  with goat cheese mousse, 49
  Parmigiano-Reggiano custards with
    romaine lettuce, anchovy dressing,
    and, 251
Parmigiano-Reggiano custards with romaine
  lettuce, anchovy dressing, and
  Parmesan crisps ("Caesar salad"),
  251, *252*
parsley:
  for chlorophyll, 247
  in red mullet with a *palette d'ail doux*
    and garlic chips, 156, 159

parsley oil, 166
  sautéed cod with cod cakes and, 142–43
parsnips:
  in braised prime beef short ribs with root
    vegetables and sautéed bone marrow,
    188–90
  sweet, black sea bass with arrowleaf
    spinach, saffron-vanilla sauce, and,
    146–47
pasta dough, 78
  for artichoke ravioli, 152–53
  in fava bean agnolotti with curry
    emulsion, 80
  in "linguine" with white clam sauce, 25
  in white corn agnolotti with summer
    truffles, 83
pasta machines, 74
pastry cream, fried, 282–83
pâte à choux, 47, *47,* 48
  in Gruyère cheese gougères, 47
pea:
  purée, 73
  soup, purée of English, with white truffle
    oil and Parmesan crisps, 37
  *see also* pea shoot(s)
peaches, poached with verjus sorbet, 269
peach palm (*pejibaye*), 68–69
"peanut butter and jellies," *307,* 308–9
peanut butter truffles, 307, *307,* 308–9
pear:
  purée, in cream of walnut soup, 268
  relish, Roquefort trifle with French butter,
    256–57
  strudel with chestnut cream and pear
    chips, 292–93
"peas and carrots" (Maine lobster pancakes
  with pea shoot salad and ginger
  carrot emulsion), 126–27, *129*
pea shoot(s):
  coulis, citrus-marinated salmon with a
    confit of navel oranges, beluga caviar,
    and, 140–41
  salad, Maine lobster pancakes with
    ginger-carrot emulsion and, 126–27
pecorino Toscano with roasted sweet
  peppers and arugula coulis, 250
*pejibaye* (peach palm), 68–69
pepper, black, 11, 180–81
pepper, roasted sweet, pecorino Toscano
  with arugula coulis and, 250
pepper, Tellicherry, 181
  syrup, in cream of blueberry soup with
    yogurt charlottes, 264–65
  whipped Brie de Meaux *en feuilleté* with
    baby mèche and, 237, 238
pepper, white, 180, 181
pepper confetti, 97
  in blini with roasted sweet peppers and
    eggplant caviar, 41
  in carpaccio of yellowfin tuna Niçoise,
    96–97
peppers, bell, *see* bell peppers, green; bell
  peppers, red; bell peppers, yellow
Perail de Brebis with frisée aux lardons,
  255, 257
Petite Basque with spiced carrot salad and
  golden raisin purée, 242
pickled:
  cherries, poached moulard duck foie gras
    *au torchon* with, 106–7
  oysters, with English cucumber
    "capellini" and dill, 24, 27

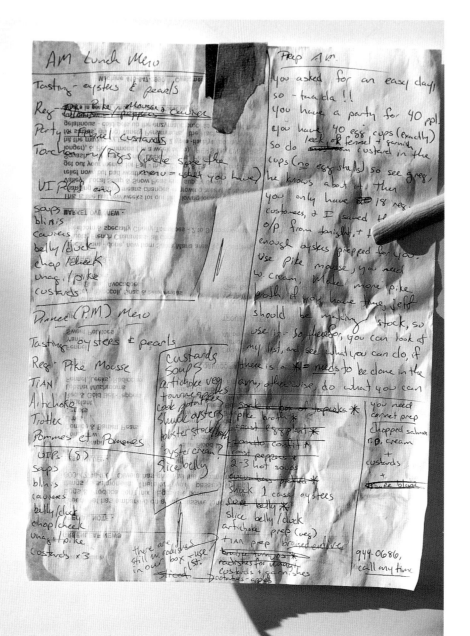